Benchmark Series

Microsoft® Word 2010

Nita Rutkosky

Pierce College at Puyallup
Puyallup, Washington

Audrey Rutkosky Roggenkamp

Pierce College at Puyallup
Puyallup, Washington

Paradigm PUBLISHING

St. Paul • Indianapolis

Managing Editor	Sonja Brown
Senior Developmental Editor	Christine Hurney
Production Editor	Donna Mears
Copy Editor	Susan Capecchi
Cover and Text Designer	Leslie Anderson
Desktop Production	Ryan Hamner, Julie Johnston, Jack Ross
Proofreader	Laura Nelson
Indexer	Sandi Schroeder

Acknowledgements: The authors, editors, and publisher thank the following instructors for their helpful suggestions during the planning and development of the books in the Benchmark Office 2010 Series: Somasheker Akkaladevi, Virginia State University, Petersburg, VA; Ed Baker, Community College of Philadelphia, Philadelphia, PA; Lynn Baldwin, Madison Area Technical College, Madison, WI; Letty Barnes, Lake Washington Technical College, Kirkland, WA; Richard Bell, Coastal Carolina Community College, Jacksonville, NC; Perry Callas, Clatsop Community College, Astoria, OR; Carol DesJardins, St. Clair County Community College, Port Huron, MI; Stacy Gee Hollins, St. Louis Community College--Florissant Valley, St. Louis, MO Sally Haywood, Prairie State College, Chicago Heights, IL; Dr. Penny Johnson, Madison Technical College, Madison, WI; Jan Kehm, Spartanburg Community College, Spartanburg, SC; Jacqueline Larsen, Asheville Buncombe Tech, Asheville, NC; Sherry Lenhart, Terra Community College, Fremont, OH; Andrea Robinson Hinsey, Ivy Tech Community College NE, Fort Wayne, IN; Bari Siddique, University of Texas at Brownsville, Brownsville, TX; Joan Splawski, Northeast Wisconsin Technical College, Green Bay, WI; Diane Stark, Phoenix College, Phoenix, AZ; Mary Van Haute, Northeast Wisconsin Technical College, Green Bay, WI; Rosalie Westerberg, Clover Park Technical College, Lakewood, WA.

The publishing team also thanks the following individuals for their contributions to this project: checking the accuracy of the instruction and exercises—Robertt (Rob) W. Neilly, Traci Post, and Lindsay Ryan; developing lesson plans, supplemental assessments, and supplemental case studies—Jan Davidson, Lambton College, Sarnia, Ontario; writing rubrics to support end-of-chapter and end-of-unit activities—Robertt (Rob) W. Neilly, Seneca College, Toronto, Ontario; writing test item banks—Jeff Johnson; writing online quiz item banks—Trudy Muller; and developing PowerPoint presentations—Janet Blum, Fanshawe College, London, Ontario.

Trademarks: Access, Excel, Internet Explorer, Microsoft, PowerPoint, and Windows are trademarks or registered trademarks of Microsoft Corporation in the United States and/or other countries. Some of the product names and company names included in this book have been used for identification purposes only and may be trademarks or registered trade names of their respective manufacturers and sellers. The authors, editors, and publisher disclaim any affiliation, association, or connection with, or sponsorship or endorsement by, such owners.

We have made every effort to trace the ownership of all copyrighted material and to secure permission from copyright holders. In the event of any question arising as to the use of any material, we will be pleased to make the necessary corrections in future printings. Thanks are due to the aforementioned authors, publishers, and agents for permission to use the materials indicated.

ISBN 978-0-76384-297-0 (Text)
ISBN 978-0-76384-300-7 (Text + CD)

Contents

Microsoft Word 2010 Level 1

Contents   **v**

Benchmark Microsoft Word 2010 is designed for students who want to learn how to use this powerful word processing program to create professional-looking documents for workplace, school, and personal communication needs. No prior knowledge of word processing is required. After successfully completing a course using this textbook, students will be able to

- Create and edit memos, letters, fliers, announcements, and reports of varying complexity
- Apply appropriate formatting elements and styles to a range of document types
- Add graphics and other visual elements to enhance written communication
- Plan, research, write, revise, and publish documents to meet specific information needs
- Given a workplace scenario requiring a written solution, assess the communication purpose and then prepare the materials that achieve the goal efficiently and effectively

In addition to mastering Word skills, students will learn the essential features and functions of computer hardware, the Windows 7 operating system, and Internet Explorer 8.0. Upon completing the text, they can expect to be proficient in using Word to organize, analyze, and present information.

Achieving Proficiency in Word 2010

Since its inception several Office versions ago, the Benchmark Series has served as a standard of excellence in software instruction. Elements of the book function individually and collectively to create an inviting, comprehensive learning environment that produces successful computer users. The following visual tour highlights the text's features.

UNIT OPENERS display the unit's four chapter titles. Each level has two units, which conclude with a comprehensive unit performance assessment.

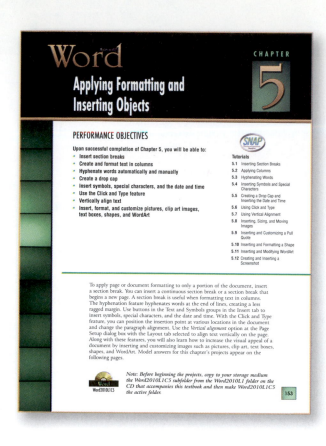

CHAPTER OPENERS present the performance objectives and an overview of the skills taught.

SNAP interactive tutorials are available to support chapter-specific skills at www.snap2010.emcp.com.

DATA FILES are provided for each chapter. A prominent note reminds students to copy the appropriate chapter data folder and make it active.

PROJECT APPROACH: Builds Skill Mastery within Realistic Context

MODEL ANSWERS provide a preview of the finished chapter projects and allow students to confirm they have created the materials accurately.

Project 1 Format a Document on Computer Input Devices **8 Parts**

You will format into columns text in a document on computer input devices, improve the readability of the document by hyphenating long words, and improve the visual appeal by inserting a drop cap.

Inserting a Section Break

♦ **Quick Steps**

Insert a Section Break
1. Click Page Layout tab.
2. Click Breaks button.
3. Click section break type in drop-down list.

HINT
If you delete a section break, the text that follows the section break takes on the formatting of the text preceding the break.

Breaks

You can change the layout and formatting of specific portions of a document by inserting section breaks. For example, you can insert section breaks and then change margins for the text between the section breaks. If you want to format specific text in a document into columns, insert a section break.

Insert a section break in a document by clicking the Page Layout tab, clicking the Breaks button in the Page Setup group, and then clicking the desired option in the *Section Breaks* section of the drop-down list. You can insert a section break that begins a new page or a continuous section break that does not begin a new page. A continuous section break separates the document into sections but does not insert a page break. Click one of the other three options in the *Section Breaks* section of the Breaks drop-down list if you want to insert a section break that begins a new page.

A section break inserted in a document is not visible in Print Layout view. Click the Draft button and a section break displays in the document as a double row of dots with the words *Section Break* in the middle. Depending on the type of section break you insert, text follows *Section Break*. For example, if you insert a continuous section break, the words *Section Break (Continuous)* display in the middle of the row of dots. To delete a section break, change to Draft view, position the insertion point on the section break, and then press the Delete key.

Project 1a Inserting a Continuous Section Break Part 1 of 8

1. Open **InputDevices.docx** and then save it with Save As and name it **WL1-C5-P1-InputDevices**.
2. Insert a continuous section break by completing the following steps:
   a. Move the insertion point to the beginning of the *Keyboard* heading.
   b. Click the Page Layout tab.
   c. Click the Breaks button in the Page Setup group and then click *Continuous* in the *Section Breaks* section of the drop-down list.
3. Click the Draft button in the view area on the Status bar and then notice the section break that displays across the screen.
4. Click the Print Layout button in the view area on the Status bar.

Step 2b
Step 2c

Removing Column Formatting

To remove column formatting using the Columns button, position the insertion point in the section containing columns, click the Page Layout tab, click the Columns button, and then click *One* at the drop-down list. You can also remove column formatting at the Columns dialog box by selecting the *One* option in the *Presets* section.

Inserting a Column Break

When formatting text into columns, Word automatically breaks the columns to fit the page. At times, column breaks may appear in an undesirable location. You can insert a column break by positioning the insertion point where you want the column to end, clicking the Page Layout tab, clicking the Breaks button, and then clicking *Column* at the drop-down list.

HINT
You can also insert a column break with the keyboard shortcut, Ctrl + Shift + Enter.

Project 1c Formatting Columns at the Columns Dialog Box Part 3 of 8

1. With **WL1-C5-P1-InputDevices.docx** open, delete the section break by completing the following steps:
   a. Click the Draft button in the view area on the Status bar.
   b. Position the insertion point on the section break and then press the Delete key.
   c. Click the Print Layout button in the view area on the Status bar.
2. Remove column formatting by clicking the Columns button in the Page Setup group in the Page Layout tab and then clicking *One* at the drop-down list.
3. Format text in columns by completing the following steps:
   a. Position the insertion point at the beginning of the first paragraph of text in the document.
   b. Click the Columns button in the Page Setup group and then click *More Columns* at the drop-down list.
   c. At the Columns dialog box, click *Two* in the *Presets* section.
   d. Click the down-pointing arrow at the right of the *Spacing* option box until *0.3"* displays.
   e. Click the *Line between* check box to insert a check mark.
   f. Click the down-pointing arrow at the right side of the *Apply to* option box and then click *This point forward* at the drop-down list.
   g. Click OK to close the dialog box.

Step 3c *Step 3e* *Step 3d* *Step 3f* *Step 3g*

MULTIPART PROJECTS provide a framework for the instruction and practice on software features. A project overview identifies tasks to accomplish and key features to use in completing the work.

STEP-BY-STEP INSTRUCTIONS guide students to the desired outcome for each project part. Screen captures illustrate what the student's screen should look like at key points.

Between project parts, the text presents instruction on the features and skills necessary to accomplish the next section of the project.

Typically, a file remains open throughout all parts of the project. Students save their work incrementally.

c. Drag the right middle sizing handle to the right side of the image.
d. Drag the bottom middle sizing handle to the bottom border of the image.
e. Click the Keep Changes button in the Close group in the Background Removal tab. (The picture should now display with the sky removed.)

20. Insert a caption by completing the following steps:
   a. Right-click the picture. (This displays the shortcut menu.)
   b. Click the *Insert Caption* option at the shortcut menu.
   c. At the Caption dialog box with the insertion point positioned in the *Caption* text box, press the spacebar and then type Uluru (Ayers Rock, Australia).
   d. Click OK. (The caption displays below and at the left side of the picture.)

21. Save, print, and then close **WL1-C5-P2-Training.docx**.

Step 19e

Step 20c

Step 20d

P**roject** **3** **Customize a Report on Robots** **2 Parts**

You will open a report on robots and then add visual appeal to the report by inserting and formatting a clip art image and a built-in text box.

Inserting a Clip Art Image

Microsoft Office includes a gallery of media images you can insert in a document such as clip art, photographs, and movie images, as well as sound clips. To insert an image in a Word document, click the Insert tab and then click the Clip Art button in the Illustrations group. This displays the Clip Art task pane at the right side of the screen as shown in Figure 5.7.

To view all picture, sound, and motion files, make sure the *Search for* text box in the Clip Art task pane does not contain any text and then click the Go button. When the desired image is visible, click the image to insert it in the document. Use buttons in the Picture Tools Format tab to format and customize the clip art image.

Unless the Clip Art task pane default settings have been customized, the task pane displays all illustrations, photographs, videos, and audio files. The *Results should be* option has a default setting of *Selected media file types*. Click the down-pointing arrow at the right side of this option to display media types. To search for a specific media type, remove the check mark before all options at the drop-down list except for the desired type. For example, if you are searching only for photograph images, remove the check mark before *Illustrations*, *Videos*, and *Audio*.

▼ **Quick Steps**

Insert Clip Art Image
1. Click Insert tab.
2. Click Clip Art button.
3. Type search word or topic.
4. Press Enter.
5. Click desired image.

HINT

You can drag a clip art image from the Clip Art task pane to your document.

Clip Art

CHAPTER REVIEW ACTIVITIES: A Hierarchy of Learning Assessments

Chapter Summary

- Group Word documents logically into folders. Create a new folder at the Open or Save As dialog box.
- You can select one or several documents at the Open dialog box. Copy, move, rename, delete, or open a document or selected documents.
- Use the *Cut*, *Copy*, and *Paste* options from the Organize button drop-down list or the Open dialog box shortcut menu to move or copy a document from one folder to another.
- Delete documents and/or folders with the *Delete* option from the Organize button drop-down list or shortcut menu.
- With options at the Save & Send tab Backstage view, you can send a document as an email attachment, save your document to SkyDrive and SharePoint, save your document in a different file format, and post your document to a special location such as a blog.
- Click the Change File Type button in the File Types category at the Save & Send tab Backstage view, and options display for saving the document in a different file format. You can also save documents in a different file format with the *Save as type* option box at the Save As dialog box.
- Move among the op[...] representing the des[...] Switch Windows bu[...] document name.
- View a portion of al[...] clicking the Arrange[...]
- Use the Minimize, [...] corner of the windo[...]
- Divide a window in[...] Split button in the [...] the same document [...]
- View the contents o[...] and then clicking th[...]
- Insert a document i[...] the Object button a[...] At the Insert File di[...]
- Preview a document[...] in the document wi[...] below the preview p[...] display size of the p[...]
- At the Print tab Bac[...] the page orientation[...] to print on one page[...] pages; and specify t[...]
- With Word's envelo[...] Envelopes and Labe[...]

CHAPTER SUMMARY captures the purpose and execution of key features.

- If you open the Envelopes and Labels dialog box in a document containing a name and address (with each line ending with a press of the Enter key), that information is automatically inserted in the *Delivery address* text box in the dialog box.
- Use Word's labels feature to print text on mailing labels, file labels, disc labels, or other types of labels.
- Word includes a number of template documents you can use to create a variety of documents. Display the list of template documents by clicking the File tab, clicking the New tab, and then clicking the Sample templates button.

Commands Review

FEATURE	RIBBON TAB, GROUP	BUTTON, OPTION	KEYBOARD SHORTCUT
Open dialog box	File	Open	Ctrl + O
Save As dialog box	File	Save As	
Print tab Backstage view	File	Print	Ctrl + P
Arrange all documents	View, Window		
Minimize document			
Maximize document			
Restore			
Split window	View, Window		
View documents side by side	View, Window		
Insert file	Insert, Text		
Envelopes and Labels dialog box with Envelopes tab selected	Mailings, Crea[...]		
Envelopes and Labels dialog box with Labels tab selected	Mailings, Cre[...]		
New tab Backstage view	File		

COMMANDS REVIEW summarizes visually the major features and alternative methods of access.

Concepts Check Test Your Knowledge

Completion: In the space provided at the right, indicate the correct term, command, or number.

1. Create a new folder with this button at the Open or Save As dialog box.

2. At the Open dialog box, the current folder path displays in this.

3. Using the mouse, select nonadjacent documents at the Open dialog box by holding down this key while clicking the desired documents.

4. Documents deleted from the hard drive are automatically sent here.

5. Copy a document to another folder without opening the document at the Open or Save As dialog box with the Organize button drop-down list or this menu.

6. The letters PDF stand for this.

7. Saving a document in this format strips out all formatting.

8. Click this button in the Window group in the View tab to arrange all open documents so a portion of each document displays.

9. Click this button and the active document fills the editing window.

10. Click this button to reduce the active document to a button on the Taskbar.

11. To display documents side by side, click this button in the Window group in the View tab.

12. Display the Insert File dialog box by clicking the Object button arrow in the Insert tab and then clicking this option.

13. Type this in the *Pages* text box at the Print tab Backstage view to print pages 3 through 6 of the open document.

14. Type this in the *Pages* text box at the Print tab Backstage view to print pages 4 and 9 of the open document.

15. The Envelopes button is located in the Create group in this tab.

16. Click the Sample templates button at this Backstage view to display a list of templates.

CONCEPTS CHECK questions assess knowledge recall.

Skills Check — Assess Your Performance

Assessment

1 APPLY CHARACTER FORMATTING TO A LEASE AGREEMENT DOCUMENT

1. Open **LeaseAgrmnt.docx**.
2. Save the document with Save As and name it **WL1-C2-A1-LeaseAgrmnt**.
3. Press Ctrl + End to move the insertion point to the end of the document and then type the text shown in Figure 2.8. Bold, italicize, and underline text as shown.
4. Select the entire document and then change the font to 12-point Candara.
5. Select and then bold *THIS LEASE AGREEMENT* located in the first paragrap...
6. Select an...
7. Select an...
8. Select an...
9. Select th... Corbel a... formatti...
10. Select th... caps form...
11. Use Form... for the re... *Premises*, *Default*, ...
12. Save, pri...

Figure 2.8 Assessment 1...

Inspection of Premise...

Lessor shall have the...
exhibit the Premises a...
Premises at any time...

Default

If Lessee fails to pay r...
Lessor may declare th...
and all rights and rem...

Late Charge

In the event that any...
of the month, Lessee...

68   Word Level 1 ■ Unit 1

SKILLS CHECK exercises ask students to create a variety of documents using multiple features without how-to directions.

Visual Benchmark — Demonstrate Your Proficiency

1 CREATE A SHAPE

1. At a blank document create the document shown in Figure 5.10 with the following specifications:
   a. Draw the shape using the *Quad Arrow Callout* located in the *Block Arrows* section.
   b. Apply the *Subtle Effect – Olive Green, Accent 3* shape style to the shape.
   c. Change the shape effect to *Soft Round* bevel.
   d. Change the height and width of the shape to 5 inches.
   e. Type the text in the shape as shown and set the text in 16-point Copperplate Gothic Bold and change the text color to dark green.
   f. Insert the truck clip art image and size and position it as shown in Figure 5.10. (If this truck clip art image is not available, choose another truck clip art image. Change the text wrap to *In Front of Text*.)
2. Center the shape on the page.
3. Save the document and name it **WL1-C5-VB1-FourCorners**.
4. Print and then close the document.

Figure 5.10 Visual Benchmark 1

VISUAL BENCHMARK assessments test students' problem-solving skills and mastery of program features.

Case Study — Apply Your Skills

Part 1
You are the office manager for the real estate company, Macadam Realty, and have been asked by the senior sales associate, Lucy Hendricks, to organize contract forms into a specific folder. Create a new folder named *RealEstate* and then copy into the folder documents that begin with the letters "RE." Ms. Hendricks has also asked you to prepare mailing labels for Macadam Realty. Include the name, Macadam Realty, and the address 100 Third Street, Suite 210, Denver, CO 80803, on the labels. Use a decorative font for the label and make the *M* in *Macadam* and the *R* in *Realty* larger and more pronounced than surrounding text. **Hint: Format text in the label by selecting text, right-clicking in the selected text, and then choosing the desired option at the shortcut menu.** Save the completed document and name it **WL1-C6-CS-P1-RELabels**. Print and then close the document.

Part 2
One of your responsibilities is to format contract forms. Open the document named **REConAgrmnt.docx** and then save it and name it **WL1-C6-CS-P2-REConAgrmnt**. The sales associate has asked you to insert signature information at the end of the document and so you decide to insert at the end of the document the file named **RESig.docx**. With **WL1-C6-CS-P2-REConAgrmnt.docx** still open, open **REBuildAgrmnt.docx**. Format the **WL1-C6-CS-P2-REConAgrmnt.docx** document so it is formatted in a manner similar to the **REBuildAgrmnt.docx** document. Consider the following when specifying formatting: margins, fonts, and paragraph shading. Save, print, and then close **WL1-C6-CS-P2-REConAgrmnt.docx**. Close **REBuildAgrmnt.docx**.

Part 3 *Help*
As part of the organization of contracts, Ms. Hendricks has asked you to insert document properties for the **REBuildAgrmnt.docx** and **WL1-C6-CS-P2-REConAgrmnt.docx** documents. Use the Help feature to learn how to insert document properties. With the information you learn from the Help feature, open each of the two documents separately, display the Info tab Backstage view, click the <u>Show All Properties</u> hyperlink, and then insert document properties in the following fields (you determine the information to type): *Title*, *Subject*, *Categories*, and *Company*. Print the document properties for each document (change the first gallery in the Print tab Backstage view to *Document Properties*). Save each document with the original name and close the documents.

Part 4
A client of the real estate company, Anna Hurley, is considering purchasing several rental properties and has asked for information on how to locate real estate rental forms. Using the Internet, locate at least three websites that offer real estate rental forms. Write a letter to Anna Hurley at 2300 South 22nd Street, Denver, CO 80205. In the letter, list the websites you found and include information on which site you thought offered the most resources. Also include in the letter that Macadam Realty is very interested in helping her locate and purchase rental properties. Save the document and name it **WL1-C6-CS-P4-RELtr**. Create an envelope for the letter and add it to the letter document. Save, print, and then close **WL1-C6-CS-P4-RELtr.docx**. (You may need to manually feed the envelope in the printer.)

240   Word Level 1 ■ Unit 2

CASE STUDY requires analyzing a workplace scenario and then planning and executing multipart projects.

Students search the Web and/or use the program's Help feature to locate additional information required to complete the Case Study.

UNIT PERFORMANCE ASSESSMENT: Cross-Disciplinary, Comprehensive Evaluation

UNIT 2

Word

Performance Assessment

Note: Before beginning unit assessments, copy to your storage medium the Word2010L1U2 subfolder from the Word2010L1 folder on the CD that accompanies this textbook and then make Word2010L1U2 the active folder.

Word2010L1U2

Assessing Proficiency

In this unit, you have learned to format text into columns; insert, format, and customize objects to enhance the visual appeal of a document; manage files, print envelopes and labels, and create documents using templates; create and edit tables; visually represent data in SmartArt diagrams and organizational charts; and use Mail Merge to create letters, envelopes, labels, and directions.

Assessment 1 Format a Technology Occupations Document

1. Open **TechOccs.docx** and then save the document with Save As and name it **WL1-U2-A01-TechOccs**.
2. Move the insertion point to the beginning of the heading *Telecommuting* and then insert the file named **CommMedia.docx**.
3. Apply the Heading 1 style to the title and the Heading 2 style to the headings in the document.
4. Change the Quick Styles set to *Formal* and change the paragraph spacing to *Open*.
5. Insert a continuous section break at the beginning of the first paragraph of text (the paragraph that begins *The march of computer technology . . .*).
6. Format the text below the section break into two columns.
7. Balance the columns on the second page.
8. Insert a pull quote of your choosing on the first page of the document that includes the text *"As the future of wireless unfolds, many new jobs will emerge as well."*
9. Create a drop cap with the first letter of the first word *The* that begins the first paragraph of text and make the drop cap two lines in height.
10. Manually hyphenate words in the document.
11. Insert page numbering that prints at the bottom of each page (you determine the page number formatting).
12. Save, print, and then close **WL1-U2-A01-TechOccs.docx**.

Assessment 2 Create a Workshop Flyer

1. Create the flyer shown in Figure U2.1 with the following specifications:
   a. Create the WordArt with the following specifications:
      • Use the *Fill - Tan, Text 2, Outline - Background 2* option (first option from the left in the top row) at the WordArt button drop-down gallery.

ASSESSING PROFICIENCY checks mastery of features.

WRITING ACTIVITIES involve applying program skills in a communication context.

Assessment 12 Merge and Print Envelopes

1. Use the Mail Merge feature to prepare envelopes for the letters created in Assessment 11.
2. Specify **WL1-U2-A11-DS.mdb** as the data source document.
3. Save the merged envelopes document and name the document **WL1-U2-A12-Envs**.
4. Print and then close **WL1-U2-A12-Envs.docx**.
5. Do not save the envelope main document.

Writing Activities

The following activities give you the opportunity to practice your writing skills along with demonstrating an understanding of some of the important Word features you have mastered in this unit. Use correct grammar, appropriate word choices, and clear sentence constructions.

Activity 1 Compose a Letter to Volunteers

You are an employee for the City of Greenwater and are responsible for coordinating volunteers for the city's Safe Night program. Compose a letter to the volunteers listed below and include the following information in the letter:
   • Safe Night event scheduled for Saturday, June 16, 2012.

Activity 2 Create a Business Letterhead

You have just opened a new mailing and shipping business and need letterhead stationery. Create a letterhead for your company in a header and/or footer. Use Word's Help feature to learn about creating a header that only displays and prints on the first page. Create the letterhead in a header that displays and prints only on the first page and include *at least* one of the following: a clip art image, a picture, a shape, a text box, and/or WordArt. Include the following information in the header:

   Global Mailing
   4300 Jackson Avenue
   Toronto, ON M4C 3X4
   (416) 555-0095
   www.emcp.net/globalmailing

Save the completed letterhead and name it **WL1-U2-Act02-Ltrhd**. Print and then close the document.

Internet Research

Create a Flyer on an Incentive Program

The owner of Terra Travel Services is offering an incentive to motivate travel consultants to increase travel bookings. The incentive is a sales contest with a grand prize of a one-week paid vacation to Cancun, Mexico. The owner has asked you to create a flyer that will be posted on the office bulletin board that includes information about the incentive program and some information about Cancun. Create this flyer using information about Cancun that you find on the Internet. Include a photo you find on a website (make sure it is not copyrighted) or include a clip art image representing travel. Include any other information or object to add visual appeal to the flyer. Save the completed flyer and name it **WL1-U2-InternetResearch**. Print and then close the document.

Job Study

Develop Recycling Program Communications

The Chief Operating Officer of Harrington Engineering has just approved your draft of the company's new recycling policy (see the file named **RecyclingPolicy.docx** located in the Word2010L1U2 folder). Edit the draft and prepare a final copy of the policy along with a memo to all employees describing the new guidelines. To support the company's energy resources conservation effort, you will send hard copies of the new policy to the Somerset Recycling Program president and to directors of Somerset Chamber of Commerce.

   Using the concepts and techniques you learned in this unit, prepare the following documents:
   • Format the recycling policy manual, including a cover page, appropriate headers and footers, and page numbers. Add at least one graphic and one diagram where appropriate. Format the document using a Quick Styles set and styles. Save the manual and name it **WL1-U2-JobStudyManual**. Print the manual.

INTERNET RESEARCH project reinforces research and word processing skills.

JOB STUDY at the end of Unit 2 presents a capstone assessment requiring critical thinking and problem solving.

Student Courseware

Student Resources CD Each Benchmark Series textbook is packaged with a Student Resources CD containing the data files required for completing the projects and assessments. A CD icon and folder name displayed on the opening page of chapters reminds students to copy a folder of files from the CD to the desired storage medium before beginning the project exercises. Directions for copying folders are printed on the inside back cover.

Internet Resource Center Additional learning tools and reference materials are available at the book-specific website at www.emcp.net/BenchmarkWord10. Students can access the same files that are on the Student Resources CD along with study aids, web links, and tips for using computers effectively in academic and workplace settings.

SNAP Training and Assessment SNAP is a web-based program offering an interactive venue for learning Microsoft Office 2010, Windows 7, and Internet Explorer 8.0. Along with a web-based learning management system, SNAP provides multimedia tutorials, performance skill items, document-based assessments, a concepts test bank, an online grade book, and a set of course planning tools. A CD of tutorials teaching the basics of Office, Windows, and Internet Explorer is also available if instructors wish to assign additional SNAP tutorial work without using the web-based SNAP program.

eBook For students who prefer studying with an eBook, the texts in the Benchmark Series are available in an electronic form. The web-based, password-protected eBooks feature dynamic navigation tools, including bookmarking, a linked table of contents, and the ability to jump to a specific page. The eBook format also supports helpful study tools, such as highlighting and note taking.

Instructor Resources

Instructor's Guide and Disc Instructor support for the Benchmark Series includes an *Instructor's Guide and Instructor Resources Disc* package. This resource includes planning information, such as Lesson Blueprints, teaching hints, and sample course syllabi; presentation resources, such as PowerPoint slide shows with lecture notes and audio support; and assessment resources, including an overview of available assessment venues, live model answers for chapter activities, and live and PDF model answers for end-of-chapter exercises. Contents of the *Instructor's Guide and Instructor Resources Disc* package are also available on the password-protected section of the Internet Resource Center for this title at www.emcp.net/BenchmarkWord10.

Computerized Test Generator Instructors can use the EXAMVIEW® Assessment Suite and test banks of multiple-choice items to create customized web-based or print tests.

Blackboard Cartridge This set of files allows instructors to create a personalized Blackboard website for their course and provides course content, tests, and the mechanisms for establishing communication via e-discussions and online group conferences. Available content includes a syllabus, test banks, PowerPoint presentations with audio support, and supplementary course materials. Upon request, the files can be available within 24–48 hours. Hosting the site is the responsibility of the educational institution.

System Requirements

This text is designed for the student to complete projects and assessments on a computer running a standard installation of Microsoft Office 2010, Professional Edition, and the Microsoft Windows 7 operating system. To effectively run this suite and operating system, your computer should be outfitted with the following:

- 1 gigahertz (GHz) processor or higher; 1 gigabyte (GB) of RAM
- DVD drive
- 15 GB of available hard-disk space
- Computer mouse or compatible pointing device

Office 2010 will also operate on computers running the Windows XP Service Pack 3 or the Windows Vista operating system.

Screen captures in this book were created using a screen resolution display setting of 1280 × 800. Refer to the *Customizing Settings* section of *Getting Started in Office 2010* following this preface for instructions on changing your monitor's resolution. Figure G.10 on page 10 shows the Microsoft Office Word ribbon at three resolutions for comparison purposes. Choose the resolution that best matches your computer; however, be aware that using a resolution other than 1280 × 800 means that your screens may not match the illustrations in this book.

About the Authors

Nita Rutkosky began teaching business education courses at Pierce College in Puyallup, Washington, in 1978. Since then she has taught a variety of software applications to students in postsecondary Information Technology certificate and degree programs. In addition to *Benchmark Office 2010,* she has co-authored *Marquee Series: Microsoft Office 2010, 2007,* and *2003; Signature Series: Microsoft Word 2010, 2007,* and *2003;* and *Using Computers in the Medical Office: Microsoft Word, Excel, and PowerPoint 2007* and *2003.* She has also authored textbooks on keyboarding, WordPerfect, desktop publishing, and voice recognition for Paradigm Publishing, Inc.

Audrey Rutkosky Roggenkamp has been teaching courses in the Business Information Technology department at Pierce College in Puyallup since 2005. Her courses have included keyboarding, skill building, and Microsoft Office programs. In addition to this title, she has co-authored *Marquee Series: Microsoft Office 2010* and *2007; Signature Series: Microsoft Word 2010* and *2007;* and *Using Computers in the Medical Office 2007* and *2003* for Paradigm Publishing, Inc.

Getting Started in Office 2010

In this textbook, you will learn to operate several computer application programs that combine to make an application "suite." This suite of programs is called Microsoft Office 2010. The programs you will learn to operate are the software, which includes instructions telling the computer what to do. Some of the application programs in the suite include a word processing program named Word, a spreadsheet program named Excel, a database program named Access, and a presentation program named PowerPoint.

Identifying Computer Hardware

The computer equipment you will use to operate the suite of programs is referred to as hardware. You will need access to a microcomputer system that should consist of the CPU, monitor, keyboard, printer, drives, and mouse. If you are not sure what equipment you will be operating, check with your instructor. The computer system shown in Figure G.1 consists of six components. Each component is discussed separately in the material that follows.

Figure G.1 Microcomputer System

CPU

CD-ROM

DVD±RW

USB drive

monitor

printer

keyboard

mouse

CPU

CPU stands for Central Processing Unit and it is the intelligence of the computer. All the processing occurs in the CPU. Silicon chips, which contain miniaturized circuitry, are placed on boards that are plugged into slots within the CPU. Whenever an instruction is given to the computer, that instruction is processed through circuitry in the CPU.

Monitor

The monitor is a piece of equipment that looks like a television screen. It displays the information of a program and the text being input at the keyboard. The quality of display for monitors varies depending on the type of monitor and the level of resolution. Monitors can also vary in size—generally from 15-inch size up to 26-inch size or larger.

Keyboard

The keyboard is used to input information into the computer. Keyboards for microcomputers vary in the number and location of the keys. Microcomputers have the alphabetic and numeric keys in the same location as the keys on a typewriter. The symbol keys, however, may be placed in a variety of locations, depending on the manufacturer. In addition to letters, numbers, and symbols, most microcomputer keyboards contain function keys, arrow keys, and a numeric keypad. Figure G.2 shows an enhanced keyboard.

Figure G.2 Keyboard

The 12 keys at the top of the keyboard, labeled with the letter F followed by a number, are called *function keys*. Use these keys to perform functions within each of the suite programs. To the right of the regular keys is a group of *special* or *dedicated keys*. These keys are labeled with specific functions that will be performed when you press the key. Below the special keys are arrow keys. Use these keys to move the insertion point in the document screen.

A keyboard generally includes three mode indicator lights. When you select certain modes, a light appears on the keyboard. For example, if you press the Caps Lock key, which disables the lowercase alphabet, a light appears next to Caps Lock. Similarly, pressing the Num Lock key will disable the special functions on the numeric keypad, which is located at the right side of the keyboard.

Disk Drives

Depending on the computer system you are using, Microsoft Office 2010 is installed on a hard drive or as part of a network system. Whether you are using Office on a hard drive or network system, you will need to have available a DVD or CD drive and a USB drive or other storage medium. You will insert the CD (compact disc) that accompanies this textbook in the DVD or CD drive and then copy folders from the CD to your storage medium. You will also save documents you complete at the computer to folders on your storage medium.

Printer

A document you create in Word is considered soft copy. If you want a hard copy of a document, you need to print it. To print documents you will need to access a printer, which will probably be either a laser printer or an ink-jet printer. A laser printer uses a laser beam combined with heat and pressure to print documents, while an ink-jet printer prints a document by spraying a fine mist of ink on the page.

Mouse

Many functions in the suite of programs are designed to operate more efficiently with a mouse. A mouse is an input device that sits on a flat surface next to the computer. You can operate a mouse with the left or the right hand. Moving the mouse on the flat surface causes a corresponding mouse pointer to move on the screen. Figure G.1 shows an illustration of a mouse.

Using the Mouse ■■■■■■■■■■■■■■■■■■■■■■■■■■■■■

The programs in the Microsoft Office suite can be operated with the keyboard and a mouse. The mouse may have two or three buttons on top, which are tapped to execute specific functions and commands. To use the mouse, rest it on a flat surface or a mouse pad. Put your hand over it with your palm resting on top of the mouse and your wrist resting on the table surface. As you move the mouse on the flat surface, a corresponding pointer moves on the screen.

When using the mouse, you should understand four terms — point, click, double-click, and drag. When operating the mouse, you may need to point to a specific command, button, or icon. Point means to position the mouse pointer on the desired item. With the mouse pointer positioned on the desired item, you may need to click a button on the mouse. Click means quickly tapping a button on the mouse once. To complete two steps at one time, such as choosing and then executing a function, double-click a mouse button. Double-click means to tap the left mouse button twice in quick succession. The term drag means to press and hold the left mouse button, move the mouse pointer to a specific location, and then release the button.

Using the Mouse Pointer

The mouse pointer will change appearance depending on the function being performed or where the pointer is positioned. The mouse pointer may appear as one of the following images:

- The mouse pointer appears as an I-beam (called the I-beam pointer) in the document screen and can be used to move the insertion point or select text.

- The mouse pointer appears as an arrow pointing up and to the left (called the arrow pointer) when it is moved to the Title bar, Quick Access toolbar, ribbon, or an option in a dialog box.

- The mouse pointer becomes a double-headed arrow (either pointing left and right, pointing up and down, or pointing diagonally) when performing certain functions such as changing the size of an object.

- In certain situations, such as moving an object or image, the mouse pointer displays with a four-headed arrow attached. The four-headed arrow means that you can move the object left, right, up, or down.

- When a request is being processed or when a program is being loaded, the mouse pointer may appear with a circle beside it. The moving circle means "please wait." When the process is completed, the circle is removed.

- The mouse pointer displays as a hand with a pointing index finger in certain functions such as Help and indicates that more information is available about the item. The mouse pointer also displays as a hand when you hover the mouse over a hyperlink.

Choosing Commands ■■■■■■■■■■■■ ■■■■■■■■■■■■■■

Once a program is open, you can use several methods in the program to choose commands. A command is an instruction that tells the program to do something. You can choose a command using the mouse or the keyboard. When a program such as Word or PowerPoint is open, the ribbon contains buttons for completing tasks and contains tabs you click to display additional buttons. To choose a button on the Quick Access toolbar or in the ribbon, position the tip of the mouse arrow pointer on a button and then click the left mouse button.

The Office suite provides access keys you can press to use a command in a program. Press the Alt key on the keyboard to display KeyTips that identify the access key you need to press to execute a command. For example, press the Alt key in a Word document with the Home tab active and KeyTips display as shown in Figure G.3. Continue pressing access keys until you execute the desired command. For example, if you want to begin spell checking a document, you would press the Alt key, press the R key on the keyboard to display the Review tab, and then press the letter S on the keyboard.

Choosing Commands from Drop-Down Lists

To choose a command from a drop-down list with the mouse, position the mouse pointer on the desired option and then click the left mouse button. To make a selection from a drop-down list with the keyboard, type the underlined letter in the desired option.

Figure G.3 Word Home Tab KeyTips

Some options at a drop-down list may be gray-shaded (dimmed), indicating that the option is currently unavailable. If an option at a drop-down list displays preceded by a check mark, that indicates that the option is currently active. If an option at a drop-down list displays followed by an ellipsis (…), a dialog box will display when that option is chosen.

Choosing Options from a Dialog Box

A dialog box contains options for applying formatting to a file or data within a file. Some dialog boxes display with tabs along the top providing additional options. For example, the Font dialog box shown in Figure G.4 contains two tabs — the Font tab and the Advanced tab. The tab that displays in the front is the active tab. To make a tab active using the mouse, position the arrow pointer on the desired tab and then click the left mouse button. If you are using the keyboard, press Ctrl + Tab or press Alt + the underlined letter on the desired tab.

Figure G.4 Word Font Dialog Box

To choose options from a dialog box with the mouse, position the arrow pointer on the desired option and then click the left mouse button. If you are using the keyboard, press the Tab key to move the insertion point forward from option to option. Press Shift + Tab to move the insertion point backward from option to option. You can also hold down the Alt key and then press the underlined letter of the desired option. When an option is selected, it displays with a blue background or surrounded by a dashed box called a marquee. A dialog box contains one or more of the following elements: text boxes, list boxes, check boxes, option buttons, measurement boxes, and command buttons.

List Boxes

Some dialog boxes such as the Word Font dialog box shown in Figure G.4 may contain a list box. The list of fonts below the *Font* option is contained in a list box. To make a selection from a list box with the mouse, move the arrow pointer to the desired option and then click the left mouse button.

Some list boxes may contain a scroll bar. This scroll bar will display at the right side of the list box (a vertical scroll bar) or at the bottom of the list box (a horizontal scroll bar). You can use a vertical scroll bar or a horizontal scroll bar to move through the list if the list is longer than the box. To move down through a list on a vertical scroll bar, position the arrow pointer on the down-pointing arrow and hold down the left mouse button. To scroll up through the list in a vertical scroll bar, position the arrow pointer on the up-pointing arrow and hold down the left mouse button. You can also move the arrow pointer above the scroll box and click the left mouse button to scroll up the list or move the arrow pointer below the scroll box and click the left mouse button to move down the list. To move through a list with a horizontal scroll bar, click the left-pointing arrow to scroll to the left of the list or click the right-pointing arrow to scroll to the right of the list.

To make a selection from a list using the keyboard, move the insertion point into the box by holding down the Alt key and pressing the underlined letter of the desired option. Press the Up and/or Down Arrow keys on the keyboard to move through the list.

In some dialog boxes where enough room is not available for a list box, lists of options are inserted in a drop-down list box. Options that contain a drop-down list box display with a down-pointing arrow. For example, the *Underline style* option at the Word Font dialog box shown in Figure G.4 contains a drop-down list. To display the list, click the down-pointing arrow to the right of the *Underline style* option box. If you are using the keyboard, press Alt + U.

Check Boxes

Some dialog boxes contain options preceded by a box. A check mark may or may not appear in the box. The Word Font dialog box shown in Figure G.4 displays a variety of check boxes within the *Effects* section. If a check mark appears in the box, the option is active (turned on). If the check box does not contain a check mark, the option is inactive (turned off). Any number of check boxes can be active. For example, in the Word Font dialog box, you can insert a check mark in any or all of the boxes in the *Effects* section and these options will be active.

To make a check box active or inactive with the mouse, position the tip of the arrow pointer in the check box and then click the left mouse button. If you are using the keyboard, press Alt + the underlined letter of the desired option.

Text Boxes

Some options in a dialog box require you to enter text. For example, the boxes below the *Find what* and *Replace with* options at the Excel Find and Replace dialog box shown in Figure G.5 are text boxes. In a text box, you type text or edit existing text. Edit text in a text box in the same manner as normal text. Use the Left and Right Arrow keys on the keyboard to move the insertion point without deleting text and use the Delete key or Backspace key to delete text.

Option Buttons

The Word Insert Table dialog box shown in Figure G.6 contains options in the *AutoFit behavior* section preceded by option buttons. Only one option button can be selected at any time. When an option button is selected, a blue circle displays in the button. To select an option button with the mouse, position the tip of the arrow pointer inside the option button and then click the left mouse button. To make a selection with the keyboard, hold down the Alt key and then press the underlined letter of the desired option.

Measurement Boxes

Some options in a dialog box contain measurements or numbers you can increase or decrease. These options are generally located in a measurement box. For example, the Word Paragraph dialog box shown in Figure G.7 contains the *Left*, *Right*, *Before*, and *After* measurement boxes. To increase a number in a measurement box, position the tip of the arrow pointer on the up-pointing arrow to the right of the desired option and then click the left mouse button. To decrease the number, click the down-pointing arrow. If you are using the keyboard, press Alt + the underlined letter of the desired option and then press the Up Arrow key to increase the number or the Down Arrow key to decrease the number.

Command Buttons

In the Excel Find and Replace dialog box shown in Figure G.5, the boxes along the bottom of the dialog box are called command buttons. Use a command button to execute or cancel a command. Some command buttons display with an ellipsis (...). A command button that displays with an ellipsis will open another dialog box. To choose a command button with the mouse, position the arrow pointer on the desired button and then click the left mouse button. To choose a command button with the keyboard, press the Tab key until the desired command button contains the marquee and then press the Enter key.

Figure G.5 Excel Find and Replace Dialog Box

Figure G.6 Word Insert Table Dialog Box

option buttons

Figure G.7 Word Paragraph Dialog Box

measurement boxes

Choosing Commands with Keyboard Shortcuts

Applications in the Office suite offer a variety of keyboard shortcuts you can use to execute specific commands. Keyboard shortcuts generally require two or more keys. For example, the keyboard shortcut to display the Open dialog box in an application is Ctrl + O. To use this keyboard shortcut, hold down the Ctrl key, type the letter O on the keyboard, and then release the Ctrl key. For a list of keyboard shortcuts, refer to the Help files.

Choosing Commands with Shortcut Menus

The software programs in the suite include menus that contain commands related to the item with which you are working. A shortcut menu appears in the file in the location where you are working. To display a shortcut menu, click the right mouse button or press Shift + F10. For example, if the insertion point is positioned in a paragraph of text in a Word document, clicking the right mouse button or pressing Shift + F10 will cause the shortcut menu shown in Figure G.8 to display in the document screen (along with the Mini toolbar).

To select an option from a shortcut menu with the mouse, click the desired option. If you are using the keyboard, press the Up or Down Arrow key until the desired option is selected and then press the Enter key. To close a shortcut menu without choosing an option, click anywhere outside the shortcut menu or press the Esc key.

Working with Multiple Programs ■■■■■■■■■■■■■■■■■■■■

As you learn the various programs in the Microsoft Office suite, you will notice how executing commands in each is very similar. For example, the steps to save, close, and print are virtually the same whether you are working in Word, Excel, or PowerPoint. This consistency between programs greatly enhances a user's ability to transfer knowledge learned in one program to another within the suite. Another appeal of Microsoft Office is the ability to have more than one program open at the same time. For example, you can open Word, create a document, and then open Excel, create a spreadsheet, and copy the spreadsheet into Word.

Figure G.8 Word Shortcut Menu

Figure G.9 Taskbar with Word, Excel, and PowerPoint Open

When you open a program, a button displays on the Taskbar containing an icon representing the program. If you open another program, a button containing an icon representing the program displays to the right of the first program button. Figure G.9 shows the Taskbar with Word, Excel, and PowerPoint open. To move from one program to another, click the button on the Taskbar representing the desired program file.

Customizing Settings

Before beginning computer projects in this textbook, you may need to customize the monitor settings and turn on the display of file extensions. Projects in the chapters in this textbook assume that the monitor display is set at 1280 by 800 pixels and that the display of file extensions is turned on.

Changing Monitor Resolutions

Before you begin learning the applications in the Microsoft Office 2010 suite, take a moment to check the display settings on the computer you are using. The ribbon in the Microsoft Office suite adjusts to the screen resolution setting of your computer monitor. Computer monitors set at a high resolution will have the ability to show more buttons in the ribbon than will a monitor set to a low resolution. The illustrations in this textbook were created with a screen resolution display set at 1280 × 800 pixels. In Figure G.10 the Word ribbon is shown three ways: at a lower screen resolution (1024 × 768 pixels), at the screen resolution featured

Figure G.10 Monitor Resolution

1024 × 768 screen resolution

1280 × 800 screen resolution

1440 × 900 screen resolution

throughout this textbook, and at a higher screen resolution (1440 × 900 pixels). Note the variances in the ribbon in all three examples. If possible, set your display to 1280 × 800 pixels to match the illustrations you will see in this textbook.

Project 1 Setting Monitor Display to 1280 by 800

1. At the Windows 7 desktop, click the Start button and then click *Control Panel*.
2. At the Control Panel dialog box, click the *Adjust screen resolution* option in the Appearance and Personalization category.
3. At the Control Panel Screen Resolution window, click the Resolution option button. (This displays a drop-down slider bar. Your drop-down slider bar may display differently than what you see in the image at the right.)
4. Drag the slider bar button on the slider bar until *1280 × 800* displays to the right of the slider button.
5. Click in the Control Panel Screen Resolution window to remove the slider bar.
6. Click the Apply button.
7. Click the Keep Changes button.
8. Click the OK button.
9. Close the Control Panel window.

Project 2 Displaying File Extensions

1. At the Windows 7 desktop, click the Start button and then click *Computer*.
2. At the Computer window, click the Organize button on the toolbar and then click *Folder and search options* at the drop-down list.
3. At the Folder Options dialog box, click the View tab.
4. Click the *Hide extensions for known file types* check box to remove the check mark.
5. Click the Apply button.
6. Click the OK button.
7. Close the Computer window.

Completing Computer Projects ■■■■■■■■■■■■■■■■■■■

Some computer projects in this textbook require that you open an existing file. Project files are saved on the Student Resources CD that accompanies this textbook. The files you need for each chapter are saved in individual folders. Before beginning a chapter, copy the necessary folder from the CD to your storage medium (such as a USB flash drive) using the Computer window. If storage capacity is an issue with your storage medium, delete any previous chapter folders before copying a chapter folder onto your storage medium.

Project 3 — Copying a Folder from the Student Resources CD

1. Insert the CD that accompanies this textbook in the CD drive. At the AutoPlay window that displays, click the Close button located in the upper right corner of the window.
2. Insert your USB flash drive in an available USB port. If an AutoPlay window displays, click the Close button.
3. At the Windows desktop, open the Computer window by clicking the Start button and then clicking *Computer* at the Start menu.
4. Double-click the CD drive in the Content pane (displays with the name *BM10StudentResources* preceded by the drive letter).
5. Double-click the desired program folder name in the Content pane.
6. Click once on the desired chapter subfolder name to select it.
7. Click the Organize button on the toolbar and then click *Copy* at the drop-down list.
8. In the Computer window Content pane, click the drive containing your storage medium.
9. Click the Organize button on the toolbar and then click *Paste* at the drop-down list.
10. Close the Computer window by clicking the Close button located in the upper right corner of the window.

Project 4 — Deleting a Folder

Note: Check with your instructor before deleting a folder.
1. Insert your storage medium (such as a USB flash drive) in the USB port.
2. At the Windows desktop, open the Computer window by clicking the Start button and then clicking *Computer* at the Start menu.
3. Double-click the drive letter for your storage medium (drive containing your USB flash drive such as *Removable Disk (F:)*).
4. Click the chapter folder in the Content pane.
5. Click the Organize button on the toolbar and then click *Delete* at the drop-down list.
6. At the message asking if you want to delete the folder, click the Yes button.
7. Close the Computer window by clicking the Close button located in the upper right corner of the window.

Using Windows 7

A computer requires an operating system to provide necessary instructions on a multitude of processes including loading programs, managing data, directing the flow of information to peripheral equipment, and displaying information. Windows 7 is an operating system that provides functions of this type (along with much more) in a graphical environment. Windows is referred to as a **graphical user interface** (GUI—pronounced *gooey*) that provides a visual display of information with features such as icons (pictures) and buttons. In this introduction, you will learn these basic features of Windows 7:

• Use desktop icons and the Taskbar to launch programs and open files or folders

• Add and remove gadgets

• Organize and manage data, including copying, moving, creating, and deleting files and folders; and create a shortcut

• Explore the Control Panel and personalize the desktop

• Use the Windows Help and Support features

• Use search tools

• Customize monitor settings

    Before using one of the software programs in the Microsoft Office suite, you will need to start the Windows 7 operating system. To do this, turn on the computer. Depending on your computer equipment configuration, you may also need to turn on the monitor and printer. If you are using a computer that is part of a network system or if your computer is set up for multiple users, a screen will display showing the user accounts defined for your computer system. At this screen, click your user account name and, if necessary, type your password and then press the Enter key. The Windows 7 operating system will start and, after a few moments, the desktop will display as shown in Figure W.1. (Your desktop may vary from what you see in Figure W.1.)

Exploring the Desktop

When Windows is loaded, the main portion of the screen is called the *desktop*. Think of the desktop in Windows as the top of a desk in an office. A business person places necessary tools—such as pencils, pens, paper, files, calculator—on the desktop to perform functions. Like the tools that are located on a desk, the desktop contains tools for operating the computer. These tools are logically grouped and placed in dialog boxes or panels that you can display using icons on the desktop. The desktop contains a variety of features for using your computer and software programs installed on the computer. The features available on the desktop are represented by icons and buttons.

Figure W.1 Windows 7 Desktop

Recycle Bin icon

Start button

Taskbar

Using Icons

Icons are visual symbols that represent programs, files, or folders. Figure W.1 identifies the Recycle Bin icon located on the Windows desktop. The Windows desktop on your computer may contain additional icons. Programs that have been installed on your computer may be represented by an icon on the desktop. Also, icons may display on your desktop representing files or folders. Double-click an icon and the program, file, or folder it represents opens on the desktop.

Using the Taskbar

The bar that displays at the bottom of the desktop (see Figure W.1) is called the Taskbar. The Taskbar, shown in Figure W.2, contains the Start button, pinned items, a section that displays task buttons representing active tasks, the notification area, and the Show Desktop button.

Figure W.2 Windows 7 Taskbar

Show desktop button

pinned items

buttons for active tabs

notification area

Click the Start button, located at the left side of the Taskbar, and the Start menu displays as shown in Figure W.3 (your Start menu may vary). You can also display the Start menu by pressing the Windows key on your keyboard or by pressing Ctrl + Esc. The left side of the Start menu contains links to the most recently and frequently used programs. The name of the currently logged on user displays at the top of the darker right portion of the menu followed by the user's libraries. The two sections below the personal libraries provide links to other Windows features, such as games, the Control Panel, and Windows Help and Support. Use the Shut down button to put the system in a power-conserving state or into a locked, shut down, or sleep mode.

To choose an option from the Start menu, drag the arrow pointer to the desired option (referred to as *pointing*) and then click the left mouse button. Pointing to options at the Start menu that are followed by a right-pointing arrow will cause a side menu to display with additional options. When a program is open, a task button representing the program appears on the Taskbar. If multiple programs are open, each program will appear as a task button on the Taskbar (a few specialized tools may not).

Manipulating Windows

When you open a program, a defined work area displays on the screen, which is referred to as a *window*. A Title bar displays at the top of a window and contains buttons at the right side for closing the window and minimizing, maximizing, and restoring the size of the window. You can open more than one window at a time and the open windows can be cascaded or stacked. Windows 7 contains a Snap feature that causes a window to "stick" to the edge of the screen when the window

Figure W.3 Start Menu

is moved to the left or right side of the screen. Move a window to the top of the screen and the window is automatically maximized. If you drag down a maximized window, the window is automatically restored down.

In addition to moving and sizing a window, you can change the display of all open windows. To do this, position the mouse pointer on the Taskbar and then click the right mouse button and a pop-up list displays with options for displaying multiple open windows. You can cascade the windows, stack the windows, and display the windows side by side.

Project 1 — Opening Programs, Switching between Programs, and Manipulating Windows

1. Open Windows 7. (To do this, turn on the computer and, if necessary, turn on the monitor and/or printer. If you are using a computer that is part of a network system or if your computer is set up for multiple users, you may need to click your user account name and, if necessary, type your password and then press the Enter key. Check with your instructor to determine if you need to complete any additional steps.)
2. When the Windows 7 desktop displays, open Microsoft Word by completing the following steps:
   a. Position the arrow pointer on the Start button on the Taskbar and then click the left mouse button.
   b. At the Start menu, click *All Programs* and then click *Microsoft Office* (this displays programs in the Office suite below Microsoft Office).
   c. Drag the arrow pointer down to *Microsoft Word 2010* and then click the left mouse button.
   d. When the Microsoft Word program is open, notice that a task button representing Word displays on the Taskbar.

Step 2d

3. Open Microsoft Excel by completing the following steps:
   a. Position the arrow pointer on the Start button on the Taskbar and then click the left mouse button.
   b. At the Start menu, click *All Programs* and then click *Microsoft Office*.
   c. Drag the arrow pointer down to *Microsoft Excel 2010* and then click the left mouse button.
   d. When the Microsoft Excel program is open, notice that a task button representing Excel displays on the Taskbar to the right of the task button representing Word.
4. Switch to the Word program by clicking the task button on the Taskbar representing Word.
5. Switch to the Excel program by clicking the task button on the Taskbar representing Excel.

Step 4

6. Restore down the Excel window by clicking the Restore Down button that displays immediately left of the Close button in the upper right corner of the screen. (This reduces the Excel window so it displays along the bottom half of the screen.)

7. Restore down the Word window by clicking the Restore Down button located immediately left of the Close button in the upper right corner of the screen.

8. Position the mouse pointer on the Word window Title bar, hold down the left mouse button, drag to the left side of the screen until an outline of the window displays in the left half of the screen, and then release the mouse button. (This "sticks" the window to the left side of the screen.)

9. Position the mouse pointer on the Excel window Title bar, hold down the left mouse button, drag to the right until an outline of the window displays in the right half of the screen, and then release the mouse button.

10. Minimize the Excel window by clicking the Minimize button that displays in the upper right corner of the Excel window Title bar.

11. Hover your mouse over the Excel button on the Taskbar and notice the Excel window thumbnail that displays above the button and then click the thumbnail. (This displays the Excel window at the right side of the screen.)

12. Cascade the Word and Excel windows by positioning the arrow pointer on an empty area on the Taskbar, clicking the right mouse button, and then clicking *Cascade windows* at the pop-up list.

13. After viewing the windows cascaded, display them stacked by right-clicking an empty area on the Taskbar and then clicking *Show windows stacked* at the pop-up list.

14. Display the desktop by right-clicking an empty area on the Taskbar and then clicking *Show the desktop* at the pop-up list.

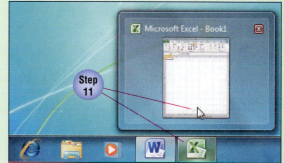

15. Display the windows stacked by right-clicking an empty area on the Taskbar and then clicking *Show open windows* at the pop-up list.

16. Position the mouse pointer on the Word window Title bar, hold down the left mouse button, drag the window to the top of the screen, and then release the mouse button. This maximizes the Word window so it fills the screen.

17. Close the Word window by clicking the Close button located in the upper right corner of the window.

18. At the Excel window, click the Maximize button located immediately left of the Close button in the upper right corner of the Excel window.

19. Close the Excel window by clicking the Close button located in the upper right corner of the window.

Using the Pinned Area

The icons that display immediately right of the Start button are pinned programs. Clicking an icon opens the program associated with the icon. Click the first icon to open the Internet Explorer web browser, click the second icon to open a window containing Libraries, and click the third icon to open the Windows media player window.

Exploring the Notification Area

The notification area is located at the right side of the Taskbar and contains icons that show the status of certain system functions such as a network connection or battery power. It also contains icons you can use to manage certain programs and Windows 7 features. The notification area also contains the system clock and date. Click the time or date in the notification area and a window displays with a clock and a calendar of the current month. Click the Change date and time settings hyperlink that displays at the bottom of the window and the Date and Time dialog box displays. To change the date and/or time, click the Change date and time button and the Date and Time Settings dialog box displays similar to the dialog box shown in Figure W.4. (If a dialog box displays telling you that Windows needs your permission to continue, click the Continue button.)

Change the month and year by clicking the left-pointing or right-pointing arrow at the top of the calendar in the *Date* section. Click the left-pointing arrow to display the previous month(s) and click the right-pointing arrow to display the next month(s).

To change the day, click the desired day in the monthly calendar that displays in the dialog box. To change the time, double-click either the hour, minute, or seconds and then type the appropriate time or use the up- and down-pointing arrows in the spin boxes to adjust the time.

Some programs, when installed, will add an icon to the notification area of the Taskbar. Display the name of the icon by positioning the mouse pointer on the icon and, after approximately one second, the icon label displays. If more icons have been inserted in the notification area than can be viewed at one time, an up-pointing arrow button displays at the left side of the notification area. Click this up-pointing arrow button and the remaining icons display.

Setting Taskbar Properties

You can customize the Taskbar with options from the Taskbar shortcut menu. Display this menu by right-clicking on an empty portion of the Taskbar. The Taskbar shortcut menu contains options for turning on or off the display of specific toolbars, specifying the display of multiple windows, displaying the Start Task Manager dialog box, locking or unlocking the Taskbar, and displaying the Taskbar and Start Menu Properties dialog box.

With options in the Taskbar and Start Menu Properties dialog box shown in Figure W.5, you can change settings for the Taskbar as well as the Start menu. Display this dialog box by right-clicking on an empty area on the Taskbar and then clicking *Properties* at the shortcut menu.

Each property is controlled by a check box. Property options containing a check mark are active. Click the option to remove the check mark and make the option inactive. If an option is inactive, clicking the option will insert a check mark in the check box and turn on the option (make it active).

Figure W.4 Date and Time Settings Dialog Box

spin boxes

Figure W.5 Taskbar and Start Menu Properties Dialog Box

Insert a check mark in this option to hide the Taskbar unless you move the mouse pointer over the location where the Taskbar should display.

Insert a check mark in this option to display icons in a reduced manner on the Taskbar.

Use this option to change the location of the Taskbar from the bottom of the desktop to the left side, right side, or top of the desktop.

Project 2 Changing Taskbar Properties

1. Make sure the Windows 7 desktop displays.
2. Change Taskbar properties by completing the following steps:
   a. Position the arrow pointer on any empty area on the Taskbar and then click the right mouse button.
   b. At the shortcut menu that displays, click *Properties*.

c. At the Taskbar and Start Menu Properties dialog box, click the *Auto-hide the taskbar* check box to insert a check mark.

d. Click the *Use small icons* check box to insert a check mark.

e. Click the button (displays with the word *Bottom*) that displays at the right side of the *Taskbar location on screen* option and then click *Right* at the drop-down list.

f. Click OK to close the dialog box.

3. Since the *Auto-hide the taskbar* check box contains a check mark, the Taskbar does not display. Display the Taskbar by moving the mouse pointer to the right side of the screen. Notice that the icons on the Taskbar are smaller.

4. Return to the default settings for the Taskbar by completing the following steps:

a. Move the mouse pointer to the right side of the screen to display the Taskbar.

b. Right-click any empty area on the Taskbar and then click *Properties* at the shortcut menu.

c. Click the *Auto-hide the taskbar* check box to remove the check mark.

d. Click the *Use small icons* check box to remove the check mark.

e. Click the button (displays with the word *Right*) that displays at the right side of the *Taskbar location on screen* option and then click *Bottom* at the drop-down list.

f. Click OK to close the dialog box.

Powering Down the Computer ■■■■■■■■■■ ■■■■■■■■■■ ■■■■

If you want to shut down Windows, close any open programs, click the Start button on the Taskbar, and then click the Shut down button as shown in Figure W.6. Click the button containing a right-pointing triangle that displays at the right side of the Shut down button and a drop-down list displays with options for powering down the computer.

In a multi-user environment, click the *Switch user* option to change users or click the *Log off* option to log off your computer, which shuts down your applications and files and makes system resources available to other users logged on to the system. If you need to walk away from your computer and you want to protect your work, consider locking the computer by clicking the *Lock* option. When you lock the computer, the desktop is hidden but the system is not shut down and the power is not conserved. To unlock the computer, click the icon on the desktop representing your account, type your password, and then press Enter. Click the *Restart* option to shut down and then restart the computer and click

Figure W.6 Shut Down Button and Power Options Button

Click this button arrow to display a list of options for switching the user, logging off or locking the computer, restarting the computer, or putting the computer in sleep mode.

Click this button to shut down your computer.

the *Sleep* option to save power without having to close all files and applications. In sleep mode, Windows saves files and information about programs and then powers down the computer to a low-power state. To "wake" the computer back up, quickly press the computer's power button.

Using Gadgets

You can add gadgets to your desktop. A gadget is a mini program providing information at a glance and easy access to frequently used tools. For example, you can add a Clock gadget to your desktop that shows the current time, a Weather gadget that displays the current temperature where you live, or a Calendar gadget that displays the current date. Gadgets are added to the Sidebar, which is a location at the right side of the Windows 7 desktop.

To view available gadgets, right-click in a blank area on the desktop and then click *Gadgets* at the shortcut menu. This displays the gadget gallery similar to what you see in Figure W.7. To add a gadget to the Sidebar, double-click the desired gadget. To remove a gadget from the Sidebar, hover the mouse pointer over the gadget and then click the Close button that displays at the upper right side of the gadget. ***Note: The Gadget option on the shortcut menu may be missing if the computer you are using is located in a school setting where customization options have been disabled. If you do not see Gadget on the shortcut menu, please skip Project 3.***

Figure W.7 Gadget Gallery

1. At the Windows 7 desktop, right-click in a blank area on the desktop and then click *Gadgets* at the shortcut menu.
2. At the Gadgets Gallery, double-click the *Clock* gadget.
3. Double-click the *Weather* gadget.
4. Double-click the *Calendar* gadget.
5. Close the Gadget Gallery by clicking the Close button located in the upper right corner of the gallery.
6. Hover your mouse over the Calendar gadget until buttons display at the right side of the gadget and then click the Larger size button. (This expands the calendar to display the days of the month.)
7. Hover your mouse over the Weather gadget and then click the Options button.
8. At the Weather dialog box that displays, type in the *Select current location* text box the name of your city followed by your state (or province) and then press Enter.
9. If a drop-down list displays with city names, scroll down the list to display your city and then click your city and state (or province).
10. Click OK to close the Weather dialog box.
11. After viewing the gadgets, remove the Clock gadget by hovering the mouse over the clock and then clicking the Close button that displays at the upper right side of the clock.
12. Close the Weather gadget by hovering the mouse over the gadget and then clicking the Close button that displays.
13. Close the Calendar gadget by hovering the mouse over the gadget and then clicking the Close button that displays.

Step 2

Step 6

Step 7

Step 11

Managing Files and Folders ▪▪▪▪▪▪▪▪▪▪▪▪▪▪▪▪▪▪▪▪▪▪▪

As you begin working with programs in Windows 7, you will create files in which data (information) is saved. A file might contain a Word document, an Excel workbook, or a PowerPoint presentation. As you begin creating files, consider creating folders into which those files will be stored. You can complete file management tasks such as creating a folder and copying and moving files and folders at the Computer window. To display the Computer window shown in Figure W.8, click the Start button on the Taskbar and then click *Computer*. The various components of the Computer window are identified in Figure W.8.

Figure W.8 Computer Window

In the Content pane of the Computer window, icons display representing each hard disk drive and removable storage medium such as a CD, DVD, or USB device connected to your computer. Next to each storage device icon, Windows provides the amount of storage space available as well as a bar with the amount of used space shaded with color. This visual cue allows you to see at a glance the proportion of space available relative to the capacity of the device. Double-click a device icon in the Content pane to change the display to show the contents stored on the device. You can display contents from another device or folder using the Navigation pane or the Address bar on the Computer window.

Copying, Moving, and Deleting Files and Folders

File and folder management activities might include copying and moving files or folders from one folder or drive to another, or deleting files or folders. The Computer window offers a variety of methods for copying, moving, and deleting files and folders. This section will provide you with steps for copying, moving, and deleting files and folders using options from the Organize button on the toolbar and the shortcut menu.

To copy a file to another folder or drive, first display the file in the Content pane by identifying the location of the file. If the file is located in the Documents folder, click the *Documents* folder in the *Libraries* section in the Navigation pane and then click the file name in the Content pane that you want to copy. Click the Organize button on the toolbar and then click *Copy* at the drop-down list. In the Navigation pane, click the location where you want to copy the file. Click the Organize button and then click *Paste* at the drop-down list. You would complete similar steps to copy and paste a folder to another location.

If the desired file is located on a storage medium such as a CD, DVD, or USB device, double-click the device in the section of the Content pane labeled *Devices with Removable Storage*. (Each removable device is assigned an alphabetic drive letter by Windows, usually starting at F or G and continuing through the alphabet depending on the number of removable devices that are currently in use.) After double-clicking the storage medium in the Content pane, navigate to the desired folder and then click the file to select it. Click the Organize button on the toolbar and then click *Copy* at the drop-down list. Navigate to the desired folder, click the Organize button, and then click *Paste* at the drop-down list.

To move a file, click the desired file in the Content pane, click the Organize button on the toolbar, and then click *Cut* at the drop-down list. Navigate to the desired location, click the Organize button, and then click *Paste* at the drop-down list.

To delete a file(s) or folder(s), click the file or folder in the Content pane in the Computer window or select multiple files or folders. Click the Organize button and then click *Delete* at the drop-down list. At the message asking if you want to move the file or folder to the Recycle Bin, click the Yes button.

In Project 4, you will insert the CD that accompanies this book into the DVD or CD drive. When the CD is inserted, the drive may automatically activate and a dialog box may display telling you that the disc or device contains more than one type of content and asking what you want Windows to do. If this dialog box displays, click the Cancel button.

Project 4 — Copying a File and Folder and Deleting a File

1. Insert the CD that accompanies this textbook into the appropriate drive. If a dialog box displays telling you that the disc or device contains more than one type of content and asking what you want Windows to do, click the Cancel button.
2. Insert your storage medium (such as a USB flash drive) in the USB port (or other drive). If an AutoPlay window displays, click the Close button.
3. At the Windows 7 desktop, click the Start button and then click *Computer* located at the right side of the Start menu.
4. Copy a file from the CD that accompanies this textbook to the drive containing your storage medium by completing the following steps:
   a. Double-click the CD drive in the Content pane containing the CD from the book.
   b. Double-click the *StudentDataFiles* folder in the Content pane.
   c. Double-click the *Windows7* folder in the Content pane.
   d. Click **WordDocument01.docx** in the Content pane.
   e. Click the Organize button on the toolbar and then click *Copy* at the drop-down list.

    f. In the Computer section in the Navigation pane, click the drive containing your storage medium. (You may need to scroll down the Navigation pane.)

    g. Click the Organize button and then click *Paste* at the drop-down list.

5. Delete ***WordDocument01.docx*** from your storage medium by completing the following steps:

    a. Make sure the contents of your storage medium display in the Content pane in the Computer window.

    b. Click ***WordDocument01.docx*** in the Content pane to select it.

    c. Click the Organize button and then click *Delete* at the drop-down list.

    d. At the message asking if you want to permanently delete the file, click the Yes button.

6. Copy the Windows7 folder from the CD to your storage medium by completing the following steps:

    a. With the Computer window open, click the drive in the *Computer* section in the Navigation pane that contains the CD that accompanies this book.

    b. Double-click *StudentDataFiles* in the Content pane.

    c. Click the *Windows7* folder in the Content pane.

    d. Click the Organize button and then click *Copy* at the drop-down list.

    e. In the *Computer* section in the Navigation pane, click the drive containing your storage medium.

    f. Click the Organize button and then click *Paste* at the drop-down list.

7. Close the Computer window by clicking the Close button located in the upper right corner of the window.

In addition to options in the Organize button drop-down list, you can use options in a shortcut menu to copy, move, and delete files or folders. To use a shortcut menu, select the desired file(s) or folder(s), position the mouse pointer on the selected item, and then click the right mouse button. At the shortcut menu that displays, click the desired option such as Copy, Cut, or Delete.

Selecting Files and Folders

You can move, copy, or delete more than one file or folder at the same time. Before moving, copying, or deleting files or folders, select the desired files or folders. To make selecting easier, consider changing the display in the Content pane to List or Details. To change the display, click the Views button arrow on the toolbar in the Computer window and then click *List* or *Details* at the drop-down list. You can also cycle through the various views by clicking the Views button. Hover your mouse over the Views button and the ScreenTip *Change your view* displays.

To select adjacent files or folders, click the first file or folder, hold down the Shift key, and then click the last file or folder. To select nonadjacent files or folders, click the first file or folder, hold down the Ctrl key, and then click any other files or folders.

1. At the Windows 7 desktop, click the Start button and then click *Computer*.
2. Copy files from the CD that accompanies this textbook to the drive containing your storage medium by completing the following steps:
   a. Make sure the CD that accompanies this textbook and your storage medium are inserted in the appropriate drives.
   b. Double-click the CD drive in the Content pane in the Computer window.
   c. Double-click the *StudentDataFiles* folder in the Content pane.
   d. Double-click the *Windows7* folder in the Content pane.
   e. Change the display to List by clicking the Views button arrow on the toolbar and then clicking *List* at the drop-down list.

Step 2e

   f. Click **WordDocument01.docx** in the Content pane.
   g. Hold down the Shift key, click **WordDocument05.docx**, and then release the Shift key. (This selects five documents.)
   h. Click the Organize button and then click *Copy* at the drop-down list.
   i. In the *Computer* section in the Navigation pane, click the drive containing your storage medium.
   j. Click the Organize button and then click *Paste* at the drop-down list.

Steps 2f-2g

3. Delete the files from your storage medium that you just copied by completing the following steps:
   a. Change the view by clicking the Views button arrow bar and then clicking *List* at the drop-down list.
   b. Click **WordDocument01.docx** in the Content pane.
   c. Hold down the Shift key, click **WordDocument05.docx**, and then release the Shift key.
   d. Position the mouse pointer on any selected file, click the right mouse button, and then click *Delete* at the shortcut menu.
   e. At the message asking if you are sure you want to permanently delete the files, click Yes.
4. Close the Computer window by clicking the Close button located in the upper right corner of the window.

Step 3d

Manipulating and Creating Folders

As you begin working with and creating a number of files, consider creating folders in which you can logically group the files. To create a folder, display the Computer window and then display in the Content pane the drive or folder where you want to create the folder. Position the mouse pointer in a blank area in the Content pane, click the right mouse button, point to *New* in the shortcut menu, and then click *Folder* at the side menu. This inserts a folder icon in the Content pane and names the folder *New folder*. Type the desired name for the new folder and then press Enter.

Project 6 — Creating a New Folder

1. At the Windows 7 desktop, open the Computer window.
2. Create a new folder by completing the following steps:
   a. Double-click in the Content pane the drive that contains your storage medium.
   b. Double-click the *Windows7* folder in the Content pane. (This opens the folder.)
   c. Click the Views button arrow and then click *List* at the drop-down list.
   d. Position the mouse pointer in a blank area in the Content pane and then click the right mouse button.
   e. Point to *New* in the shortcut menu and then click *Folder* at the side menu.

Step 2e

   f. Type **SpellCheckFiles** and then press Enter. (This changes the name from *New folder* to *SpellCheckFiles*.)
3. Copy **WordSpellCheck01.docx**, **WordSpellCheck02.docx**, and **WordSpellCheck03.docx** into the SpellCheckFiles folder you just created by completing the following steps:
   a. Click the Views button arrow and then click *List* at the drop-down list. (Skip this step if *List* is already selected.)
   b. Click once on the file named **WordSpellCheck01.docx** located in the Content pane.
   c. Hold down the Shift key, click once on the file named **WordSpellCheck03.docx**, and then release the Shift key. (This selects three documents.)
   d. Click the Organize button and then click *Copy* at the drop-down list.
   e. Double-click the *SpellCheckFiles* folder in the Content pane.
   f. Click the Organize button and then click *Paste* at the drop-down list.

Step 2f

4. Delete the SpellCheckFiles folder and its
   contents by completing the following steps:
   a. Click the Back button (contains a left-
      pointing arrow) located at the left side
      of the Address bar.
   b. With the SpellCheckFiles folder selected in
      the Content pane, click the Organize button
      and then click *Delete* at the drop-down list.
   c. At the message asking you to confirm the
      deletion, click Yes.
5. Close the window by clicking the Close button located in the upper right corner of the window.

Using the Recycle Bin

Deleting the wrong file can be a disaster but Windows 7 helps protect your work with the Recycle Bin. The Recycle Bin acts just like an office wastepaper basket; you can "throw away" (delete) unwanted files, but you can "reach in" to the Recycle Bin and take out (restore) a file if you threw it away by accident.

Deleting Files to the Recycle Bin

A file or folder or selected files or folders you delete from the hard drive are sent automatically to the Recycle Bin. If you want to permanently delete files or folders from the hard drive without first sending them to the Recycle Bin, select the desired file(s) or folder(s), right click on one of the selected files or folders, hold down the Shift key, and then click *Delete* at the shortcut menu.

Files and folders deleted from a USB flash drive or disc are deleted permanently. (Recovery programs are available, however, that will help you recover deleted files or folders. If you accidentally delete a file or folder from a USB flash drive or disc, do not do anything more with the USB flash drive or disc until you can run a recovery program.)

You can delete files in the manner described earlier in this section and you can also delete a file by dragging the file icon to the Recycle Bin. To do this, click the desired file in the Content pane in the Computer window, drag the file icon on top of the Recycle Bin icon on the desktop until the text *Move to Recycle Bin* displays, and then release the mouse button.

Restoring Files from the Recycle Bin

To restore a file from the Recycle Bin, double-click the Recycle Bin icon on the desktop. This opens the Recycle Bin window shown in Figure W.9. (The contents of the Recycle Bin will vary.) To restore a file, click the file you want restored and then click the Restore this item button on the toolbar. This removes the file from the Recycle Bin and returns it to its original location. You can also restore a file by positioning the mouse pointer on the file, clicking the right mouse button, and then clicking *Restore* at the shortcut menu.

Figure W.9 Recycle Bin Window

toolbar

Navigation pane

Content pane

Details pane

Project 7 Deleting Files to and Restoring Files from the Recycle Bin

Before beginning this project, check with your instructor to determine if you can copy files to the hard drive.

1. At the Windows 7 desktop, open the Computer window.
2. Copy files from your storage medium to the Documents folder on your hard drive by completing the following steps:
   a. Double-click in the Content pane the drive containing your storage medium.
   b. Double-click the *Windows7* folder in the Content pane.
   c. Click the Views button arrow and then click *List* at the drop-down list. (Skip this step if *List* is already selected.)
   d. Click **WordSpellCheck01.docx** in the Content pane.
   e. Hold down the Shift key, click **WordSpellCheck03.docx**, and then release the Shift key.
   f. Click the Organize button and then click *Copy* at the drop-down list.
   g. Click the *Documents* folder in the *Libraries* section in the Navigation pane.
   h. Click the Organize button and then click *Paste* at the drop-down list.

Step 2g

3. Delete to the Recycle Bin the files you just copied by completing the following steps:
   a. With **WordSpellCheck01.docx** through **WordSpellCheck03.docx** selected in the Content pane, click the Organize button and then click *Delete* at the drop-down list.
   b. At the message asking you if you are sure you want to move the items to the Recycle Bin, click Yes.
4. Close the Computer window.
5. At the Windows 7 desktop, display the contents of the Recycle Bin by double-clicking the Recycle Bin icon.
6. Restore the files you just deleted by completing the following steps:
   a. Select **WordSpellCheck01.docx** through **WordSpellCheck03.docx** in the Recycle Bin Content pane. (If these files are not visible, you will need to scroll down the list of files in the Content pane.)
   b. Click the Restore the selected items button on the toolbar.

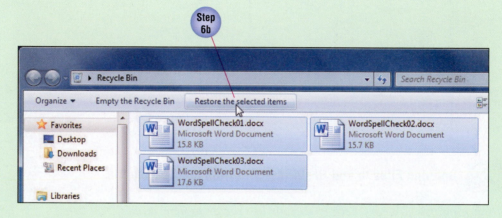

7. Close the Recycle Bin by clicking the Close button located in the upper right corner of the window.
8. Display the Computer window.
9. Click the *Documents* folder in the *Libraries* section in the Navigation pane.
10. Delete the files you restored.
11. Close the Computer window.

Emptying the Recycle Bin

Just like a wastepaper basket, the Recycle Bin can get full. To empty the Recycle Bin, position the arrow pointer on the Recycle Bin icon on the desktop and then click the right mouse button. At the shortcut menu that displays, click the *Empty Recycle Bin* option. At the message asking if you want to permanently delete the items, click Yes. You can also empty the Recycle Bin by displaying the Recycle Bin window and then clicking the Empty the Recycle Bin button on the toolbar. At the message asking if you want to permanently delete the items, click Yes. To delete a specific file from the Recycle Bin window, click the desired file in the Recycle Bin window, click the Organize button, and then *Delete* at the drop-down list. At the message asking if you want to permanently delete the file, click Yes. When you empty the Recycle Bin, the files cannot be recovered by the Recycle Bin or by Windows 7. If you have to recover a file, you will need to use a file recovery program.

Before beginning this project, check with your instructor to determine if you can delete files/folders from the Recycle Bin.

1. At the Windows 7 desktop, double-click the Recycle Bin icon.
2. At the Recycle Bin window, empty the contents by clicking the Empty the Recycle Bin button on the toolbar.
3. At the message asking you if you want to permanently delete the items, click Yes.
4. Close the Recycle Bin by clicking the Close button located in the upper right corner of the window.

Creating a Shortcut ■■■■■■■■■■■■■■■■■■■■■■■

If you use a file or program on a consistent basis, consider creating a shortcut to the file or program. A shortcut is a specialized icon that represents very small files that point the operating system to the actual item, whether it is a file, a folder, or an application. If you create a shortcut to a Word document, the shortcut icon is not the actual document but a path to the document. Double-click the shortcut icon and Windows 7 opens the document in Word.

One method for creating a shortcut is to display the Computer window and then make active the drive or folder where the file is located. Right-click the desired file, point to *Send To,* and then click *Desktop (create shortcut).* You can easily delete a shortcut icon from the desktop by dragging the shortcut icon to the Recycle Bin icon. This deletes the shortcut icon but does not delete the file to which the shortcut pointed.

Project 9   **Creating a Shortcut**

1. At the Windows 7 desktop, display the Computer window.
2. Double-click the drive containing your storage medium.
3. Double-click the *Windows7* folder in the Content pane.
4. Change the display of files to a list by clicking the Views button arrow and then clicking *List* at the drop-down list. (Skip this step if *List* is already selected.)
5. Create a shortcut to the file named **WordLetter01.docx** by right-clicking **WordLetter01.docx**, pointing to *Send to,* and then clicking *Desktop (create shortcut).*

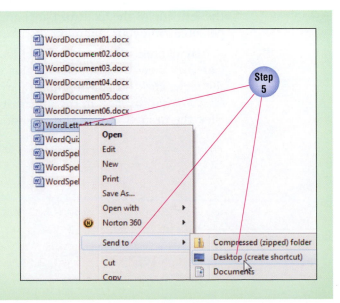

6. Close the Computer window.
7. Open Word and the file named **WordLetter01.docx** by double-clicking the *WordLetter01.docx* shortcut icon on the desktop.
8. After viewing the file in Word, exit Word by clicking the Close button that displays in the upper right corner of the window.
9. Delete the *WordLetter01.docx* shortcut icon by completing the following steps:
   a. At the desktop, position the mouse pointer on the *WordLetter01.docx* shortcut icon.
   b. Hold down the left mouse button, drag the icon on top of the Recycle Bin icon, and then release the mouse button.

Step 7

Exploring the Control Panel ■■■■■■■■■■■ ■■■■■■■ ■■ ■■■■

The Control Panel, shown in Figure W.10, contains a variety of icons you can use to customize the appearance and functionality of your computer as well as access and change system settings. Display the Control Panel by clicking the Start button on the Taskbar and then clicking *Control Panel* at the Start menu. The Control Panel organizes settings into categories to make them easier to find. Click a category icon and the Control Panel displays lower-level categories and tasks within each of them.

Hover your mouse over a category icon in the Control Panel and a ScreenTip displays with an explanation of what options are available. For example, if you hover the mouse over the Appearance and Personalization icon, a ScreenTip displays with information about the tasks available in the category such as changing the appearance of desktop items, applying a theme or screen saver to your computer, or customizing the Start menu and Taskbar.

If you click a category icon in the Control Panel, the Control Panel displays all of the available subcategories and tasks in the category. Also, the categories display in text form at the left side of the Control Panel. For example, if you click the Appearance and Personalization category icon, the Control Panel displays as shown in Figure W.11. Notice how the Control Panel categories display at the left side of the Control Panel and options for changing the appearance and personalizing your computer display in the middle of the Control Panel.

By default, the Control Panel displays categories of tasks in what is called Category view. You can change this view to *Large icons* or *Small icons*. To change the view, click the down-pointing arrow that displays at the right side of the text *View by* that displays in the upper right corner of the Control Panel, and then click the desired view at the drop-down list (see Figure W.10).

Figure W.10 The Control Panel

Click a category icon or hyperlink to display all of the category's options.

Use this option to change views.

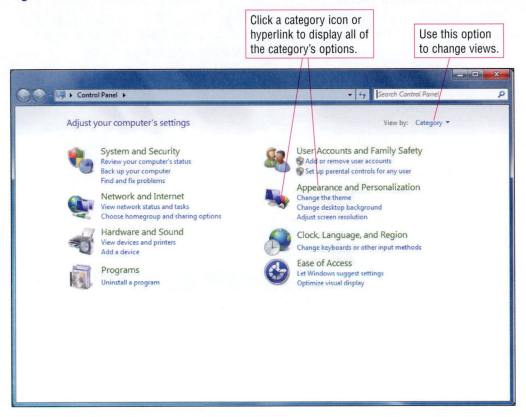

Figure W.11 Appearance and Personalization Window

Click this option to return to the main Control Panel.

lower-level categories

task hyperlinks

Click a category to display category options.

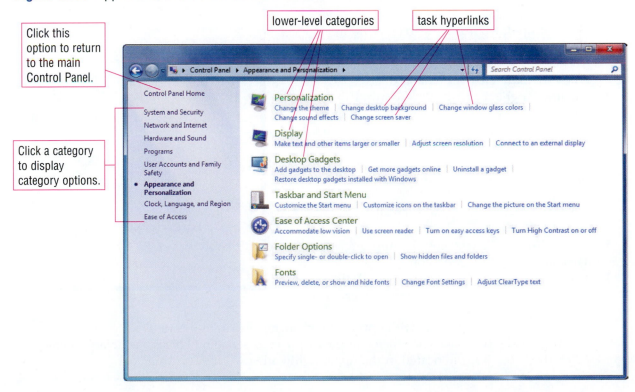

Project 10 Changing the Desktop Theme

1. At the Windows 7 desktop, click the Start button and then click *Control Panel* at the Start menu.
2. At the Control Panel, click the Appearance and Personalization category icon.

3. Click the <u>Change the theme</u> hyperlink that displays below the Personalization category in the panel at the right in the Control Panel.
4. At the window that displays with options for changing visuals and sounds on your computer, click the *Landscapes* theme.

5. Click the <u>Desktop Background</u> hyperlink that displays in the lower left corner of the panel at the right.
6. Click the button that displays below the text *Change picture every* and then click *10 Seconds* at the drop-down list. (This tells Windows to change the picture on your desktop every 10 seconds.)
7. Click the Save changes button that displays in the lower right corner of the Control Panel.
8. Click the Close button located in the upper right corner to close the Control Panel.
9. Look at the picture that displays as the background at the desktop. Wait for 10 seconds and then look at the second picture that displays.
10. Click the Start button and then click *Control Panel* at the Start menu.
11. At the Control Panel, click the Appearance and Personalization category icon.
12. Click the <u>Change the theme</u> hyperlink that displays below the Personalization category in the panel at the right.

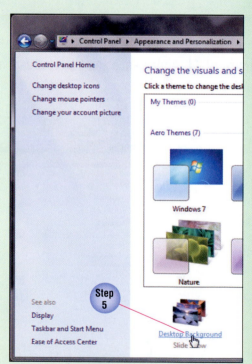

13. At the window that displays with options for changing visuals and sounds on your computer, click the *Windows 7* theme in the *Aero Themes* section. (This is the default theme.)
14. Click the Close button located in the upper right corner of the Control Panel.

Searching in the Control Panel

The Control Panel contains a large number of options for customizing the appearance and functionality of your computer. If you want to customize a feature and are not sure where the options for the feature are located, search for the feature. To do this, display the Control Panel and then type the name of the desired feature. By default, the insertion point is positioned in the *Search Control Panel* text box. When you type the feature name in the Search Control Panel, options related to the feature display in the Control Panel.

Project 11 — Customizing the Mouse

1. Click the Start button and then click *Control Panel*.
2. At the Control Panel, type **mouse**. (The insertion point is automatically located in the *Search Control Panel* text box when you open the Control Panel. When you type *mouse*, features for customizing the mouse display in the Control Panel.)
3. Click the Mouse icon that displays in the Control Panel.
4. At the Mouse Properties dialog box, notice the options that display. (The *Switch primary and secondary buttons* option might be useful, for example, if you are left-handed and want to switch the buttons on the mouse.)
5. Click the Cancel button to remove the dialog box.
6. At the Control Panel, click the Change the mouse pointer display or speed hyperlink.

7. At the Mouse Properties dialog box with the Pointer Options tab selected, click the *Display pointer trails* check box in the *Visibility* section to insert a check mark.
8. Drag the button on the slider bar (located below the *Display pointer trails* check box) approximately to the middle of the bar.
9. Click OK to close the dialog box.
10. Close the Control Panel.
11. Move the mouse pointer around the screen to see the pointer trails as well as the speed at which the mouse moves.

Displaying Personalize Options with a Shortcut Command

In addition to the Control Panel, you can display customization options with a command from a shortcut menu. Display a shortcut menu by positioning the mouse pointer in the desired position and then clicking the right mouse button. For example, display a shortcut menu with options for customizing the desktop by positioning the mouse pointer in an empty area on the desktop and then clicking the right mouse button. At the shortcut menu that displays, click the desired shortcut command.

Project 12 | Customizing with a Shortcut Command

1. At the Windows 7 desktop, position the mouse pointer in an empty area on the desktop, click the right mouse button, and then click *Personalize* at the shortcut menu.
2. At the Control Panel Appearance and Personalization window that displays, click the <u>Change mouse pointers</u> hyperlink that displays at the left side of the window.
3. At the Mouse Properties dialog box, click the Pointer Options tab.
4. Click in the *Display pointer trails* check box to remove the check mark.
5. Click OK to close the dialog box.
6. At the Control Panel Appearance and Personalization window, click the <u>Screen Saver</u> hyperlink that displays in the lower right corner of the window.
7. At the Screen Saver Settings dialog box, click the option button below the *Screen saver* option and then click *Ribbons* at the drop-down list.
8. Check the number in the *Wait* text box. If a number other than *1* displays, click the down-pointing arrow in the spin box at the right side of the text box until *1* displays. (This tells Windows to display the screen saver after one minute of inactivity.)
9. Click OK to close the dialog box.
10. Close the Control Panel by clicking the Close button located in the upper right corner of the window.

11. Do not touch the mouse or keyboard and wait over one minute for the screen saver to display. After watching the screen saver, move the mouse. (This redisplays the desktop.)
12. Right-click in an empty area on the desktop and then click *Personalize* at the shortcut menu.
13. At the Control Panel Appearance and Personalization window, click the <u>Screen Saver</u> hyperlink.
14. At the Screen Saver Settings dialog box, click the option button below the *Screen saver* option and then click *(None)* at the drop-down list.
15. Click OK to close the dialog box.
16. Close the Control Panel Appearance and Personalization window.

Exploring Windows Help and Support ▪▪▪▪▪▪▪▪▪▪▪▪▪▪▪▪▪▪▪

Windows 7 includes an on-screen reference guide providing information, explanations, and interactive help on learning Windows features. Get help at the Windows Help and Support window shown in Figure W.12. Display this window by clicking the Start button and then clicking *Help and Support* at the Start menu. Use buttons in the window toolbar to display the opening Windows Help and Support window, print the current information, display a list of contents, get customer support or other types of services, and display a list of Help options.

Figure W.12 Windows Help and Support Window

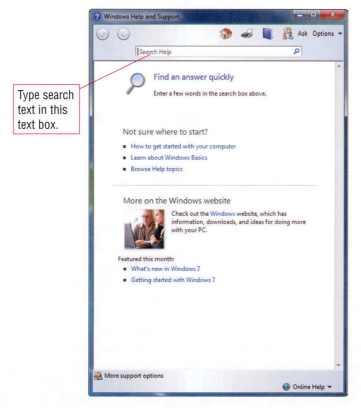

Type search text in this text box.

1. At the Windows 7 desktop, click the Start button and then click *Help and Support* at the Start menu.
2. At the Windows Help and Support window, click the <u>Learn about Windows Basics</u> hyperlink.
3. Click a hyperlink that interests you, read the information, and then click the Back button on the Windows Help and Support window toolbar. (The Back button is located in the upper left corner of the window.)
4. Click another hyperlink that interests you and then read the information.
5. Click the Help and Support home button that displays on the window toolbar. (This returns you to the opening Windows Help and Support window.)
6. Click in the *Search Help* text box, type **delete files**, and then press Enter.
7. Click the <u>Delete a file or folder</u> hyperlink that displays in the window.
8. Read the information that displays about deleting files or folders and then click the Print button on the window toolbar.
9. At the Print dialog box, click the Print button.
10. Click the Close button to close the Windows Help and Support window.

Using Search Tools ■

The Start menu contains a search tool you can use to quickly find a program or file on your computer. To use the search tool, click the Start button and then type the first few characters of the program or file for which you are searching in the *Search programs and files* text box. As you type characters in the text box, a pop-up list displays with program names or file names that begin with the characters. As you continue typing characters, the search tool refines the list.

You can also search for programs or files with the search text box in the Computer window. The search text box displays in the upper right corner of the Computer window at the right side of the Address bar. If you want to search a specific folder, make that folder active in the Content pane and then type the search text in the text box.

When conducting a search, you can use the asterisk (*) as a wildcard character in place of any letters, numbers, or symbols within a file name. For example, in the following project you will search for file names containing *check* by typing ***check** in the search text box. The asterisk indicates that the file name can start with any letter but it must contain the letters *check* somewhere in the file name.

Project 14   Searching for Programs and Files

1. At the Windows 7 desktop, click the Start button.
2. With the insertion point positioned in the *Search programs and files* text box, type **paint**. (Notice as you type the letters that Windows displays programs and/or files that begin with the same letters you are typing or that are associated with the same letters in a keyword. Notice that the Paint program displays below the heading *Programs* at the top of the list. Depending on the contents stored in the computer you are using, additional items may display below Paint.)

3. Click *Paint* that displays below the *Programs* heading.
4. Close the Paint window.
5. Click the Start button and then click *Computer*.
6. At the Computer window, double-click the icon representing your storage medium.
7. Double-click the *Windows7* folder.
8. Click in the search text box located at the right of the Address bar and then type **document**. (As you begin typing the letters, Windows filters the list of files in the Content pane to those that contain the letters you type. Notice that the Address bar displays *Search Results in Windows7* to indicate that the files that display matching your criteria were limited to the current folder.)
9. Select the text *document* that displays in the search text box and then type ***check**. (Notice that the Content pane displays file names containing the letters *check* no matter how the file name begins.)
10. Double-click **WordSpellCheck02.docx** to open the document in Word.
11. Close the document and exit Word by clicking the Close button located in the upper right corner of the window.
12. Close the Computer window.

Browsing the Internet Using Internet Explorer 8.0

Microsoft Internet Explorer 8.0 is a web browser program with options and features for displaying sites as well as navigating and searching for information on the Internet. The *Internet* is a network of computers connected around the world. Users access the Internet for several purposes: to communicate using instant messaging and/or email, to subscribe to newsgroups, to transfer files, to socialize with other users around the globe in chat rooms, and also to access virtually any kind of information imaginable.

Using the Internet, people can find a phenomenal amount of information for private or public use. To use the Internet, three things are generally required: an Internet Service Provider (ISP), a program to browse the Web (called a *web browser*), and a *search engine*. In this section, you will learn how to:

- Navigate the Internet using URLs and hyperlinks
- Use search engines to locate information
- Download web pages and images

You will use the Microsoft Internet Explorer web browser to locate information on the Internet. Uniform Resource Locators, referred to as URLs, are the method used to identify locations on the Internet. The steps for browsing the Internet vary but generally include: opening Internet Explorer, typing the URL for the desired site, navigating the various pages of the site, navigating to other sites using links, and then closing Internet Explorer.

To launch Internet Explorer 8.0, click the Internet Explorer icon on the Taskbar at the Windows desktop. Figure IE.1 identifies the elements of the Internet Explorer, version 8.0, window. The web page that displays in your Internet Explorer window may vary from what you see in Figure IE.1.

If you know the URL for the desired website, click in the Address bar, type the URL, and then press Enter. The website's home page displays in a tab within the Internet Explorer window. URLs (Uniform Resource Locators) are the method used to identify locations on the Internet. The format of a URL is *http://server-name.path*. The first part of the URL, *http*, stands for HyperText Transfer Protocol, which is the protocol or language used to transfer data within the World Wide Web. The colon and slashes separate the protocol from the server name. The server name is the second component of the URL. For example, in the URL http://www.microsoft.com, the server name is *microsoft*. The last part of the URL specifies the domain to which the server belongs. For example, *.com* refers to "commercial" and establishes that the URL is a commercial company. Examples of other domains include *.edu* for "educational," *.gov* for "government," and *.mil* for "military."

Figure IE.1 Internet Explorer Window

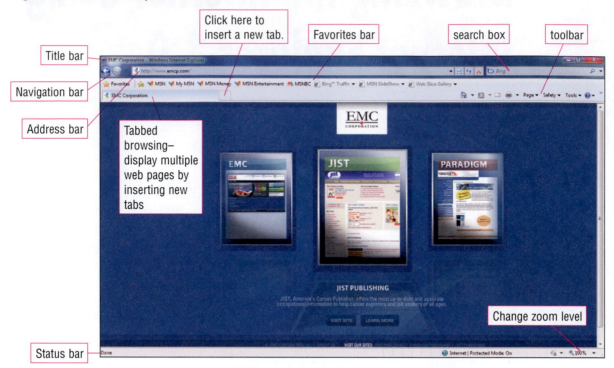

Title bar

Navigation bar

Address bar

Click here to insert a new tab.

Favorites bar

search box

toolbar

Tabbed browsing–display multiple web pages by inserting new tabs

JIST PUBLISHING

JIST, America's Career Publisher, offers the most up-to-date and accurate occupational information to help career explorers and job seekers of all ages.

VISIT SITE   LEARN MORE

Change zoom level

Status bar

Project 1   **Browsing the Internet Using URLs**

1. Make sure you are connected to the Internet through an Internet Service Provider and that the Windows desktop displays. (Check with your instructor to determine if you need to complete steps for accessing the Internet such as typing a user name and password to log on.)

2. Launch Microsoft Internet Explorer by clicking the Internet Explorer icon located on the Taskbar located at the bottom of the Windows desktop.

3. At the Internet Explorer window, explore the website for Yosemite National Park by completing the following steps:

   a. Click in the Address bar, type **www.nps.gov/yose**, and then press Enter.

   b. Scroll down the home page for Yosemite National Park by clicking the down-pointing arrow on the vertical scroll bar located at the right side of the Internet Explorer window.

   c. Print the home page by clicking the Print button located on the Internet Explorer toolbar. (Some websites have a printer friendly button you can click to print the page.)

Step 3a

Step 3c

Step 3b

4. Explore the website for Glacier National Park by completing the following steps:
   a. Click in the Address bar, type **www.nps.gov/glac**, and then press Enter.
   b. Print the home page by clicking the Print button located on the Internet Explorer toolbar.
5. Close Internet Explorer by clicking the Close button (contains an X) located in the upper right corner of the Internet Explorer window.

Navigating Using Hyperlinks ▪▪▪▪▪▪▪▪▪▪▪▪▪▪▪▪▪▪▪▪▪▪▪▪

Most web pages contain "hyperlinks" that you click to connect to another page within the website or to another site on the Internet. Hyperlinks may display in a web page as underlined text in a specific color or as images or icons. To use a hyperlink, position the mouse pointer on the desired hyperlink until the mouse pointer turns into a hand, and then click the left mouse button. Use hyperlinks to navigate within and between sites on the Internet. The navigation bar in the Internet Explorer window contains a Back button that, when clicked, takes you to the previous web page viewed. If you click the Back button and then want to return to the previous page, click the Forward button. You can continue clicking the Back button to back your way out of several linked pages in reverse order since Internet Explorer maintains a history of the websites you visit.

Project 2   Navigating Using Hyperlinks

1. Make sure you are connected to the Internet and then click the Internet Explorer icon on the Taskbar.
2. At the Internet Explorer window, display the White House web page and navigate in the page by completing the following steps:
   a. Click in the Address bar, type **whitehouse.gov**, and then press Enter.
   b. At the White House home page, position the mouse pointer on a hyperlink that interests you until the pointer turns into a hand, and then click the left mouse button.
   c. At the linked web page, click the Back button. (This returns you to the White House home page.)
   d. At the White House home page, click the Forward button to return to the previous web page viewed.
   e. Print the web page by clicking the Print button on the Internet Explorer toolbar.
3. Display the website for Amazon.com and navigate in the site by completing the following steps:
   a. Click in the Address bar, type **www.amazon.com**, and then press Enter.

b. At the Amazon.com home page, click a hyperlink related to books.

c. When a book web page displays, click the Print button on the Internet Explorer toolbar.

4. Close Internet Explorer by clicking the Close button (contains an X) located in the upper right corner of the Internet Explorer window.

Searching for Specific Sites ■■■■■■■■■■■■■■■■■■■■■■■■■■■■

If you do not know the URL for a specific site or you want to find information on the Internet but do not know what site to visit, complete a search with a search engine. A search engine is a software program created to search quickly and easily for desired information. A variety of search engines are available on the Internet, each offering the opportunity to search for specific information. One method for searching for information is to click in the search box located to the right of the Address bar, type a keyword or phrase related to your search, and then click the Search button or press Enter. Another method for completing a search is to visit the website for a search engine and use options at the site.

Bing is Microsoft's online search portal and is the default search engine used by Internet Explorer. Bing organizes search results by topic category and provides related search suggestions.

Project 3 **Searching for Information by Topic**

1. Start Internet Explorer.

2. At the Internet Explorer window, search for sites on bluegrass music by completing the following steps:

a. Click in the search box (may display *Bing*) located at the right side of the Address bar.

b. Type **bluegrass music** and then press Enter.

c. When a list of sites displays in the Bing results window, click a site that interests you.

d. When the page displays, click the Print button.

3. Use the Yahoo! search engine to find sites on bluegrass music by completing the following steps:

a. Click in the Address bar, type **www.yahoo.com**, and then press Enter.

b. At the Yahoo! website, with the insertion point positioned in the search text box, type **bluegrass music** and then press Enter. (Notice that the sites displayed vary from sites displayed in the earlier search.)

c. Click hyperlinks until a website displays that interests you.

d. Print the page.

4. Use the Google search engine to find sites on jazz music by completing the following steps:
   a. Click in the Address bar, type **www.google.com**, and then press Enter.
   b. At the Google website, with the insertion point positioned in the search text box, type **jazz music** and then press Enter.
   c. Click a site that interests you.
   d. Print the page.
5. Close Internet Explorer.

Using a Metasearch Engine ▪▪▪▪▪▪▪▪▪▪▪▪▪▪▪▪▪▪

Bing, Yahoo!, and Google are search engines that search the Web for content and display search results. In addition to individual search engines, you can use a metasearch engine, such as Dogpile, that sends your search text to other search engines and then compiles the results in one list. With a metasearch engine, you type the search text once and then access results from a wider group of search engines. The Dogpile metasearch engine provides search results from Google, Yahoo!, Bing, and Ask.

Project 4   Searching with a Metasearch Search Engine

1. At the Windows desktop, click the Internet Explorer icon on the Taskbar.
2. Click in the Address bar.
3. Type **www.dogpile.com** and then press Enter.
4. At the Dogpile website, type **jazz music** in the search text box and then press Enter.
5. Click a hyperlink that interests you.
6. Close the Internet Explorer window.

Completing Advanced Searches for Specific Sites ▪■▪■▪■▪■▪

Web Search

The Internet contains an enormous amount of information. Depending on what you are searching for on the Internet and the search engine you use, some searches can result in several thousand "hits" (sites). Wading through a large number of sites can be very time-consuming and counterproductive. Narrowing a search to very specific criteria can greatly reduce the number of hits for a search. To narrow a search, use the advanced search options offered by the search engine.

Project 5   Narrowing a Search

1. Start Internet Explorer.
2. Search for sites on skydiving in Oregon by completing the following steps:
   a. Click in the Address bar, type **www.yahoo.com**, and then press Enter.
   b. At the Yahoo! home page, click the Web Search button next to the search text box.
   c. Click the <u>more</u> hyperlink located above the search text box and then click Advanced Search at the drop-down list.
   d. At the Advanced Web Search page, click in the search text box next to *all of these words*.
   e. Type **skydiving Oregon tandem static line**. (This limits the search to web pages containing all of the words typed in the search text box.)
   f. Click the Yahoo! Search button.
   g. When the list of websites displays, click a hyperlink that interests you.
   h. Click the Back button until the Yahoo! Advanced Web Search page displays.
   i. Click in the *the exact phrase* text box and then type **skydiving in Oregon**.
   j. Click the *Only .com domains* in the *Site/Domain* section.
   k. Click the Yahoo! Search button.
   l. When the list of websites displays, click a hyperlink that interests you.
   m. Print the page.
3. Close Internet Explorer.

Step 2c

Web | Images | Video | Local | Shopping | more ˅
Answers
Directory
Jobs
News
Sports
All Search Services
Advanced Search
Preferences
Advertising Programs

© 2010 Yahoo! | Page Tour | ... | ... Subm...

Step 2e

YAHOO!® SEARCH   Yahoo! - Search Home - Help

Advanced Web Search

You can use the options on this page to create a very specific search. Just fill in the fields you need for your current search.

[Yahoo! Search]

Show results with	all of these words	skydiving Oregon tandem static line	any part of the page ▼
	the exact phrase		any part of the page ▼
	any of these words		any part of the page ▼
	none of these words		any part of the page ▼

Step 2i

YAHOO!® SEARCH   Yahoo! - Search Home - Help

Advanced Web Search

You can use the options on this page to create a very specific search. Just fill in the fields you need for your current search.

[Yahoo! Search]

Show results with	all of these words	skydiving Oregon tandem static line	any part of the page ▼
	the exact phrase	skydiving in Oregon	any part of the page ▼
	any of these words		any part of the page ▼
	none of these words		any part of the page ▼

Tip: Use these options to look for an exact phrase or to exclude pages containing certain words. You can also limit your search to certain parts of pages.

Step 2k

Updated   anytime ▼

Site/Domain
○ Any domain
● Only .com domains   ○ Only .edu domains
○ Only .gov domains   ○ Only .org domains

Step 2j

Downloading Images, Text, and Web Pages from the Internet ▪▪▪▪

The image(s) and/or text that display when you open a web page as well as the web page itself can be saved as a separate file. This separate file can be viewed, printed, or inserted in another file. The information you want to save in a separate file is downloaded from the Internet by Internet Explorer and saved in a folder of your choosing with the name you specify. Copyright laws protect much of the information on the Internet. Before using information downloaded from the Internet, check the site for restrictions. If you do use information, make sure you properly cite the source.

Project 6 Downloading Images and Web Pages

1. Start Internet Explorer.
2. Download a web page and image from Banff National Park by completing the following steps:
   a. Search for sites on the Internet for Banff National Park.
   b. From the list of sites that displays, choose a site that contains information about Banff National Park and at least one image of the park.
   c. Save the web page as a separate file by clicking the Page button on the Internet Explorer toolbar and then clicking *Save As* at the drop-down list.
   d. At the Save Webpage dialog box, type **BanffWebPage**.
   e. Navigate to the drive containing your storage medium and then click the Save button.

3. Save an image file by completing the following steps:
   a. Right-click an image that displays at the website. (The image that displays may vary from what you see below.)
   b. At the shortcut menu that displays, click *Save Picture As*.
   c. At the Save Picture dialog box, type **BanffImage** in the *File name* text box.

Step
3b

Step
3c

   d. Navigate to the drive containing your storage medium and then click the Save button.
4. Close Internet Explorer.

Project 7   Opening the Saved Web Page and Image in a Word Document

1. Open Microsoft Word by clicking the Start button on the Taskbar, clicking *All Programs*, clicking *Microsoft Office*, and then clicking *Microsoft Word 2010*.
2. With Microsoft Word open, insert the image in a document by completing the following steps:
   a. Click the Insert tab and then click the Picture button in the Illustrations group.
   b. At the Insert Picture dialog box, navigate to the drive containing your storage medium and then double-click *BanffImage.jpg*.
   c. When the image displays in the Word document, print the document by pressing Ctrl + P and then clicking the Print button.
   d. Close the document by clicking the File tab and then clicking the Close button. At the message asking if you want to save the changes, click *Don't Save*.
3. Open the **BanffWebPage.mht** file by completing the following steps:
   a. Click the File tab and then click the Open button.
   b. At the Open dialog box, navigate to the drive containing your storage medium and then double-click *BanffWebPage.mht*.
   c. Preview the web page(s) by pressing Ctrl + P. At the Print tab Backstage view, preview the page shown at the right side of the Backstage view.
4. Close Word by clicking the Close button (contains an X) that displays in the upper right corner of the screen.

Step
2b

Step
3b

Microsoft Word

Level 1

Unit 1 ■ Editing and Formatting Documents

Preparing Documents

PERFORMANCE OBJECTIVES

Upon successful completion of Chapter 1, you will be able to:

- **Open Microsoft Word**
- **Create, save, name, print, open, and close a Word document**
- **Exit Word**
- **Edit a document**
- **Move the insertion point within a document**
- **Scroll within a document**
- **Select text in a document**
- **Use the Undo and Redo buttons**
- **Check spelling and grammar in a document**
- **Use the Help feature**

Tutorials

1.1 Creating, Saving, and Printing a Document

1.2 Using the AutoCorrect Feature

1.3 Previewing and Printing Documents

1.4 Opening and Pinning a Document

1.5 Editing a Document

1.6 Using the Spelling and Grammar Feature

1.7 Using the Help Feature

In this chapter, you will learn to create, save, name, print, open, close, and edit a Word document as well as complete a spelling and grammar check. You will also learn about the Help feature, which is an on-screen reference manual providing information on features and commands for each program in the Office suite. Before continuing, make sure you read the *Getting Started* section presented at the beginning of this book. This section contains information about computer hardware and software, using the mouse, executing commands, and exploring Help files. Model answers for this chapter's projects appear on the following page.

Word2010L1C1

Note: Before beginning the projects, copy to your storage medium the Word2010L1C1 subfolder from the Word2010L1 folder on the CD that accompanies this textbook. Steps on how to copy a folder are presented on the inside of the back cover of this textbook. Do this every time you start a chapter's projects.

The traditional chronological resume lists your work experience in reverse-chronological order (starting with your current or most recent position). The functional style deemphasizes the "where" and "when" of your career and instead groups similar experience, talents, and qualifications regardless of when they occurred.

Like the chronological resume, the hybrid resume includes specifics about where you worked, when you worked there, and what your job titles were. Like a functional resume, a hybrid resume emphasizes your most relevant qualifications in an expanded summary section, in several "career highlights" bullet points at the top of your resume, or in project summaries.

Created:
Thursday, December 6, 2012
Note: The two paragraphs will become the 2nd and 3rd paragraphs in the 5th section.

Project 1 Prepare a Word Document

WL1-C1-P1-Computers.docx

The majority of new jobs being created in the United States today involve daily work with computers. Computer-related careers include technical support jobs, sales and training, programming and applications development, network and database administration, and computer engineering.

A technician is an entry-level worker who installs and maintains hardware and/or software. Technical sales and technical training jobs emphasize interpersonal skills as much as they do technical skills. Programming is one of the most difficult and highly skilled jobs in the industry. Programmers create new software, such as Microsoft Windows or computer games, and often have college degrees. Software engineers are programmers trained to create software in teams with other programmers. Application developers are similar to programmers, but they use existing software such as a database to create applications for business solutions. Application development jobs include database administration, network administration, and systems analysis. Database and network administration involve overseeing and maintaining databases and networks, respectively. Systems analysts design information systems or evaluate and improve existing ones.

Project 2 Save and Edit a Word Document

WL1-C1-P2-CompCareers.docx

COMPUTER KEYBOARDS

To enter commands into a computer or to enter data into it, a user needs an input device. An input device can be built into the computer, like the keyboard in a laptop, or it can be connected to the computer by a cable. Some input devices, like remote keyboards, send directions to the computer by means of an infrared signal.

Keyboards can be external devices that are attached by a cable, or they can be attached to the CPU case itself as they are in laptops. Most keyboards today are QWERTY keyboards, which take their name from the first six keys at the left of the first row of letters. The QWERTY design was invented in the early days of mechanical typewriters to slow down typists and thus keep keys from jamming.

The DVORAK keyboard is an alternative to the QWERTY keyboard. On the DVORAK keyboard, the most commonly used keys are placed close to the user's fingertips and this increases typing speed. You can install software on a QWERTY keyboard that emulates a DVORAK keyboard. The ability to emulate other keyboards is convenient especially when working with foreign languages.

Project 4 Insert and Delete Text

WL1-C1-P4-CompKeyboards.docx

ON THE HORIZON

The march of computer technology continues to change the nature of our jobs and workplaces. Considering the global economic and technology scene, some major changes in occupations involve changes in communications media, work locations, and communications tools.

Communications Media

One key to being successful in our modern, technological world is spotting a trend early and adjusting one's career direction accordingly. For example, 80 percent of daily newspaper readers are over 50 years old. Young readers are not as interested in the printed word, and each year the industry suffers from a shrinking number of subscriptions. The young are still reading, but they are reading online media sites rather than the printed page. Websites make excellent dynamic newspapers, as they can be changed at will, they require no printing or distribution costs, and they do not require the newspaper delivery person to go door to door asking for payment. This gradual switch to the new media is causing many jobs to change. The number of printing and lithography jobs is shrinking, but web developers and graphic artists are in demand.

Industry-morphing trends are sweeping away many traditional approaches to the marketing and distribution of products. Increasingly, music and movies are being downloaded versus being bought on a disc. Fewer movies are being rented, while more people are watching them on-demand through their cable systems. Once a successful approach is discovered, every type of media that can be digitized rather than produced and distributed in physical form will come under increasing pressure to modernize in order to match the competition. Individuals managing career paths need to be aware of these trends and avoid becoming part of a downsizing effort.

Telecommuting

Telecommuting, sometimes called telework, involves working via computer from home or while traveling rather than going to the office on a daily basis. Approximately 25 million Americans telecommute at least one day per week. Telework plans have been especially successful for commissioned salespeople, who are often more productive when away from the office environment.

Project 5 Complete a Spelling and Grammar Check

WL1-C1-P5-TechOccTrends.docx

P roject **1** **Prepare a Word Document** **2 Parts**

You will create a short document containing information on computers and then save, print, and close the document.

Opening Microsoft Word

Microsoft Office 2010 contains a word processing program named Word that you can use to create, save, edit, and print documents. The steps to open Word may vary depending on your system setup. Generally, to open Word, you would click the Start button on the Taskbar at the Windows desktop, point to *All Programs*, click *Microsoft Office*, and then click *Microsoft Word 2010*.

Start

▼ **Quick Steps**

Open Word
1. Click Start button.
2. Point to *All Programs*.
3. Click *Microsoft Office*.
4. Click *Microsoft Word 2010*.

Creating, Saving, Printing, and Closing a Document

When Microsoft Word is open, a blank document displays as shown in Figure 1.1. The features of the document screen are described in Table 1.1.

At a blank document, type information to create a document. A document is any information you choose — for instance, a letter, report, term paper, table, and so on. Some things to consider when typing text are:

- **Word Wrap:** As you type text to create a document, you do not need to press the Enter key at the end of each line because Word wraps text to the next line. A word is wrapped to the next line if it begins before the right margin and continues past the right margin. The only times you need to press Enter are to end a paragraph, create a blank line, or end a short line.

- **AutoCorrect:** Word contains a feature that automatically corrects certain words as you type them. For example, if you type the word *adn* instead of *and*, Word automatically corrects it when you press the spacebar after the word. AutoCorrect will also superscript the letters that follow an ordinal number (a number indicating a position in a series). For example, if you type *2nd* and then press the spacebar or Enter key, Word will convert this ordinal number to 2nd.

- **Automatic Spell Checker:** By default, Word will automatically insert a red wavy line below words that are not contained in the Spelling dictionary or automatically corrected by AutoCorrect. This may include misspelled words, proper names, some terminology, and some foreign words. If you type a word not recognized by the Spelling dictionary, leave it as written if the word is correct. However, if the word is incorrect, you have two choices — you can delete the word and then type it correctly, or you can position the I-beam pointer on the word, click the right mouse button, and then click the correct spelling in the pop-up list.

- **Automatic Grammar Checker:** Word includes an automatic grammar checker. If the grammar checker detects a sentence containing a grammatical error, a green wavy line is inserted below the sentence. You can leave the sentence as written or position the mouse I-beam pointer on the sentence, click the *right* mouse button, and a pop-up list will display with possible corrections.

- **Spacing Punctuation:** Typically, Word uses Calibri as the default typeface, which is a proportional typeface. (You will learn more about typefaces in Chapter 2.) When typing text in a proportional typeface, space once (rather than twice) after

HINT

To avoid opening the same program twice, use the Taskbar to see which programs are open.

HINT

A book icon displays in the Status bar. A check mark on the book indicates no spelling errors detected in the document by the spell checker, while an X in the book indicates errors. Double-click the book icon to move to the next error. If the book icon is not visible, right-click the Status bar and then click the *Spelling and Grammar Check* option at the pop-up list.

Figure 1.1 Blank Document

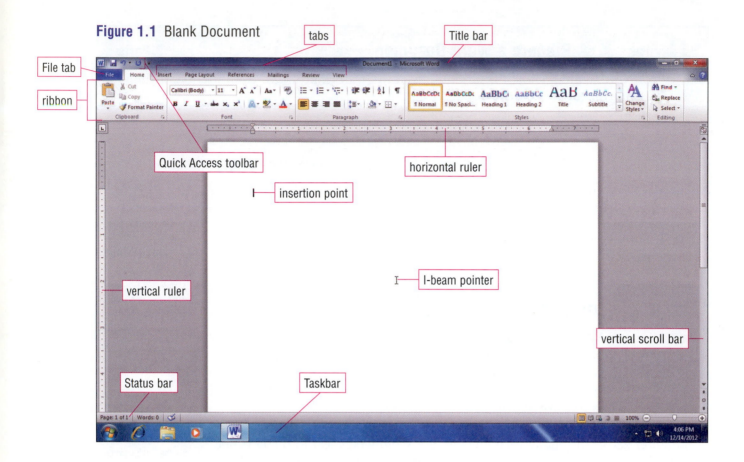

Table 1.1 Microsoft Word Screen Features

Feature	Description
File tab	Click the File tab and the Backstage view displays containing buttons and tabs for working with and managing documents.
Horizontal ruler	Used to set margins, indents, and tabs.
I-beam pointer	Used to move the insertion point or to select text.
Insertion point	Indicates location of next character entered at the keyboard.
Quick Access toolbar	Contains buttons for commonly used commands.
Ribbon	Area containing the tabs and commands divided into groups.
Status bar	Displays number of pages and words, View buttons, and the Zoom slider bar.
Title bar	Displays document name followed by program name.
Tabs	Contains commands and features organized into groups.
Taskbar	Divided into three sections—the Start button, the task buttons area, and the notification area.
Vertical ruler	Used to set top and bottom margins.
Vertical scroll bar	Used to view various parts of the document.

end-of-sentence punctuation such as a period, question mark, or exclamation point, and after a colon. Proportional typeface is set closer together, and extra white space at the end of a sentence or after a colon is not needed.

- **Option Buttons:** As you insert and edit text in a document, you may notice an option button popping up in your text. The name and appearance of this option button varies depending on the action. If a word you type is corrected by AutoCorrect, if you create an automatic list, or if autoformatting is applied to text, the AutoCorrect Options button appears. Click this button to undo the specific automatic action. If you paste text in a document, the Paste Options button appears near the text. Click this button to display the Paste Options gallery with buttons for controlling how the pasted text is formatted.

- **AutoComplete:** Microsoft Word and other Office applications include an AutoComplete feature that inserts an entire item when you type a few identifying characters. For example, type the letters *Mond* and *Monday* displays in a ScreenTip above the letters. Press the Enter key or press F3 and Word inserts *Monday* in the document.

Using the New Line Command

A Word document is based on a template that applies default formatting. Some basic formatting includes 1.15 line spacing and 10 points of spacing after a paragraph. Each time you press the Enter key, a new paragraph begins and 10 points of spacing is inserted after the paragraph. If you want to move the insertion point down to the next line without including the additional 10 points of spacing, use the New Line command, Shift + Enter.

Project 1a · Creating a Document · Part 1 of 2

1. Follow the instructions in this chapter to open Microsoft Word or check with your instructor for specific instructions.
2. At a blank document, type the information shown in Figure 1.2 with the following specifications:
    a. Correct any errors highlighted by the spell checker as they occur.
    b. Space once after end-of-sentence punctuation.
    c. After typing *Created:* press Shift + Enter to move the insertion point to the next line without adding 10 points of additional spacing.
    d. To insert the word *Thursday* located towards the end of the document, type **Thur** and then press F3. (This is an example of the AutoComplete feature.)
    e. To insert the word *December*, type **Dece** and then press the Enter key. (This is another example of the AutoComplete feature.)
    f. Press Shift + Enter after typing *December 6, 2012*.
    g. When typing the last line (the line containing the ordinal numbers), type the ordinal number text and AutoCorrect will automatically convert the letters in the ordinal numbers to superscript.
3. When you are finished typing the text, press the Enter key once.

Figure 1.2 Project 1a

The traditional chronological resume lists your work experience in reverse-chronological order (starting with your current or most recent position). The functional style deemphasizes the "where" and "when" of your career and instead groups similar experience, talents, and qualifications regardless of when they occurred.

Like the chronological resume, the hybrid resume includes specifics about where you worked, when you worked there, and what your job titles were. Like a functional resume, a hybrid resume emphasizes your most relevant qualifications in an expanded summary section, in several "career highlights" bullet points at the top of your resume, or in project summaries.

Created:
Thursday, December 6, 2012
Note: The two paragraphs will become the 2nd and 3rd paragraphs in the 5th section.

▼ **Quick Steps**

Save a Document
1. Click Save button.
2. Type document name.
3. Click Save button in dialog box.

Save a document approximately every 15 minutes or when interrupted.

Save

Saving a Document

Save a document if you want to use it in the future. You can use a variety of methods to save a document such as clicking the Save button on the Quick Access toolbar, clicking the File tab and then clicking the Save As button, or using the keyboard shortcut Ctrl + S. To save a document, click the Save button on the Quick Access toolbar. At the Save As dialog box shown in Figure 1.3, type the name of the document and then press Enter or click the Save button located in the lower right corner of the dialog box.

Figure 1.3 Save As Dialog Box

Naming a Document

Document names created in Word and other applications in the Office suite can be up to 255 characters in length, including drive letter and any folder names, and may include spaces. File names cannot include any of the following characters:

forward slash (/)	question mark (?)
backslash (\)	quotation mark (")
greater than sign (>)	colon (:)
less than sign (<)	semicolon (;)
asterisk (*)	pipe symbol (|)

Printing a Document

Click the File tab and the Backstage view displays as shown in Figure 1.4. Use buttons and tabs at this view to work with and manage documents such as opening, closing, saving, and printing a document. If you want to remove the Backstage view without completing an action, click the File tab, click any other tab in the ribbon, or press the Esc key on your keyboard.

Many of the computer exercises you will be creating will need to be printed. A printing of a document on paper is referred to as *hard copy* and a document displayed in the screen is referred to as *soft copy*. Print a document with options at the Print tab Backstage view shown in Figure 1.5. To display this view, click the File tab and then click the Print tab. You can also display the Print tab Backstage view by pressing the keyboard shortcut, Ctrl + P.

The left side of the Print tab Backstage view displays three categories—Print, Printer, and Settings. Click the Print button in the Print category to send the

Quick Steps

Print a Document
Click Quick Print button.
OR
1. Click File tab.
2. Click Print tab.
3. Click Print button.

Close a Document
1. Click File tab.
2. Click Close button.
OR
Press Ctrl + F4.

Figure 1.4 Backstage View

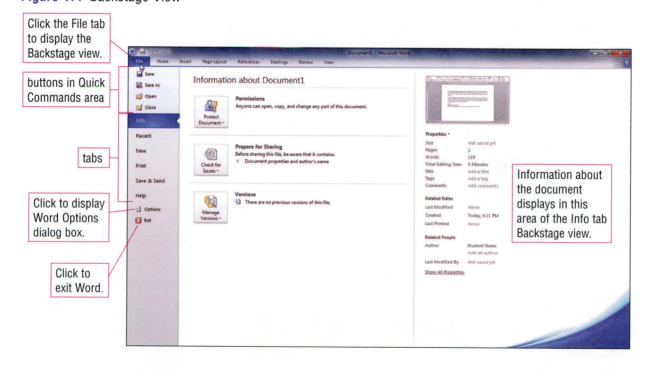

Click the File tab to display the Backstage view.

buttons in Quick Commands area

tabs

Click to display Word Options dialog box.

Click to exit Word.

Information about the document displays in this area of the Info tab Backstage view.

Figure 1.5 Print Tab Backstage View

Print Preview

Click the Print button to send the document to the specified printer.

Print tab

Navigation buttons

slider bar

document to the printer and specify the number of copies you want printed with the *Copies* option. Use the gallery in the Printer category to specify the desired printer. The Settings category contains a number of galleries, each with options for specifying how you want your document printed such as whether or not you want the pages collated when printed; the orientation, page size, and margins of your document; and how many pages of your document you want to print on a page.

Quick Print

Another method for printing a document is to insert the Quick Print button on the Quick Access toolbar and then click the button. This sends the document directly to the printer without displaying the Print tab Backstage view. To insert the button on the Quick Access toolbar, click the Customize Quick Access Toolbar button that displays at the right side of the toolbar and then click *Quick Print* at the drop-down list. To remove the Quick Print button from the Quick Access toolbar, right-click on the button and then click the *Remove from Quick Access Toolbar* option that displays in the drop-down list.

Closing a Document

When you save a document, it is saved on your storage medium and remains in the document screen. To remove the document from the screen, click the File tab and then click the Close button or use the keyboard shortcut, Ctrl + F4. When you close a document, the document is removed and a blank screen displays. At this screen, you can open a previously saved document, create a new document, or exit the Word program.

1. Save the document you created for Project 1a and name it **WL1-C1-P1-Computers** (for Word Level 1, Chapter 1, Project 1 and the document refers to computers) by completing the following steps:
   a. Click the Save button on the Quick Access toolbar.
   b. At the Save As dialog box, navigate to the Word2010L1Cl folder on your storage medium. (To do this, click the drive representing your storage medium in the Navigation pane and then double-click the Word2010L1C1 folder.
   c. Click in the *File name* text box (this selects any text in the box), type **WL1-C1-P1-Computers**, and then press Enter.
2. Print the document by clicking the File tab, clicking the Print tab, and then at the Backstage view, clicking the Print button.

3. Close the document by clicking the File tab and then clicking the Close button.

Project 2   Save and Edit a Word Document   2 Parts

You will open a document located in the Word2010L1C1 folder on your storage medium, add text to the document, and then save the document with a new name.

Creating a New Document ▪▪▪▪▪▪▪▪▪▪▪▪▪▪

When you close a document, a blank screen displays. If you want to create a new document, display a blank document. To do this, click the File tab, click the New tab, and then click the Create button that displays below the image of the blank document at the right side of the New tab Backstage view. You can also open a new document using the keyboard shortcut, Ctrl + N, or by inserting a New

▼ **Quick Steps**

Create a New Document
1. Click File tab.
2. Click New tab.
3. Click Create button.

button on the Quick Access toolbar. To insert the button, click the Customize Quick Access Toolbar button that displays at the right side of the toolbar and then click *New* at the drop-down list.

Opening a Document ■■■■■■■■■■■■■■■■■■■■■■■

▼ Quick Steps

Open a Document
1. Click File tab.
2. Click Open button.
3. Double-click document name.

After you save and close a document, you can open it at the Open dialog box shown in Figure 1.6. To display this dialog box, click the File tab and then click the Open button. You can also display the Open dialog box using the keyboard shortcut, Ctrl + O, or by inserting an Open button on the Quick Access toolbar. To insert the button, click the Customize Quick Access Toolbar button that displays at the right side of the toolbar and then click *Open* at the drop-down list. At the Open dialog box, open a document by double-clicking the document name.

If you want to see a list of the most recently opened documents, click the File tab and then click the Recent tab. This displays the Recent tab Backstage view containing a list of the most recently opened documents. To open a document from the list, scroll down the list and then click the desired document.

The Recent tab Backstage view contains the *Quickly access this number of Recent Documents* option that displays at the bottom of the screen. Click the option to insert a check mark in the check box and the four most recently opened document names display below the four options (*Save*, *Save As*, *Open*, and *Close*) in the Quick Commands area. By default, four document names display. You can change this number with the option box that displays at the right side of the *Quickly access this number of Recent Documents* option.

Figure 1.6 Open Dialog Box

Pinning a Document ▪▪▪▪▪▪▪▪▪▪▪▪▪▪▪▪▪▪▪▪▪▪▪▪

When you click the File tab and then click the Recent tab, the Recent Documents list displays with the most recently opened documents. If you want a document to remain in the list, "pin" the document to the list by clicking the pin button that displays at the right side of the document name. This changes the dimmed gray stick pin to a blue stick pin. The next time you display the Recent Documents list, the document you "pinned" displays at the top of the list. To "unpin" the document, click the pin button to change it from a blue pin to a dimmed gray pin. You can pin more than one document to the list.

Project 2a **Opening and Pinning/Unpinning a Document**   **Part 1 of 2**

1. Open the **CompCareers.docx** document by completing the following steps:
   a. Click the File tab and then click the Open button in the Quick Commands area.
   b. At the Open dialog box, make sure the Word2010L1C1 folder on your storage medium is the active folder.
   c. Double-click *CompCareers.docx* in the Content pane.

2. Close **CompCareers.docx**.
3. Open **FutureSoftware.docx** by completing steps similar to those in Step 1.
4. Close **FutureSoftware.docx**.
5. Pin the **CompCareers.docx** document to the Recent Documents list by completing the following steps:
   a. Click the File tab. (If the Recent tab Backstage view does not display, click the Recent tab.)
   b. Click the dimmed gray stick pin that displays at the right side of the document

   CompCareers.docx. (This moves the document to the top of the list and changes the dimmed gray stick pin to a blue stick pin.)
6. Click *CompCareers.docx* at the top of the Recent Documents list to open the document.
7. With the insertion point positioned at the beginning of the document, type the text shown in Figure 1.7.
8. Unpin the **CompCareers.docx** from the Recent Documents list by completing the following steps:
   a. Click the File tab and then click the Recent tab.
   b. At the Recent Documents list, click the blue stick pin that displays at the right of the **CompCareers.docx** document name. (This changes the pin from a blue stick pin to a dimmed gray stick pin.)
   c. Click the File tab to return to the document.

Figure 1.7 Project 2a

The majority of new jobs being created in the United States today involve daily work with computers. Computer-related careers include technical support jobs, sales and training, programming and applications development, network and database administration, and computer engineering.

▼ **Quick Steps**

Save a Document with Save As
1. Click File tab.
2. Click Save As button.
3. Navigate to desired folder.
4. Type document name.
5. Press Enter.

Exit Word
1. Click File tab.
2. Click Exit button.
OR
Click Close button.

Save any open documents before exiting Word.

Saving a Document with Save As ■■■■■■■■■■■■■

If you open a previously saved document and want to give it a new name, use the Save As button at the Backstage view rather than the Save button. Click the File tab and then click the Save As button and the Save As dialog box displays. At this dialog box, type the new name for the document and then press Enter.

Exiting Word ■■■■■■■■■■■■■■■■■■■■■■■

When you are finished working with Word and have saved all necessary information, exit Word by clicking the File tab and then clicking the Exit button located below the Help tab. You can also exit the Word program by clicking the Close button located in the upper right corner of the screen.

Project 2b   Saving a Document with Save As   Part 2 of 2

1. With **CompCareers.docx** open, save the document with a new name by completing the following steps:
   a. Click the File tab and then click the Save As button.
   b. At the Save As dialog box, press the Home key on your keyboard to move the insertion point to the beginning of the file name and then type **WL1-C1-P2-**. (Pressing the Home key saves you from having to type the entire document name.)
   c. Press the Enter key.
2. Print the document by clicking the File tab, clicking the Print tab, and then clicking the Print button at the Print tab Backstage view. (If your Quick Access toolbar contains the Quick Print button, you can click the button to send the document directly to the printer.)
3. Close the document by pressing Ctrl + F4.

You will open a previously created document, save it with a new name, and then use scrolling and browsing techniques to move the insertion point to specific locations in the document.

Editing a Document ■■■■■■■■■■■■■■■■■■■■■■■■■■■■

When editing a document, you may decide to insert or delete text. To edit a document, use the mouse, the keyboard, or the mouse combined with the keyboard to move the insertion point to specific locations in the document. To move the insertion point using the mouse, position the I-beam pointer where you want the insertion point located and then click the left mouse button.

You can also scroll in a document, which changes the text display but does not move the insertion point. Use the mouse with the *vertical scroll bar*, located at the right side of the screen, to scroll through text in a document. Click the up scroll arrow at the top of the vertical scroll bar to scroll up through the document and click the down scroll arrow to scroll down through the document. The scroll bar contains a scroll box that indicates the location of the text in the document screen in relation to the remainder of the document. To scroll up one screen at a time, position the arrow pointer above the scroll box (but below the up scroll arrow) and then click the left mouse button. Position the arrow pointer below the scroll box and click the left button to scroll down a screen. If you hold down the left mouse button, the action becomes continuous. You can also position the arrow pointer on the scroll box, hold down the left mouse button, and then drag the scroll box along the scroll bar to reposition text in the document screen. As you drag the scroll box along the vertical scroll bar in a longer document, page numbers display in a box at the right side of the document screen.

Project 3a **Scrolling in a Document**   Part 1 of 2

1. Open **InterfaceApps.docx** (from the Word2010L1C1 folder you copied to your storage medium.)
2. Save the document with Save As and name it **WL1-C1-P3-InterfaceApps**.
3. Position the I-beam pointer at the beginning of the first paragraph and then click the left mouse button.
4. Click the down scroll arrow on the vertical scroll bar several times. (This scrolls down lines of text in the document.) With the mouse pointer on the down scroll arrow, hold down the left mouse button and keep it down until the end of the document displays.
5. Position the mouse pointer on the up scroll arrow and hold down the left mouse button until the beginning of the document displays.
6. Position the mouse pointer below the scroll box and then click the left mouse button. Continue clicking the mouse button (with the mouse pointer positioned below the scroll box) until the end of the document displays.
7. Position the mouse pointer on the scroll box in the vertical scroll bar. Hold down the left mouse button, drag the scroll box to the top of the vertical scroll bar, and then release the mouse button. (Notice that the document page numbers display in a box at the right side of the document screen.)
8. Click in the title at the beginning of the document. (This moves the insertion point to the location of the mouse pointer.)

Moving the Insertion Point to a Specific Page

Previous
Page

Select Browse
Object

Next Page

Along with scrolling options, Word also contains navigation buttons for moving the insertion point to specific locations. Navigation buttons display toward the bottom of the vertical scroll bar and include the Previous Page button, the Select Browse Object button, and the Next Page button. The full names of and the tasks completed by the Previous and Next buttons vary depending on the last navigation completed. Click the Select Browse Object button and a palette of browsing choices displays. You will learn more about the Select Browse Object button in the next section.

Word includes a Go To option you can use to move the insertion point to a specific page within a document. To move the insertion point to a specific page, click the Find button arrow located in the Editing group in the Home tab and then click *Go To* at the drop-down list. At the Find and Replace dialog box with the Go To tab selected, type the page number in the *Enter page number* text box and then press Enter. Click the Close button to close the dialog box.

Browsing in a Document

The Select Browse Object button located toward the bottom of the vertical scroll bar contains options for browsing through a document. Click this button and a palette of browsing choices displays. Use the options on the palette to move the insertion point to various features in a Word document. Position the arrow pointer on an option in the palette and the option name displays above the options (the option name may display below the options). The options on the palette and the location of the options vary depending on the last function performed.

Moving the Insertion Point with the Keyboard

To move the insertion point with the keyboard, use the arrow keys located to the right of the regular keyboard. You can also use the arrow keys on the numeric keypad. If you use these keys, make sure Num Lock is off. Use the arrow keys together with other keys to move the insertion point to various locations in the document as shown in Table 1.2.

When moving the insertion point, Word considers a word to be any series of characters between spaces. A paragraph is any text that is followed by a stroke of the Enter key. A page is text that is separated by a soft or hard page break. If you open a previously saved document, you can move the insertion point to where the insertion point was last located when the document was closed by pressing Shift + F5.

Table 1.2 Insertion Point Movement Commands

To move insertion point	Press
One character left	Left Arrow
One character right	Right Arrow
One line up	Up Arrow
One line down	Down Arrow

continues

Table 1.2 Insertion Point Movement Commands, continued

To move insertion point	Press
One word to the left	Ctrl + Left Arrow
One word to the right	Ctrl + Right Arrow
To end of a line	End
To beginning of a line	Home
To beginning of current paragraph	Ctrl + Up Arrow
To beginning of next paragraph	Ctrl + Down Arrow
Up one screen	Page Up
Down one screen	Page Down
To top of previous page	Ctrl + Page Up
To top of next page	Ctrl + Page Down
To beginning of document	Ctrl + Home
To end of document	Ctrl + End

Project 3b **Moving the Insertion Point and Browsing in a Document** **Part 2 of 2**

1. With **WL1-C1-P3-InterfaceApps.docx** open, move the insertion point to page 3 by completing the following steps:
   a. Click the Find button arrow located in the Editing group in the Home tab and then click *Go To* at the drop-down list.
   b. At the Find and Replace dialog box with the Go To tab selected, type 3 in the *Enter page number* text box and then press Enter.
   c. Click the Close button to close the Find and Replace dialog box.

2. Click the Previous Page button located immediately above the Select Browse Object button on the vertical scroll bar. (This moves the insertion point to page 2.)

3. Click the Previous Page button again. (This moves the insertion point to page 1.)
4. Click the Next Page button located immediately below the Select Browse Object button on the vertical scroll bar. (This moves the insertion point to the beginning of page 2.)

5. Move to the beginning of page 3 by completing the following steps:
   a. Click the Select Browse Object button.
   b. At the palette of browsing choices, click the last choice in the bottom row (*Browse by Page*). (This moves the insertion point to page 3.)
6. Press Ctrl + Home to move the insertion point to the beginning of the document.
7. Practice using the keyboard commands shown in Table 1.2 to move the insertion point within the document.
8. Close **WL1-C1-P3-InterfaceApps.docx**.

Step 5b

Step 5a

Project 4 Insert and Delete Text   2 Parts

You will open a previously created document, save it with a new name, and then make editing changes to the document. The editing changes include selecting, inserting, and deleting text.

Inserting and Deleting Text

Editing a document may include inserting and/or deleting text. To insert text in a document, position the insertion point in the desired location and then type the text. Existing characters move to the right as you type the text. A number of options are available for deleting text. Some deletion commands are shown in Table 1.3.

Selecting Text ■■ ■ ■ ■ ■ ■ ■ ■ ■ ■ ■ ■ ■ ■ ■ ■ ■ ■ ■ ■

You can use the mouse and/or keyboard to select a specific amount of text. Once selected, you can delete the text or perform other Word functions involving the selected text. When text is selected, it displays with a blue background as shown in Figure 1.8 and the Mini toolbar displays in a dimmed fashion and contains options for common tasks. Move the mouse pointer over the Mini toolbar and it becomes active. (You will learn more about the Mini toolbar in Chapter 2.)

Table 1.3 Deletion Commands

To delete	Press
Character right of insertion point	Delete key
Character left of insertion point	Backspace key
Text from insertion point to beginning of word	Ctrl + Backspace
Text from insertion point to end of word	Ctrl + Delete

Figure 1.8 Selected Text and Mini Toolbar

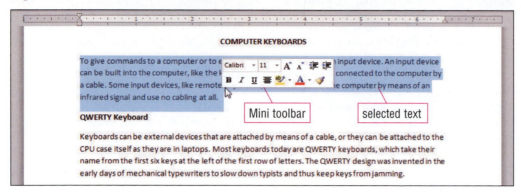

Selecting Text with the Mouse

Use the mouse to select a word, line, sentence, paragraph, or the entire document. Table 1.4 indicates the steps to follow to select various amounts of text. To select a specific amount of text such as a line or a paragraph, the instructions in the table tell you to click in the selection bar. The selection bar is the space located toward the left side of the document screen between the left edge of the page and the text. When the mouse pointer is positioned in the selection bar, the pointer turns into an arrow pointing up and to the right (instead of to the left).

To select an amount of text other than a word, sentence, or paragraph, position the I-beam pointer on the first character of the text to be selected, hold down the left mouse button, drag the I-beam pointer to the last character of the text to be selected, and then release the mouse button. You can also select all text between the current insertion point and the I-beam pointer. To do this, position the insertion point where you want the selection to begin, hold down the Shift key, click the I-beam pointer at the end of the selection, and then release the Shift key. To cancel a selection using the mouse, click anywhere in the document screen outside the selected text.

HINT

To select text vertically, hold down the Alt key while dragging with the mouse.

Table 1.4 Selecting with the Mouse

To select	Complete these steps using the mouse
A word	Double-click the word.
A line of text	Click in the selection bar to the left of the line.
Multiple lines of text	Drag in the selection bar to the left of the lines.
A sentence	Hold down the Ctrl key, then click anywhere in the sentence.
A paragraph	Double-click in the selection bar next to the paragraph or triple-click anywhere in the paragraph.
Multiple paragraphs	Drag in the selection bar.
An entire document	Triple-click in the selection bar.

Selecting Text with the Keyboard

If text is selected, any character you type replaces the selected text.

To select a specific amount of text using the keyboard, turn on the Selection Mode by pressing the F8 function key. With the Selection Mode activated, use the arrow keys to select the desired text. If you want to cancel the selection, press the Esc key and then press any arrow key. You can customize the Status bar to display text indicating that the Selection Mode is activated. To do this, right-click any blank location on the Status bar and then click *Selection Mode* at the pop-up list. When you press F8 to turn on the Selection Mode, the words *Extend Selection* display on the Status bar. You can also select text with the commands shown in Table 1.5.

Project 4a Editing a Document   Part 1 of 2

1. Open **CompKeyboards.docx**. (This document is located in the Word2010L1C1 folder you copied to your storage medium.)
2. Save the document with Save As and name it **WL1-C1-P4-CompKeyboards**.
3. Change the word *give* in the first sentence of the first paragraph to *enter*.
4. Change the second *to* in the first sentence to *into*.
5. Delete the words *means of* in the first sentence in the *QWERTY Keyboard* section.
6. Select the words *and use no cabling at all* and the period that follows located at the end of the last sentence in the first paragraph, and then press the Delete key.
7. Insert a period immediately following the word *signal*.
8. Delete the heading line containing the text *QWERTY Keyboard* using the Selection Mode by completing the following steps:
   a. Position the insertion point immediately before the *Q* in *QWERTY*.
   b. Press F8 to turn on the Selection Mode.
   c. Press the Down Arrow key.
   d. Press the Delete key.
9. Complete steps similar to those in Step 8 to delete the heading line containing the text *DVORAK Keyboard*.
10. Begin a new paragraph with the sentence that reads *Keyboards have different physical appearances.* by completing the following steps:
    a. Position the insertion point immediately left of the *K* in *Keyboards* (the first word of the fifth sentence in the last paragraph).
    b. Press the Enter key.
11. Save **WL1-C1-P4-CompKeyboards.docx**.

Table 1.5 Selecting with the Keyboard

To select	Press
One character to right	Shift + Right Arrow
One character to left	Shift + Left Arrow
To end of word	Ctrl + Shift + Right Arrow
To beginning of word	Ctrl + Shift + Left Arrow
To end of line	Shift + End
To beginning of line	Shift + Home
One line up	Shift + Up Arrow
One line down	Shift + Down Arrow
To beginning of paragraph	Ctrl + Shift + Up Arrow
To end of paragraph	Ctrl + Shift + Down Arrow
One screen up	Shift + Page Up
One screen down	Shift + Page Down
To end of document	Ctrl + Shift + End
To beginning of document	Ctrl + Shift + Home
Entire document	Ctrl + A or click Select button in Editing group and then Select All

Using the Undo and Redo Buttons

If you make a mistake and delete text that you did not intend to, or if you change your mind after deleting text and want to retrieve it, you can use the Undo or Redo buttons on the Quick Access toolbar. For example, if you type text and then click the Undo button, the text will be removed. You can undo text or commands. For example, if you add formatting such as bolding to text and then click the Undo button, the bolding is removed.

If you use the Undo button and then decide you do not want to reverse the original action, click the Redo button. For example, if you select and underline text and then decide to remove underlining, click the Undo button. If you then decide you want the underlining back on, click the Redo button. Many Word actions can be undone or redone. Some actions, however, such as printing and saving, cannot be undone or redone.

Word maintains actions in temporary memory. If you want to undo an action performed earlier, click the Undo button arrow. This causes a drop-down list to display. To make a selection from this drop-down list, click the desired action and the action, along with any actions listed above it in the drop-down list, is undone.

You cannot undo a save.

Undo

Redo

1. With **WL1-C1-P4-CompKeyboards.docx** open, delete the last sentence in the last paragraph using the mouse by completing the following steps:
   a. Position the I-beam pointer anywhere in the sentence that begins *All keyboards have modifier keys . . . .*
   b. Hold down the Ctrl key and then click the left mouse button.

> install software on a QWERTY keyboard that emulates a DVORAK keyboard. The ability to emulate other keyboards is convenient especially when working with foreign languages.
>
> Keyboards have different physical appearances. Many keyboards have a separate numeric keypad, like that of a calculator, containing numbers and mathematical operators. Some keyboards are sloped and "broken" into two pieces to reduce strain. All keyboards have modifier keys that enable the user to change the symbol or character entered when a given key is pressed.

Steps 1a-1b

   c. Press the Delete key.
2. Delete the last paragraph by completing the following steps:
   a. Position the I-beam pointer anywhere in the last paragraph (the paragraph that begins *Keyboards have different physical appearances*).
   b. Triple-click the left mouse button.
   c. Press the Delete key.

Step 3

3. Undo the deletion by clicking the Undo button on the Quick Access toolbar.
4. Redo the deletion by clicking the Redo button on the Quick Access toolbar.
5. Select the first sentence in the second paragraph and then delete it.
6. Select the first paragraph in the document and then delete it.

Step 7a   **Step 7b**

7. Undo the two deletions by completing the following steps:
   a. Click the Undo button arrow.
   b. Click the *second* Clear listed in the drop-down list. (This will redisplay the first sentence in the second paragraph as well as displaying the first paragraph. The sentence will be selected.)
8. Click outside the sentence to deselect it.
9. Save, print, and then close **WL1-C1-P4-CompKeyboards.docx**.

Project 5   Complete a Spelling and Grammar Check   1 Part

You will open a previously created document, save it with a new name, and then check the spelling and grammar in the document.

Checking the Spelling and Grammar in a Document ■■■

Two tools for creating thoughtful and well-written documents include a spelling checker and a grammar checker. The spelling checker finds misspelled words and offers replacement words. It also finds duplicate words and irregular capitalizations. When you spell check a document, the spelling checker compares the words in your document with the words in its dictionary. If the spelling checker finds a match, it passes over the word. If a match is not found for the word, the spelling checker will stop, select the word, and offer replacements.

The grammar checker will search a document for errors in grammar, punctuation, and word usage. The spelling checker and the grammar check can help you create a well-written document, but do not replace the need for proofreading. To complete a spelling and grammar check, click the Review tab and then click the Spelling & Grammar button in the Proofing group. You can also begin spelling and grammar checking by pressing the keyboard shortcut, F7. As the spelling and grammar checker selects text, make a choice from some of the options in the Spelling and Grammar dialog box as shown in Table 1.6.

By default, a spelling and grammar check are both completed on a document. If you want to check only the spelling in a document and not the grammar, remove the check mark from the *Check grammar* check box located in the lower left corner of the Spelling and Grammar dialog box. When spell checking a document, you can temporarily leave the Spelling and Grammar dialog box, make corrections in the document, and then resume spell checking by clicking the Resume button.

▼ **Quick Steps**

Check Spelling and Grammar
1. Click Review tab.
2. Click Spelling & Grammar button.
3. Change or ignore errors.
4. Click OK.

HINT

Complete a spelling and grammar check on a portion of a document by selecting the text first and then clicking the Spelling & Grammar button.

Spelling & Grammar

Table 1.6 Spelling and Grammar Dialog Box Buttons

Button	Function
Ignore Once	During spell checking, skips that occurrence of the word; in grammar checking, leaves currently selected text as written.
Ignore All	During spell checking, skips that occurrence of the word and all other occurrences of the word in the document.
Ignore Rule	During grammar checking, leaves currently selected text as written and ignores the current rule for remainder of the grammar check.
Add to Dictionary	Adds selected word to the spelling check dictionary.
Delete	Deletes the currently selected word(s).
Change	Replaces selected word in sentence with selected word in *Suggestions* list box.
Change All	Replaces selected word in sentence with selected word in *Suggestions* list box and all other occurrences of the word.
AutoCorrect	Inserts selected word and correct spelling of word in AutoCorrect dialog box.
Explain	During grammar checking, displays grammar rule information about the selected text.
Undo	Reverses most recent spelling and grammar action.
Next Sentence	Accepts manual changes made to sentence and then continues grammar checking.
Options	Displays a dialog box with options for customizing a spelling and grammar check.

1. Open **TechOccTrends.docx**.
2. Save the document with Save As and name it **WL1-C1-P5-TechOccTrends**.
3. Click the Review tab.
4. Click the Spelling & Grammar button in the Proofing group.
5. The spelling checker selects the word *tecnology*. The proper spelling is selected in the *Suggestions* list box, so click the Change button (or Change All button).
6. The spelling checker selects the word *occupatoins*. The proper spelling of the word is selected in the *Suggestions* list box, so click the Change button (or Change All button).
7. The grammar checker selects the sentence that begins *One key to being successful . . .* and displays *trends* and *a trend* in the *Suggestions* list box. Click *a trend* in the *Suggestions* list box and then click the Change button.
8. The grammar checker selects the sentence that begins *Young reader are not as interested . . .* and displays *reader is* and *readers are* in the *Suggestions* text box. Click the Explain button, read the information about subject-verb agreement that displays in the Word Help window,

and then click the Close button located in the upper right corner of the Word Help window.
9. Click *readers are* in the *Suggestions* text box and then click the Change button.
10. The spelling checker selects *excelent*. The proper spelling is selected in the *Suggestions* list box, so click the Change button.
11. The grammar checker selects the sentence that begins *The number of printing and lithography job's is shrinking . . . .* Click the Explain button, read the information about plural or possessive that displays in the Word Help window, and then click the Close button located in the upper right corner of the Word Help window.
12. With *jobs* selected in the *Suggestions* list box, click the Change button.
13. The spelling checker selects the word *sucessful* and offers *successful* in the *Suggestions* text box. Since this word is misspelled in another location in the document, click the Change All button.

14. The spelling checker selects the word *are* that is used twice in a row. Click the Delete button to delete the word.
15. When the message displays telling you that the spelling and grammar check is complete, click the OK button.
16. Save, print, and then close **WL1-C1-P5-TechOccTrends .docx**.

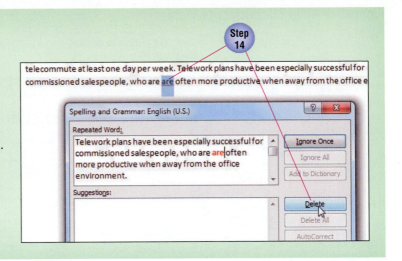

Step 14

P̶roject **6** **Use the Help Feature**   **2 Parts**

You need to learn more about selecting text and saving a document so you decide to use Help to research these features.

Using Help

Word's Help feature is an on-screen reference manual containing information about all Word features and commands. Word's Help feature is similar to Windows Help and the Help features in Excel, PowerPoint, and Access. Get help by clicking the Microsoft Word Help button located in the upper right corner of the screen (a question mark in a circle) or by pressing the keyboard shortcut, F1. This displays the Word Help window. In this window, type a topic, feature, or question in the Search text box and then press Enter. Topics related to the search text display in the Word Help window. Click a topic that interests you. If the topic window contains a <u>Show All</u> hyperlink in the upper right corner, click this hyperlink and the information expands to show all help information related to the topic. When you click the <u>Show All</u> hyperlink, it becomes the <u>Hide All</u> hyperlink.

The Help tab Backstage view, shown in Figure 1.9, contains an option for displaying the Word Help window as well as other options. To display the Help tab Backstage view, click the File tab and then click the Help tab. At the Help tab Backstage view, click the Microsoft Office Help button in the *Support* section to display the Word Help window and click the Getting Started button to access the Microsoft website that displays information about getting started with Word 2010. Click the Contact Us button in the *Support* section and the Microsoft Support website displays. Click the Options button in the *Tools for Working With Office* section and the Word Options dialog box displays. You will learn about this dialog box in a later chapter. Click the Check for Updates button and the Microsoft Update website displays with information on available updates. The right side of the Help tab Backstage view displays information about Office and Word.

▼ **Quick Steps**

Use Help Feature
1. Click Microsoft Word Help button.
2. Type topic, feature, or question.
3. Press Enter.
4. Click desired topic.

Figure 1.9 Help Tab Backstage View

Click this button to display the Word Help window.

Click this button to display the Microsoft website with information on getting started with Word.

Click this button to display the Microsoft Support website.

Click this button to display the Word Options dialog box.

Click this button to display the Microsoft Update website.

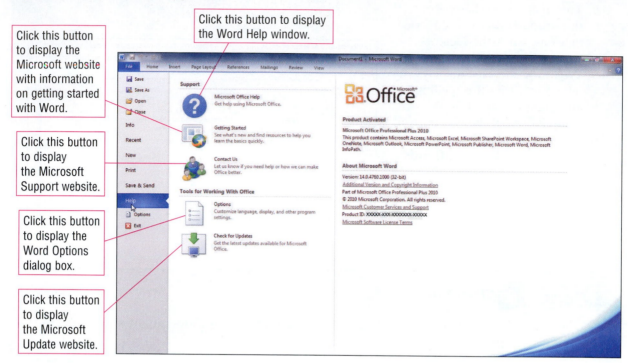

Project 6a   **Using the Help Feature**   Part 1 of 2

1. At a blank document, click the Microsoft Word Help button located in the upper right corner of the screen.
2. At the Word Help window, type **save a document** in the Search text box.
3. Press the Enter key.
4. When the list of topics displays, click the Save a document in Word hyperlink. (If your Word Help window does not display the online options, check the lower right corner of the window. If the word *Offline* displays, click *Offline* and then click the *Show content from Office.com* option at the drop-down list.)
5. Click the Show All hyperlink that displays in the upper right corner of the window.

6. Read the information about saving a document.
7. Print the information by clicking the Print button located toward the top of the Word Help window.
8. At the Print dialog box, click the Print button.
9. Click the Close button to close the Word Help window.
10. Click the File tab and then click the Help tab.
11. Click the Getting Started button in the *Support* section. (You must be connected to the Internet to display the web page.)

12. Look at the information that displays at the website and then click the Close button located in the upper right corner of the web page.
13. Click the File tab and then click the Help tab.
14. Click the Contact Us button, look at the information that displays at the website, and then close the web page.

Getting Help in a Dialog Box or Backstage View

Some dialog boxes, as well as the Backstage view, contain a Help button you can click to display a help window with specific information about the dialog box or Backstage view. After reading and/or printing the information, close a dialog box by clicking the Close button located in the upper right corner of the dialog box or close the Backstage view by clicking the File tab or clicking any other tab in the ribbon.

Project 6b   Getting Help in a Dialog Box and Backstage View   Part 2 of 2

1. At a blank document, click the File tab and then click the Save As button.
2. At the Save As dialog box, click the Help button located in the upper right corner of the dialog box.
3. Read the information about saving files and then click the Close button located in the upper right corner of the dialog box.
4. Close the Save As dialog box.
5. Click the File tab.
6. At the Backstage view, click the Help button located in the upper right corner of the window.
7. Click the Introducing Backstage hyperlink.
8. Read the information about the Backstage view.
9. Close the Word Help window and then click the File tab to return to the document.

Chapter Summary

- Refer to Figure 1.1 and Table 1.1 for a listing of key word screen features.
- The Quick Access toolbar is located above the File tab and contains buttons for commonly used commands.
- Click the File tab and the Backstage view displays containing tabs and buttons for working with and managing documents
- The ribbon area contains tabs with commands and options divided into groups.
- The insertion point displays as a blinking vertical line and indicates the position of the next character to be entered in the document.
- Document names can contain a maximum of 255 characters, including the drive letter and folder names, and may include spaces.
- The insertion point can be moved throughout the document without interfering with text by using the mouse, the keyboard, or the mouse combined with the keyboard.
- The scroll box on the vertical scroll bar indicates the location of the text in the document in relation to the remainder of the document.
- Click the Select Browse Object button located at the bottom of the vertical scroll bar to display options for browsing through a document.
- You can move the insertion point by character, word, screen, or page, and from the first to the last character in a document. Refer to Table 1.2 for keyboard insertion point movement commands.
- You can delete text by character, word, line, several lines, or partial page using specific keys or by selecting text using the mouse or the keyboard.
- You can select a specific amount of text using the mouse or the keyboard. Refer to Table 1.4 for information on selecting with the mouse and refer to Table 1.5 for information on selecting with the keyboard.
- Use the Undo button on the Quick Access toolbar if you change your mind after typing, deleting, or formatting text and want to undo the action. Use the Redo button to redo something that had been undone with the Undo button.
- The spelling checker matches the words in your document with the words in its dictionary. If a match is not found, the word is selected and possible corrections are suggested. The grammar checker searches a document for errors in grammar, style, punctuation, and word usage. When a grammar error is detected, display information about the error by clicking the Explain button at the Spelling & Grammar dialog box.
- Word's Help feature is an on-screen reference manual containing information about all Word features and commands. Click the Microsoft Word Help button or press F1 to display the Word Help window.
- Click the File tab and then click the Help tab to display the Help tab Backstage view.
- Some dialog boxes, as well as the Backstage view, contain a Help button you can click to display information specific to the dialog box or Backstage view.

Commands Review

FEATURE	RIBBON TAB, GROUP	BUTTON, OPTION	FILE TAB	KEYBOARD SHORTCUT
Close document			Close	Ctrl + F4
Exit Word		X	Exit	
Find and Replace dialog box with Go To tab selected	Home, Editing	🔍, Go To		Ctrl + G
Help tab Backstage view			Help	
New blank document			New, Create	Ctrl + N
Open dialog box			Open	Ctrl + O
Print tab Backstage view			Print	Ctrl + P
Save document		💾	Save	Ctrl + S
Select document	Home, Editing	▸, Select All		Ctrl + A
Spelling and Grammar dialog box	Review, Proofing	ABC		F7
Word Help window		❓		F1

Concepts Check Test Your Knowledge

Completion: In the space provided at the right, indicate the correct term, symbol, or command.

1. This toolbar contains the Save button. _____

2. Click this tab to display the Backstage view. _____

3. This is the area located toward the top of the screen that contains tabs with commands and options divided into groups. _____

4. This bar, located toward the bottom of the screen, displays number of pages and words, View buttons, and the Zoom slider bar. _____

5. This tab is selected by default. _____

6. This feature automatically corrects certain words as you type them. _____

7. This feature inserts an entire item when you type a few identifying characters and then press Enter or F3. _____

8. This is the keyboard shortcut to display the Print tab Backstage view. _____

9. This is the keyboard shortcut to close a document. _____

10. This is the keyboard shortcut to display a new blank document. _____

11. Use this keyboard shortcut to move the insertion point to the beginning of the previous page. _____

12. Use this keyboard shortcut to move the insertion point to the end of the document. _____

13. Press this key on the keyboard to delete the character left of the insertion point. _____

14. Using the mouse, do this to select one word. _____

15. To select various amounts of text using the mouse, you can click in this bar. _____

16. Click this tab to display the Spelling & Grammar button in the Proofing group. _____

17. This is the keyboard shortcut to display the Word Help window. _____

Skills Check Assess Your Performance

Assessment

1 TYPE AND EDIT A DOCUMENT ON FUZZY LOGIC

1. Open Word and then type the text in Figure 1.10. Correct any errors highlighted by the spell checker and space once after end-of-sentence punctuation.
2. Make the following changes to the document:
   a. Delete *AI* in the first sentence of the first paragraph and then insert *artificial intelligence*.
   b. Insert the words *for approximations and* between the words *allowing* and *incomplete* located in the first sentence of the first paragraph.
   c. Insert the words *or numerical* between the words *yes/no* and *information* in the second sentence of the first paragraph.
   d. Delete the words *hard to come by* in the last sentence of the first paragraph and replace with the word *rare*.
   e. Insert the letters *SQL* between the words *logic* and *database* in the last sentence of the second paragraph.

    f. Move the insertion point immediately left of the period at the end of the last sentence of the last paragraph, type a comma, and then insert the words *and trade shares on the Tokyo Stock Exchange*. Delete the word *and* before the words *automobile transmissions* in the last sentence.

    g. Join the first and second paragraphs.

    h. Delete the name *Marie Solberg* and then type your first and last names.

3. Save the document and name it **WL1-C1-A1-FuzzyLogic**.

4. Print and then close **WL1-C1-A1-FuzzyLogic.docx**.

Figure 1.10 Assessment 1

Fuzzy Logic

The fuzzy logic branch of AI attempts to model human reasoning by allowing incomplete input data. Instead of demanding precise yes/no information, fuzzy logic systems allow users to input "fuzzy" data. The terminology used by the system is deliberately vague and includes terms such as very probable, somewhat decreased, reasonable, or very slight. This is an attempt to simulate real-world conditions, where precise answers are hard to come by.

A fuzzy logic system attempts to work more naturally with the user by piecing together an answer in a manner similar to that used by a traditional expert system. Fuzzy logic database queries seem significantly more human than traditional queries.

Fuzzy logic systems are much more common in Japan than they are in the United States, where traditional expert systems and neural networks tend to be favored. In Japan, microprocessors specially designed by Toshiba and Hitachi to use fuzzy logic operate subways, consumer electronics, and automobile transmissions.

Created by Marie Solberg
Monday, October 1, 2012
Note: Please insert this information between 4th and 5th sections.

Assessment

2   CHECK THE SPELLING AND GRAMMAR OF A COMPUTER SOFTWARE DOCUMENT

1. Open **FutureSoftware.docx**.

2. Save the document with Save As and name it **WL1-C1-A2-FutureSoftware**.

3. Complete a spelling and grammar check on the document. You determine what to change and what to leave as written.

4. Insert the sentence *Wizards are small programs designed to assist users by automating tasks.* between the third and fourth sentences in the *User-Friendly System Software* section.

5. Move the insertion point to the end of the document, type your first and last names, press Shift + Enter, and then type the current date.

6. Save, print, and then close **WL1-C1-A2-FutureSoftware.docx**.

Assessment

3 CREATE A DOCUMENT DESCRIBING KEYBOARD SHORTCUTS

1. Click the Microsoft Word Help button, type **keyboard shortcuts,** and then press Enter.
2. At the Word Help window, click the <u>Keyboard shortcuts for Microsoft Word</u> hyperlink.
3. At the keyboard shortcut window, click the <u>Show All</u> hyperlink.
4. Read through the information in the Word Help window.
5. Create a document describing four keyboard shortcuts.
6. Save the document and name it **WL1-C1-A3-KeyboardShortcuts.**
7. Print and then close **WL1-C1-A3-KeyboardShortcuts.docx.**

Visual Benchmark Demonstrate Your Proficiency

CREATE A COVER PAGE

1. At a blank document, press the Enter key three times and then type the personal business letter shown in Figure 1.11 on the next page by following the directions in red.
2. Save the completed letter and name it **WL1-C1-VB-CoverLtr.**
3. Print and then close the document.

Figure 1.11 Visual Benchmark

4520 South Park Street *(press Shift + Enter)*
Newark, NJ 07122 *(press Shift + Enter)*
(Current date) *(press Enter two times)*

Mrs. Sylvia Hammond *(press Shift + Enter)*
Sales Director, Eastern Division *(press Shift + Enter)*
Grand Style Products *(press Shift + Enter)*
1205 Sixth Street *(press Shift + Enter)*
Newark, NJ 07102 *(press Enter)*

Dear Mrs. Hammond: *(press Enter)*

Thank you for agreeing to meet with me next Wednesday. Based on our initial conversation, it seems that my ability to sell solutions rather than products is a good fit for your needs as you seek to expand your visibility in the region. *(press Enter)*

As noted in the enclosed resume, I have led an under-performing product division to generating 33 percent of total revenue (up from 5 percent) at our location, and delivering, from a single location, 25 percent of total sales for our 20-site company. Having completed this turnaround over the last 5 years, I'm eager for new challenges where my proven skills in sales, marketing, and program/event planning can contribute to a company's bottom line. *(press Enter)*

I have been thinking about the challenges you described in building your presence at the retail level, and I have some good ideas to share at our meeting. I am excited about the future of Grand Style Products and eager to contribute to your growth. *(press Enter)*

Sincerely, *(press Enter two times)*

(Student Name) *(press Enter)*

Enclosure

Case Study — Apply Your Skills

Part 1

You are the assistant to Paul Brewster, the training coordinator at a medium-sized service-oriented business. You have been asked by Mr. Brewster to prepare a document for Microsoft Word users within the company explaining how to use the Save As command when saving a document rather than the Save command. Save the document and name it **WL1-C1-CS-SaveAs**. Print and then close the document.

Part 2

Mr. Brewster would like a document containing a brief summary of some basic Word commands for use in Microsoft Word training classes. He has asked you to prepare a document containing the following information:

- A brief explanation on how to move the insertion point to a specific page
- Keyboard shortcuts to move the insertion point to the beginning and end of a text line and beginning and end of a document
- Commands to delete text from the insertion point to the beginning of the word and from the insertion point to the end of the word
- Steps to select a word, a sentence, a paragraph, and an entire document using the mouse.
- Keyboard shortcut to select the entire document

Save the document and name it **WL1-C1-CS-WordCommands**. Print and then close the document.

Part 3

According to Mr. Brewster, the company is considering updating the Resources Department computers to Microsoft Office 2010. He has asked you to use the Internet to go to the Microsoft home page at www.microsoft.com and then use the search feature to find information on the system requirements for Office Professional Plus 2010. When you find the information, type a document that contains the Office Professional Plus 2010 system requirements for the computer and processor, memory, hard disk space, and operating system. Save the document and name it **WL1-C1-CS-SystemReq**. Print and then close the document.

Word Microsoft®

Formatting Characters and Paragraphs

PERFORMANCE OBJECTIVES

Upon successful completion of Chapter 2, you will be able to:

- Change the font and font effects
- Format selected text with buttons on the Mini toolbar
- Apply styles from Quick Styles sets
- Apply themes
- Change the alignment of text in paragraphs
- Indent text in paragraphs
- Increase and decrease spacing before and after paragraphs
- Repeat the last action
- Automate formatting with Format Painter
- Change line spacing in a document
- Reveal and compare formatting

Tutorials

A Word document is based on a template that applies default formatting. Some of the default formats include 11-point Calibri, line spacing of 1.15, 10 points of spacing after each paragraph, and left-aligned text. The appearance of a document in the document screen and how it looks when printed is called the *format*. In this chapter, you will learn about character formatting that can include such elements as changing the typeface, type size, and typestyle as well as applying font effects such as bolding and italicizing. The Paragraph group in the Home tab includes buttons for applying formatting to paragraphs of text. In Word, a paragraph is any amount of text followed by the press of the Enter key. In this chapter, you will learn to apply paragraph formatting to text such as changing text alignment, indenting text, applying formatting with Format Painter, and changing line spacing. Model answers for this chapter's projects appear on the following pages.

Word
Word2010L1C2

Note: Before beginning the projects, copy to your storage medium the Word2010L1C2 subfolder from the Word2010L1 folder on the CD that accompanies this textbook and then make Word2010L1C2 the active folder.

Project 1 — GLOSSARY OF TERMS

A

Access time: The time a storage device spends locating a particular file.
Aggregation software: E-commerce software application that combines online activities to provide one-stop shopping for consumers.
Analog signals: Signals composed of continuous waves transmitted at a certain frequency range over a medium, such as a telephone line.

B

Backup: A second copy kept of valuable data.
Bandwidth: The number of *bits* that can be transferred per second over a given medium or network.
Beta-testing: One of the last steps in software development that involves allowing outside people to use the software to see if it works as designed.

C

Chinese abacus: Pebbles strung on a rod inside a frame. Pebbles in the upper part of an abacus correspond to 5×10^0, or 5, for the first column; 5×10^1, or 50, for the second column; 5×10^2, or 500, for the third column; and so on.
Chip: A thin wafer of *silicon* containing electronic circuitry that performs various functions, such as mathematical calculations, storage, or controlling computer devices.
Cluster: A group of two or more sectors on a disk, which is the smallest unit of storage space used to store data.
Coding: A term used by programmers to refer to the act of writing source code.
Crackers: A term coined by computer hackers for those who intentionally enter (or hack) computer systems to damage them.

CREATED BY SUSAN ASHBY
WEDNESDAY, FEBRUARY 22, 2012

Project 1 Apply Character Formatting
WL1-C2-P1-CompTerms.docx

Project 2 — COMMERCIAL LIFE CYCLE

The software life cycle is the term used to describe the phases involved in the process of creating, testing, and releasing new commercial software products. This cycle is similar to the process used in developing information systems, except that in this case the cycle focuses on the creation and release of a software program, not the development of a customized information system. The commercial software life cycle is repeated every time a new version of a program is needed. The phases in the software life cycle include the following: proposal and planning, design, implementation, testing, and public release.

PROPOSAL AND PLANNING

In the proposal and planning phase of a new software product, software developers will describe the proposed software program and what it is supposed to accomplish. In the case of existing software, the proposal and planning stage can be used to describe any new features and improvements. Older software programs are often revised to take advantage of new hardware or software developments and to add new functions or features.

DESIGN

Developers are ready to begin the design process once the decision has been made to create or upgrade a software program. This step produces specifications documenting the details of the software to be written by programmers. Developers use problem-solving steps to determine the appropriate specifications.

IMPLEMENTATION

The implementation phase of the software life cycle is usually the most difficult. Development teams often spend late nights and weekends writing code and making it work. If the planning and design efforts have been successful, this phase should go well, but unanticipated problems inevitably crop up and have to be solved. The end result of the implementation phase is the production of a prototype called an alpha product, which is used by the development team for testing purposes. The alpha product can be revised to incorporate any improvements suggested by team members.

TESTING

A quality assurance (QA) team usually develops a testing harness, which is a scripted set of tests that a program must undergo before being considered ready for public release. These tests might cover events such as very large input loads, maximum number of users, running on several different platforms, and simulated power outages. Once testing is finished, a beta version of the software program is created for testing outside of the development group, often by a select group of knowledgeable consumers. Any suggestions they make can be used to improve the product before it is released to the general public. Once the beta version is finalized, the user manual can be written or updated. At this point, the software developers would send the master CDs to duplicators for mass production.

PUBLIC RELEASE AND SUPPORT

When the product is deemed ready for widespread use, it is declared "gold" and released to the public. The software life cycle now goes back to the beginning phases as software developers think of new ways to improve the product.

Project 2 Apply Styles and Themes
WL1-C2-P2-SoftwareCycle.docx

Project 3 — PROPERTY PROTECTION ISSUES

The ability to link computers through the Internet offers many advantages. With linked computers, we can quickly and easily communicate with other users around the world, sharing files and other data with a few simple keystrokes. The convenience provided by linking computers through the Internet also has some drawbacks. Computer viruses can travel around the world in seconds, damaging programs and files. Hackers can enter into systems without authorization and steal or alter data. In addition, the wealth of information on the Web and the increased ease with which it can be copied have made plagiarizing easy. Plagiarism is using others' ideas and creations (their intellectual property) without permission.

All of these ethical issues revolve around property rights, the right of someone to protect and control the things he or she owns. A solid legal framework ensuring the protection of personal property exists, but computers have created many new issues that challenge conventional interpretations of these laws.

Intellectual Property

Intellectual property includes just about anything that can be created by the agency of the human mind. To encourage innovation and improvement and thus benefit society as a whole, our legal system grants patents to those who invent new and better ways of doing things. A patent awards ownership of an idea or invention to its creator for a fixed number of years. This allows the inventor the right to charge others for the use of the invention. To encourage and protect artistic and literary endeavors, authors and artists are awarded copyrights to the material they create, allowing them the right to control the use of their works and charge others for their use. Patent and copyright violation is punishable by law, and prosecutions and convictions are frequent. The legal framework protecting intellectual property has come under constant challenge as technology has moved forward.

With the Internet, accessing and copying written works that may be protected is easy. Today, authors are increasingly dismayed to find copies of their works appearing on the Internet without their permission. The same problem occurs with graphic and artistic images on the Internet, such as photographs and artwork. Once placed on the Web, they can be copied and reused numerous times. Unauthorized copying of items appearing on websites is difficult and sometimes even technically impossible to prevent.

Page 1

Fair Use

Situations exist in which using work written by others is permissible. Using another person's material without permission is allowed as long as the use is acknowledged, is used for noncommercial purposes, and involves only the use of limited excerpts of protected material, such as no more than 300 words of prose and one line of poetry. Such a right is called fair use and is dealt with under the U.S. Copyright Act, Section 107. Here, in part, is what the Fair Use law states:

> [A] copyrighted work, including such use by reproduction in copies or phonorecords or by any other means specified by that section, for purposes such as criticism, comment, news reporting, teaching (including multiple copies for classroom use), scholarship, or research, is not an infringement of copyright.

Even under the Fair Use provision, describing the source of the material is important. Plagiarism may be punished by law, and in many educational institutions it can result in suspension or even expulsion.

Intellectual Property Protection

The problem faced by intellectual property owners in the digital age is twofold. First, new technology has presented new difficulties in interpreting previous understandings dealing with the protection of intellectual property, such as difficulties applying the Fair Use provision to Internet material. Second, the new technical capabilities brought about by digital technologies have greatly increased the ease with which intellectual property can be appropriated and used without authorization, making policing and protecting intellectual property very difficult. Intellectual property owners have formed new organizations to ensure the protection of their property.

REFERENCES

Fuller, Floyd and Brian Larson. (2010) *Computers: Understanding Technology* (pp. 659–661). St. Paul, MN: Paradigm Publishing.

Myerson, Jean A. (2008) *Intellectual Properties* (pp. 123–126). New Orleans, LA: Robicheaux Publishing House.

Patterson, Margaret and Montgomery Littleton. (2011) *Issues of Plagiarism*. Chicago, IL: Lansing and Edelman Publishers.

Page 2

Project 3 Apply Paragraph Formatting and Use Format Painter
WL1-C2-P3-IntelProp.docx

Talbot, Lenora J. and Marcella S. Angleton. (2010) *Internet Considerations.* Portland, OR: Pacific Blue Publishing Group.

Prepared by Clarissa Markham
Edited by Joshua Streeter

Solving Problems

In groups or individually, brainstorm possible solutions to the issues presented.

- Computers currently offer both *visual* and *audio* communications. Under development are devices and technologies that will allow users to smell various types of products while looking at them in the computer screen. What are some new applications of this technology for the food industry? Can you think of other industries that could use this capability?

- Picture yourself working in the Information Technology department of a mid-sized company. Your responsibilities include evaluating employees' computer system needs and recommending equipment purchases. Recently, the company president hired a new employee and you must evaluate her computer system needs. Considering that you have a budget of $5,500 for equipping the new employee with the computer system (or systems), research possible configurations and prepare a report outlining your recommendations, including costs. Assume that for her office she needs a complete system, including a system unit, monitor, printer, speakers, keyboard, and mouse.

Page 3

Project 4 Format Computer Issues Document

WL1-C2-P4-CompIssues.docx

Project 1 Apply Character Formatting   **4 Parts**

You will open a document containing a glossary of terms, add additional text, and then format the document by applying character formatting.

Changing Fonts

The Font group shown in Figure 2.1 contains a number of buttons you can use to apply character formatting to text in a document. The top row contains buttons for changing the font and font size as well as buttons for increasing and decreasing the size of the font changing the text case, and clearing formatting. You can remove character formatting (as well as paragraph formatting) applied to text by clicking the Clear Formatting button in the Font group. Remove only character formatting from selected text by pressing the keyboard shortcut, Ctrl + spacebar. The bottom row contains buttons for applying typestyles such as bold, italic, and underline and for applying text effects, highlighting, and color.

HINT
Change the default font by selecting the desired font at the Font dialog box and then clicking the Set As Default button.

A Word document is based on a template that formats text in 11-point Calibri. You may want to change this default to some other font for such reasons as changing the mood of the document, enhancing the visual appeal, and increasing the readability of the text. A font consists of three elements — typeface, type size, and typestyle.

HINT
Use a serif typeface for text-intensive documents.

A typeface is a set of characters with a common design and shape and can be decorative or plain and either monospaced or proportional. Word refers to typeface as *font*. A monospaced typeface allots the same amount of horizontal space for each

Figure 2.1 Font Group Buttons

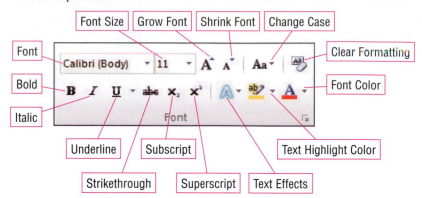

character while a proportional typeface allots a varying amount of space for each character. Proportional typefaces are divided into two main categories: *serif* and *sans serif*. A serif is a small line at the end of a character stroke. Consider using a serif typeface for text-intensive documents because the serifs help move the reader's eyes across the page. Use a sans serif typeface for headings, headlines, and advertisements.

Microsoft added six new fonts in Office 2007 that are available in Office 2010 including the default, Calibri, as well as Cambria, Candara, Consolas, Constantia, and Corbel. Calibri, Candara, and Corbel are sans serif typefaces; Cambria and Constantia are serif typefaces; and Consolas is monospaced. These six typefaces as well as some other popular typefaces are shown in Table 2.1.

Type size is generally set in proportional size. The size of proportional type is measured vertically in units called *points*. A point is approximately $1/72$ of an inch — the higher the point size, the larger the characters. Within a typeface, characters may have a varying style. Type styles are divided into four main categories: regular, bold, italic, and bold italic.

Use the Font button in the Font group to change the font and the Font Size button to change the size. When you select text and then click the Font button arrow, a drop-down gallery displays of font options. Hover your mouse pointer over a font option and the selected text in the document displays with the font applied. You can continue hovering your mouse pointer over different font options to see how the selected text displays in the specified font. The Font button drop-down gallery is an example of the *live preview* feature, which allows you to see how the font formatting affects your text without having to return to the document. The live preview feature is also available when you click the Font Size button arrow.

Table 2.1 Serif and Sans Serif Typefaces

Serif Typefaces	Sans Serif Typefaces	Monospaced Typefaces
Cambria	Calibri	Consolas
Constantia	Candara	Courier New
Times New Roman	Corbel	Lucida Console
Bookman Old Style	Arial	MS Gothic

1. Open **CompTerms.docx**.
2. Save the document with Save As and name it **WL1-C2-P1-CompTerms**.
3. Change the typeface to Cambria by completing the following steps:
   a. Select the entire document by pressing Ctrl + A. (You can also select all text in the document by clicking the Select button in the Editing group and then clicking *Select All* at the drop-down list.)
   b. Click the Font button arrow, scroll down the Font drop-down gallery until *Cambria* displays, and then hover the mouse pointer over *Cambria*. This displays a live preview of the text set in Cambria.
   c. Click the mouse button on *Cambria*.

Steps
3b-3c

4. Change the type size to 14 by completing the following steps:
   a. With the text in the document still selected, click the Font Size button arrow.
   b. At the drop-down gallery that displays, hover the mouse pointer on *14* and look at the live preview of the text with 14 points applied.
   c. Click the left mouse button on *14*.

Step
4a

Steps
4b-4c

5. At the document screen, deselect the text by clicking anywhere in the document.
6. Change the type size and typeface by completing the following steps:
   a. Press Ctrl + A to select the entire document.
   b. Click three times on the Shrink Font button in the Font group. (This decreases the size to 10 points.)
   c. Click twice on the Grow Font button. (This increases the size of the font to 12 points.)

Step
6b

Step
6c

d. Click the Font button arrow, scroll down the drop-down gallery, and then click *Constantia*. (The most recently used fonts display at the beginning of the document, followed by a listing of all fonts.)
7. Save **WL1-C2-P1-CompTerms.docx**.

Choosing a Typestyle

Apply a particular typestyle to text with the Bold, Italic, or Underline buttons in the bottom row in the Font group. You can apply more than one style to text. For example, you can bold and italicize the same text or apply all three styles to the same text. Click the Underline button arrow and a drop-down gallery displays with underlining options such as a double line, dashed line, and thicker underline. Click the *Underline Color* option at the Underline button drop-down gallery and a side menu displays with color options.

Project 1b **Applying Character Formatting to Text as You Type** **Part 2 of 4**

1. With **WL1-C2-P1-CompTerms.docx** open, press Ctrl + Home to move the insertion point to the beginning of the document.
2. Type a heading for the document by completing the following steps:
   a. Click the Bold button in the Font group. (This turns on bold.)
   b. Click the Underline button in the Font group. (This turns on underline.)
   c. Type **Glossary of Terms**.
3. Press Ctrl + End to move the insertion point to the end of the document.

Step 2a Step 2b

Step 2c

4. Type the text shown in Figure 2.2 with the following specifications:
   a. While typing the document, make the appropriate text bold as shown in the figure by completing the following steps:
      1) Click the Bold button in the Font group. (This turns on bold.)
      2) Type the text.
      3) Click the Bold button in the Font group. (This turns off bold.)
   b. While typing the document, italicize the appropriate text as shown in the figure by completing the following steps:
      1) Click the Italic button in the Font group.
      2) Type the text.
      3) Click the Italic button in the Font group.
5. After typing the text, press the Enter key twice and then press Ctrl + Home to move the insertion point to the beginning of the document.

6. Change the underlining below the title by completing the following steps:
   a. Select the title <u>Glossary of Terms</u>.
   b. Click the Underline button arrow and then click the third underline option from the top of the drop-down gallery.
   c. Click the Underline button arrow, point to the *Underline Color* option, and then click the Red color (second color option from the left) in the *Standard Colors* section.

7. With the title still selected, change the font size to 14 points.
8. Save **WL1-C2-P1-CompTerms.docx**.

Figure 2.2 Project 1b

C

Chip: A thin wafer of *silicon* containing electronic circuitry that performs various functions, such as mathematical calculations, storage, or controlling computer devices.

Cluster: A group of two or more *sectors* on a disk, which is the smallest unit of storage space used to store data.

Coding: A term used by programmers to refer to the act of writing source code.

Crackers: A term coined by computer hackers for those who intentionally enter (or hack) computer systems to damage them.

Choosing a Font Effect

Apply font effects with some of the buttons in the top and bottom rows in the Font group or clear all formatting from selected text with the Clear Formatting button. Change the case of text with the Change Case button drop-down list. Click the Change Case button in the top row in the Font group and a drop-down list displays with the options *Sentence case, lowercase, UPPERCASE, Capitalize Each Word,* and *tOGGLE cASE*. You can also change the case of selected text with the keyboard shortcut, Shift + F3. Each time you press Shift + F3, selected text cycles through the case options.

Change Case

Clear Formatting

Strikethrough

Subscript

Superscript

Text Effects

Text Highlight
Color

Font Color

The bottom row in the Font group contains buttons for applying font effects. Use the Strikethrough button to draw a line through selected text. This has a practical application in some legal documents in which deleted text must be retained in the document. Use the Subscript button to create text that is lowered slightly below the line such as the chemical formula H_2O. Use the Superscript button to create text that is raised slightly above the text line such as the mathematical equation four to the third power (written as 4^3). Click the Text Effects button in the bottom row and a drop-down gallery displays with effect options. Use the Text Highlight Color button to highlight specific text in a document and use the Font Color button to change the color of text.

Using Keyboard Shortcuts

Several of the buttons in the Font group have keyboard shortcuts. For example, you can press Ctrl + B to turn on bold or press Ctrl + I to turn on italics. Position the mouse pointer on a button and an enhanced ScreenTip displays with the name of the button; the keyboard shortcut, if any; a description of the action performed by the button; and sometimes access to the Word Help window. Table 2.2 identifies the keyboard shortcuts available for buttons in the Font group.

Formatting with the Mini Toolbar

When you select text, the Mini toolbar displays in a dimmed fashion above the selected text. Hover the mouse pointer over the Mini toolbar and it becomes active. Click a button on the Mini toolbar to apply formatting to selected text.

Table 2.2 Font Button Keyboard Shortcuts

Font Group Button	Keyboard Shortcut
Font	Ctrl + Shift + F
Font Size	Ctrl + Shift + P
Grow Font	Ctrl + Shift + >
Shrink Font	Ctrl + Shift + <
Bold	Ctrl + B
Italic	Ctrl + I
Underline	Ctrl + U
Subscript	Ctrl + =
Superscript	Ctrl + Shift + +
Change Case	Shift + F3

1. With **WL1-C2-P1-CompTerms.docx** open, move the insertion point to the beginning of the term *Chip*, press the Enter key, and then press the Up Arrow key. Type the text shown in Figure 2.3. Create the superscript numbers by clicking the Superscript button, typing the number, and then clicking the Superscript button.

2. Change the case of text and remove underlining from the title by completing the following steps:
   a. Select the title *Glossary of Terms*.
   b. Click the Change Case button in the Font group and then click *UPPERCASE* at the drop-down list.
   c. Click the Underline button to remove underlining.
   d. Click the Text Effects button in the font group and then click the *Gradient Fill - Blue, Accent 1* option (fourth option from the left in the third row) at the drop-down gallery.

3. Strike through text by completing the following steps:
   a. Select the words and parentheses *(or hack)* in the *Crackers* definition.
   b. Click the Strikethrough button in the Font group.

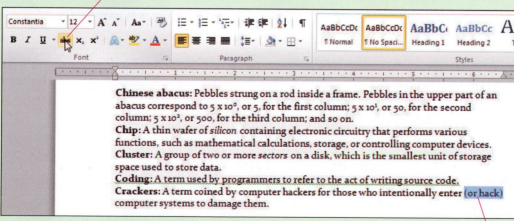

4. Change the font color by completing the following steps:
   a. Press Ctrl + A to select the entire document.

b. Click the Font Color button arrow.

c. Click the Dark Red color (first color option in the *Standard Colors* section) at the drop-down gallery.

d. Click in the document to deselect text.

5. Highlight text in the document by completing the following steps:

   a. Click the Text Highlight Color button arrow in the Font group and then click the yellow color at the drop-down palette. (This causes the mouse pointer to display as an I-beam pointer with a highlighter pen attached.)

   b. Select the term *Beta-testing* and the definition that follows.

   c. Click the Text Highlight Color button arrow and then click the turquoise color (third color from the left in the top row).

   d. Select the term *Cluster* and the definition that follows.

   e. Click the Text Highlight Color button arrow and then click the yellow color at the drop-down gallery.

   f. Click the Text Highlight Color button to turn off highlighting.

6. Apply italic formatting using the Mini toolbar by completing the following steps:

   a. Select the text *one-stop shopping* located in the definition for the term *Aggregation software*. (When you select the text, the Mini toolbar displays.)

   b. Click the Italic button on the Mini toolbar.

   c. Select the word *bits* located in the definition for the term *Bandwidth* and then click the Italic button on the Mini toolbar.

7. Save **WL1-C2-P1-CompTerms.docx**.

Figure 2.3 Project 1c

Chinese abacus: Pebbles strung on a rod inside a frame. Pebbles in the upper part of an abacus correspond to 5×10^0, or 5, for the first column; 5×10^1, or 50, for the second column; 5×10^2, or 500, for the third column; and so on.

Figure 2.4 Font Dialog Box

Choose a typeface in this list box. Use the scroll bar at the right side of the box to view available typefaces.

Choose a typestyle in this list box. The options in the box may vary depending on the selected typeface.

Choose a type size in this list box, or select the current measurement in the top box and then type the desired measurement.

Apply font effects to text by inserting a check mark in the desired effect check box.

This area displays a preview of text with the selected formatting applied.

Click this button to change the default font.

Click this button to display the Format Text Effects dialog box that contains text formatting options.

Changing Fonts at the Font Dialog Box

In addition to buttons in the Font group, you can use options at the Font dialog box shown in Figure 2.4 to change the typeface, type size, and typestyle of text as well as apply font effects. Display the Font dialog box by clicking the Font group dialog box launcher. The dialog box launcher is a small square containing a diagonal-pointing arrow that displays in the lower right corner of the Font group.

▼ **Quick Steps**

Change Font and Apply Effects
1. Select text if necessary.
2. Click Font group dialog box launcher.
3. Choose desired options at dialog box.
4. Click OK.

Project 1d   **Changing the Font at the Font Dialog Box**   Part 4 of 4

1. With **WL1-C2-P1-CompTerms.docx** open, press Ctrl + End to move the insertion point to the end of the document. (Make sure the insertion point is positioned a double space below the last line of text.)

2. Type **Created by Susan Ashby** and then press the Enter key.

3. Type **Wednesday, February 22, 2012**.

4. Change the font to 13-point Candara and the color to dark blue by completing the following steps:
   a. Press Ctrl + A to select the entire document.
   b. Click the Font group dialog box launcher.

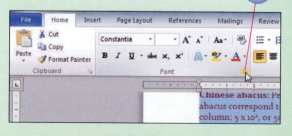

Step 4b

c. At the Font dialog box, click the up-pointing arrow at the right side of the *Font* list box to scroll up the list box and then click *Candara*.

d. Click in the *Size* text box and then type **13**.

e. Click the down-pointing arrow at the right side of the *Font color* list box and then click a dark blue color of your choosing at the drop-down color palette.

f. Click OK to close the dialog box.

5. Double underline text by completing the following steps:

a. Select *Wednesday, February 22, 2012*.

b. Click the Font group dialog box launcher.

c. At the Font dialog box, click the down-pointing arrow at the right side of the *Underline style* option box and then click the double-line option at the drop-down list.

d. Click OK to close the dialog box.

6. Change text to small caps by completing the following steps:

a. Select the text *Created by Susan Ashby* and *Wednesday, February 22, 2012*.

b. Display the Font dialog box.

c. Click the *Small caps* option in the *Effects* section. (This inserts a check mark in the check box.)

d. Click OK to close the dialog box.

7. Save, print, and then close **WL1-C2-P1-CompTerms.docx**.

Project 2 **Apply Styles and Themes**   **3 Parts**

You will open a document containing information on the life cycle of software, apply styles to text, and then change the Quick Styles set. You will also apply a theme and then change the theme colors and fonts.

Applying Styles from a Quick Styles Set ■ ■ ■ ■ ■ ■ ■ ■ ■ ■

A Word document contains a number of predesigned formats grouped into style sets called Quick Styles. Several thumbnails of the styles in the default Quick Styles set display in the Styles group in the Home tab. Display additional styles by clicking the More button that displays at the right side of the style thumbnails. This displays a drop-down gallery of style choices. To apply a style, position the insertion point in the text or paragraph of text to which you want the style applied, click the More button at the right side of the style thumbnails in the Styles group, and then click the desired style at the drop-down gallery.

A Word document contains some default formatting including 10 points of spacing after paragraphs and a line spacing of 1.15. (You will learn more about these formatting options later in this chapter.) You can remove this default formatting as well as any character formatting applied to text in your document by applying the No Spacing style to your text. This style is located in the Styles group.

Changing the Quick Styles Set

Word contains a number of Quick Styles sets containing styles you can use to apply formatting to a document. To change to a different Quick Styles set, click the Change Styles button in the Styles group in the Home tab and then point to Style Set. This displays a side menu with Quick Styles sets. Click the desired set and the style formatting changes for the styles in the set.

▼ **Quick Steps**

Apply a Style
1. Position insertion point in desired text or paragraph of text.
2. Click More button in Styles group.
3. Click desired style.

Change Quick Styles Set
1. Click Change Styles button.
2. Point to *Style Set*.
3. Click desired set.

More

Change Styles

Project 2a   **Applying Quick Styles**   **Part 1 of 3**

1. Open **SoftwareCycle.docx**.
2. Save the document with Save As and name it **WL1-C2-P2-SoftwareCycle**.
3. Remove the 10 points of spacing after paragraphs and change the line spacing to 1 by completing the following steps:
   a. Press Ctrl + A to select the entire document.
   b. Click the No Spacing style in the Styles group in the Home tab.

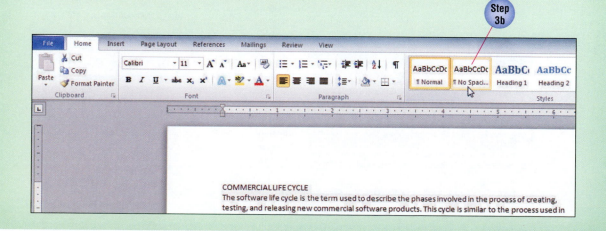

Step 3b

---

4. Position the insertion point on any character in the title *COMMERCIAL LIFE CYCLE* and then click the Heading 1 style that displays in the Styles group.

5. Position the insertion point on any character in the heading *Proposal and Planning* and then click the Heading 2 style that displays in the Styles group.

6. Position the insertion point on any character in the heading *Design* and then click the Heading 2 style in the Styles group.

7. Apply the Heading 2 style to the remaining headings (*Implementation, Testing,* and *Public Release and Support*).

8. Click the Change Styles button in the Styles group, point to *Style Set*, and then click *Modern*. (Notice how the Heading 1 and Heading 2 formatting changes.)

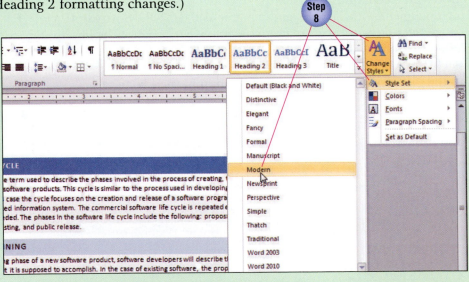

9. Save and then print **WL1-C2-P2-SoftwareCycle.docx**.

Applying a Theme ■■■■■■■■■■■■■■■■■■■■■■

Word provides a number of themes you can use to format text in your document. A theme is a set of formatting choices that include a color theme (a set of colors), a font theme (a set of heading and body text fonts), and an effects theme (a set of lines and fill effects). To apply a theme, click the Page Layout tab and then click the Themes button in the Themes group. At the drop-down gallery that displays, click the desired theme. You can hover the mouse pointer over a theme and the live preview feature will display your document with the theme formatting applied. With the live preview feature you can see how the theme formatting affects your document before you make your final choice. Applying a theme is an easy way to give your document a professional look.

▼ **Quick Steps**

Apply a Theme
1. Click Page Layout tab.
2. Click Themes button.
3. Click desired theme.

Themes

Project 2b **Applying a Theme to Text in a Document** **Part 2 of 3**

1. With **WL1-C2-P2-SoftwareCycle.docx** open, click the Page Layout tab and then click the Themes button in the Themes group.
2. At the drop-down gallery, hover your mouse pointer over several different themes and notice how the text formatting changes in your document.
3. Scroll down the drop-down gallery and then click the *Module* theme.
4. Save and then print **WL1-C2-P2-SoftwareCycle.docx**.

Changing Themes

You can change a theme with the three buttons that display at the right side of the Themes button. A theme contains specific color formatting, which you can change with options from the Theme Colors button in the Themes group. Click this button and a drop-down gallery displays with named color schemes. The names of the color schemes correspond to the names of the themes. Each theme applies specific fonts, which you can change with options from the Theme Fonts button in the Themes group. Click this button and a drop-down gallery displays with font choices. Each font group in the drop-down gallery contains two choices. The first choice in the group is the font that is applied to headings and the second choice is the font that is applied to body text in the document. If you are formatting a document containing graphics with lines and fills, you can apply a specific theme effect with options at the Theme Effects drop-down gallery.

▼ **Quick Steps**

Change Theme Color
1. Click Page Layout tab.
2. Click Theme Colors button.
3. Click desired theme color.

Change Theme Fonts
1. Click Page Layout tab.
2. Click Theme Fonts button.
3. Click desired theme fonts.

Theme Colors

Theme Fonts

Theme Effects

The buttons in the Themes group display a visual representation of the current theme. If you change the theme colors, the small color squares in the Themes button and the Theme Colors button reflect the change. Changing the theme fonts and the *As* on the Themes button as well as the uppercase *A* on the Theme Fonts button reflect the change. If you change the theme effects, the circle in the Theme Effects button reflects the change.

 Project 2c   **Changing a Theme**   **Part 3 of 3**

1. With **WL1-C2-P2-SoftwareCycle.docx** open, click the Theme Colors button in the Themes group and then click *Foundry* at the drop-down gallery. (Notice how the colors in the title and headings change.)
2. Click the Theme Fonts button and then click the *Apex* option. (Notice how the document text font changes.)
3. Save, print, and then close **WL1-C2-P2-SoftwareCycle.docx**.

Project 3   **Apply Paragraph Formatting and Use Format Painter**   **6 Parts**

You will open a report on intellectual property and fair use issues and then format the report by changing the alignment of text in paragraphs, applying spacing before and after paragraphs of text, and repeating the last formatting action.

Changing Paragraph Alignment ■■■■■■■■■■■■■■■■■■

By default, paragraphs in a Word document are aligned at the left margin and ragged at the right margin. Change this default alignment with buttons in the Paragraph group in the Home tab or with keyboard shortcuts as shown in Table 2.3.

You can change the alignment of text in paragraphs before you type the text or you can change the alignment of existing text. If you change the alignment before typing text, the alignment formatting is inserted in the paragraph mark.

Table 2.3 Paragraph Alignment Buttons and Keyboard Shortcuts

To align text	Paragraph Group Button	Keyboard Shortcut
At the left margin	☰	Ctrl + L
Between margins	☰	Ctrl + E
At the right margin	☰	Ctrl + R
At the left and right margins	☰	Ctrl + J

Center

Show/Hide ¶

Align Text
Left

Align Text
Right

As you type text and press Enter, the paragraph formatting is continued. For example, if you click the Center button in the Paragraph group, type text for the first paragraph, and then press the Enter key, the center alignment formatting is still active and the insertion point displays centered between the left and right margins. To display the paragraph symbols in a document, click the Show/Hide ¶ button in the Paragraph group. With the Show/Hide ¶ button active (displays with an orange background), nonprinting formatting symbols display such as the paragraph symbol ¶ indicating a press of the Enter key or a dot indicating a press of the spacebar.

To return paragraph alignment to the default (left-aligned), click the Align Text Left button in the Paragraph group. You can also return all paragraph formatting to the default with the keyboard shortcut, Ctrl + Q. This keyboard shortcut removes paragraph formatting from selected text. If you want to remove all formatting from selected text including character and paragraph formatting, click the Clear Formatting button in the Font group.

To change the alignment of existing text in a paragraph, position the insertion point anywhere within the paragraph. You do not need to select the entire paragraph. To change the alignment of several adjacent paragraphs in a document, select a portion of the first paragraph through a portion of the last paragraph. You do not need to select all of the text in the paragraphs.

HINT

Align text in a document so the message of the document can be followed and the page is attractive.

Project 3a Changing Paragraph Alignment   Part 1 of 6

1. Open **IntelProp.docx**. (Some of the default formatting in this document has been changed.)
2. Save the document with Save As and name it **WL1-C2-P3-IntelProp**.
3. Click the Show/Hide ¶ button in the Paragraph group in the Home tab to turn on the display of nonprinting characters.

Step 3

4. Press Ctrl + A to select the entire document and then change the alignment to Justify by clicking the Justify button in the Paragraph group in the Home tab.
5. Press Ctrl + End to move the insertion point to the end of the document.
6. Press the Enter key once.
7. Press Ctrl + E to move the insertion point to the middle of the page.
8. Type **Prepared by Clarissa Markham**.
9. Press Shift + Enter and then type **Edited by Joshua Streeter**.

Step 4

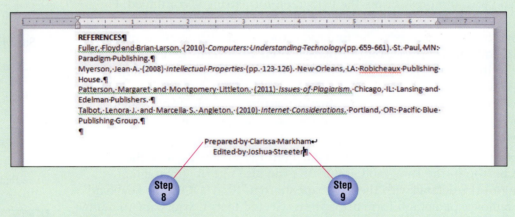

Step 8

Step 9

10. Click the Show/Hide ¶ button in the Paragraph group in the Home tab to turn off the display of nonprinting characters.
11. Save **WL1-C2-P3-IntelProp.docx**.

Changing Alignment at the Paragraph Dialog Box

▼ **Quick Steps**

Change Paragraph Alignment
Click desired alignment button in Paragraph group in Home tab.
OR
1. Click Paragraph group dialog box launcher.
2. Click *Alignment* option down-pointing arrow.
3. Click desired alignment.
4. Click OK.

Along with buttons in the Paragraph group and keyboard shortcuts, you can also change paragraph alignment with the Alignment option at the Paragraph dialog box shown in Figure 2.5. Display this dialog box by clicking the Paragraph group dialog box launcher. At the Paragraph dialog box, click the down-pointing arrow at the right side of the *Alignment* option box. At the drop-down list that displays, click the desired alignment option and then click OK to close the dialog box.

Figure 2.5 Paragraph Dialog Box with Alignment Options

Change paragraph alignment by clicking this down-pointing arrow and then clicking the desired alignment at the drop-down list.

Use these options to specify spacing before and after paragraphs.

Project 3b **Changing Paragraph Alignment at the Paragraph Dialog Box** **Part 2 of 6**

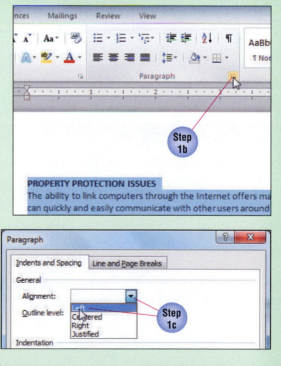

1. With **WL1-C2-P3-IntelProp.docx** open, change paragraph alignment by completing the following steps:
   a. Select the entire document.
   b. Click the Paragraph group dialog box launcher.
   c. At the Paragraph dialog box with the Indents and Spacing tab selected, click the down-pointing arrow at the right of the *Alignment* list box and then click *Left*.
   d. Click OK to close the dialog box.
   e. Deselect the text.
2. Change paragraph alignment by completing the following steps:
   a. Press Ctrl + End to move the insertion point to the end of the document.
   b. Position the insertion point on any character in the text *Prepared by Clarissa Markham*.
   c. Click the Paragraph group dialog box launcher.
   d. At the Paragraph dialog box with the Indents and Spacing tab selected, click the down-pointing arrow at the right of the *Alignment* list box and then click *Right*.

Step 1b

Step 1c

Indenting Text in Paragraphs ■ ■ ■ ■ ■ ■ ■ ■ ■ ■ ■ ■ ■ ■ ■

By now you are familiar with the word wrap feature of Word, which ends lines and wraps the insertion point to the next line. To indent text from the left margin, the right margin, or both, use the indent buttons in the Paragraph group, in the Page Layout tab, keyboard shortcuts, options from the Paragraph dialog box, markers on the Ruler, or use the Alignment button on the Ruler. Figure 2.6 identifies indent markers and the Alignment button on the Ruler. Refer to Table 2.4 for methods for indenting text in a document. If the Ruler is not visible, display the Ruler by clicking the View Ruler button located at the top of the vertical scroll bar.

Figure 2.6 Ruler and Indent Markers

Alignment button · First Line Indent marker · Left Indent marker · Hanging Indent marker · Right Indent marker

Table 2.4 Methods for Indenting Text

Indent	Methods for Indenting
First line of paragraph	• Press the Tab key.
	• Display Paragraph dialog box, click the down-pointing arrow to the right of the *Special* list box, click *First line*, and then click OK.
	• Drag the First Line Indent marker on the Ruler.
	• Click the Alignment button located at the left side of the Ruler until the First Line Indent button displays and then click on the Ruler at the desired location.

continues

Table 2.4 Methods for Indenting Text, continued

Indent	Methods for Indenting
Text from left margin	• Click the Increase Indent button in the Paragraph group in the Home tab to increase the indent or click the Decrease Indent button to decrease the indent. • Insert a measurement in the *Indent Left* measurement button in the Paragraph group in the Page Layout tab. • Press Ctrl + M to increase the indent or press Ctrl + Shift + M to decrease the indent. • Display the Paragraph dialog box, type the desired indent measurement in the *Left* measurement box, and then click OK. • Drag the left indent marker on the Ruler.
Text from right margin	• Insert a measurement in the *Indent Right* measurement button in the Paragraph group in the Page Layout tab. • Display the Paragraph dialog box, type the desired indent measurement in the *Right* measurement box, and then click OK. • Drag the right indent marker on the Ruler.
All lines of text except the first (called a hanging indent)	• Press Ctrl + T. (Press Ctrl + Shift + T to remove hanging indent.) • Display the Paragraph dialog box, click the down-pointing arrow to the right of the *Special* list box, click *Hanging*, and then click OK. • Click the Alignment button located at the left side of the Ruler until the Hanging Indent button displays and then click on the Ruler at the desired location.
Text from both left and right margins	• Display the Paragraph dialog box, type the desired indent measurement in the *Left* measurement box, type the desired measurement in the *Right* measurement box, and then click OK. • Insert a measurement in the *Indent Right* and *Indent Left* measurement buttons in the Paragraph group in the Page Layout tab. • Drag the left indent marker on the Ruler; then drag the right indent marker on the Ruler.

Project 3c **Indenting Paragraphs** **Part 3 of 6**

1. With **WL1-C2-P3-IntelProp.docx** open, indent the first line of text in paragraphs by completing the following steps:
   a. Select the first two paragraphs of text in the document (the text after the title *PROPERTY PROTECTION ISSUES* and before the heading *Intellectual Property*.
   b. Position the mouse pointer on the First Line Indent marker on the Ruler, hold down the left mouse button, drag the marker to the 0.5-inch mark, and then release the mouse button.

c. Select the paragraphs of text in the *Intellectual Property* section and then drag the First Line Indent marker on the Ruler to the 0.5-inch mark.

d. Select the paragraphs of text in the *Fair Use* section, click the Alignment button located at the left side of the Ruler until the First Line Indent button displays, and then click on the Ruler at the 0.5-inch mark.

e. Position the insertion point on any character in the paragraph of text below the *Intellectual Property Protection* heading, make sure the First Line Indent button displays in the Alignment button, and then click at the 0.5-inch mark on the Ruler.

2. Since the text in the second paragraph in the *Fair Use* section is a quote, you need to indent the text from the left and right margins by completing the following steps:

   a. Position the insertion point anywhere within the second paragraph in the *Fair Use* section (the paragraph that begins *[A] copyrighted work, including such . . .*).

   b. Click the Paragraph group dialog box launcher.

   c. At the Paragraph dialog box, with the Indents and Spacing tab selected, select the current measurement in the *Left* measurement box and then type **0.5**.

   d. Select the current measurement in the *Right* measurement box and then type **0.5**.

   e. Click the down-pointing arrow at the right side of the *Special* list box and then click *(none)* at the drop-down list.

   f. Click OK or press Enter.

3. Create a hanging indent for the first paragraph in the *REFERENCES* section by positioning the insertion point anywhere in the first paragraph below *REFERENCES* and then pressing Ctrl + T.

4. Create a hanging indent for the second paragraph in the *REFERENCES* section by completing the following steps:

   a. Position the insertion point anywhere in the second paragraph in the *REFERENCES* section.

   b. Make sure the Ruler is displayed. (If it is not, click the View Ruler button located at the top of the vertical scroll bar.)

   c. Click the Alignment button located at the left side of the Ruler until the Hanging Indent button displays.

   d. Click on the 0.5-inch mark on the Ruler.

5. Create a hanging indent for the third
   and fourth paragraphs by completing the following
   steps:
   a. Select a portion of the third and fourth
      paragraphs.
   b. Click the Paragraph group dialog box launcher.
   c. At the Paragraph dialog box with the Indents and
      Spacing tab selected, click the down-pointing
      arrow at the right side of the *Special* list box and
      then click *Hanging* at the drop-down list.
   d. Click OK or press Enter.
6. Save **WL1-C2-P3-IntelProp.docx**.

Step
5c

Spacing Before and After Paragraphs ■■■■■■■■■ ■ ■■■

By default, Word applies 10 points of additional spacing after a paragraph. You
can remove this spacing, increase or decrease the spacing, and insert spacing above
the paragraph. To change spacing before or after a paragraph, use the *Spacing
Before* and *Spacing After* measurement boxes located in the Paragraph group in the
Page Layout tab, or the *Before* and/or *After* options at the Paragraph dialog box
with the Indents and Spacing tab selected. You can also add spacing before and
after paragraphs at the Line and Paragraph Spacing button drop-down list.

Spacing before or after a paragraph is part of the paragraph and will be
moved, copied, or deleted with the paragraph. If a paragraph, such as a heading,
contains spacing before it, and the paragraph falls at the top of a page, Word
ignores the spacing.

Spacing before or after paragraphs is added in points and a vertical inch
contains approximately 72 points. To add spacing before or after a paragraph you
would click the Page Layout tab, select the current measurement in the *Spacing
Before* or the *Spacing After* measurement box, and then type the desired number
of points. You can also click the up- or down-pointing arrows at the right side of
the *Spacing Before* and *Spacing After* measurement boxes to increase or decrease the
amount of spacing.

HINT

Line spacing
determines the amount
of vertical space
between lines while
paragraph spacing
determines the amount
of space above or
below paragraphs of
text.

Repeating the Last Action ■■■■■■■■ ■■■■■■■ ■ ■■■

If you apply formatting to text and then want to apply the same formatting to
other text in the document, consider using the Repeat command. To use this
command, apply the desired formatting, move the insertion point to the next
location where you want the formatting applied, and then press the F4 function
key or press Ctrl + Y.

▼ **Quick Steps**

Repeat Last Action
Press F4.
OR
Press Ctrl + Y.

1. With **WL1-C2-P3-IntelProp.docx** open, add 6 points of spacing before and after each paragraph in the document by completing the following steps:
   a. Select the entire document.
   b. Click the Page Layout tab.
   c. Click once on the up-pointing arrow at the right side of the *Spacing Before* measurement box in the Paragraph group (this inserts *6 pt* in the box).
   d. Click once on the up-pointing arrow at the right side of the *Spacing After* measurement box in the Paragraph group (this inserts *6 pt* in the text box).

2. Add an additional 6 points of spacing above the headings by completing the following steps:
   a. Position the insertion point on any character in the heading *Intellectual Property* and then click once on the up-pointing arrow at the right side of the *Spacing Before* measurement box (this changes the measurement to *12 pt*).

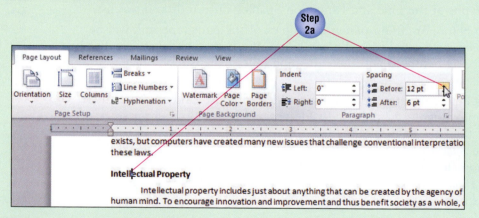

   b. Position the insertion point on any character in the heading *Fair Use* and then press F4. (F4 is the Repeat command.)
   c. Position the insertion point on any character in the heading *Intellectual Property Protection* and then press F4.
   d. Position the insertion point on any character in the heading *REFERENCES* and then press Ctrl + Y. (Ctrl + Y is also the Repeat command.)
3. Save **WL1-C2-P3-IntelProp.docx**.

Formatting with Format Painter ■■■■■■■■■■■■■■■■■■

▼ Quick Steps

Format with Format Painter
1. Format text.
2. Double-click Format Painter button.
3. Select text.
4. Click Format Painter button.

The Clipboard group in the Home tab contains a button for copying formatting and displays in the Clipboard group as a paintbrush. To use the Format Painter button, position the insertion point on a character containing the desired formatting, click the Format Painter button, and then select text to which you want the formatting applied. When you click the Format Painter button, the mouse I-beam pointer displays with a paintbrush attached. If you want to apply formatting a single time, click the Format Painter button once. If you want to apply the formatting in more than one location in the document, double-click the Format Painter button and then select text to which you want formatting applied. When you are finished, click the Format Painter button to turn it off. You can also turn off Format Painter by pressing the Esc key.

Format Painter

Project 3e   **Formatting Headings with the Format Painter**   Part 5 of 6

1. With **WL1-C2-P3-IntelProp.docx** open, click the Home tab.
2. Select the entire document and then change the font to 12-point Cambria.
3. Select the title *PROPERTY PROTECTION ISSUES*, click the Center button in the Paragraph group, and then change the font to 16-point Candara bold.
4. Apply 16-point Candara bold formatting to the *REFERENCES* heading by completing the following steps:
   a. Click on any character in the title *PROPERTY PROTECTION ISSUES*.
   b. Click once on the Format Painter button in the Clipboard group.
   c. Press Ctrl + End to move the insertion point to the end of the document and then click on any character in the heading *REFERENCES*. (This applies the 16-point Candara bold formatting and centers the text.)

Step 4b

5. With the insertion point positioned on any character in the heading *REFERENCES*, add an additional 6 points of spacing before the heading (for a total of 12 points before the heading).
6. Select the heading *Intellectual Property* and then change the font to 14-point Candara bold.
7. Use the Format Painter button and apply 14-point Candara bold formatting to the other headings by completing the following steps:
   a. Position the insertion point on any character in the heading *Intellectual Property*.
   b. Double-click the Format Painter button in the Clipboard group.
   c. Using the mouse, select the heading *Fair Use*.
   d. Using the mouse, select the heading *Intellectual Property Protection*.
   e. Click once on the Format Painter button in the Clipboard group. (This turns off the feature.)
   f. Deselect the heading.
8. Save **WL1-C2-P3-IntelProp.docx**.

Changing Line Spacing ■■■■ ■■■■■■ ■■■■■■ ■■■■■

▼ Quick Steps

Change Line Spacing
1. Click Line and Paragraph Spacing button in Paragraph group.
2. Click desired option at drop-down list.
OR
Press shortcut command keys.
OR
1. Click Paragraph group dialog box launcher.
2. Click *Line Spacing* option down-pointing arrow.
3. Click desired line spacing option.
4. Click OK.
OR
1. Click Paragraph group dialog box launcher.
2. Type line measurement in *At* text box.
3. Click OK.

Line and
Paragraph
Spacing

The default line spacing for a document is 1.15. (The line spacing for the **IntelProp.docx** document, which you opened at the beginning of Project 3, had been changed to single.) In certain situations, Word automatically adjusts the line spacing. For example, if you insert a large character or object such as a graphic, Word increases the line spacing of that specific line. But you also may sometimes encounter a writing situation in which you decide to change the line spacing for a section or for the entire document.

Change line spacing using the Line and Paragraph Spacing button in the Paragraph group in the Home tab, with keyboard shortcuts, or with options from the Paragraph dialog box. Table 2.5 displays the keyboard shortcuts to change line spacing.

You can also change line spacing at the Paragraph dialog box with the *Line spacing* option or the *At* option. If you click the down-pointing arrow at the right side of the *Line spacing* option, a drop-down list displays with a variety of spacing options. For example, to change the line spacing to double you would click *Double* at the drop-down list. You can type a specific line spacing measurement in the *At* text box. For example, to change the line spacing to 1.75, type *1.75* in the *At* text box.

Table 2.5 Line Spacing Keyboard Shortcuts

Press	To change line spacing to
Ctrl + 1	single spacing
Ctrl + 2	double spacing
Ctrl + 5	1.5 line spacing

Project 3f **Changing Line Spacing** **Part 6 of 6**

1. With **WL1-C2-P3-IntelProp.docx** open, change the line spacing for all paragraphs to double spacing by completing the following steps:
   a. Select the entire document.
   b. Click the Line and Paragraph Spacing button located in the Paragraph group in the Home tab.
   c. Click *2.0* at the drop-down list.
2. With the entire document still selected, press Ctrl + 5. (This changes the line spacing to 1.5 line spacing.)

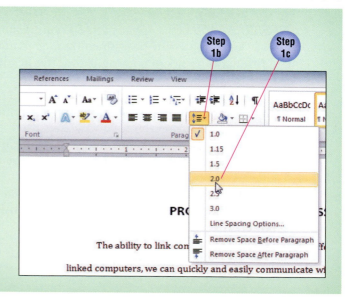

3. Change the line spacing to 1.3 using the Paragraph dialog box by completing the following steps:
   a. With the entire document still selected, click the Paragraph group dialog box launcher.
   b. At the Paragraph dialog box, make sure the Indents and Spacing tab is selected, click inside the *At* text box, and then type 1.3. (This text box is located to the right of the *Line spacing* list box.)
   c. Click OK or press Enter.
   d. Deselect the text.
4. Save, print, and then close **WL1-C2-P3-IntelProp.docx**.

Step 3b

Project **4**   **Format Computer Issues Document**   **3 Parts**

You will open a document containing two computer-related problems to solve, apply predesigned paragraph spacing, reveal the formatting, compare the formatting, and make formatting changes.

Changing Paragraph Spacing with the Change Styles Button

The Change Styles button in the Styles group in the Home tab contains a Paragraph Spacing option you can use to apply predesigned paragraph spacing to text in a document. Click the Change Styles button and then point to *Paragraph Spacing* and a side menu displays. Hover your mouse over an option at the side menu and, after a moment, a ScreenTip displays with information about the formatting applied by the option. For example, if you hover the mouse over the *Compact* option at the side menu, a ScreenTip displays telling you that the Compact option will change the spacing before paragraphs to zero points, the spacing after paragraphs to four points, and the line spacing to one. Use options at the *Paragraph Spacing* side menu to quickly apply paragraph spacing to text in your document.

1. Open **CompIssues.docx**.
2. Save the document with Save As and name it **WL1-C2-P4-CompIssues**.
3. Change the paragraph spacing using the Change Styles button by completing the following steps:
   a. Click the Change Styles button in the Styles group in the Home tab.
   b. Point to *Paragraph Spacing* at the drop-down list.
   c. Hover the mouse over each of the paragraph spacing options beginning with *Compact* and read the ScreenTip that displays for each option explaining the paragraph spacing applied by the option.
   d. Click the *Double* option at the side menu.
4. Scroll through the document and notice the paragraph spacing.
5. Change the paragraph spacing by clicking the Change Styles button, pointing to *Paragraph Spacing*, and then clicking *Relaxed* at the side menu.
6. Save **WL1-C2-P4-CompIssues.docx**.

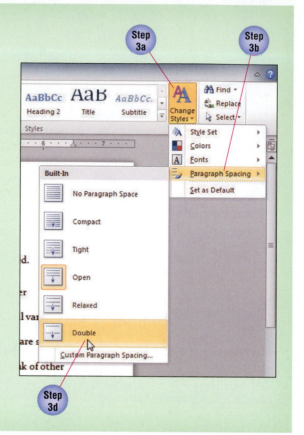

Revealing Formatting ■■■■■■ ■ ■ ■ ■ ■ ■ ■ ■

Display formatting applied to specific text in a document at the Reveal Formatting task pane as shown in Figure 2.7. The Reveal Formatting task pane displays font, paragraph, and section formatting applied to text where the insertion point is positioned or to selected text. Display the Reveal Formatting task pane with the keyboard shortcut Shift + F1. Generally, a minus symbol precedes *Font* and *Paragraph* and a plus symbol precedes *Section* in the *Formatting of selected text* section of the Reveal Formatting task pane. Click the minus symbol to hide any items below a heading and click the plus symbol to reveal items. Some of the items below headings in the *Formatting of selected text* section are hyperlinks. Click a hyperlink and a dialog box displays with the specific option.

1. With **WL1-C2-P4-CompIssues.docx** open, press Shift + F1 to display the Reveal Formatting task pane.
2. Click anywhere in the heading *Solving Problems* and then notice the formatting information that displays in the Reveal Formatting task pane.
3. Click in the bulleted paragraph and notice the formatting information that displays in the Reveal Formatting task pane.

Figure 2.7 Reveal Formatting Task Pane

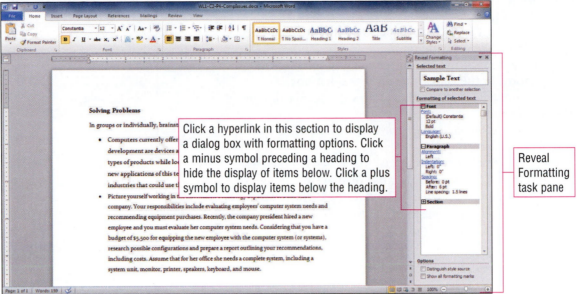

Click a hyperlink in this section to display a dialog box with formatting options. Click a minus symbol preceding a heading to hide the display of items below. Click a plus symbol to display items below the heading.

Reveal Formatting task pane

Comparing Formatting

Along with displaying formatting applied to text, you can use the Reveal Formatting task pane to compare formatting of two text selections to determine what formatting is different. To compare formatting, select the first instance of formatting to be compared, click the *Compare to another selection* check box, and then select the second instance of formatting to compare. Any differences between the two selections display in the *Formatting differences* list box.

▼ **Quick Steps**

Compare Formatting
1. Press Shift + F1 to display Reveal Formatting task pane.
2. Click or select text.
3. Click *Compare to another selection* check box.
4. Click or select text.

Project 4c   **Comparing Formatting**   **Part 3 of 3**

1. With **WL1-C2-P4-CompIssues.docx** open, make sure the Reveal Formatting task pane displays. If it does not, turn it on by pressing Shift + F1.
2. Select the first bulleted paragraph (the paragraph that begins *Computers currently offer both . . .*).
3. Click the *Compare to another selection* check box to insert a check mark.
4. Select the second bulleted paragraph (the paragraph that begins *Picture yourself working in the . . .*).
5. Determine the formatting differences by reading the information in the *Formatting differences* list box. (The list box displays *12 pt -> 11 pt* below the Font: hyperlink, indicating that the difference is point size.)
6. Format the second bulleted paragraph so it is set in 12-point size.
7. Click the *Compare to another selection* check box to remove the check mark.
8. Select the word *visual* that displays in the first sentence in the first bulleted paragraph.

9. Click the *Compare to another selection* check box to insert a check mark.
10. Select the word *audio* that displays in the first sentence of the first bulleted paragraph.
11. Determine the formatting differences by reading the information in the *Formatting differences* list box.
12. Format the word *audio* so it matches the formatting of the word *visual*.
13. Click the *Compare to another selection* check box to remove the check mark.
14. Close the Reveal Formatting task pane by clicking the Close button (contains an X) that displays in the upper right corner of the task pane.
15. Save, print, and then close **WL1-C2-P4-CompIssues.docx**.

Chapter Summary

- A font consists of three parts: typeface, type size, and typestyle.
- A typeface (font) is a set of characters with a common design and shape. Typefaces are either monospaced, allotting the same amount of horizontal space to each character, or proportional, allotting a varying amount of space for each character. Proportional typefaces are divided into two main categories: serif and sans serif.
- Type size is measured in point size; the higher the point size, the larger the characters.
- A typestyle is a variation of style within a certain typeface. You can apply typestyle formatting with some of the buttons in the Font group.
- With some of the buttons in the Font group, you can apply font effects such as superscript, subscript, and strikethrough.
- The Mini toolbar automatically displays above selected text. Use buttons on this toolbar to apply formatting to selected text.
- With options at the Font dialog box, you can change the font, font size, and font style and apply specific effects. Display this dialog box by clicking the Font group dialog box launcher.
- A Word document contains a number of predesigned formats grouped into style sets called Quick Styles. Change to a different Quick Styles set by clicking the Change Styles button in the Styles group in the Home tab, pointing to Style Set, and then clicking the desired set.
- Apply a theme and change theme colors, fonts, and effects with buttons in the Themes group in the Page Layout tab.
- By default, paragraphs in a Word document are aligned at the left margin and ragged at the right margin. Change this default alignment with buttons in the Paragraph group, at the Paragraph dialog box, or with keyboard shortcuts.

- To turn on or off the display of nonprinting characters such as paragraph marks, click the Show/Hide ¶ button in the Paragraph group.

- Indent text in paragraphs with indent buttons in the Paragraph group in the Home tab, buttons in the Paragraph group in the Page Layout tab, keyboard shortcuts, options from the Paragraph dialog box, markers on the Ruler, or use the Alignment button on the Ruler.

- Increase and/or decrease spacing before and after paragraphs using the *Spacing Before* and *Spacing After* measurement boxes in the Paragraph group in the Page Layout tab, or using the *Before* and/or *After* options at the Paragraph dialog box.

- Use the Format Painter button in the Clipboard group in the Home tab to copy formatting already applied to text to different locations in the document.

- Change line spacing with the Line and Paragraph Spacing button in the Paragraph group in the Home tab, keyboard shortcuts, or options from the Paragraph dialog box.

- Display the Reveal Formatting task pane to display formatting applied to text. Use the *Compare to another selection* option in the task pane to compare formatting of two text selections to determine what formatting is different.

Commands Review

FEATURE	RIBBON TAB, GROUP	BUTTON	KEYBOARD SHORTCUT
Bold text	Home, Font	**B**	Ctrl + B
Center-align text	Home, Paragraph	≡	Ctrl + E
Change case of text	Home, Font	Aa ▾	Shift + F3
Change Quick Styles set	Home, Styles	A̲A	
Clear all formatting	Home, Font	A̲	
Clear character formatting			Ctrl + spacebar
Clear paragraph formatting			Ctrl + Q
Decrease font size	Home, Font	A▾	Ctrl + <
Display nonprinting characters	Home, Paragraph	¶	Ctrl + Shift + *
Font	Home, Font	Calibri (Body) ▾	
Font color	Home, Font	A̲ ▾	
Font dialog box	Home, Font	▣	Ctrl + Shift + F

FEATURE	RIBBON TAB, GROUP	BUTTON	KEYBOARD SHORTCUT
Format Painter	Home, Clipboard		Ctrl + Shift + C
Highlight text	Home, Font		
Increase font size	Home, Font		Ctrl + >
Italicize text	Home, Font		Ctrl + I
Justify-align text	Home, Paragraph		Ctrl + J
Left-align text	Home, Paragraph		Ctrl + L
Line spacing	Home, Paragraph		Ctrl + 1 (single) Ctrl + 2 (double) Ctrl + 5 (1.5)
Paragraph dialog box	Home, Paragraph		
Repeat last action			F4 or Ctrl + Y
Reveal Formatting task pane			Shift + F1
Right-align text	Home, Paragraph		Ctrl + R
Spacing after paragraph	Page Layout, Paragraph	After: 0 pt	
Spacing before paragraph	Page Layout, Paragraph	Before: 0 pt	
Strikethrough text	Home, Font		
Subscript text	Home, Font		Ctrl + =
Superscript text	Home, Font		Ctrl + Shift + +
Text Effects	Home, Font		
Theme Colors	Page Layout, Themes		
Theme Effects	Page Layout, Themes		
Theme Fonts	Page Layout, Themes		
Themes	Page Layout, Themes		
Underline text	Home, Font		Ctrl + U

Concepts Check Test Your Knowledge

Completion: In the space provided at the right, indicate the correct term, symbol, or command.

1. The Bold button is located in this group in the Home tab.

2. Click this button in the Font group to remove all formatting from selected text.

3. Proportional typefaces are divided into two main categories, serif and this.

4. This is the keyboard shortcut to italicize selected text.

5. This term refers to text that is raised slightly above the regular text line.

6. This automatically displays above selected text.

7. Click this to display the Font dialog box.

8. A Word document contains a number of predesigned formats grouped into style sets called this.

9. Apply a theme and change theme colors, fonts, and effects with buttons in the Themes group in this tab.

10. This is the default paragraph alignment.

11. Click this button in the Paragraph group to turn on the display of nonprinting characters.

12. Return all paragraph formatting to normal with this keyboard shortcut.

13. Click this button in the Paragraph group in the Home tab to align text at the right margin.

14. In this type of paragraph, the first line of text remains at the left margin and the remaining lines of text are indented to the first tab.

15. Repeat the last action by pressing F4 or with this keyboard shortcut.

16. Use this button in the Clipboard group in the Home tab to copy formatting already applied to text to different locations in the document.

17. Change line spacing to 1.5 with this keyboard shortcut.

18. Press these keys to display the Reveal Formatting task pane.

Skills Check Assess Your Performance

Assessment

1 APPLY CHARACTER FORMATTING TO A LEASE AGREEMENT DOCUMENT

1. Open **LeaseAgrmnt.docx**.
2. Save the document with Save As and name it **WL1-C2-A1-LeaseAgrmnt**.
3. Press Ctrl + End to move the insertion point to the end of the document and then type the text shown in Figure 2.8. Bold, italicize, and underline text as shown.
4. Select the entire document and then change the font to 12-point Candara.
5. Select and then bold *THIS LEASE AGREEMENT* located in the first paragraph.
6. Select and then bold *DOLLARS* located in the *Rent* section.
7. Select and then bold *DOLLARS* located in the *Damage Deposit* section.
8. Select and then italicize *12 o'clock midnight* in the *Term* section.
9. Select the title *LEASE AGREEMENT* and then change the font to 18-point Corbel and the font color to dark blue. (Make sure the title retains the bold formatting.)
10. Select the heading *Term*, change the font to 14-point Corbel, and apply small caps formatting. (Make sure the heading retains the bold formatting.)
11. Use Format Painter to change the formatting to small caps in 14-point Corbel for the remaining headings (*Rent, Damage Deposit, Use of Premises, Condition of Premises, Alterations and Improvements, Damage to Premises, Inspection of Premises, Default*, and *Late Charge*).
12. Save, print, and then close **WL1-C2-A1-LeaseAgrmnt.docx**.

Figure 2.8 Assessment 1

Inspection of Premises

Lessor shall have the right at all reasonable times during the term of this Agreement to exhibit the Premises and to display the usual *for sale, for rent,* or *vacancy* signs on the Premises at any time within <u>forty-five</u> days before the expiration of this Lease.

Default

If Lessee fails to pay rent when due and the default continues for <u>seven</u> days thereafter, Lessor may declare the entire balance immediately due and payable and may exercise any and all rights and remedies available to Lessor.

Late Charge

In the event that any payment required to be paid by Lessee is not made by the 10th day of the month, Lessee shall pay to Lessor a *late fee* in the amount of **$50**.

Assessment

2 APPLY STYLES, A QUICK STYLES SET, AND A THEME TO A HARDWARE TECHNOLOGY DOCUMENT

1. Open **FutureHardware.docx**.
2. Save the document with Save As and name it **WL1-C2-A2-FutureHardware**.
3. Apply the Heading 1 style to the title *ON THE HORIZON*.
4. Apply the Heading 2 style to the headings in the document (*Increased Optical Disc Storage Capacity, Improved Monitors, Holographic Storage*, and *Electronic Paper*).
5. Change the Quick Styles set to *Fancy*.
6. Apply the *Foundry* theme.
7. Change the theme colors to *Aspect*.
8. Change the theme fonts to *Flow*.
9. Change the paragraph spacing to Relaxed. ***Hint: Use the* Paragraph Spacing *option at the Change Styles button drop-down list.***
10. Highlight the second sentence in the *Increased Optical Disc Storage Capacity* section.
11. Highlight the second sentence in the *Holographic Storage* section.
12. Save, print, and then close **WL1-C2-A2-FutureHardware.docx**.

Assessment

3 APPLY CHARACTER AND PARAGRAPH FORMATTING TO AN EMPLOYEE PRIVACY DOCUMENT

1. Open **WorkplacePrivacy.docx**.
2. Save the document with Save As and name it **WL1-C2-A3-WorkplacePrivacy**.
3. Move the insertion point to the beginning of the document and then type **WORKPLACE PRIVACY** centered.
4. Select text from the beginning of the first paragraph to the end of the document (make sure you select the blank line at the end of the document) and then make the following changes:
   a. Change the line spacing to 1.5.
   b. Change the spacing after to 0 points.
   c. Indent the first line of each paragraph 0.5 inch.
   d. Change the alignment to Justify.
5. Move the insertion point to the end of the document and, if necessary, drag the First Line Indent marker on the Ruler back to 0″. Type the text shown in Figure 2.9. (Hang indent text as shown in Figure 2.9.)
6. Select the entire document and then change the font to Constantia.
7. Select the title *WORKPLACE PRIVACY* and then change the font to 14-point Calibri bold and apply the *Gradient Fill - Orange, Accent 6, Inner Shadow* text effect (second option from the left in the fourth row in the Text Effects button drop-down gallery).
8. Apply the same formatting to the title *BIBLIOGRAPHY* that you applied to the title *WORKPLACE PRIVACY*.
9. Save, print, and then close **WL1-C2-A3-WorkplacePrivacy.docx**.

Figure 2.9 Assessment 3

BIBLIOGRAPHY

Amaral, H. G. (2011). *Privacy in the workplace,* 2nd edition (pp. 103-112). Denver, CO:
  Goodwin Publishing Group.

Cuevas, R. A. (2010). *Employer and employee rights* (pp. 18-35). Los Angeles, CA:
  North Ridge Publishing Company.

Forsyth, S. M. (2011). *Protecting your privacy* (pp. 23-31). San Francisco, CA:
  Roosevelt & Carson Publishing.

Visual Benchmark Demonstrate Your Proficiency

CREATE AN ACTIVE LISTENING REPORT

1. At a blank document, press the Enter key twice, and then type the document shown in Figure 2.10. Set the body text in 12-point Cambria, the title in 16-point Candara bold, the headings in 14-point Candara bold, change the paragraph spacing after the headings to 6 points, and then apply additional formatting so the document appears as shown in the figure.
2. Save the document and name it **WL1-C2-VB-ActiveListen**.
3. Print and then close the document.

Figure 2.10 Visual Benchmark

ACTIVE LISTENING SKILLS

Speaking and listening is a two-way activity. When the audience pays attention, the speaker gains confidence, knowing that his or her message is being received and appreciated. At the same time, alert listeners obtain information, hear an amusing or interesting story, and otherwise benefit from the speaker's presentation.

Become an Active Listener

Active listeners pay attention to the speaker and to what is being said. They are respectful of the speaker and eager to be informed or entertained. In contrast, *passive listeners* "tune out" the presentation and may even display rudeness by not paying attention to the speaker. Here are ways in which you can become an active listener:

Listen with a purpose: Stay focused on what the speaker is saying and you will gain useful information or hear a suspenseful story narrated well. Try to avoid letting your attention wander.

Be courteous: Consider that the speaker spent time preparing for the presentation and thus deserves your respect.

Take brief notes: If the speaker is providing information, take brief notes on the main ideas. Doing so will help you understand and remember what is being said. If you have questions or would like to hear more about a particular point, ask the speaker for clarification after the presentation.

Practice Active Listening Skills in Conversation

Most people have had the experience of being in a one-way conversation in which one person does all the talking and the others just listen. In fact, this is not a conversation, which is by definition an exchange of information and ideas. In a true conversation, everyone has the chance to be heard. Do not monopolize the conversation. Give the other person or persons an opportunity to talk. Pay attention when others are speaking and show your interest in what is being said by making eye contact and asking questions. Avoid interrupting since this shows your disinterest and also suggests that what you have to say is more important.

Case Study Apply Your Skills

Part 1

You work for your local chamber of commerce and are responsible for assisting the Office Manager, Teresa Alexander. Ms. Alexander would like to maintain consistency in articles submitted for publication in the monthly chamber newsletter. She wants you to explore various decorative and plain fonts. She would like you to choose two handwriting fonts, two decorative fonts, and two plain fonts and then prepare a document containing an illustration of each of these fonts. Save the document and name it **WL1-C2-CS-Fonts**. Print and then close the document.

Part 2

Ms. Alexander has asked you to write a short article for the upcoming chamber newsletter. In the article, she would like you to describe an upcoming event at your school, a local college or university, or your local community. Effectively use at least two of the fonts you wrote about in the document you prepared for Case Study Part 1. Save the document and name it **WL1-C2-CS-Article**. Print and then close the document.

Part 3

When preparing the monthly newsletter, additional fonts may be necessary. Ms. Alexander has asked you to research the steps needed to install new fonts on your computer. Use the Help feature to research the steps and then prepare a document listing the steps. Format the document with appropriate headings and fonts. Save the document and name it **WL1-C2-CS-DownloadFonts**. Print and then close the document.

Help

Word

Microsoft®

Customizing Paragraphs

PERFORMANCE OBJECTIVES

Upon successful completion of Chapter 3, you will be able to:

- Apply numbering and bulleting formatting to text
- Insert paragraph borders and shading
- Apply custom borders and shading
- Sort paragraph text
- Set, clear, and move tabs on the Ruler and at the Tabs dialog box
- Cut, copy, and paste text in a document
- Copy and paste text between documents

Tutorials

3.1 Creating Bulleted and Numbered Lists

3.2 Applying Custom Borders and Shading

3.3 Adding a Border and Shading to Selected Text

3.4 Sorting Text in Paragraphs

3.5 Setting Tabs Using the Ruler

3.6 Setting Tabs Using the Tabs Dialog Box

3.7 Cutting, Copying, and Pasting Text

3.8 Using the Office Clipboard

As you learned in Chapter 2, Word contains a variety of options for formatting text in paragraphs. In this chapter you will learn how to insert numbers and bullets in a document, how to apply borders and shading to paragraphs of text in a document, how to sort paragraphs of text, and how to manipulate tabs on the Ruler and at the Tabs dialog box. Editing some documents might include selecting and then deleting, moving, or copying text. You can perform this type of editing with buttons in the Clipboard group in the Home tab or with keyboard shortcuts. Model answers for this chapter's projects appear on the following pages.

Word2010L1C3

Note: Before beginning the projects, copy to your storage medium the Word2010L1C3 subfolder from the Word2010L1 folder on the CD that accompanies this textbook and then make Word2010L1C3 the active folder.

Project 1 — Technology Information

Technology Information Questions

1. Is programming just for professionals?
2. Could a bit of training as a programmer help your career?
3. Which elements in the procedure of creating a macro are similar to the steps in developing a program?
4. What kinds of networks are used in your local area?
5. How can networks improve efficiency?

Technology Timeline: Computers in the Workplace

- 1900 to 1930: Most Americans grow up on farms and live in rural communities.
- 1930 to 1940: Number of factory workers increases and cities swell in population; soon they outnumber rural communities.
- 1950s: Computers invade the business environment and the number of office "white-collar" workers increases.
- 1980: Personal computers enter the workplace and office workers become knowledge workers. Office workers outnumber factory workers in the job market.
- 1993: The Internet becomes publicly available and millions go online. Farmers number less than three percent of the population.
- 2002 to 2010: Seven of the ten fastest-growing occupations, according to the U.S. Department of Labor, are computer-specific jobs. The other three are desktop publishers, personal and home-care aides, and medical assistants.

Technology Career Questions

1. What is your ideal technical job?
2. Which job suits your personality?
3. Which is your first-choice certificate?
4. How does the technical job market look in your state right now? Is the job market wide open or are the information technology career positions limited?

Project 1 Format a Document on Computer Technology
WL1-C3-P1-TechInfo.docx

Project 2 — Online Shopping

Online Shopping

Online shopping, also called electronic shopping or e-shopping, is defined as using a computer, modem, browser, and the Internet to locate, examine, purchase, and pay for products.

Many businesses encourage consumers to shop online because it saves employee time, thus reducing staff needs and saving money for the company. For example, some major airlines offer special discounts to travelers who purchase their tickets over the Internet, and most are eliminating paper tickets altogether.

Advantages of Online Shopping

For the consumer, online shopping offers several distinct advantages over traditional shopping methods. Some of these conveniences include:

- Convenience. With e-shopping, you can browse merchandise and make purchases whenever you want from the privacy and comfort of your home or office.
- Ease of comparison shopping. E-shopping allows you to quickly find comparable items at similar stores and locate those venues with the best quality and lowest prices.
- Greater selection. Because they are not restricted by available shelf space, online stores can offer you an almost unlimited number of products.
- More product information. At many online stores, you can find detailed information about a wide variety of products, an advantage often unavailable in traditional stores.

Online Shopping Venues

Just as consumers can visit a variety of bricks-and-mortar retail outlets, such as stores and shopping malls, Internet shoppers can browse several types of online shopping venues, including online stores, superstores, and shopping malls.

Online Shopping Safety Tips

The number one concern about shopping online is security. The truth is, shopping online is safe and secure if you know what to look for. Following these guidelines can help you avoid trouble.

1. Only buy at secure sites.
2. Never provide your social security number.
3. Look for sites that follow privacy rules from a privacy watchdog such as TRUSTe.
4. Find out the privacy policy of shopping sites before you buy.
5. Keep current on the latest Internet scams.
6. Answer only the minimum questions when filling out forms.

REFERENCES

Claussen, Morgan. "Online Shopping Tips," *Technology Bytes*, October 2, 2012.
Fairmont, Gerald. "Securing Your Privacy," emcpnews.com, August 5, 2012.
Weyman, Jennifer. "Safe Online Shopping," *Computing Standards*, September 10, 2012.

Project 2 Customize a Document on Online Shopping
WL1-C3-P2-OnlineShop.docx

Project 3 — Workshops

WORKSHOPS

Title	Price	Date
Quality Management	$240	Friday, February 3
Staff Development	229	Friday, February 17
Streamlining Production	175	Monday, March 5
Managing Records	150	Tuesday, March 27
Customer Service Training	150	Thursday, March 29
Sales Techniques	125	Tuesday, April 10

TRAINING DATES

January 3	February 7
January 12	February 15
January 24	February 21
January 26	February 23

TABLE OF CONTENTS

Project 3 Prepare a Document on Workshops and Training Dates
WL1-C3-P3-Tabs.docx

Project 4 — Online Shopping Tips

Online Shopping Safety Tips

The number one concern about shopping online is security. The truth is, shopping online is safe and secure if you know what to look for. Following these guidelines should help you avoid trouble.

Find out the privacy policy of shopping sites before you buy. Ask what information they gather, how that information will be used, and whether they share that information.

Only buy at secure sites. Secure sites use encryption to scramble your credit card information so that no one except the site can read it. When you enter a secure site, you'll get a pop-up notice in your browser, and then an icon of a closed lock will appear at the bottom of the browser.

Keep current with the latest Internet scams. The U.S. Consumer Gateway reports on Internet scams and tells you what actions the Federal Trade Commission has taken against Internet scammers. The Internet Fraud Watch, run by the National Consumers League, is a great source as well.

Never provide your social security number. A legitimate site will not ask you for your social security number.

Look for sites that follow privacy rules from a privacy watchdog such as TRUSTe. TRUSTe (www.truste.org) is a nonprofit group that serves as a watchdog for Internet privacy. It allows sites to post an online seal if the site adheres to TRUSTe's Internet privacy policies.

Answer only the minimum questions when filling out forms. Many sites put an asterisk next to the questions that must be answered, so only answer those.

Project 4 Move and Copy Text in a Document on Online Shopping Tips
WL1-C3-P4-ShoppingTips.docx

TECHNICAL SUPPORT TEAM
Staff Meeting
Wednesday, March 14, 2012
3:00 to 4:30 p.m., Room 20

TECHNICAL SUPPORT TEAM
Staff Meeting
Wednesday, March 14, 2012
3:00 to 4:30 p.m., Room 20

TECHNICAL SUPPORT TEAM
Staff Meeting
Wednesday, March 14, 2012
3:00 to 4:30 p.m., Room 20

TECHNICAL SUPPORT TEAM
Staff Meeting
Wednesday, March 14, 2012
3:00 to 4:30 p.m., Room 20

TECHNICAL SUPPORT TEAM
Staff Meeting
Wednesday, March 14, 2012
3:00 to 4:30 p.m., Room 20

TECHNICAL SUPPORT TEAM
Staff Meeting
Wednesday, March 14, 2012
3:00 to 4:30 p.m., Room 20

TECHNICAL SUPPORT TEAM
Staff Meeting
Wednesday, March 14, 2012
3:00 to 4:30 p.m., Room 20

CONTRACT NEGOTIATION ITEMS

1. The Employer agrees that, during the term of this Agreement, it shall not cause or initiate any lockout of Employees.

2. During the term of this Agreement, the **LWU**, its members, and its representatives agree not to engage in, authorize, sanction, or support any strike, slowdown, or other acts of curtailment or work stoppage.

3. Employees transferring to another location at their own request due to bidding or exercise of seniority shall be provided with space-available transportation with no service charge for self and family.

4. Each employee requested by **RM** to be away from regular base on duty shall receive expenses.

5. An employee shall report to his/her **RM** supervisor that he/she is ill and unable to work at least two (2) hours prior to the start of his/her shift, if at all possible.

6. If **RM**, at any time, grants additional sick leave or assistance to any employee, the **LWU** will deem this a precedence requiring additional sick leave or assistance in any other case.

Project 5 Copy Text in a Staff Meeting Announcement
WL1-C3-P5-StaffMtg.docx

Project 6 Create a Contract Negotiations Document
WL1-C3-P6-NegotiateItems.docx

Project 1 — Format a Document on Computer Technology — 5 Parts

You will open a document containing information on computer technology, type numbered text in the document, and apply numbering and bullet formatting to paragraphs in the document.

Applying Numbering and Bullets

Automatically number paragraphs or insert bullets before paragraphs using buttons in the Paragraph group. Use the Bullets button to insert bullets before specific paragraphs and use the Numbering button to insert numbers.

Numbering

Bullets

Numbering Paragraphs

If you type *1.*, press the spacebar, type a paragraph of text, and then press the Enter key, Word indents the number approximately 0.25 inch from the left margin and then hang indents the text in the paragraph approximately 0.5 inch from the left margin. Additionally, *2.* is inserted 0.25 inch from the left margin at the beginning of the next paragraph. Continue typing items and Word inserts the next number in the list. To turn off numbering, press the Enter key twice or click the Numbering button in the Paragraph group. (You can also remove paragraph formatting from a paragraph, including automatic numbering, with the keyboard shortcut, Ctrl + Q. Remove all formatting including character and paragraph formatting from selected text by clicking the Clear Formatting button in the Font group.)

▼ Quick Steps

Type Numbered Paragraphs
1. Type 1.
2. Press spacebar.
3. Type text.
4. Press Enter.

If you press the Enter key twice between numbered paragraphs, the automatic number is removed. To turn it back on, type the next number in the list (and the period) followed by a space. Word will automatically indent the number and hang indent the text.

When the AutoFormat feature inserts numbering and indents text, the AutoCorrect Options button displays. Click this button and a drop-down list displays with options for undoing and/or stopping the automatic numbering. An AutoCorrect Options button also displays when AutoFormat inserts automatic bulleting in a document. If you want to insert a line break without inserting a bullet or number, you do not need to turn off the automatic numbering/bulleting and then turn it back on again. Instead, simply press Shift + Enter to insert the line break.

| Project 1a | Typing Numbered Paragraphs | Part 1 of 5 |

1. Open **TechInfo.docx**.
2. Save the document with Save As and name it **WL1-C3-P1-TechInfo**.
3. Press Ctrl + End to move the insertion point to the end of the document and then type the text shown in Figure 3.1. Bold and center the title *Technology Career Questions*. When typing the numbered paragraphs, complete the following steps:
   a. Type 1. and then press the spacebar.
   b. Type the paragraph of text and then press the Enter key. (This moves the insertion point down to the next line, inserts *2.* indented 0.25 inch from the left margin, and also indents the first paragraph of text approximately 0.5 inch from the left margin. Also, the AutoCorrect Options button displays. Use this button if you want to undo or stop automatic numbering.)
   c. Continue typing the remaining text. (Remember, you do not need to type the paragraph number and period — these are automatically inserted.)
   d. After typing the last question, press the Enter key twice. (This turns off paragraph numbering.)
4. Save **WL1-C3-P1-TechInfo.docx**.

Figure 3.1 Project 1a

Technology Career Questions

1. What is your ideal technical job?
2. Which job suits your personality?
3. Which is your first-choice certificate?
4. How does the technical job market look in your state right now? Is the job market wide open or are the information technology career positions limited?

If you do not want automatic numbering in a document, turn off the feature at the AutoCorrect dialog box with the AutoFormat As You Type tab selected as shown in Figure 3.2. To display this dialog box, click the File tab and then click the Options button located below the Help tab. At the Word Options dialog box, click the *Proofing* option located in the left panel and then click the AutoCorrect Options button that displays in the *AutoCorrect options* section of the dialog box. At the

Figure 3.2 AutoCorrect Dialog Box with AutoFormat As You Type Tab Selected

Remove the check mark from this check box to turn off automatic numbering.

Remove the check mark from this check box to turn off automatic bulleting.

AutoCorrect dialog box, click the AutoFormat As You Type tab and then click the *Automatic numbered lists* check box to remove the check mark. Click OK to close the AutoCorrect dialog box and then click OK to close the Word Options dialog box.

You can also automate the creation of numbered paragraphs with the Numbering button in the Paragraph group. To use this button, type the text (do not type the number) for each paragraph to be numbered, select the paragraphs to be numbered, and then click the Numbering button in the Paragraph group. You can insert or delete numbered paragraphs in a document.

▼ **Quick Steps**

Create Numbered Paragraph
1. Select text.
2. Click Numbering button.

Project 1b   **Inserting Paragraph Numbering**   **Part 2 of 5**

1. With **WL1-C3-P1-TechInfo.docx** open, apply numbers to paragraphs by completing the following steps:
   a. Select the five paragraphs of text in the *Technology Information Questions* section.
   b. Click the Numbering button in the Paragraph group.

Step 1b

Step 1a

Technology Inform

Is programming just for professionals?

Does your school employ programmers?

Could a bit of training as a programmer help your care

Which elements in the procedure of creating a macro

How can networks improve efficiency?

2. Add text between paragraphs 4 and 5 in the *Technology Information Questions* section by completing the following steps:
   a. Position the insertion point immediately to the right of the question mark at the end of the fourth paragraph.
   b. Press Enter.
   c. Type **What kinds of networks are used in your local area?**
3. Delete the second question (paragraph) in the *Technology Information Questions* section by completing the following steps:
   a. Select the text of the second paragraph. (You will not be able to select the number.)
   b. Press the Delete key.
4. Save **WL1-C3-P1-TechInfo.docx**.

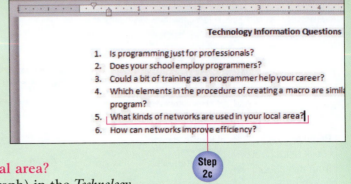

Technology Information Questions

1. Is programming just for professionals?
2. Does your school employ programmers?
3. Could a bit of training as a programmer help your career?
4. Which elements in the procedure of creating a macro are similar program?
5. What kinds of networks are used in your local area?
6. How can networks improve efficiency?

Step 2c

Bulleting Paragraphs

▼ **Quick Steps**

Type Bulleted Paragraphs
1. Type *, >, or - symbol.
2. Press spacebar.
3. Type text.
4. Press Enter.

Create Bulleted Paragraphs
1. Select text.
2. Click Bullets button.

In addition to automatically numbering paragraphs, Word's AutoFormat feature will create bulleted paragraphs. Bulleted lists with hanging indents are automatically created when a paragraph begins with the symbol *, >, or -. Type one of the symbols, press the spacebar, type text, and then press Enter. The AutoFormat feature inserts a bullet approximately 0.25 inch from the left margin and indents the text following the bullet another 0.25 inch. You can turn off the automatic bulleting feature at the AutoCorrect dialog box with the AutoFormat As You Type tab selected. You can demote or promote bulleted text by pressing the Tab key to demote text or pressing Shift + Tab to promote bulleted text. Word uses different bullets for demoted text.

You can also create bulleted paragraphs with the Bullets button in the Paragraph group. To create bulleted paragraphs using the Bullets button, type the text (do not type the bullet) of the paragraphs, select the paragraphs, and then click the Bullets button in the Paragraph group.

Project 1c   **Typing and Inserting Bulleted Text**   **Part 3 of 5**

1. With **WL1-C3-P1-TechInfo.docx** open, press Ctrl + End to move the insertion point to the end of the document and then press the Enter key once.
2. Type the heading *Technology Timeline: Computer Design* in bold as shown in Figure 3.3 and then press the Enter key.
3. Type a greater than symbol (**>**), press the spacebar, type the text of the first bulleted paragraph in Figure 3.3, and then press the Enter key.
4. Press the Tab key (this demotes the bullet to a hollow circle) and then type the bulleted text.
5. Press the Enter key (this displays another hollow circle bullet), type the bulleted text, and then press the Enter key.
6. Press Shift + Tab (this promotes the bullet to an arrow), type the bulleted text, and then press the Enter key twice (this turns off bullets).

7. Promote bulleted text by positioning the insertion point at the beginning of the text *1958: Jack Kilby, an engineer . . .* and then pressing Shift + Tab. Promote the other hollow circle bullet to an arrow. (The four paragraphs of text should be preceded by an arrow bullet.)

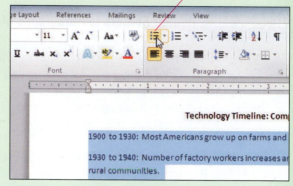

8. Format the paragraphs of text in the *Technology Timeline: Computers in the Workplace* section as a bulleted list by completing the following steps:
   a. Select the paragraphs of text in the *Technology Timeline: Computers in the Workplace* section.
   b. Click the Bullets button in the Paragraph group. (Word will insert the same arrow bullets that you inserted in Step 2. Word keeps the same bullet formatting until you choose a different bullet style.)
9. Save and then print **WL1-C3-P1-TechInfo.docx**. (This document will print on two pages.)

Figure 3.3 Project 1c

Technology Timeline: Computer Design

➢ 1937: Dr. John Atanasoff and Clifford Berry design and build the first electronic digital computer.
  o 1958: Jack Kilby, an engineer at Texas Instruments, invents the integrated circuit, thereby laying the foundation for fast computers and large-capacity memory.
  o 1981: IBM enters the personal computer field by introducing the IBM-PC.
➢ 2004: Wireless computer devices, including keyboards, mice, and wireless home networks, become widely accepted among users.

Inserting Paragraph Borders and Shading

Every paragraph you create in Word contains an invisible frame. You can apply a border to the frame around the paragraph. You can apply a border to specific sides of the paragraph or to all sides, you can customize the type of border lines, and you can add shading and fill to the border. Add borders and shading to paragraphs in a document using the Borders and Shading buttons in the Paragraph group or options from the Borders and Shading dialog box.

Inserting Paragraph Borders

When a border is added to a paragraph of text, the border expands and contracts as text is inserted or deleted from the paragraph. You can create a border around a single paragraph or a border around selected paragraphs. One method for creating a border is to use options from the Borders button in the Paragraph group. Click the Borders button arrow and a drop-down list displays. At the drop-down list, click the option that will insert the desired border. For example, to insert a border at the bottom of the paragraph, click the *Bottom Border* option. Clicking an option

▼ **Quick Steps**

Apply Border
1. Select text.
2. Click Borders button.

Borders

will add the border to the paragraph where the insertion point is located. To add a border to more than one paragraph, select the paragraphs first and then click the desired option.

1. With **WL1-C3-P1-TechInfo.docx** open, select text from the beginning of the title *Technology Timeline: Computer Design* through the four bulleted paragraphs of text below and then press the Delete key.
2. Insert an outside border to specific text by completing the following steps:
   a. Select text from the title *Technology Information Questions* through the five numbered paragraphs of text.
   b. In the Paragraph group, click the Borders button arrow.
   c. At the Borders drop-down list, click the *Outside Borders* option.
3. Select text from the title *Technology Timeline: Computers in the Workplace* through the six bulleted paragraphs of text and then click the Borders button in the Paragraph group. (The button will apply the border option that was previously selected.)
4. Select text from the title *Technology Career Questions* through the four numbered paragraphs of text below and then click the Borders button in the Paragraph group.
5. Save and then print **WL1-C3-P1-TechInfo. docx**.

Adding Paragraph Shading

With the Shading button in the Paragraph group you can add shading to text in a document. Select text you want to shade and then click the Shading button. This applies a background color behind the text. Click the Shading button arrow and a Shading drop-down gallery displays.

Paragraph shading colors display in themes in the drop-down gallery. Use one of the theme colors or click one of the standard colors that displays at the bottom of the gallery. Click the *More Colors* option and the Colors dialog box displays. At the Colors dialog box with the Standard tab selected, click the desired color or click the Custom tab and then specify a custom color.

1. With **WL1-C3-P1-TechInfo.docx** open, apply paragraph shading and change border lines by completing the following steps:
   a. Position the insertion point on any character in the title *Technology Information Questions*.
   b. Click the Borders button arrow and then click *No Border* at the drop-down list.
   c. Click the Borders button arrow and then click *Bottom Border* at the drop-down list.
   d. Click the Shading button arrow and then click the *Purple, Accent 4, Lighter 60%* option.
2. Apply the same formatting to the other titles by completing the following steps:
   a. With the insertion point positioned on any character in the title *Technology Information Questions*, double-click the Format Painter button in the Clipboard group.
   b. Select the title *Technology Timeline: Computers in the Workplace*.
   c. Select the title *Technology Career Questions*.
   d. Click the Format Painter button in the Clipboard group.
3. Remove the paragraph border and apply shading to paragraphs by completing the following steps:
   a. Select the numbered paragraphs of text below the *Technology Information Questions* title.
   b. Click the Borders button arrow and then click *No Border* at the drop-down list.
   c. Click the Shading button arrow and then click the *Purple, Accent 4, Lighter 80%* option.
4. Select the bulleted paragraphs of text below the *Technology Timeline: Computers in the Workplace* title, click the Borders button, and then click the Shading button. (Clicking the Borders button will apply the previous border option, which was *No Border*. Clicking the Shading button will apply the previous shading option, which was *Purple, Accent 4, Lighter 80%*.)
5. Select the numbered paragraphs of text below the *Technology Career Questions* title, click the Borders button, and then click the Shading button.
6. Save, print, and then close **WL1-C3-P1-TechInfo.docx**.

You will open a document containing information on online shopping, apply and customize borders and shading, and then sort text in the document.

Customizing Borders and Shading

If you want to further customize paragraph borders and shading, use options at the Borders and Shading dialog box. Display this dialog box by clicking the Borders button arrow and then clicking *Borders and Shading* at the drop-down list. Click the Borders tab and options display for customizing the border; click the Shading tab and shading options display. As you learned in a previous section, you can add borders to a paragraph with the Borders button in the Paragraph group. If you want to further customize borders, use options at the Borders and Shading dialog box with the Borders tab selected as shown in Figure 3.4. At the Borders and Shading dialog box, specify the desired border, style, color, and width. Click the Shading tab and the dialog box displays with shading options.

Figure 3.4 Borders and Shading Dialog Box with the Borders Tab Selected

Click the Shading tab to display options for fill colors and patterns.

Click the sides, top, or bottom of this preview area to insert or remove a border.

---

1. Open **OnlineShop.docx**.
2. Save the document with Save As and name it **WL1-C3-P2-OnlineShop**.
3. Make the following changes to the document:
   a. Insert 12 points of space before and 6 points of space after the headings *Online Shopping, Advantages of Online Shopping, Online Shopping Venues, Online Shopping Safety Tips*, and *REFERENCES*. (Do this with the *Spacing Before* and *Spacing After* measurement boxes in the Page Layout tab.)
   b. Center the *REFERENCES* title.

4. Insert a custom border and add shading to a heading by completing the following steps:
   a. Move the insertion point to any character in the heading *Online Shopping*.
   b. Click the Borders button arrow and then click *Borders and Shading* at the drop-down list.
   c. At the Borders and Shading dialog box with the Borders tab selected, click the down-pointing arrow at the right side of the *Color* option box and then click the *Dark Blue* color in the *Standard Colors* section.
   d. Click the down-pointing arrow at the right of the *Width* option box and then click *1 pt* at the drop-down list.

   e. Click the top border of the box in the *Preview* section of the dialog box.
   f. Click the down scroll arrow in the *Style* list box and then click the first thick/thin line.
   g. Click the down-pointing arrow at the right side of the *Color* option box and then click the *Dark Blue* color in the *Standard Colors* section.
   h. Click the bottom border of the box in the *Preview* section of the dialog box.

i. Click the Shading tab.
j. Click the down-pointing arrow at the right side of the *Fill* option box and then click *Olive Green, Accent 3, Lighter 60%*.
k. Click OK to close the dialog box.

5. Use Format Painter to apply the same border and shading formatting to the remaining headings by completing the following steps:
a. Position the insertion point on any character in the heading *Online Shopping*.
b. Double-click the Format Painter button in the Clipboard group in the Home tab.
c. Select the heading *Advantages of Online Shopping*.
d. Select the heading *Online Shopping Venues*.
e. Select the heading *Online Shopping Safety Tips*.
f. Click the Format Painter button once.

6. Move the insertion point to any character in the heading *Online Shopping* and then remove the 12 points of spacing above.
7. Save **WL1-C3-P2-OnlineShop.docx**.

Sorting Text in Paragraphs ■■■■■■■■■■■■■■■■■

▼ **Quick Steps**

Sort Paragraphs of Text
1. Click Sort button.
2. Make any needed changes at Sort Text dialog box.
3. Click OK.

Sort

You can sort text arranged in paragraphs alphabetically by the first character. The first character can be a number, symbol (such as $ or #), or letter. Type paragraphs you want to sort at the left margin or indented to a tab stop. Unless you select specific paragraphs for sorting, Word sorts the entire document.

To sort text in paragraphs, open the document. If the document contains text you do not want sorted, select the specific paragraph you do want sorted. Click the Sort button in the Paragraph group and the Sort Text dialog box displays. At this dialog box, click OK. If you select text and then display the dialog box the *Sort by* option is set at *Paragraphs*. If the text you select is numbers, then *Numbers* displays in the Sort Text dialog box.

Project 2b   **Sorting Paragraphs Alphabetically**   **Part 2 of 2**

1. With **WL1-C3-P2-OnlineShop.docx** open, sort the bulleted text alphabetically by completing the following steps:
a. Select the bulleted paragraphs in the *Advantages of Online Shopping* section.
b. Click the Sort button in the Paragraph group.
c. At the Sort Text dialog box, make sure *Paragraphs* displays in the *Sort by* option box and the *Ascending* option is selected.
d. Click OK.

2. Sort the numbered paragraphs by completing the following steps:
a. Select the numbered paragraphs in the *Online Shopping Safety Tips* section.

b. Click the Sort button in the Paragraph group.

c. Click OK at the Sort Text dialog box.

3. Sort alphabetically the three paragraphs of text below the *REFERENCES* title by completing the following steps:

a. Select the paragraphs of text below the *REFERENCES* title.

b. Click the Sort button in the Paragraph group.

c. Click the down-pointing arrow at the right side of the *Type* list box and then click *Text* at the drop-down list.

d. Click OK.

4. Save, print, and then close **WL1-C3-P2-OnlineShop.docx**.

 Project **3** **Prepare a Document on Workshops and Training Dates**   **4 Parts**

- You will set and move tabs on the Ruler and at the Tabs dialog box and type tabbed text about workshops, training dates, and a table of contents.

Manipulating Tabs ▪■▪■▪■▪■▪■▪■▪■▪■▪■▪■▪■▪

When you work with a document, Word offers a variety of default settings such as margins and line spacing. One of these defaults is a left tab set every 0.5 inch. In some situations, these default tabs are appropriate; in others, you may want to create your own. Two methods exist for setting tabs. Tabs can be set on the Ruler or at the Tabs dialog box.

Manipulating Tabs on the Ruler

Use the Ruler to set, move, and delete tabs. If the Ruler is not visible, click the View Ruler button located at the top of the vertical scroll bar. The Ruler displays left tabs set every 0.5 inch. These default tabs are indicated by tiny vertical lines along the bottom of the Ruler. With a left tab, text aligns at the left edge of the tab. The other types of tabs that can be set on the Ruler are center, right, decimal, and bar. Use the Alignment button that displays at the left side of the Ruler to specify tabs. Each time you click the Alignment button, a different tab or paragraph alignment symbol displays. Table 3.1 shows the tab alignment buttons and what type of tab each will set.

Table 3.1 Tab Alignment Buttons

Tab Alignment Button	Type of Tab	Tab Alignment Button	Type of Tab
L	Left tab	⊥	Decimal tab
⊥	Center tab	I	Bar tab
⌐	Right tab		

Setting Tabs

▼ **Quick Steps**

Set Tabs on Ruler
1. Click Alignment button on Ruler.
2. Click desired location on Ruler.

When setting tabs on the Ruler, a dotted guideline displays to help align tabs.

Position the insertion point in any paragraph of text, and tabs for the paragraph appear on the Ruler.

To set a left tab on the Ruler, make sure the left alignment symbol (see Table 3.1) displays in the Alignment button. Position the arrow pointer just below the tick mark (the marks on the Ruler) where you want the tab symbol to appear and then click the left mouse button. When you set a tab on the Ruler, any default tabs to the left are automatically deleted by Word. Set a center, right, decimal, or bar tab on the Ruler in a similar manner.

Before setting a tab on the Ruler, click the Alignment button at the left side of the Ruler until the appropriate tab symbol displays and then set the tab. If you change the tab symbol in the Alignment button, the symbol remains until you change it again or you exit Word. If you exit and then reenter Word, the tab symbol returns to the default of left tab.

If you want to set a tab at a specific measurement on the Ruler, hold down the Alt key, position the arrow pointer at the desired position, and then hold down the left mouse button. This displays two measurements in the white portion in the Ruler. The first measurement displays the location of the arrow pointer on the Ruler in relation to the left margin. The second measurement is the distance from the location of the arrow pointer on the Ruler to the right margin. With the left mouse button held down, position the tab symbol at the desired location and then release the mouse button and the Alt key.

If you change tab settings and then create columns of text using the New Line command, Shift + Enter, the tab formatting is stored in the paragraph mark at the end of the columns. If you want to make changes to the tab settings for text in the columns, position the insertion point anywhere within the columns (all of the text in the columns does not have to be selected) and then make the changes.

Project 3a | Setting Left, Center, and Right Tabs on the Ruler | Part 1 of 4

1. At a new blank document, type **WORKSHOPS** centered and bolded as shown in Figure 3.5.
2. Press the Enter key and then return the paragraph alignment back to left and turn off bold for the new paragraph.
3. Set a left tab at the 0.5-inch mark, a center tab at the 3.25-inch mark, and a right tab at the 6-inch mark by completing the following steps:
   a. Click the Show/Hide ¶ button in the Paragraph group in the Home tab to turn on the display of nonprinting characters.
   b. Make sure the Ruler is displayed. (If not, click the View Ruler button located at the top of the vertical scroll bar.)
   c. Make sure the left tab symbol displays in the Alignment button at the left side of the Ruler.
   d. Position the arrow pointer on the 0.5-inch mark on the Ruler and then click the left mouse button.

e. Position the arrow pointer on the Alignment button at the left side of the Ruler and then click the left mouse button until the center tab symbol displays (see Table 3.1).

f. Position the arrow pointer below the 3.25-inch mark on the Ruler. Hold down the Alt key and then the left mouse button. Make sure the first measurement on the Ruler displays as *3.25"* and then release the mouse button and the Alt key.

g. Position the arrow pointer on the Alignment button at the left side of the Ruler and then click the left mouse button until the right tab symbol displays (see Table 3.1).

h. Position the arrow pointer below the 6-inch mark on the Ruler. Hold down the Alt key and then the left mouse button. Make sure the first measurement on the Ruler displays as *6"* and then release the mouse button and the Alt key.

4. Type the text in columns as shown in Figure 3.5. Press the Tab key before typing each column entry and press Shift + Enter after typing the text in the third column.

5. After typing the last column entry, press the Enter key twice.

6. Press Ctrl + Q to remove paragraph formatting (tab settings).

7. Click the Show/Hide ¶ button to turn off the display of nonprinting characters.

8. Save the document and name it **WL1-C3-P3-Tabs**.

Figure 3.5 Project 3a

WORKSHOPS

Title	Price	Date
Quality Management	$240	Friday, February 3
Staff Development	229	Friday, February 17
Streamlining Production	175	Monday, March 5
Managing Records	150	Tuesday, March 27
Customer Service Training	150	Thursday, March 29
Sales Techniques	125	Tuesday, April 10

Moving Tabs and Deleting Tabs

After a tab has been set on the Ruler, it can be moved to a new location. To move a tab, position the arrow pointer on the tab symbol on the Ruler, hold down the left mouse button, drag the symbol to the new location on the Ruler, and then release the mouse button. To delete a tab from the Ruler, position the arrow pointer on the tab symbol you want deleted, hold down the left mouse button, drag the symbol down into the document, and then release the mouse button.

Project 3b **Moving Tabs** **Part 2 of 4**

1. With **WL1-C3-P3-Tabs.docx** open, position the insertion point on any character in the first entry in the tabbed text.
2. Position the arrow pointer on the left tab symbol at the 0.5-inch mark, hold down the left mouse button, drag the left tab symbol to the 1-inch mark on the Ruler, and then release the mouse button. *Hint: Use the Alt key to help you precisely position the tab symbol.*

3. Position the arrow pointer on the right tab symbol at the 6-inch mark, hold down the left mouse button, drag the right tab symbol to the 5.5-inch mark on the Ruler, and then release the mouse button. *Hint: Use the Alt key to help you precisely position the tab symbol.*
4. Save **WL1-C3-P3-Tabs.docx**.

Manipulating Tabs at the Tabs Dialog Box

▼ **Quick Steps**

Set Tabs at Tabs Dialog Box
1. Click Paragraph group dialog box launcher.
2. Click Tabs button.
3. Specify tab positions, alignments, and leader options.
4. Click OK.

Use the Tabs dialog box shown in Figure 3.6 to set tabs at a specific measurement. You can also use the Tabs dialog box to set tabs with preceding leaders and clear one tab or all tabs. To display the Tabs dialog box, click the Paragraph group dialog box launcher. At the Paragraph dialog box, click the Tabs button located in the bottom left corner of the dialog box.

Figure 3.6 Tabs Dialog Box

Clearing Tabs and Setting Tabs

At the Tabs dialog box, you can clear an individual tab or all tabs. To clear all tabs, click the Clear All button. To clear an individual tab, specify the tab position, and then click the Clear button.

At the Tabs dialog box, you can set a left, right, center, or decimal tab as well as a bar. (For an example of a bar tab, refer to Figure 3.7.) You can also set a left, right, center, or decimal tab with preceding leaders. To change the type of tab at the Tabs dialog box, display the dialog box and then click the desired tab in the Alignment section. Type the desired measurement for the tab in the *Tab stop position* text box.

Project 3c **Setting Left Tabs and a Bar Tab at the Tabs Dialog Box** **Part 3 of 4**

1. With **WL1-C3-P3-Tabs.docx** open, press Ctrl + End to move the insertion point to the end of the document.
2. Type the title **TRAINING DATES** bolded and centered as shown in Figure 3.7, press the Enter key, return the paragraph alignment back to left, and then turn off bold.
3. Display the Tabs dialog box and then set left tabs and a bar tab by completing the following steps:
   a. Click the Paragraph group dialog box launcher.
   b. At the Paragraph dialog box, click the Tabs button located in the lower left corner of the dialog box.
   c. Make sure *Left* is selected in the *Alignment* section of the dialog box.
   d. Type **1.75** in the *Tab stop position* text box.
   e. Click the Set button.
   f. Type **4** in the *Tab stop position* text box and then click the Set button.
   g. Type **3.25** in the *Tab stop position* text box, click *Bar* in the *Alignment* section, and then click the Set button.
   h. Click OK to close the Tabs dialog box.

Step 3g

Step 3h

4. Type the text in columns as shown in Figure 3.7. Press the Tab key before typing each column entry and press Shift + Enter to end each line.
5. After typing *February 23*, complete the following steps:
   a. Press the Enter key.
   b. Clear tabs by displaying the Tabs dialog box, clicking the Clear All button, and then clicking OK.
   c. Press the Enter key.
6. Remove the 10 points of spacing after the last entry in the text by completing the following steps:
   a. Position the insertion point on any character in the *January 26* entry.
   b. Click the Page Layout tab.
   c. Click twice on the down-pointing arrow at the right side of the *Spacing After* measurement box. (This changes the measurement to *0 pt*.)
7. Save **WL1-C3-P3-Tabs.docx**.

Figure 3.7 Project 3c

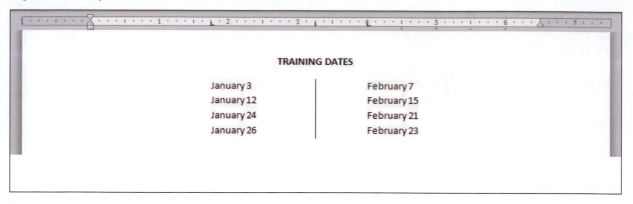

Setting Leader Tabs

The four types of tabs can also be set with leaders. Leaders are useful in a table of contents or other material where you want to direct the reader's eyes across the page. Figure 3.8 shows an example of leaders. Leaders can be periods (.), hyphens (-), or underlines (_). To add leaders to a tab, click the type of leader desired in the *Leader* section of the Tabs dialog box.

Project 3d **Setting a Left Tab and a Right Tab with Dot Leaders** **Part 4 of 4**

1. With **WL1-C3-P3-Tabs.docx** open, press Ctrl + End to move the insertion point to the end of the document.
2. Type the title **TABLE OF CONTENTS** bolded and centered as shown in Figure 3.8.
3. Press the Enter key and then return the paragraph alignment back to left and turn off bold.
4. Set a left tab and a right tab with dot leaders by completing the following steps:
   a. Click the Paragraph group dialog box launcher.
   b. Click the Tabs button located in the lower left corner of the Paragraph dialog box.
   c. At the Tabs dialog box, make sure *Left* is selected in the *Alignment* section of the dialog box.
   d. With the insertion point positioned in the *Tab stop position* text box, type **1** and then click the Set button.
   e. Type **5.5** in the *Tab stop position* text box.
   f. Click *Right* in the *Alignment* section of the dialog box.
   g. Click *2 ......* in the *Leader* section of the dialog box and then click the Set button.
   h. Click OK to close the dialog box.
5. Type the text in columns as shown in Figure 3.8. Press the Tab key before typing each column entry and press Shift + Enter to end each line.
6. Save, print, and then close **WL1-C3-P3-Tabs.docx**.

Figure 3.8 Project 3d

P roject **4** **Move and Copy Text in a Document on**   **2 Parts**
                Online Shopping Tips

You will open a document containing information on online shopping safety tips and then cut, copy, and paste text in the document.

Cutting, Copying, and Pasting Text ■■■■■■■■■■■■■■

Cut

When editing a document, you may need to delete specific text, move text to a different location in the document, and/or copy text to various locations in the document. You can complete these activities using buttons in the Clipboard group in the Home tab.

Paste

Deleting Selected Text

Word offers different methods for deleting text from a document. To delete a single character, you can use either the Delete key or the Backspace key. To delete more than a single character, select the text, and then press the Delete key on the keyboard or click the Cut button in the Clipboard group. If you press the Delete key, the text is deleted permanently. (You can restore deleted text with the Undo button on the Quick Access toolbar.) The Cut button in the Clipboard group will remove the selected text from the document and insert it in the ***Clipboard***. Word's Clipboard is a temporary area of memory. The Clipboard holds text while it is being moved or copied to a new location in the document or to a different document.

H I N T

The Clipboard contents are deleted when the computer is turned off. Text you want to save permanently should be saved as a separate document.

Cutting and Pasting Text

To move text to a different location in the document, select the text, click the Cut button in the Clipboard group, position the insertion point at the location where you want the text inserted, and then click the Paste button in the Clipboard group.

You can also move selected text with a shortcut menu. To do this, select the text and then position the insertion point inside the selected text until it turns into an arrow pointer. Click the right mouse button and then click *Cut* at the shortcut menu. Position the insertion point where you want the text inserted, click the right mouse button, and then click *Paste* at the shortcut menu. Keyboard shortcuts are also available for cutting and pasting text. Use Ctrl + X to cut text and Ctrl + V to insert text.

▼ Quick Steps

Move Selected Text
1. Select text.
2. Click Cut button.
3. Move to desired location.
4. Click Paste button.

When selected text is cut from a document and inserted in the Clipboard, it stays in the Clipboard until other text is inserted in the Clipboard. For this reason, you can paste text from the Clipboard more than just once. For example, if you cut text to the Clipboard, you can paste this text in different locations within the document or other documents as many times as desired.

Moving Text by Dragging with the Mouse

You can also use the mouse to move text. To do this, select text to be moved and then position the I-beam pointer inside the selected text until it turns into an arrow pointer. Hold down the left mouse button, drag the arrow pointer (displays with a gray box attached) to the location where you want the selected text inserted, and then release the button. If you drag and then drop selected text in the wrong location, immediately click the Undo button.

Project 4a **Moving and Dragging Selected Text** **Part 1 of 2**

1. Open **ShoppingTips.docx**.
2. Save the document with Save As and name it **WL1-C3-P4-ShoppingTips**.
3. Move a paragraph by completing the following steps:
   a. Select the paragraph that begins with *Only buy at secure sites.* including the blank line below the paragraph.
   b. Click the Cut button in the Clipboard group in the Home tab.
   c. Position the insertion point at the beginning of the paragraph that begins with *Look for sites that follow . . . .*
   d. Click the Paste button in the Clipboard group. (If the first and second paragraphs are not separated by a blank line, press the Enter key once.)

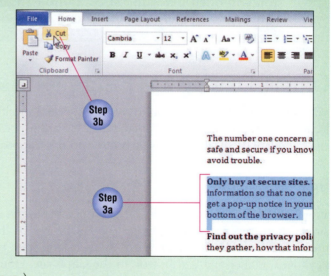

4. Following steps similar to those in Step 3, move the paragraph that begins with *Never provide your social . . .* so it is positioned before the paragraph that begins *Look for sites that follow privacy . . .* and after the paragraph that begins *Only buy at secure . . . .*
5. Use the mouse to select the paragraph that begins with *Keep current with the latest Internet . . .* including one blank line below the paragraph.
6. Move the I-beam pointer inside the selected text until it becomes an arrow pointer.
7. Hold down the left mouse button, drag the arrow pointer (displays with a small gray box attached) so that the insertion point, which displays as a grayed vertical bar, is positioned at the beginning of the paragraph that begins with *Never provide your social . . . ,* and then release the mouse button.
8. Deselect the text.
9. Save **WL1-C3-P4-ShoppingTips.docx**.

Using the Paste Options Button

When selected text is pasted, the Paste Options button displays in the lower right corner of the text. Click this button (or press the Ctrl key on the keyboard) and the *Paste Options* gallery displays as shown in Figure 3.9. Use options from this gallery to specify how you want information pasted in the document. Hover the mouse over a button in the gallery and the live preview displays the text in the document as it will appear when pasted. By default, pasted text retains the formatting of the selected text. You can choose to match the formatting of the pasted text with the formatting where the text is pasted or paste only the text without retaining formatting. To determine the function of a button in the *Paste Options* gallery, hover the mouse over a button and a ScreenTip displays with an explanation of the button function as well as the keyboard shortcut. For example, hover the mouse pointer over the first button from the left in the *Paste Options* gallery and the ScreenTip displays with the information *Keep Source Formatting (K)*. Click this button or press the letter *K* on the keyboard and the pasted text keeps its original formatting.

Paste Options

Figure 3.9 Paste Options Button Drop-down List

Click the option that specifies the formatting you desire for the pasted text.

Project 4b　**Using the Paste Options Button**　　　　　　　　　**Part 2 of 2**

1. With **L1-C3-P4-ShoppingTips.docx** open, open **Tip.docx**.
2. Select the paragraph of text in the document including the blank line below the paragraph and then click the Copy button in the Clipboard group.
3. Close **Tip.docx**.
4. Move the insertion point to the end of the document.
5. Click the Paste button in the Clipboard group.
6. Click the Paste Options button that displays at the end of the paragraph and then click the middle button in the Paste Options gallery (Merge Formatting (M) button). (This changes the font so it matches the formatting of the other paragraphs in the document.)

7. Save, print, and then close **WL1-C3-P4-ShoppingTips.docx**.

Project **5** Copy Text in a Staff Meeting Announcement   1 Part

You will copy and paste text in a document announcing a staff meeting for the Technical Support Team.

Copying and Pasting Text

▼ **Quick Steps**

Copy Selected Text
1. Select text.
2. Click Copy button.
3. Move to desired location.
4. Click Paste button.

Copy

Copying selected text can be useful in documents that contain repetitive portions of text. You can use this function to insert duplicate portions of text in a document instead of retyping the text. After you have selected text, copy the text to a different location with the Copy and Paste buttons in the Clipboard group in the Home tab or using the mouse. You can also use the keyboard shortcut, Ctrl + C, to copy text.

To use the mouse to copy text, select the text and then position the I-beam pointer inside the selected text until it becomes an arrow pointer. Hold down the left mouse button and hold down the Ctrl key. Drag the arrow pointer (displays with a small gray box and a box containing a plus symbol) to the location where you want the copied text inserted (make sure the insertion point, which displays as a grayed vertical bar, is positioned in the desired location) and then release the mouse button and then the Ctrl key.

Project 5   Copying Text   Part 1 of 1

1. Open **StaffMtg.docx**.
2. Save the document with Save As and name it **WL1-C3-P5-StaffMtg**.
3. Copy the text in the document to the end of the document by completing the following steps:
   a. Select all of the text in the document and include one blank line below the text. *Hint: Click the Show/Hide ¶ button to turn on the display of nonprinting characters. When you select the text, select one of the paragraph markers below the text.*
   b. Click the Copy button in the Clipboard group.
   c. Move the insertion point to the end of the document.
   d. Click the Paste button in the Clipboard group.
4. Copy the text again at the end of the document. To do this, position the insertion point at the end of the document and then click the Paste button in the Clipboard group. (This inserts a copy of the text from the Clipboard.)
5. Select all of the text in the document using the mouse and include one blank line below the text. (Consider turning on the display of nonprinting characters.)
6. Move the I-beam pointer inside the selected text until it becomes an arrow pointer.
7. Hold down the Ctrl key and then the left mouse button. Drag the arrow pointer (displays with a box with a plus symbol inside) to the end of the document, release the mouse button, and then release the Ctrl key.
8. Deselect the text.

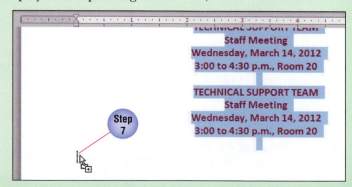

9. Make sure all text fits on one page. If not, consider deleting any extra blank lines.
10. Save, print, and then close **WL1-C3-P5-StaffMtg.docx**.

Project **6** **Create a Contract Negotiations Document** **1 Part**

You will use the Clipboard to copy and paste paragraphs to and from paragraphs in separate documents to create a contract negotiations document.

Using the Clipboard ▪▪■■▪■■▪▪■■▪▪▪▪▪■■▪■▪

Use the Clipboard to collect and paste multiple items. You can collect up to 24 different items and then paste them in various locations. To display the Clipboard task pane, click the Clipboard group dialog box launcher located in the lower right corner of the Clipboard group. The Clipboard task pane displays at the left side of the screen in a manner similar to what you see in Figure 3.10.

Select text or an object you want to copy and then click the Copy button in the Clipboard group. Continue selecting text or items and clicking the Copy button. To insert an item, position the insertion point in the desired location and then click the option in the Clipboard task pane representing the item. Click the Paste All button to paste all of the items in the Clipboard into the document. If the copied item is text, the first 50 characters display beside the button on the Clipboard task pane. When all desired items are inserted, click the Clear All button to remove any remaining items.

▼ **Quick Steps**

Use Clipboard
1. Click Clipboard group dialog box launcher.
2. Select and copy desired text.
3. Move to desired location.
4. Click desired option in Clipboard task pane.

You can copy items to the Clipboard from various Office applications and then paste them into any Office file.

Clear All

Figure 3.10 Clipboard Task Pane

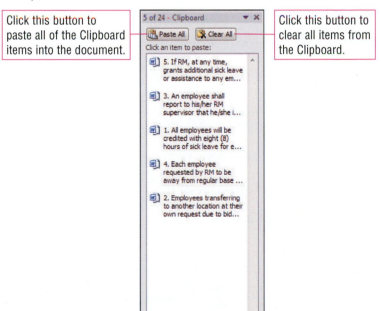

Click this button to paste all of the Clipboard items into the document.

Click this button to clear all items from the Clipboard.

1. Open **ContractItems.docx**.
2. Turn on the display of the Clipboard task pane by clicking the Clipboard group dialog box launcher. (If the Clipboard task pane list box contains any text, click the Clear All button located toward the top of the task pane.)
3. Select paragraph 1 in the document (the 1. is not selected) and then click the Copy button in the Clipboard group.
4. Select paragraph 3 in the document (the 3. is not selected) and then click the Copy button in the Clipboard group.
5. Close **ContractItems.docx**.
6. Paste the paragraphs by completing the following steps:
   a. Press Ctrl + N to display a new blank document. (If the Clipboard task pane does not display, click the Clipboard group dialog box launcher.)
   b. Type **CONTRACT NEGOTIATION ITEMS** centered and bolded.
   c. Press the Enter key, turn off bold, and return the paragraph alignment back to left.
   d. Click the Paste All button in the Clipboard task pane to paste both paragraphs in the document.
   e. Click the Clear All button in the Clipboard task pane.
7. Open **UnionContract.docx**.
8. Select and then copy each of the following paragraphs:
   a. Paragraph 2 in the *Transfers and Moving Expenses* section.
   b. Paragraph 4 in the *Transfers and Moving Expenses* section.
   c. Paragraph 1 in the *Sick Leave* section.
   d. Paragraph 3 in the *Sick Leave* section.
   e. Paragraph 5 in the *Sick Leave* section.
9. Close **UnionContract.docx**.
10. Make sure the insertion point is positioned at the end of the document and then paste the paragraphs by completing the following steps:
    a. Click the button in the Clipboard task pane representing paragraph 2. (When the paragraph is inserted in the document, the paragraph number changes to 3.)
    b. Click the button in the Clipboard task pane representing paragraph 4.
    c. Click the button in the Clipboard task pane representing paragraph 3.
    d. Click the button in the Clipboard task pane representing paragraph 5.
11. Click the Clear All button located toward the top of the Clipboard task pane.
12. Close the Clipboard task pane.
13. Save the document and name it **WL1-C3-P6-NegotiateItems**.
14. Print and then close **WL1-C3-P6-NegotiateItems.docx**.

Step 2

Step 6d

Step 10a

Step 11

Chapter Summary

- Number paragraphs with the Numbering button in the Paragraph group in the Home tab and insert bullets before paragraphs with the Bullets button.

- Remove all paragraph formatting from a paragraph by pressing the keyboard shortcut, Ctrl + Q, and remove all character and paragraph formatting by clicking the Clear Formatting button in the Font group.

- The AutoCorrect Options button displays when the AutoFormat feature inserts numbers. Click this button to display options for undoing and/or stopping automatic numbering.

- Bulleted lists with hanging indents are automatically created when a paragraph begins with *, >, or -. The type of bullet inserted depends on the type of character entered.

- You can turn off automatic numbering and bullets at the AutoCorrect dialog box with the AutoFormat As You Type tab selected.

- A paragraph created in Word contains an invisible frame and you can insert a border around this frame. Click the Borders button arrow to display a drop-down list of border choices.

- Apply shading to text by clicking the Shading button arrow and then clicking the desired color at the drop-down gallery.

- Use options at the Borders and Shading dialog box with the Borders tab selected to add a customized border to a paragraph or selected paragraphs and use options with Shading tab selected to add shading or a pattern to a paragraph or selected paragraphs.

- With the Sort button in the Paragraph group in the Home tab, you can sort text arranged in paragraphs alphabetically by the first character, which includes numbers, symbols, or letters.

- By default, tabs are set every 0.5 inch. These settings can be changed on the Ruler or at the Tabs dialog box.

- Use the Alignment button at the left side of the Ruler to select a left, right, center, or decimal tab. When you set a tab on the Ruler, any default tabs to the left are automatically deleted.

- After a tab has been set on the Ruler, it can be moved or deleted using the mouse pointer.

- At the Tabs dialog box, you can set any of the four types of tabs as well as a bar tab at a specific measurement. You can also set tabs with preceding leaders and clear one tab or all tabs. Preceding leaders can be periods, hyphens, or underlines.

- Cut, copy, and paste text using buttons in the Clipboard group or with keyboard shortcuts.

- When selected text is pasted, the Paste Options button displays in the lower right corner of the text. Click the button and the *Paste Options* gallery displays with buttons for specifying how you want information pasted in the document.

- With the Office Clipboard, you can collect up to 24 items and then paste them in various locations in a document.

Commands Review

FEATURE	RIBBON TAB, GROUP	BUTTON, OPTION	KEYBOARD SHORTCUT
Borders	Home, Paragraph		
Borders and Shading dialog box	Home, Paragraph	, Borders and Shading	
Bullets	Home, Paragraph		
Clear character and paragraph formatting	Home, Font		
Clear paragraph formatting			Ctrl + Q
Clipboard task pane	Home, Clipboard		
Copy text	Home, Clipboard		Ctrl + C
Cut text	Home, Clipboard		Ctrl + X
New Line command			Shift + Enter
Numbering	Home, Paragraph		
Paragraph dialog box	Home, Paragraph		
Paste text	Home, Clipboard		Ctrl + V
Shading	Home, Paragraph		
Sort Text dialog box	Home, Paragraph		
Tabs dialog box	Home, Paragraph	, Tabs	

Concepts Check Test Your Knowledge

Completion: In the space provided at the right, indicate the correct term, symbol, or command.

1. The Numbering button is located in this group in the Home tab. _____

2. Automate the creation of bulleted paragraphs with this button in the Home tab. _____

3. This button displays when the AutoFormat feature inserts numbers. _____

4. You can turn off automatic numbering and bullets at the AutoCorrect dialog box with this tab selected. _____

5. Bulleted lists with hanging indents are automatically created when you begin a paragraph with the asterisk symbol (*), the hyphen (-), or this symbol.   _____

6. The Borders button is located in this group in the Home tab.   _____

7. Use options at this dialog box to add a customized border to a paragraph or selected paragraphs.   _____

8. Sort text arranged in paragraphs alphabetically by the first character, which includes numbers, symbols, or this.   _____

9. By default, each tab is set apart from the other by this measurement.   _____

10. This is the default tab type.   _____

11. When setting tabs on the Ruler, choose the tab type with this button.   _____

12. Tabs can be set on the Ruler or here.   _____

13. This group in the Home tab contains the Cut, Copy, and Paste buttons.   _____

14. To copy selected text with the mouse, hold down this key while dragging selected text.   _____

15. With this task pane, you can collect up to 24 items and then paste the items in various locations in the document.   _____

Skills Check Assess Your Performance

Assessment

1 APPLY PARAGRAPH FORMATTING TO A COMPUTER ETHICS DOCUMENT

1. Open **CompEthics.docx**.
2. Save the document with Save As and name it **WL1-C3-A1-CompEthics**.
3. Move the insertion point to the end of the document and then type the text shown in Figure 3.11. Apply bullet formatting as shown in the figure.
4. Change the Quick Styles set to *Formal*.
5. Apply the Heading 1 style to the three headings in the document.
6. Apply the Paper theme.
7. Select the paragraphs of text in the *COMPUTER ETHICS* section and then apply numbering formatting.
8. Select the paragraphs of text in the *TECHNOLOGY TIMELINE* section and then apply bullet formatting.
9. Insert the following paragraph of text between paragraphs 2 and 3 in the *Computer Ethics* section: **Find sources relating to the latest federal and/or state legislation on privacy protection.**

10. Apply Blue-Gray, Accent 6, Lighter 60% paragraph shading to the three headings in the document.
11. Apply Gold, Accent 3, Lighter 80% paragraph shading to the numbered paragraphs in the *COMPUTER ETHICS* section and the bulleted paragraphs in the *TECHNOLOGY TIMELINE* and *ACLU FAIR ELECTRONIC MONITORING POLICY* sections.
12. Save, print, and then close **WL1-C3-A1-CompEthics.docx**.

Figure 3.11 Assessment 1

ACLU Fair Electronic Monitoring Policy

➢ Notice to employees of the company's electronic monitoring practices
➢ Use of a signal to let an employee know he or she is being monitored
➢ Employee access to all personal data collected through monitoring
➢ No monitoring of areas designed for the health or comfort of employees
➢ The right to dispute and delete inaccurate data
➢ A ban on the collection of data unrelated to work performance
➢ Restrictions on the disclosure of personal data to others without the employee's consent

Assessment

2 TYPE TABBED TEXT AND APPLY FORMATTING TO A COMPUTER SOFTWARE DOCUMENT

1. Open **ProdSoftware.docx**.
2. Save the document with Save As and name it **WL1-C3-A2-ProdSoftware**.
3. Move the insertion point to the end of the document and then type the tabbed text as shown in Figure 3.12. Before typing the text in columns, set left tabs at the 0.75-inch, 2.75-inch, and 4.5-inch marks on the Ruler.
4. Apply the Heading 1 style to the three headings in the document (*Productivity Software, Personal-Use Software*, and *Software Training Schedule*).
5. Change the Quick Styles set to *Distinctive*.
6. Apply the Elemental theme.
7. Select the productivity software categories in the *PRODUCTIVITY SOFTWARE* section (from *Word processing* through *Computer-aided design*) and then sort the text alphabetically.
8. With the text still selected, apply bullet formatting.
9. Select the personal-use software categories in the *PERSONAL-USE SOFTWARE* section (from *Personal finance software* through *Games and entertainment software*) and then sort the text alphabetically.
10. With the text still selected, apply bullet formatting.
11. Apply a single-line border to the top and a double-line border to the bottom of the three headings in the document and then apply paragraph shading of your choosing to each heading.
12. Position the insertion point on the first line of tabbed text below the *SOFTWARE TRAINING SCHEDULE* heading and then insert 12 points of spacing before the paragraph.
13. Select the text in columns and then move the tab symbols on the Ruler as follows:
    a. Move the tab at the 0.75-inch mark to the 1-inch mark.
    b. Move the tab at the 4.5-inch mark to the 4-inch mark.
14. Save, print, and then close **WL1-C3-A2-ProdSoftware.docx**.

Figure 3.12 Assessment 2

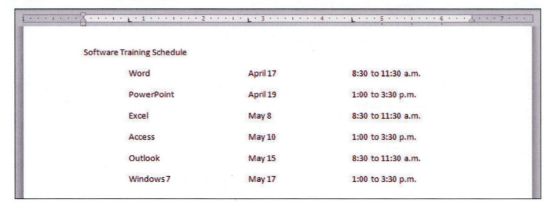

Software Training Schedule

Word	April 17	8:30 to 11:30 a.m.
PowerPoint	April 19	1:00 to 3:30 p.m.
Excel	May 8	8:30 to 11:30 a.m.
Access	May 10	1:00 to 3:30 p.m.
Outlook	May 15	8:30 to 11:30 a.m.
Windows 7	May 17	1:00 to 3:30 p.m.

Assessment

3 TYPE AND FORMAT A TABLE OF CONTENTS DOCUMENT

1. At a new blank document, type the document shown in Figure 3.13 with the following specifications:
   a. Change the font to 11-point Cambria.
   b. Bold and center the title as shown.
   c. Before typing the text in columns, display the Tabs dialog box and then set left tabs at the 1-inch mark and the 1.5-inch mark, and a right tab with dot leaders at the 5.5-inch mark.
2. Save the document and name it **WL1-C3-A3-TofC**.
3. Print **WL1-C3-A3-TofC.docx**.
4. Select the text in columns and then move the tab symbols on the Ruler as follows:
   a. Delete the left tab symbol that displays at the 1.5-inch mark.
   b. Set a new left tab at the 0.5-inch mark.
   c. Move the right tab at the 5.5-inch mark to the 6-inch mark.

Figure 3.13 Assessment 3

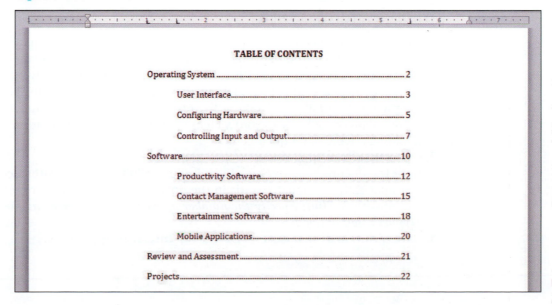

TABLE OF CONTENTS

Operating System	2
User Interface	3
Configuring Hardware	5
Controlling Input and Output	7
Software	10
Productivity Software	12
Contact Management Software	15
Entertainment Software	18
Mobile Applications	20
Review and Assessment	21
Projects	22

5. Apply paragraph borders and shading of your choosing to enhance the visual appeal of the document.
6. Save, print, and then close **WL1-C3-A3-TofC.docx**.

Assessment

4   FORMAT A BUILDING CONSTRUCTION AGREEMENT DOCUMENT

1. Open **ConstructAgrmnt.docx**.
2. Save the document with Save As and name it **WL1-C3-A4-ConstructAgrmnt**.
3. Select and then delete the paragraph that begins *Supervision of Work*.
4. Select and then delete the paragraph that begins *Exclusions*.
5. Move the paragraph that begins *Financing Arrangements* above the paragraph that begins *Start of Construction*.
6. Open **AgrmntItems.docx**.
7. Turn on the display of the Clipboard and then clear all the contents, if necessary.
8. Select and then copy the first paragraph.
9. Select and then copy the second paragraph.
10. Select and then copy the third paragraph.
11. Close **AgrmntItems.docx**.
12. With **WL1-C3-A4-ConstructAgrmnt.docx** open, turn on the display of the Clipboard and then paste the *Supervision* paragraph *above* the *Changes and Alterations* paragraph and merge the formatting. (Make sure you position the insertion point *above* the paragraph before you paste the text.)
13. Paste the *Pay Review* paragraph *above* the *Possession of Residence* paragraph and merge the formatting.
14. Clear all items from the Clipboard and then close the Clipboard.
15. Check the spacing between paragraphs. Insert or delete blank lines to maintain consistent spacing.
16. Save, print, and then close **L1-C3-A4-ConstructAgrmnt.docx**.

Assessment

5   HYPHENATE WORDS IN A REPORT

1. In some Word documents, especially documents with left and right margins wider than 1 inch, the right margin may appear quite ragged. If the paragraph alignment is changed to justified, the right margin will appear even, but there will be extra space added throughout the line. In these situations, hyphenating long words that fall at the end of the text line provides the document with a more balanced look. Use Word's Help feature to learn how to automatically hyphenate words in a document.
2. Open **InterfaceApps.docx**.
3. Save the document with Save As and name it **WL1-C3-A5-InterfaceApps**.
4. Automatically hyphenate words in the document, limiting the consecutive hyphens to 2. ***Hint: Specify the number of consecutive hyphens at the Hyphenation dialog box.***
5. Save, print, and then close **WL1-C3-A5-InterfaceApps.docx**.

Visual Benchmark   Demonstrate Your Proficiency

CREATE A RESUME

1. At a blank document, click the No Spacing style and then type the resume document shown in Figure 3.14 on page 104. Apply character and paragraph formatting as shown in the figure. Insert six points of spacing after the heading *PROFESSIONAL EXPERIENCE* and after the heading *EDUCATION*. Change the font size of the name, DEVON CHAMBERS, to 16 points.
2. Save the document and name it **WL1-C3-VB-Resume.**
3. Print and then close the document.

Case Study   Apply Your Skills

Part 1

You are the assistant to Gina Coletti, manager of La Dolce Vita, an Italian restaurant. She has been working on updating and formatting the lunch menu. She has asked you to complete the menu by opening the **Menu.docx** document (located in the Word2010L1C3 folder), determining how the appetizer section is formatted, and then applying the same formatting to the *Soups and Salads*; *Sandwiches, Calzones and Burgers*; and *Individual Pizzas* sections. Save the document and name it **WL1-C3-CS-Menu**. Print and then close the document.

Part 2

Ms. Coletti has reviewed the completed menu and is pleased with the menu but wants to add a page border around the entire page to increase visual interest. Open **WL1-C3-CS-Menu.docx** and then save the document and name it **WL1-C3-CS-MenuPgBorder**. Display the Borders and Shading dialog box with the Page Border tab selected and then experiment with the options available. Apply an appropriate page border to the menu (consider applying an art page border). Save, print, and then close **WL1-C3-CS-MenuPgBorder.docx**.

Part 3

Each week, the restaurant offers daily specials. Ms. Coletti has asked you to open and format the text in the **MenuSpecials.docx** document. She has asked you to format the specials menu in a similar manner as the main menu but to make some changes to make it unique from the main menu. Apply the same page border to the specials menu document that you applied to the main menu document. Save the document and name it **WL1-C3-CS-MenuSpecials**. Print and then close the document.

Part 4

You have been asked by the head chef to research a new recipe for an Italian dish. Using the Internet, find a recipe that interests you and then prepare a Word document containing the recipe and ingredients. Use bullets before each ingredient and use numbering for each step in the recipe preparation. Save the document and name it **WL1-C3-CS-Recipe**. Print and then close the document.

Figure 3.14 Visual Benchmark

DEVON CHAMBERS

344 North Anderson Road – Oklahoma City, OK 73177 – (404) 555-3228

PROFILE

Business manager with successful track record at entrepreneurial start-up and strong project management skills. Keen ability to motivate and supervise employees, strong hands-on experience with customer service, marketing, and operations. Highly organized and motivated professional looking to leverage strengths in leadership and organizational skills in a project coordinator role.

PROFESSIONAL EXPERIENCE

Midwest Deli, Oklahoma City, OK ....02/10 to present
Assistant Manager
- Coordinated the opening of a new business, which included budgeting start-up costs, establishing relationships with vendors, ordering supplies, purchasing and installing equipment, and marketing the business to the community
- Manage business personnel, which includes recruitment, interviewing, hiring, training, motivating staff, and conflict resolution
- Manage daily business operations through customer satisfaction, quality control, employee scheduling, process improvement, and maintaining product inventory

Marin Associates, Shawnee, OK ....06/08 to 06/09
Projects Coordinator
- Developed and maintained a secure office network and installed and repaired computers
- Provided support for hardware and software issues
- Directed agency projects such as equipment purchases, office reorganization, and building maintenance and repair

Moore Insurance Agency, Shawnee, OK ....04/06 to 04/08
Administrative Assistant
- Prepared documents and forms for staff and clients
- Organized and maintained paper and electronic files and scheduled meetings and appointments
- Disseminated information using the telephone, mail services, websites, and email

EDUCATION

Associate of Arts, Business 2010
Oklahoma City Community College

TECHNOLOGY SKILLS
- Proficient in Microsoft Word, Excel, and PowerPoint
- Knowledgeable in current and previous versions of the Windows operating system
- Experience with networking, firewalls, and security systems

REFERENCES
Professional and personal references available upon request.

Formatting Pages

PERFORMANCE OBJECTIVES

Upon successful completion of Chapter 4, you will be able to:

- **Change document views**
- **Navigate in a document with the Navigation pane**
- **Change margins, page orientation, and paper size in a document**
- **Format pages at the Page Setup dialog box**
- **Insert a page break, blank page, and cover page**
- **Insert page numbering**
- **Insert and edit predesigned headers and footers**
- **Insert a watermark, page color, and page border**
- **Find and replace text and formatting**

Tutorials

A document generally displays in Print Layout view. You can change this default view with buttons in the View area on the Status bar or with options in the View tab. Use the Navigation pane to navigate in a document. A Word document, by default, contains 1-inch top, bottom, left, and right margins. You can change these default margins with the Margins button in the Page Setup group in the Page Layout tab or with options at the Page Setup dialog box. You can insert a variety of features in a Word document including a page break, blank page, and cover page as well as page numbers, headers, footers, a watermark, page color, and page border. Use options at the Find and Replace dialog box to search for specific text or formatting and replace with other text or formatting. Model answers for this chapter's projects appear on the following pages.

Word2010L1C4

Note: Before beginning the projects, copy to your storage medium the Word2010L1C4 subfolder from the Word2010L1 folder on the CD that accompanies this textbook and then make Word2010L1C4 the active folder.

NETIQUETTE GUIDELINES

Distance conveys a degree of anonymity, and as a result, many people feel less inhibited in online situations than in their everyday lives. This lessening of inhibitions sometimes leads people to drop their normal standards of decorum when communicating online. In response, good cybercitizens have developed, over the years, an informal set of guidelines for online behavior called *netiquette.* Netiquette can be summarized by three simple precepts: Remember that there is a human being on the other end of your communication, treat that human being with respect, and do not transmit any message that you wouldn't be willing to communicate face to face. Some specific guidelines include:

- Be careful what you write about others. Assume that anyone about whom you are writing will read your comments or receive them by some circuitous route.
- Be truthful. Do not pretend to be someone or something that you are not.
- Be brief. Receiving and reading messages costs time and money.
- Use titles that accurately and concisely describe the contents of email and other postings.
- Consider your audience, and use language that is appropriate. Excessive use of jargon in a nontechnical chat room, for example, can be bad manners, and remember that children sometimes join chat rooms.
- Avoid offensive language, especially comments that might be construed as racist or sexist.
- Remember that the law still applies in cyberspace. Do not commit illegal acts online, such as libeling or slandering others, and do not joke about committing illegal acts.
- Be careful with humor and sarcasm. One person's humorous comment can be another person's boorish or degrading remark.
- Do not post a message more than once.
- Generally speaking, avoid putting words into full capitals. Online, all-caps is considered SHOUTING.
- If you are following up a previous message or posting, summarize that message or posting.
- Do not post irrelevant messages, referred to in hacker's jargon as spam.
- Do not post messages whose sole purpose is to sucker others into an irrelevant or unimportant discussion. Such messages are known as trolls.
- Read existing follow-up postings and don't repeat what has already been said.
- Respect other people's intellectual property. Don't post, display, or otherwise provide access to materials belonging to others, and cite references as appropriate.
- Temper online expressions of hostility; in hacker's jargon, avoid excessive flaming of others.
- Never send online chain letters.
- Some email programs allow one to place a signature containing text and graphics at the end of a mailing. Remember that elaborate materials take up valuable transmission time, and do not overdo these signatures.
- Limit the length of typed lines to less than 78 characters, and avoid unusual formatting.
- Identify any financial interests related to an email message or posting. If you are selling something, make that fact clear.
- Do not send email to people who might have no interest in it. In particular, avoid automatically copying email to large numbers of people.
- Online messages can be quite informal, but try, nevertheless, to express yourself using proper spelling, capitalization, grammar, usage, and punctuation.
- Avoid chastising others for their online typos. To err is human. To forgive is good cybercitizenship.

Project 2 Format a Document on Online Etiquette Guidelines
WL1-C4-P2-Netiquette.docx

2012

Computer Devices

Student Name
Drake Computing
1/1/2012

Cover Page

Project 3 Customize a Report on Computer Input and Output Devices
WL1-C4-P3-CompDevices.docx

COMPUTER INPUT DEVICES

Engineers have been especially creative in designing new ways to get information into computers. Some input methods are highly specialized and unusual, while common devices often undergo redesign to improve their capabilities or their ergonomics, the ways in which they affect people physically. Some common input devices include keyboards, mice, trackballs, and touchpads.

KEYBOARD

A keyboard can be an external device that is attached by means of a cable, or it can be attached to the CPU case itself as it is for laptop computers. Most keyboards today are QWERTY keyboards, which take their name from the first six keys at the left of the first row of letters. An alternative, the DVORAK keyboard, places the most commonly used keys close to the user's fingertips and speeds typing.

Many keyboards have a separate numeric keypad, like that of a calculator, containing numbers and mathematical operators. All keyboards have modifier keys that enable the user to change the symbol or character that is entered when a given key is pressed. The Shift key, for example, makes a letter uppercase. Keyboards also have special cursor keys that enable the user to change the position on the screen of the cursor, a symbol that appears on the monitor to show where in a document the next change will appear. Most keyboards also have function keys, labeled F1, F2, F3, and so on. These keys allow the user to issue commands by pressing a single key.

Page 1

MOUSE

Graphical operating systems contain many elements that a user can choose by pointing at them. Such elements include buttons, tools, pull-down menus, and icons for file folders, programs, and document files. Often pointing to and clicking on one of these elements is more convenient than using the cursor or arrow keys on the keyboard. This pointing and clicking can be done by using a mouse. The mouse is the second most common input device, after the keyboard. A mouse operates by moving the cursor on the computer screen to correspond to movements made with the mouse.

TRACKBALL

A trackball is like an upside-down mouse. A mouse is moved over a pad. A trackball remains stationary, and the user moves the ball with his or her fingers or palm. One or more buttons for choosing options are incorporated into the design of the trackball.

TOUCHPAD AND TOUCHSCREEN

A touchpad feels less mechanical than a mouse or trackball because the user simply moves a finger on the pad. A touchpad has two parts. One part acts as a button, while the other emulates a mouse pad on which the user traces the location of the cursor with a finger. People with carpal tunnel syndrome find touchpads and trackballs easier to use than mice. Many portable computers have built-in trackballs or touchpads as input devices.

A touchscreen allows the user to choose options by pressing the appropriate part of the screen. Touchscreens are widely used in bank ATMs and in kiosks at retail outlets and in tourist areas.

Page 2

Page 3

To get information into a computer, a person uses an input device. To get information out, a person uses an output device. Some common output devices include monitors, printers, and speakers.

MONITOR

A monitor, or screen, is the most common output device used with a personal computer. A monitor creates a visual display and is either built into the CPU case or attached as an external device by means of a cable. Sometimes the cable is connected to a circuit board called a video card placed into an expansion slot in the CPU.

The most common monitors use either a thin film transistor (TFT) active matrix liquid crystal display (LCD) or a plasma display. Plasma displays have a very true level of color reproduction compared with LCDs. Emerging display technologies include surface-conduction electron-emitter displays (SED) and organic light emitting diodes (OLED).

PRINTER

After monitors, printers are the most important output devices. The print quality produced by these devices is measured in dpi, or dots per inch. As with screen resolution, the greater the number of dots per inch, the better the quality. The earliest printers for personal computers were dot matrix printers that used perforated computer paper. These impact printers worked something like typewriters, transferring the image of a character by using pins to strike a ribbon.

A laser printer uses a laser beam to create points of electrical charge on a cylindrical drum. Toner, composed of particles of ink with a negative electrical charge, sticks to the charged points on the

Page 3

3 | P a g e

---

4 | P a g e

Page 4

Page 1 (top-right document)

The Internet is having trouble keeping up with the rapid increase in users and the increased workload created by the popularity of bandwidth-intensive applications such as music and video files. The broadband connections needed to enjoy these new applications are not evenly distributed. Several ongoing projects promise to provide solutions for these problems in the future. Once these connectivity problems are dealt with, people around the world will be able to enjoy the new web services that are only a few short years away.

SATELLITE INTERNET CONNECTIONS

Many people living in remote or sparsely populated areas are not served by broadband Internet connections. Cable or optical fiber networks are very expensive to install and maintain, and ISPs are not interested in providing service to areas or individuals unless they think it will be profitable. One hope for people without broadband connections is provided by satellite TV networks. Remote ISPs connect to the satellite network using antennae attached to their servers. Data is relayed to and from ISP servers to satellites, which are in turn connected to an Internet backbone access point. While the connection speeds might not be as fast as those offered by regular land-based broadband access, they are faster than the service twisted-pair cable can offer and much better than no access at all.

SECOND INTERNET

A remedy for the traffic clogging the information highway is **Internet2**, a revolutionary new type of Internet currently under development. When fully operational, Internet2 will enable large research universities in the United States to

Page 1

May 4, 2012

Project 4 Add Elements to a Report on the Future of the Internet

WL1-C4-P4-InternetFuture.docx

Page 2 (bottom-left document)

collaborate and share huge amounts of complex scientific information at amazing speeds. Led by over 170 universities working in partnership with industry and government, the Internet2 consortium is developing and deploying advanced network technologies and applications.

Internet2 is a testing ground for universities to work together and develop advanced Internet technologies such as telemedicine, digital libraries, and virtual laboratories. Internet2 universities will be connected to an ultrahigh-speed network called the Abilene backbone. Each university will use state-of-the-art equipment to take advantage of transfer speeds provided by the network.

INTERNET SERVICES FOR A FEE

Industry observers predict that large portals such as AOL, MSN, and Yahoo! will soon determine effective structures and marketing strategies to get consumers to pay for Internet services. This new market, called bring-your-own-access (BYOA), will combine essential *content*, for example, news and weather, with *services*, such as search, directory, email, IM, and online shopping, into a new product with monthly access charges. But to entice current and potential customers into the BYOA market, ISP and telecom companies must offer improvements in the area of security, privacy, and ease of use. Additionally, they are expected to develop new ways to personalize content and add value to the current range of Internet services.

Page 2

May 4, 2012

Page 3 (bottom-right document)

INTERNET IN 2030

Ray Kurzweil, a computer futurist, has looked ahead to the year 2030 and visualized a Web that offers no clear distinctions between real and simulated environments and people. Among the applications he sees as very possible are computerized displays in eyeglasses that could offer simultaneous translations of foreign language conversations, nanobots (microscopic robots) that would work with our brains to extend our mental capabilities, and sophisticated avatars (simulated on-screen persons) that people will interact with online. Technologies that allow people to project their feelings as well as their images and voices may usher in a period when people could "be" with another person even though they are physically hundreds or even thousands of miles apart.

Page 3

May 4, 2012

ROBOTS AS ANDROIDS

Robotic factories are increasingly commonplace, especially in heavy manufacturing, where tolerance of repetitive movements, great strength, and untiring precision are more important than flexibility. Robots are especially useful in hazardous work, such as defusing bombs or handling radioactive materials. They also excel in constructing tiny components like those found inside notebook computers, which are often too small for humans to assemble.

Most people think of robots in science fiction terms, which generally depict them as androids, or simulated humans. Real robots today do not look human at all and, judged by human standards, they are not very intelligent. The task of creating a humanlike body has proven incredibly difficult. Many technological advances in visual perception, audio perception, touch, dexterity, locomotion, and navigation need to occur before robots that look and act like human beings will live and work among us.

VISUAL PERCEPTION

Visual perception is an area of great complexity. A large percentage of the human brain is dedicated to processing data coming from the eyes. As our most powerful sense, sight is the primary means through which we understand the world around us. A single camera is not good enough to simulate the eye. Two cameras are needed to give stereoscopic vision, which allows depth and movement perception. Even with two cameras, visual perception is incomplete because the cameras cannot understand or translate what they see. Processing the image is the difficult part. In order for a robot to move through a room full of furniture it must build a mental map of that room, complete with obstacles. The robot must judge the distance and size of objects before it can figure out how to move around them.

AUDIO PERCEPTION

Audio perception is less complex than visual perception, but no less important. People respond to audible cues about their surroundings and the people they are with without even thinking about it. Listeners can determine someone's emotional state just by hearing the person's voice. A car starting up when someone crosses the street prompts the walker to glance in that direction to check for danger. Identifying a single voice and interpreting what is being said amid accompanying background noise is a task that is among the most important for human beings—and the most difficult.

TACTILE PERCEPTION

Tactile perception, or touch, is another critical sense. Robots can be built with any level of strength, since they are made of steel and motors. How does a robot capable of lifting a car pick up an egg in the dark without dropping or crushing it? The answer is through a sense of touch. The robot must not only be able to feel an object, but also be able to sense how much pressure it is applying to that object. With this feedback it can properly judge how hard it should squeeze. This is a very difficult area, and it may prove that simulating the human hand is even more difficult than simulating the human mind.

Related to touch is the skill of dexterity, or hand-eye coordination. The challenge is to create a robot that can perform small actions, such as soldering tiny joints or placing a chip at a precise spot in a circuit board within half a millimeter.

LOCOMOTION

Locomotion includes broad movements such as walking. Getting a robot to move around is not easy. This area of robotics is challenging, as it requires balance within an endlessly changing set of variables. How does the program adjust for walking up a hill, or down a set of stairs? What if the wind is blowing hard or a foot slips? Currently most mobile robots work with wheels or treads, which limits their mobility in some circumstances but makes them much easier to control.

NAVIGATION

Related to perception, navigation deals with the science of moving a mobile robot through an environment. Navigation is not an isolated area of artificial intelligence, as it must work closely with a visual system or some other kind of perception system. Sonar, radar, mechanical "feelers," and other systems have been subjects of experimentation. A robot can plot a course to a location using an internal "map" built up by a navigational perception system. If the course is blocked or too difficult, the robot must be smart enough to backtrack so it can try another plan.

Page 1

Page 2

Project 5 Format a Report on Robots

WL1-C4-P5-Robots.docx

RENT AGREEMENT

THIS RENT AGREEMENT (hereinafter referred to as the "Agreement") is made and entered into this ___ day of _____, 2012, by and between Tracy Hartford and Michael Iwami.

Term

Tracy Hartford rents to Michael Iwami and Michael Iwami rents from Tracy Hartford the described premises together with any and all appurtenances thereto, for a term of _____ year(s), such term beginning on _____, and ending at 12 o'clock midnight on _____.

Rent

The total rent for the term hereof is the sum of _____ DOLLARS ($_____) payable on the ____ day of each month of the term. All such payments shall be made to Tracy Hartford at Tracy Hartford's address on or before the due date and without demand.

Damage Deposit

Upon the due execution of this Agreement, Michael Iwami shall deposit with Tracy Hartford the sum of _____ DOLLARS ($_____), receipt of which is hereby acknowledged by Tracy Hartford, as security for any damage caused to the Premises during the renting term hereof. Such deposit shall be returned to Michael Iwami, without interest, and minus any set off for damages to the Premises upon the termination of this renting Agreement.

Use of Premises

The Premises shall be used and occupied by Michael Iwami and Michael Iwami's immediately family, exclusively, as a private single family dwelling, and no part of the Premises shall be used at any time during the term of this Agreement by Michael Iwami for the purpose of carrying on any business, profession, or trade of any kind, or for any purpose other than as a private single family dwelling. Michael Iwami shall not allow any other person, other than Michael Iwami's immediate family or transient relatives and friends who are guests of Michael Iwami, to use or occupy the Premises without first obtaining Tracy Hartford's written consent to such use.

Condition of Premises

Michael Iwami stipulates, represents, and warrants that Michael Iwami has examined the Premises, and that they are at the time of this Agreement in good order, repair, and in a safe, clean, and tenantable condition.

Alterations and Improvements

Michael Iwami shall make no alterations to the buildings or improvements on the Premises without the prior written consent of Tracy Hartford. Any and all alterations, changes, and/or improvements

built, constructed, or placed on the Premises by Michael Iwami shall, unminus otherwise provided by written agreement between Tracy Hartford and Michael Iwami, be and become the property of Tracy Hartford and remain on the Premises at the expiration or earlier termination of this Agreement.

Damage to Premises

In the event Premises are destroyed or rendered wholly unlivable, by fire, storm, earthquake, or other casualty not caused by the negligence of Michael Iwami, this Agreement shall terminate from such time except for the purpose of enforcing rights that may have then accrued hereunder.

Page 1

Page 2

Project 6 Format a Lease Agreement Document

WL1-C4-P6-LeaseAgrmnt.docx

Changing the View ■■■■■■■■■■■■■■■■■■■■■■

By default a Word document displays in Print Layout view. This view displays the document on the screen as it will appear when printed. Other views are available such as Draft and Full Screen Reading. Change views with buttons in the View area on the Status bar or with options in the View tab. The buttons in the View area on the Status bar are identified in Figure 4.1. Along with the View buttons, the Status bar also contains a Zoom slider bar as shown in Figure 4.1. Drag the button on the Zoom slider bar to increase or decrease the size of display, or click the Zoom Out button to decrease size and click the Zoom In to increase size.

Click the 100% that displays at the left side of the Zoom slider bar to display the Zoom dialog box.

Zoom Out

Zoom In

Displaying a Document in Draft View

Change to Draft view and the document displays in a format for efficient editing and formatting. At this view, margins and other features such as headers and footers do not display on the screen. Change to Draft view by clicking the Draft button in the View section on the Status bar or click the View tab and then click the Draft button in the Document Views group.

Displaying a Document in Full Screen Reading View

The Full Screen Reading view displays a document in a format for easy viewing and reading. Change to Full Screen Reading view by clicking the Full Screen Reading button in the View section on the Status bar or by clicking the View tab and then clicking the Full Screen Reading button in the Document Views group.

Navigate in Full Screen Reading view using the keys on the keyboard as shown in Table 4.1. You can also navigate in Full Screen Reading view with options from the View Options button that displays toward the top right side of the screen or with the Next Screen and Previous Screen buttons located at the top of the window and also located at the bottom of each page.

You can customize the Full Screen Reading view with some of the options from the View Options drop-down list. Display this list by clicking the View Options button located in the upper right corner of the Full Screen Reading window.

Draft

Full Screen Reading

Figure 4.1 View Buttons and Zoom Slider Bar

Table 4.1 Keyboard Commands in Full Screen Reading View

Press this key	To complete this action
Page Down key or spacebar	Move to the next page or section
Page Up key or Backspace key	Move to the previous page or section
Right Arrow key	Move to next page
Left Arrow key	Move to previous page
Home	Move to first page in document
End	Move to last page in document
Esc	Return to Print Layout

Navigating Using the Navigation Pane

Quick Steps

Display Navigation Pane
1. Click View tab.
2. Click *Navigation Pane* check box.

Word includes a number of features you can use to navigate in a document. Along with the navigation features you have already learned, you can also navigate using the Navigation pane shown in Figure 4.2. When you click the *Navigation Pane* check box in the Show group in the View tab, the Navigation pane displays at the left side of the screen and includes a Search text box and a pane with three tabs. Click the first tab to display titles and headings with styles applied in the Navigation pane. Click a title or heading in the pane to move the insertion point to that title or heading. Click the second tab to display thumbnails of each page in the pane. Click a thumbnail to move the insertion point to the specific page. Click the third tab to browse the current search results in the document. Close the Navigation pane by clicking the *Navigation Pane* check box in the Show group in the View tab or by clicking the Close button located in the upper right corner of the pane.

Figure 4.2 Navigation Pane

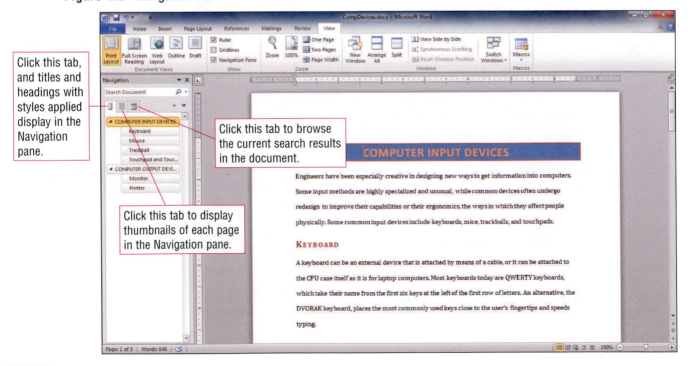

Click this tab, and titles and headings with styles applied display in the Navigation pane.

Click this tab to browse the current search results in the document.

Click this tab to display thumbnails of each page in the Navigation pane.

1. Open **CompDevices.docx**.
2. Click the Draft button located in the View section on the Status bar.

Step 2

3. Using the mouse, drag the Zoom slider bar button to the left to decrease the size of the document display to approximately 60%. (The percentage displays at the left side of the Zoom Out button.)
4. Drag the Zoom slider bar button back to the middle until *100%* displays at the left side of the Zoom Out button.

Step 3

5. Click the Print Layout button in the View section on the Status bar.
6. Click the Full Screen Reading button located in the View section on the Status bar.
7. Click the View Options button located toward the top of the viewing window and then click *Show Two Pages* at the drop-down list.

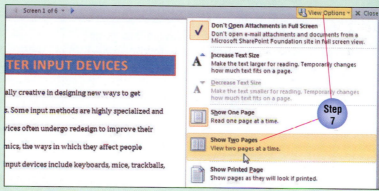

Step 7

8. Click the Next Screen button to display the next two pages in the viewing window.
9. Click the Previous Screen button to display the previous two pages.

Step 8

10. Click the View Options button located toward the top of the viewing window and then click *Show One Page* at the drop-down list.
11. Practice navigating using the actions shown in Table 4.1. (Try all of the actions in Table 4.1 except pressing the Esc key since that action will close Full Screen Reading view.)
12. Increase the size of the text by clicking the View Options button and then clicking the *Increase Text Size* option.

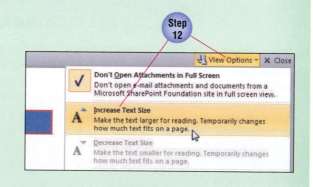

Step 12

13. Press the Home key to display the first viewing page.
14. Decrease the size of the text by clicking the View Options button and then clicking the *Decrease Text Size* option.
15. Click the Close button located in the upper right corner of the screen.

16. Click the View tab and then click the *Navigation Pane* check box.
17. Click the *COMPUTER OUTPUT DEVICES* title that displays in the Navigation pane.

18. Click the *Keyboard* heading that displays in the Navigation pane.
19. Click the middle tab in the Navigation pane. (This displays page thumbnails in the pane.).
20. Click the number 3 thumbnail in the Navigation pane.
21. Click the number 1 thumbnail in the Navigation pane.
22. Close the Navigation pane by clicking the Close button located in the upper right corner of the Navigation pane.

Hiding/Showing White Space in Print Layout View ■■■■■■■■■■■■■■■■■■■■■■■

▼ **Quick Steps**

Hide White Space
1. Position mouse pointer at top of page until pointer displays as *Hide White Space* icon.
2. Double-click left mouse button.

Show White Space
1. Position mouse pointer on thin line separating pages until pointer displays as *Show White Space* icon.
2. Double-click left mouse button.

In Print Layout view, a page displays as it will appear when printed including the white space at the top and bottom of the page representing the default margins. To save space on the screen in Print Layout view, you can remove the white space by positioning the mouse pointer at the top edge or bottom edge of a page or between pages until the pointer displays as the *Hide White Space* icon and then double-clicking the left mouse button. To redisplay the white space, position the mouse pointer on the thin, black line separating pages until the pointer turns into the *Show White Space* icon and then double-click the left mouse button.

Hide White Space

Show White Space

1. With **CompDevices.docx** open, make sure the document displays in Print Layout view.
2. Press Ctrl + Home to move the insertion point to the beginning of the document.
3. Hide the white spaces at the top and bottom of pages by positioning the mouse pointer at the top edge of the page until the pointer turns into the *Hide White Space* icon and then double-clicking the left mouse button.
4. Scroll through the document and notice the display of pages.
5. Redisplay the white spaces at the top and bottom of pages by positioning the mouse pointer on any thin, black, horizontal line separating pages until the pointer turns into the *Show White Space* icon and then double-clicking the left mouse button.
6. Close **CompDevices.docx**.

Project 2   Format a Document on Online Etiquette Guidelines   2 Parts

You will open a document containing information on guidelines for online etiquette and then change the margins, page orientation, and page size.

Changing Page Setup ▪▪▪▪▪▪▪▪▪▪▪▪▪▪▪▪

The Page Setup group in the Page Layout tab contains a number of options for affecting pages in a document. With options in the group you can perform such actions as changing margins, orientation, and page size and inserting page breaks. The Pages group in the Insert tab contains three buttons for inserting a page break, blank page, and cover page.

Margins

Changing Margins

Change page margins with options at the Margins drop-down list as shown in Figure 4.3. To display this list, click the Page Layout tab and then click the Margins button in the Page Setup group. To change the margins, click one of the preset margins that display in the drop-down list. Be aware that most printers contain a required margin (between one-quarter and three-eighths inch) because printers cannot print to the edge of the page.

▼ **Quick Steps**

Change Margins
1. Click Page Layout tab.
2. Click Margins button.
3. Click desired margin option.

Change Page Orientation
1. Click Page Layout tab.
2. Click Orientation button.
3. Click desired orientation.

Changing Page Orientation

Click the Orientation button in the Page Setup group in the Page Layout tab and two options display — *Portrait* and *Landscape*. At the portrait orientation, which is the default, the page is 11 inches tall and 8.5 inches wide. At the landscape orientation, the page is 8.5 inches tall and 11 inches wide. Change the page orientation and the page margins automatically change.

Figure 4.3 Margins Drop-down List

Click the Margins button to display this drop-down list of margin options.

Click the *Custom Margins* option to display the Page Setup dialog box with the Margins tab selected.

▼ **Quick Steps**

Change Page Size
1. Click Page Layout tab.
2. Click Size button.
3. Click desired size option.

Size

Changing Page Size

By default, Word uses a page size of 8.5 inches wide and 11 inches tall. You can change this default setting with options at the Size drop-down list. Display this drop-down list by clicking the Size button in the Page Setup group in the Page Layout tab.

Project 2a **Changing Margins, Page Orientation, and Size**   **Part 1 of 2**

1. Open **Netiquette.docx**.
2. Save the document with Save As and name it **WL1-C4-P2-Netiquette**.
3. Click the Page Layout tab.
4. Click the Margins button in the Page Setup group and then click the *Office 2003 Default* option.
5. Click the Orientation button in the Page Setup group.
6. Click *Landscape* at the drop-down list.

7. Scroll through the document and notice how the text displays on the page in landscape orientation.
8. Click the Orientation button in the Page Setup group and then click *Portrait* at the drop-down list. (This changes the orientation back to the default.)
9. Click the Size button in the Page Setup group.
10. Click the A5 option (displays with *5.83″ × 8.27″* below *A5*). If this option is not available, choose an option with a similar size.
11. Scroll through the document and notice how the text displays on the page.
12. Click the Size button and then click *Legal* (displays with *8.5″ × 14″* below *Legal*).
13. Scroll through the document and notice how the text displays on the page.
14. Click the Size button and then click *Letter* (displays with *8.5″ × 11″* below *Letter*). (This returns the size back to the default.)
15. Save **WL1-C4-P2-Netiquette.docx**.

Changing Margins at the Page Setup Dialog Box

The Margins button in the Page Setup group provides you with a number of preset margins. If these margins do not fit your needs, you can set specific margins at the Page Setup dialog box with the Margins tab selected as shown in Figure 4.4. Display this dialog box by clicking the Page Setup group dialog box launcher or by clicking the Margins button and then clicking *Custom Margins* at the bottom of the drop-down list.

To change margins, select the current measurement in the *Top*, *Bottom*, *Left*, or *Right* text box, and then type the new measurement. You can also increase a measurement by clicking the up-pointing arrow at the right side of the text box. Decrease a measurement by clicking the down-pointing arrow. As you make changes to the margin measurements at the Page Setup dialog box, the sample page in the *Preview* section illustrates the effects of the margin changes.

Changing Paper Size at the Page Setup Dialog Box

The Size button drop-down list contains a number of preset page sizes. If these sizes do not fit your needs, you can specify page size at the Page Setup dialog box with the Paper tab selected. Display this dialog box by clicking the Size button in the Page Setup group and then clicking *More Paper Sizes* that displays at the bottom of the drop-down list.

▼ **Quick Steps**

Change Margins at Page Setup Dialog Box
1. Click Page Layout tab.
2. Click Page Setup group dialog box launcher.
3. Specify desired margins.
4. Click OK.

Change Page Size at Page Setup Dialog Box
1. Click Page Layout tab.
2. Click Size button.
3. Click *More Paper Sizes* at drop-down list.
4. Specify desired size.
5. Click OK.

Figure 4.4 Page Setup Dialog Box with Margins Tab Selected

Notice the default settings for the top, bottom, left, and right margins.

Project 2b Changing Margins at the Page Setup Dialog Box

1. With **WL1-C4-P2-Netiquette.docx** open, make sure the Page Layout tab is selected.
2. Click the Page Setup group dialog box launcher.
3. At the Page Setup dialog box with the Margins tab selected, click the down-pointing arrow at the right side of the *Top* text box until *0.5"* displays.
4. Click the down-pointing arrow at the right side of the *Bottom* text box until *0.5"* displays.
5. Select the current measurement in the *Left* text box and then type **0.75**.
6. Select the current measurement in the *Right* text box and then type **0.75**.
7. Click OK to close the dialog box.
8. Click the Size button in the Page Setup group and then click *More Paper Sizes* at the drop-down list.
9. At the Page Setup dialog box with the Paper tab selected, click the down-pointing arrow at the right side of the *Paper size* option, scroll down the list box, and then click *A4* at the drop-down list.
10. Click OK to close the dialog box.

Step 3

Step 4

Step 5

Step 6

Step 9

11. Scroll through the document and notice how the text displays on the page.
12. Click the Size button in the Page Setup group and then click *Letter* at the drop-down list.
13. Save, print, and then close **WL1-C4-P2-Netiquette.docx**.

Project **3** **Customize a Report on Computer Input and Output Devices**　　　**3 Parts**

You will open a document containing information on computer input and output devices and then insert page breaks, a blank page, a cover page, and page numbering.

Inserting a Page Break

With the default top and bottom margins of one inch, approximately nine inches of text print on the page. At approximately the ten-inch mark, Word automatically inserts a page break. You can insert your own page break in a document with the keyboard shortcut, Ctrl + Enter, or with the Page Break button in the Pages group in the Insert tab.

A page break inserted by Word is considered a *soft* page break and a page break inserted by you is considered a *hard* page break. Soft page breaks automatically adjust if you add or delete text from a document. A hard page break does not adjust and is therefore less flexible than a soft page break. If you add or delete text from a document with a hard page break, check the break to determine whether it is still in a desirable location. In Draft view, a hard page break displays as a row of dots with the words *Page Break* in the center. To delete a page break, position the insertion point immediately below the page break and then press the Backspace key or change to Draft view, position the insertion point on the page break, and then press the Delete key.

▼ **Quick Steps**

Insert Page Break
1. Click Insert tab.
2. Click Page Break button.
OR
Press Ctrl + Enter.

Page Break

Project 3a **Inserting Page Breaks**　　　**Parts 1 of 3**

1. Open **CompDevices.docx**.
2. Save the document with Save As and name it **WL1-C4-P3-CompDevices**.
3. Change the top margin by completing the following steps:
   a. Click the Page Layout tab.
   b. Click the Page Setup group dialog box launcher.
   c. At the Page Setup dialog box, click the Margins tab and then type **1.5** in the *Top* text box.
   d. Click OK to close the dialog box.

4. Insert a page break at the beginning of the heading *Mouse* by completing the following steps:
   a. Position the insertion point at the beginning of the heading *Mouse* (located toward the bottom of page 1).

b. Click the Insert tab and then click the Page Break button in the Pages group.

5. Move the insertion point to the beginning of the title *COMPUTER OUTPUT DEVICES* (located at the bottom of page 2) and then insert a page break by pressing Ctrl + Enter.

6. Move the insertion point to the beginning of the heading *Printer* and then press Ctrl + Enter to insert a page break.

7. Delete the page break by completing the following steps:

   a. Click the Draft button in the view area on the Status bar.

   b. With the insertion point positioned at the beginning of the heading *Printer*, press the Backspace key. (This displays the page break in the document.)

   c. Press the Backspace key again to delete the page break.

   d. Click the Print Layout button in the view area of the Status bar.

8. Pressing the Backspace key removed the formatting from the Printer heading. Apply formatting by completing the following steps;

   a. Move the insertion point to any character in the heading *Monitor*.

   b. Click the Home tab and then click once on the Format Painter button.

   c. Select the heading *Printer*.

9. Save **WL1-C4-P3-CompDevices.docx**.

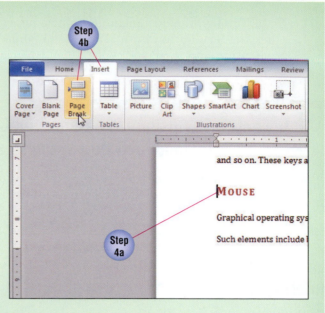

Inserting a Blank Page

Blank Page

▼ Quick Steps

Insert Blank Page
1. Click Insert tab.
2. Click Blank Page button.

Insert Cover Page
1. Click Insert tab.
2. Click Cover Page button.
3. Click desired cover page at drop-down list.

Click the Blank Page button in the Pages group in the Insert tab to insert a blank page at the position of the insertion point. This might be useful in a document where you want to insert a blank page for an illustration, graphic, or figure.

Inserting a Cover Page

If you are preparing a document for distribution to others or you want to simply improve the visual appeal of your document, consider inserting a cover page. With the Cover Page button in the Pages group in the Insert tab, you can insert a predesigned and formatted cover page and then type personalized text in specific locations on the page. Click the Cover Page button and a drop-down list displays. The drop-down list provides a visual representation of the cover page. Scroll through the list and then click the desired cover page.

HINT

A cover page provides a polished and professional look to a document.

Cover Page

A predesigned cover page contains location placeholders where you can enter specific information. For example, a cover page might contain the placeholder *[Type the document title]*. Click anywhere in the placeholder text and the placeholder text is selected. With the placeholder text selected, type the desired text. You can delete a placeholder by clicking anywhere in the placeholder text, clicking the placeholder tab, and then pressing the Delete key.

1. With **WL1-C4-P3-CompDevices.docx** open, create a blank page by completing the following steps:

   a. Move the insertion point to the beginning of the heading *Touchpad and Touchscreen* located on the second page.

   b. Click the Insert tab.

   c. Click the Blank Page button in the Pages group.

2. Insert a cover page by completing the following steps:

   a. Press Ctrl + Home to move the insertion point to the beginning of the document.

   b. Click the Cover Page button in the Pages group.

   c. At the drop-down list, scroll down and then click the *Motion* cover page.

   d. Click anywhere in the placeholder text *[Type the document title]* and then type **Computer Devices**.

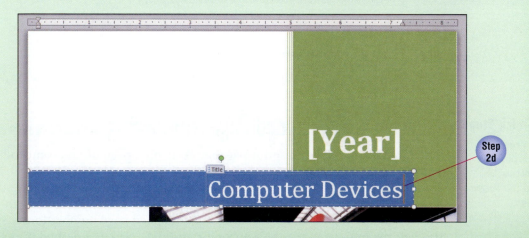

e. Click the placeholder text *[Year]*. Click the down-pointing arrow that displays at the right side of the placeholder and then click the Today button that displays at the bottom of the drop-down calendar.

f. Click anywhere in the placeholder text *[Type the company name]* and then type **Drake Computing**. (If a name displays in the placeholder, select the name and then type **Drake Computing**.)

g. Click anywhere in the placeholder text *[Type the author name]* and then type your first and last names. (If a name displays in the placeholder, select the name and then type your first and last names.)

3. Remove the blank page you inserted in Step 1 by completing the following steps:

a. Move the insertion point immediately right of the period that ends the last sentence in the paragraph of text in the *Trackball* heading (located toward the bottom of page 3).

b. Press the Delete key on the keyboard approximately six times until the heading *Touch Pad and Touch Screen* displays on page 3.

4. Save **WL1-C4-P3-CompDevices.docx**.

Step 2e

Step 2f

TRACKBALL

A trackball is like an upside-down mouse. A mouse is moved over a pad stationary, and the user moves the ball with his or her fingers or palm. choosing options are incorporated into the design of the trackball.

Step 3b

TOUCHPAD AND TOUCHSCREEN

A touchpad feels less mechanical than a mouse or trackball because the

---

Inserting Predesigned Page Numbering ■ ■ ■ ■ ■ ■ ■ ■ ■ ■ ■

Word, by default, does not print page numbers on a page. If you want to insert page numbering in a document, use the Page Number button in the Header & Footer group in the Insert tab. When you click the Page Number button, a drop-down list displays with options for specifying the page number location. Point to an option at this list and a drop-down list displays of predesigned page number formats. Scroll through the options in the drop-down list and then click the desired option. If you want to change the format of page numbering in a document, double-click the page number, select the page number text, and then apply the desired formatting. You can remove page numbering from a document by clicking the Page Number button and then clicking *Remove Page Numbers* at the drop-down list.

1. With **WL1-C4-P3-CompDevices.docx** open, insert page numbering by completing the following steps:
   a. Move the insertion point so it is positioned on any character in the title *COMPUTER INPUT DEVICES*.
   b. Click the Insert tab.
   c. Click the Page Number button in the Header & Footer group and then point to *Top of Page*.
   d. Scroll through the drop-down list and then click the *Brackets 2* option.

2. Double-click the document to make it active and then scroll through the document and notice the page numbering that displays at the top of each page except the cover page. (The cover page and text are divided by a section break, which you will learn more about in Chapter 5. Word considers the cover page as page 1 but does not include the numbering on the page.)

3. Remove the page numbering by clicking the Insert tab, clicking the Page Number button, and then clicking *Remove Page Numbers* at the drop-down list.

4. Click the Page Number button, point to *Bottom of Page*, scroll down the drop-down list and then click the *Accent Bar 2* option.

5. Double-click in the document to make it active.

6. Save, print, and then close **WL1-C4-P3-CompDevices.docx**.

You will open a document containing information on the future of the Internet, insert a predesigned header and footer in the document, remove a header, and format and delete header and footer elements.

Inserting Predesigned Headers and Footers ■■■■■■■■■

▼ **Quick Steps**

Insert Predesigned Header
1. Click Insert tab.
2. Click Header button.
3. Click desired option at drop-down list.
4. Type text in specific placeholders in header.

Header

Text that appears at the top of every page is called a *header* and text that appears at the bottom of every page is referred to as a *footer*. Headers and footers are common in manuscripts, textbooks, reports, and other publications. Insert a predesigned header in a document by clicking the Insert tab and then clicking the Header button in the Header & Footer group. This displays the Header drop-down list. At this list, click the desired predesigned header option and the header is inserted in the document. Headers and footers are visible in Print Layout view but not Draft view.

A predesigned header or footer may contain location placeholders where you can enter specific information. For example, a header might contain the placeholder *[Type the document title]*. Click anywhere in the placeholder text and all of the placeholder text is selected. With the placeholder text selected, type the desired text. You can delete a placeholder by clicking anywhere in the placeholder text, clicking the placeholder tab, and then pressing the Delete key.

P**roject 4a**   **Inserting a Predesigned Header in a Document**   Part 1 of 3

1. Open **InternetFuture.docx**.
2. Save the document with Save As and name it **WL1-C4-P4-InternetFuture**.
3. Make the following changes to the document:
   a. Select the entire document, change the line spacing to *2*, and then deselect the document.
   b. Apply the Heading 1 style to the title *FUTURE OF THE INTERNET*.
   c. Apply the Heading 2 style to the headings *Satellite Internet Connections*, *Second Internet*, *Internet Services for a Fee*, and *Internet in 2030*.
   d. Change the Quick Styles set to *Formal*. ***Hint: Use the Change Styles button in the Styles group in the Home tab.***
   e. Apply the Origin theme by clicking the Page Layout tab, clicking the Themes button, and then clicking *Origin* at the drop-down gallery.
   f. Move the insertion point to the beginning of the heading *INTERNET IN 2030* (located toward the bottom of page 2) and then insert a page break by clicking the Insert tab and then clicking the Page Break button in the Pages group.

4. Press Ctrl + Home to move the insertion point to the beginning of the document and then insert a header by completing the following steps:

a. If necessary, click the Insert tab.

b. Click the Header button in the Header & Footer group.

c. Scroll to the bottom of the drop-down list that displays and then click *Tiles*.

d. Click anywhere in the placeholder text *[Type the document title]* and then type **Future of the Internet**.

e. Click anywhere in the placeholder text *[Year]* and then type the current year.

f. Double-click in the document text. (This makes the document text active and dims the header.)

5. Scroll through the document to see how the header will print.

6. Save and then print **WL1-C4-P4-InternetFuture.docx**.

Insert a predesigned footer in the same manner as inserting a header. Click the Footer button in the Header & Footer group in the Insert tab and a drop-down list displays similar to the Header drop-down list. Click the desired footer and the predesigned footer formatting is applied to the document.

Removing a Header or Footer

Remove a header from a document by clicking the Insert tab and then clicking the Header button in the Header & Footer group. At the drop-down list that displays, click the *Remove Header* option. Complete similar steps to remove a footer.

▼ **Quick Steps**

Insert Predesigned Footer
1. Click Insert tab.
2. Click Footer button.
3. Click desired option at drop-down list.
4. Type text in specific placeholders in footer.

Footer

Project 4b   **Removing a Header and Inserting a Predesigned Footer**   **Part 2 of 3**

1. With **WL1-C4-P4-InternetFuture.docx** open, press Ctrl + Home to move the insertion point to the beginning of the document.

2. Remove the header by clicking the Insert tab, clicking the Header button in the Header & Footer group, and then clicking the *Remove Header* option at the drop-down menu.

3. Insert a footer in the document by completing the following steps:

   a. Click the Footer button in the Header & Footer group.

   b. Click *Alphabet* at the drop-down list.

Step 2

Step 3a

Step 3b

   c. Click anywhere in the placeholder text *[Type text]* and then type **Future of the Internet**.

   d. Double-click in the document text. (This makes the document text active and dims the footer.)

4. Scroll through the document to see how the footer will print.

5. Save and then print **WL1-C4-P4-InternetFuture.docx**.

Step 3c

You can double-click a header or footer in Print Layout view to display the header or footer pane for editing.

Editing a Predesigned Header or Footer

Predesigned headers and footers contain elements such as page numbers and a title. You can change the formatting of the element by clicking the desired element and then applying the desired formatting. You can also select and then delete an item.

Project 4c   **Formatting and Deleting Header and Footer Elements**   **Part 3 of 3**

1. With **WL1-C4-P4-InternetFuture.docx** open, remove the footer by clicking the Insert tab, clicking the Footer button, and then clicking *Remove Footer* at the drop-down list.

2. Insert and then format a header by completing the following steps:
   a. Click the Header button in the Header & Footer group in the Insert tab, scroll in the drop-down list, and then click *Motion (Odd Page)*. (This header inserts the document title as well as the page number.)
   b. Delete the document title from the header by clicking anywhere in the text *FUTURE OF THE INTERNET*, selecting the text, and then pressing the Delete key.
   c. Double-click in the document text.
3. Insert and then format a footer by completing the following steps:
   a. Click the Insert tab.
   b. Click the Footer button, scroll down the drop-down list, and then click *Motion (Odd Page)*.
   c. Click on any character in the date that displays in the footer, select the date, and then type the current date.
   d. Select the date, turn on bold, and then change the font size to 12.
   e. Double-click in the document text.
4. Scroll through the document to see how the header and footer will print.
5. Save, print, and then close **WL1-C4-P4-InternetFuture.docx**.

---

 roject **5** **Format a Report on Robots**   **2 Parts**

You will open a document containing information on the difficulties of creating a humanlike robot and then insert a watermark, change page background color, and insert a page border.

Formatting the Page Background ▪▪▪▪▪▪▪▪▪▪▪▪▪

The Page Background group in the Page Layout tab contains three buttons for customizing a page background. Click the Watermark button and choose a predesigned watermark from a drop-down list. If a document is going to be viewed on-screen or on the Web, consider adding a page color. In Chapter 3, you learned how to apply borders and shading to text at the Borders and Shading dialog box. This dialog box also contains options for inserting a page border.

Inserting a Watermark

A *watermark* is a lightened image that displays behind text in a document. Using watermarks is an excellent way to add visual appeal to a document. Word provides a number of predesigned watermarks you can insert in a document. Display these watermarks by clicking the Watermark button in the Page Background group in the Page Layout tab. Scroll through the list of watermarks and then click the desired option.

▼ Quick Steps

Insert Watermark
1. Click Page Layout tab.
2. Click Watermark button.
3. Click desired option at drop-down list.

Change Page Color
1. Click Page Layout tab.
2. Click Page Color button.
3. Click desired option at color palette.

Watermark

Changing Page Color

Page Color

Use the Page Color button in the Page Background group to apply background color to a document. This background color is intended for viewing a document on-screen or on the Web. The color is visible on the screen but does not print. Insert a page color by clicking the Page Color button and then clicking the desired color at the color palette.

Project 5a Inserting a Watermark and Page Color

Part 1 of 2

1. Open **Robots.docx** and then save the document with Save As and name it **WL1-C4-P5-Robots**.
2. Apply the Heading 1 style to the title *ROBOTS AS ANDROIDS* and the Heading 3 style to the five headings in the document. (You may need to click the Heading 2 style to display the Heading 3 style.)
3. Change the Quick Styles set to *Thatch* and then center the document title *ROBOTS AS ANDROIDS*.
4. Change the top margin to 1.5 inches.
5. Apply the Aspect theme.
6. Insert a page break at the beginning of the heading *Tactile Perception*.
7. Insert a watermark by completing the following steps:
   a. Move the insertion point to the beginning of the document.
   b. Click the Page Layout tab.
   c. Click the Watermark button in the Page Background group.
   d. At the drop-down list, click the *CONFIDENTIAL 1* option.
8. Scroll through the document and notice how the watermark displays behind the text.
9. Remove the watermark and insert a different one by completing the following steps:
   a. Click the Watermark button in the Page Background group and then click *Remove Watermark* at the drop-down list.
   b. Click the Watermark button and then click *DO NOT COPY 1* at the drop-down list.
10. Scroll through the document and notice how the watermark displays.
11. Move the insertion point to the beginning of the document.
12. Click the Page Color button in the Page Background group and then click *Dark Green, Accent 4, Lighter 80%* at the color palette.
13. Save **WL1-C4-P5-Robots.docx**.

Step 7b

Step 7c

Step 7d

Step 9b

Step 12

Inserting a Page Border

To improve the visual appeal of a document, consider inserting a page border. When you insert a page border in a multiple-page document, the border prints on each page. To insert a page border, click the Page Borders button in the Page Background group in the Page Layout tab. This displays the Borders and Shading dialog box with the Page Border tab selected as shown in Figure 4.5. At this dialog box, you can specify the border style, color, and width.

The dialog box contains an option for inserting a page border containing an image. To display the images available, click the down-pointing arrow at the right side of the *Art* list box. Scroll down the drop-down list and then click the desired image. (This feature may need to be installed the first time you use it.)

▼ **Quick Steps**

Insert Page Border
1. Click Page Layout tab.
2. Click Page Borders button.
3. Specify desired options at dialog box.

Page Borders

Changing Page Border Options

By default, a page border displays and prints 24 points from the top, left, right, and bottom edges of the page. Some printers, particularly inkjet printers, have a nonprinting area around the outside edges of the page that can interfere with the printing of a border. Before printing a document with a page border, click the File tab and then click the Print tab. Look at the preview of the page at the right side of the Print tab Backstage view and determine whether the entire border is visible. If a portion of the border is not visible in the preview page (generally at the bottom and right side of the page), consider changing measurements at the Border and Shading Options dialog box shown in Figure 4.6. You can also change measurements at the Border and Shading Options dialog box to control the location of the page border on the page.

Display the Border and Shading Options dialog box by clicking the Page Layout tab and then clicking the Page Borders button. At the Borders and Shading dialog box with the Page Border tab selected, click the Options button that displays in the lower right corner of the dialog box. The options at the Border and Shading Options dialog box change depending on whether you click the Options button at the Borders and Shading dialog box with the Borders tab selected or the Page Border tab selected.

Figure 4.5 Borders and Shading Dialog Box with Page Border Tab Selected

Click this down-pointing arrow to scroll through a list of page border styles.

Click this down-pointing arrow to display a list of width points.

Click this down-pointing arrow to display a list of art border images.

Preview the page border in this section.

Click this down-pointing arrow to display a palette of page border colors.

Figure 4.6 Border and Shading Options Dialog Box

Increase these measurements to move the page border away from the edge of the page or decrease the measurements to move the page border closer to the edge of the page.

Change this option to *Text* to specify the distance from the text to the page border.

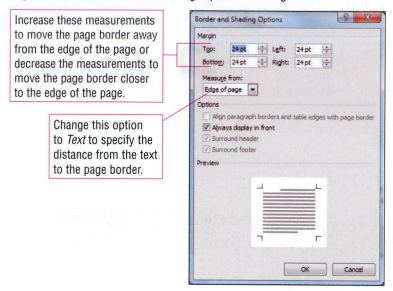

If your printer contains a nonprinting area and the entire page border will not print, consider increasing the spacing from the page border to the edge of the page. Do this with the *Top, Left, Bottom,* and/or *Right* measurement boxes. The *Measure from* option box has a default setting of *Edge of page.* You can change this option to *Text,* which changes the top and bottom measurements to *1 pt* and the left and right measurements to *4 pt* and moves the page border into the page. Use the measurement boxes to specify the distance you want the page border displayed and printed from the text in the document.

Project 5b   **Inserting a Page Border**   **Part 2 of 2**

1. With **WL1-C4-P5-Robots.docx** open, remove the page color by clicking the Page Color button in the Page Background group in the Page Layout tab and then clicking *No Color* at the color palette.
2. Insert a page border by completing the following steps:
   a. Click the Page Borders button in the Page Background group in the Page Layout tab.
   b. Click the *Box* option in the *Setting* section.
   c. Scroll down the list of line styles in the *Style* list box until the end of the list displays and then click the third line from the end.
   d. Click the down-pointing arrow at the right of the *Color* list box and then click *Red, Accent 2, Darker 25%* at the color palette.
   e. Click OK to close the dialog box.

3. Increase the spacing from the page border to the edges of the page by completing the following steps:
   a. Click the Page Borders button in the Page Background group in the Page Layout tab.
   b. At the Borders and Shading dialog box with the Page Border tab selected, click the Options button located in the lower right corner.
   c. At the Border and Shading Options dialog box, click the up-pointing arrow at the right side of the *Top* measurement box until *31 pt* displays. (This is the maximum measurement allowed.)
   d. Increase the measurement for the *Left, Bottom,* and *Right* measurement boxes to *31 pt.*
   e. Click OK to close the Border and Shading Options dialog box.
   f. Click OK to close the Borders and Shading dialog box.

4. Save **WL1-C4-P5-Robots.docx** and then print only page 1.
5. Insert an image page border and change the page border spacing options by completing the following steps:
   a. Click the Page Borders button in the Page Background group in the Page Layout tab.
   b. Click the down-pointing arrow at the right side of the *Art* list box and then click the border image shown below (located approximately one-third of the way down the drop-down list).
   c. Click the Options button located in the lower right corner of the Borders and Shading dialog box.
   d. At the Border and Shading Options dialog box, click the down-pointing arrow at the right of the *Measure from* option box and then click *Text* at the drop-down list.
   e. Click the up-pointing arrow at the right of the *Top* measurement box until *10 pt* displays.
   f. Increase the measurement for the *Bottom* measurement to *10 pt* and the measurement in the *Left* and *Right* measurement boxes to *14 pt.*
   g. Click the *Surround header* check box to remove the check mark.
   h. Click the *Surround footer* check box to remove the check mark.
   i. Click OK to close the Border and Shading Options dialog box.
   j. Click OK to close the Borders and Shading dialog box.
6. Save, print, and then close **WL1-C4-P5-Robots.docx**.

You will open a lease agreement document, search for specific text and replace it with other text, and then search for specific formatting and replace it with other formatting.

Finding and Replacing Text and Formatting ■■■■■■■□□

Quick Steps

Find Text
1. Click Find button in Home tab.
2. Type search text.
3. Click Next Search Result button.

Find

Replace

With Word's Find feature you can search for specific characters or formatting. With the Find and Replace feature, you can search for specific characters or formatting and replace them with other characters or formatting. The Find button and the Replace button are located in the Editing group in the Home tab.

Click the Find button in the Editing group in the Home tab (or press the keyboard shortcut, Ctrl + F) and the Navigation pane displays at the left side of the screen with the third tab selected. Hover the mouse over the third tab and a ScreenTip displays with the information *Browse the results from your current search*. With this tab selected, type search text in the Search text box and any occurrence of the text in the document is highlighted and a fragment of the text surrounding the search text displays in a thumbnail in the Navigation pane. For example, search for *Lessee* in the WL1-C4-P6-LeaseAgrmnt.docx document and the screen displays as shown in Figure 4.7. Notice that any occurrence of *Lessee* displays highlighted in yellow in the document and the Navigation pane displays thumbnails of text surrounding the occurrences of *Lessee*.

Figure 4.7 Navigation Pane Showing Search Results

Click this down-pointing arrow to display a drop-down list with options for displaying find and replace dialog boxes and options for specifying what you want to find in the document.

Type search text in this text box.

Click this button to move to the next occurrence of search text.

Click this button to move to the previous occurrence of search text.

Text thumbnails display search text in document and text surrounding the search text.

Occurrences of search text are highlighted in the document.

Click a text thumbnail in the Navigation pane and the occurrence of the search text is selected in the document. If you hover your mouse over a text thumbnail in the Navigation pane, the page number location displays in a small box near the mouse pointer. You can also move to the next occurrence of the search text by clicking the Next Search Result button located towards the upper right side of the Navigation pane. Click the Previous Search Result button to move to the previous occurrence of the search text.

Click the down-pointing arrow at the right side of the Search text box and a drop-down list displays with options for displaying dialog boxes such as the Find Options dialog box or the Find and Replace dialog box and also options for specifying what you want to find in the document such as figures, tables, and equations.

You can also highlight search text in a document with options at the Find and Replace dialog box with the Find tab selected. Display this dialog box by clicking the Find button arrow in the Editing group in the Home tab and then clicking *Advanced Find* at the drop-down list. You can also display the Find and Replace dialog box by clicking the down-pointing arrow at the right side of the Search text box in the Navigation pane with the Find tab selected and then clicking the *Advanced Find* option at the drop-down list. To highlight find text, type the search text in the *Find what* text box, click the Reading Highlight button, and then click *Highlight All* at the drop-down list. All occurrences of the text in the document are highlighted. To remove highlighting, click the Reading Highlight button and then click *Clear Highlighting* at the drop-down list.

Project 6a   **Finding and Highlighting Text**   **Part 1 of 4**

1. Open **LeaseAgrmnt.docx** and then save the document with Save As and name it **WL1-C4-P6-LeaseAgrmnt**.
2. Find all occurrences of *lease* by completing the following steps:
   a. Click the Find button in the Editing group in the Home tab.
   b. Type **lease** in the search text box in the Navigation pane.
   c. After a moment, all occurrences of *lease* in the document are highlighted and text thumbnails display in the Navigation pane. Click a couple of the text thumbnails in the Navigation pane to select the text in the document.
   d. Click the Previous Search Result button to select the previous occurrence of *lease* in the document.
3. Use the Find and Replace dialog box with the Find tab selected to highlight all occurrences of *Premises* in the document by completing the following steps:
   a. Click in the document and press Ctrl + Home to move the insertion point to the beginning of the document.
   b. Click the down-pointing arrow at the right side of the search text box in the Navigation pane and then click *Advanced Find* at the drop-down list.

c. At the Find and Replace dialog box with the Find tab selected (and *lease* selected in the *Find what* text box), type **Premises**.

d. Click the Reading Highlight button and then click *Highlight All* at the drop-down list.

e. Click in the document to make it active and then scroll through the document and notice the occurrences of highlighted text.

f. Click in the dialog box to make it active.

g. Click the Reading Highlight button and then click *Clear Highlighting* at the drop-down list.

h. Click the Close button to close the Find and Replace dialog box.

4. Close the Navigation pane by clicking the Close button that displays in the upper right corner of the pane.

Finding and Replacing Text

▼ **Quick Steps**

Find and Replace Text
1. Click Replace button in Home tab.
2. Type search text.
3. Press Tab key.
4. Type replace text.
5. Click Replace or Replace All button.

If the Find and Replace dialog box is in the way of specific text, drag the dialog box to a different location.

To find and replace text, click the Replace button in the Editing group in the Home tab or use the keyboard shortcut, Ctrl + H. This displays the Find and Replace dialog box with the Replace tab selected as shown in Figure 4.8. Type the text you want to find in the *Find what* text box, press the Tab key, and then type the replacement text.

The Find and Replace dialog box contains several command buttons. Click the Find Next button to tell Word to find the next occurrence of the characters. Click the Replace button to replace the characters and find the next occurrence. If you know that you want all occurrences of the characters in the *Find what* text box replaced with the characters in the *Replace with* text box, click the Replace All button. This replaces every occurrence from the location of the insertion point to the beginning or end of the document (depending on the search direction). Click the Cancel button to close the Find and Replace dialog box.

Figure 4.8 Find and Replace Dialog Box with the Replace Tab Selected

Type search text in the *Find what* text box.

Type replacement text in the *Replace with* text box.

Project 6b **Finding and Replacing Text** **Part 2 of 4**

1. With **WL1-C4-P6-LeaseAgrmnt.docx** open, make sure the insertion point is positioned at the beginning of the document.

2. Find all occurrences of *Lessor* and replace with *Tracy Hartford* by completing the following steps:

    a. Click the Replace button in the Editing group in the Home tab.

    b. At the Find and Replace dialog box with the Replace tab selected, type **Lessor** in the *Find what* text box.

    c. Press the Tab key to move the insertion point to the *Replace with* text box.

    d. Type **Tracy Hartford**.

    e. Click the Replace All button.

    f. At the message *Word has completed its search of the document and has made 11 replacements*, click OK. (Do not close the Find and Replace dialog box.)

3. With the Find and Replace dialog box still open, complete steps similar to those in Step 2 to find all occurrences of *Lessee* and replace with *Michael Iwami*.

4. Close the Find and Replace dialog box.

5. Save **WL1-C4-P6-LeaseAgrmnt.docx**.

Choosing Check Box Options

The Find and Replace dialog box contains a variety of check boxes with options you can choose for completing a search. To display these options, click the More button located at the bottom of the dialog box. This causes the Find and Replace dialog box to expand as shown in Figure 4.9. Each option and what will occur if

Figure 4.9 Expanded Find and Replace Dialog Box

Specify search options with options in this section.

it is selected is described in Table 4.2. To remove the display of options, click the Less button. (The Less button was previously the More button.) Note that if you make a mistake when replacing text, you can close the Find and Replace dialog box and then click the Undo button on the Quick Access toolbar.

Table 4.2 Options at the Expanded Find and Replace Dialog Box

Choose this option	*To*
Match case	Exactly match the case of the search text. For example, if you search for *Book* and select the *Match case* option, Word will stop at *Book* but not *book* or *BOOK*.
Find whole words only	Find a whole word, not a part of a word. For example, if you search for *her* and did not select *Find whole words only*, Word would stop at *there*, *here*, *hers*, etc.
Use wildcards	Search for wildcards, special characters, or special search operators.
Sounds like	Match words that sound alike but are spelled differently such as *know* and *no*.
Find all word forms	Find all forms of the word entered in the *Find what* text box. For example, if you enter *hold*, Word will stop at *held* and *holding*.
Match prefix	Find only those words that begin with the letters in the *Find what* text box. For example, if you enter *per*, Word will stop at words such as *perform* and *perfect* but skip words such as *super* and *hyperlink*.
Match suffix	Find only those words that end with the letters in the *Find what* text box. For example, if you enter *ly*, Word will stop at words such as *accurately* and *quietly* but skip over words such as *catalyst* and *lyre*.
Ignore punctuation characters	Ignore punctuation within characters. For example, if you enter *US* in the *Find what* text box, Word will stop at *U.S.*
Ignore white space characters	Ignore spaces between letters. For example, if you enter *F B I* in the *Find what* text box, Word will stop at *FBI*.

Project 6c   Finding and Replacing Word Forms and Suffixes   Part 3 of 4

1. With **WL1-C4-P6-LeaseAgrmnt.docx** open, make sure the insertion point is positioned at the beginning of the document.
2. Find all word forms of the word *lease* and replace with *rent* by completing the following steps:
   a. Click the Replace button in the Editing group in the Home tab.
   b. At the Find and Replace dialog box with the Replace tab selected, type **lease** in the *Find what* text box.

c. Press the Tab key and then type **rent** in the *Replace with* text box.

d. Click the More button.

e. Click the *Find all word forms (English)* option. (This inserts a check mark in the check box.)

f. Click the Replace All button.

g. At the message telling you that Replace All is not recommended with Find All Word Forms, click OK.

h. At the message *Word has completed its search of the document and has made 6 replacements*, click OK.

i. Click the *Find all word forms* option to remove the check mark.

3. Find the word *less* and replace with the word *minus* and specify that you want Word to find only those words that end in *less* by completing the following steps:

a. At the expanded Find and Replace dialog box, select the text in the *Find what* text box and then type **less**.

b. Select the text in the *Replace with* text box and then type **minus**.

c. Click the *Match suffix* check box to insert a check mark and tell Word to find only words that end in *less*.

d. Click the Replace All button.

e. At the message telling you that 2 replacements were made, click OK.

f. Click the *Match suffix* check box to remove the check mark.

g. Click the Less button.

h. Close the Find and Replace dialog box.

4. Save **WL1-C4-P6-LeaseAgrmnt.docx**.

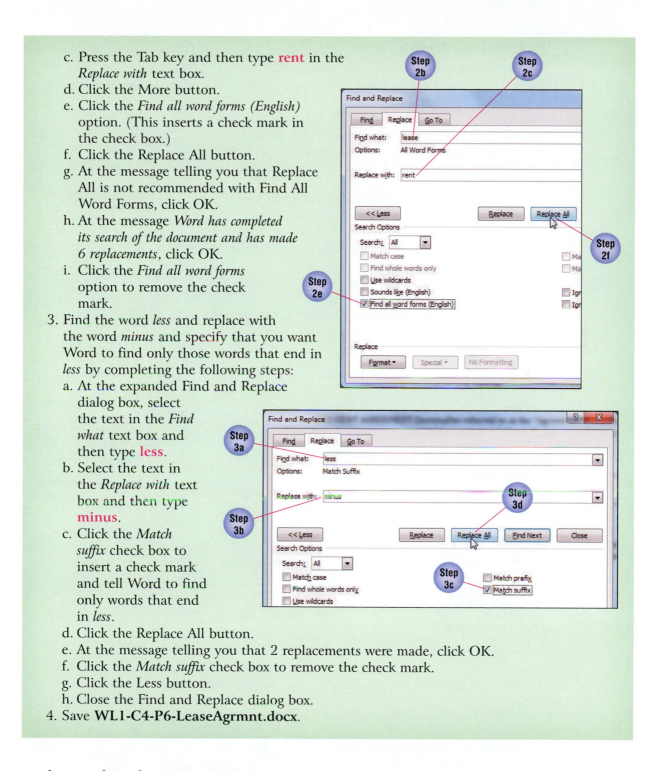

Finding and Replacing Formatting

With options at the Find and Replace dialog box with the Replace tab selected, you can search for characters containing specific formatting and replace them with other characters or formatting. To specify formatting in the Find and Replace dialog box, click the More button and then click the Format button that displays toward the bottom of the dialog box. At the pop-up list that displays, identify the type of formatting you want to find.

1. With **WL1-C4-P6-LeaseAgrmnt.docx** open, move the insertion point to the beginning of the document.
2. Find text set in 12-point Candara bold dark red and replace it with text set in 14-point Calibri bold dark blue by completing the following steps:
   a. Click the Replace button in the Editing group.
   b. At the Find and Replace dialog box, press the Delete key. (This deletes any text that displays in the *Find what* text box.)
   c. Click the More button. (If a check mark displays in any of the check boxes, click the option to remove the check mark.)
   d. With the insertion point positioned in the *Find what* text box, click the Format button located toward the bottom of the dialog box and then click *Font* at the pop-up list.
   e. At the Find Font dialog box, change the Font to *Candara*, the Font style to *Bold*, the Size to *12*, and the Font color to *Dark Red* (first color option from the left in the *Standard Colors* section).

Step 2d

Step 2e

Step 2i

   f. Click OK to close the Find Font dialog box.
   g. At the Find and Replace dialog box, click inside the *Replace with* text box and then delete any text that displays.
   h. Click the Format button located toward the bottom of the dialog box and then click *Font* at the pop-up list.
   i. At the Replace Font dialog box, change the Font to *Calibri*, the Font style to *Bold*, the Size to *14*, and the Font color to *Dark Blue* (second color option from the right in the *Standard Colors* section).
   j. Click OK to close the Replace Font dialog box.

k. At the Find and Replace dialog box, click the Replace All button.
l. At the message telling you that the search of the document is complete and eight replacements were made, click OK.
m. Click in the Find what text box and then click the No Formatting button.
n. Click in the Replace with text box and then click the No Formatting button.
o. Click the Less button.
p. Close the Find and Replace dialog box.
3. Save, print, and then close **WL1-C4-P6-LeaseAgrmnt.docx**.

Chapter Summary

- You can change the document view with buttons in the View section on the Status bar or with options in the View tab.

- Print Layout is the default view, which can be changed to other views such as Draft view or Full Screen Reading view.

- The Draft view displays the document in a format for efficient editing and formatting.

- Use the Zoom slider bar to change the percentage of the display.

- Full Screen Reading view displays a document in a format for easy viewing and reading.

- Navigate in a document using the Navigation pane. Display the pane by clicking the *Navigation Pane* check box in the Show group in the View tab.

- By default, a Word document contains 1-inch top, bottom, left, and right margins. Change margins with preset margin settings at the Margins button drop-down list or with options at the Page Setup dialog box with the Margins tab selected.

- The default page orientation is portrait, which can be changed to landscape with the Orientation button in the Page Setup group in the Page Layout tab.

- The default page size is 8.5 by 11 inches, which can be changed with options at the Size drop-down list or options at the Page Setup dialog box with the Paper tab selected.

- The page break that Word inserts automatically is a soft page break. A page break that you insert is a hard page break. Insert a page break with the Page Break button in the Pages group in the Insert tab or by pressing Ctrl + Enter.

- Insert a predesigned and formatted cover page by clicking the Cover Page button in the Pages group in the Insert tab and then clicking the desired option at the drop-down list.

- Insert predesigned and formatted page numbering by clicking the Page Number button in the Header & Footer group in the Insert tab, specifying the desired location of page numbers, and then clicking the desired page numbering option.

- You can insert predesigned headers and footers in a document with the Header button and the Footer button in the Header & Footer group in the Insert tab.

- A watermark is a lightened image that displays behind text in a document. Use the Watermark button in the Page Background group in the Page Layout tab to insert a watermark.

- Insert page color in a document with the Page Color button in the Page Background group. Page color is designed for viewing a document on-screen and does not print.
- Click the Page Borders button in the Page Background group and the Borders and Shading dialog box with the Page Border tab selected displays. Use options at this dialog box to insert a page border or an image page border in a document.
- Use the Find feature to search for specific characters or formatting. Use the Find and Replace feature to search for specific characters or formatting and replace with other characters or formatting.
- At the Find and Replace dialog box, click the Find Next button to find the next occurrence of the characters and/or formatting. Click the Replace button to replace the characters or formatting and find the next occurrence, or click the Replace All button to replace all occurrences of the characters or formatting.
- Click the More button at the Find and Replace dialog box to display additional options for completing a search.

Commands Review

FEATURE	RIBBON TAB, GROUP	BUTTON, OPTION	KEYBOARD SHORTCUT
Blank page	Insert, Pages		
Borders and Shading dialog box with Page Border tab selected	Page Layout, Page Background		
Border and Shading Options dialog box	Page Layout, Page Background	, Options	
Cover page	Insert, Pages		
Draft view	View, Document Views		
Find and Replace dialog box with Find tab selected	Home, Editing	, Advanced Find	
Find and Replace dialog box with Replace tab selected	Home, Editing		Ctrl + H
Footer	Insert, Header & Footer		
Full Screen Reading view	View, Document Views		
Header	Insert, Header & Footer		
Margins	Page Layout, Page Setup		
Navigation Pane	View, Show		Ctrl + F
Orientation	Page Layout, Page Setup		
Page break	Insert, Pages		Ctrl + Enter

FEATURE	RIBBON TAB, GROUP	BUTTON, OPTION	KEYBOARD SHORTCUT
Page color	Page Layout, Page Background		
Page numbering	Insert, Header & Footer		
Page Setup dialog box with Margins tab selected	Page Layout, Page Setup	, Custom Margins OR	
Page Setup dialog box with Paper tab selected	Page Layout, Page Setup	, *More Paper Sizes*	
Page size	Page Layout, Page Setup		
Print Layout view	View, Document Views		
Watermark	Page Layout, Page Background		

Concepts Check Test Your Knowledge

Completion: In the space provided at the right, indicate the correct term, symbol, or command.

1. This is the default measurement for the top, bottom, left, and right margins.

2. This view displays a document in a format for efficient editing and formatting.

3. This view displays a document in a format for easy viewing and reading.

4. The Navigation pane check box is located in this group in the View tab.

5. To remove white space, double-click this icon.

6. This is the default page orientation.

7. Set specific margins at this dialog box with the Margins tab selected.

8. Press these keys on the keyboard to insert a page break.

9. The Cover Page button is located in the Pages group in this tab.

10. Text that appears at the top of every page is called this.

11. A footer displays in Print Layout view, but not this view.

12. A lightened image that displays behind text in a document is called this. _____

13. Change the position of the page border from the edge of the page with options at this dialog box. _____

14. The Page Borders button displays in this group in the Page Layout tab. _____

15. If you want to replace every occurrence of what you are searching for in a document, click this button at the Find and Replace dialog box. _____

16. Click this option at the Find and Replace dialog box if you are searching for a word and all of its forms. _____

Skills Check Assess Your Performance

Assessment

1 FORMAT A SOFTWARE LIFE CYCLE DOCUMENT AND CREATE A COVER PAGE

1. Open **SoftwareCycle.docx** and then save the document with Save As and name it **WL1-C4-A1-SoftwareCycle**.
2. Select the entire document, change the line spacing to *2*, and then deselect the document.
3. Apply the Heading 1 style to the title of the document and apply the Heading 2 style to the headings in the document.
4. Change the Quick Styles set to *Fancy*.
5. Select the entire document and then remove italic formatting.
6. Change the theme colors to *Elemental*. (Make sure you change the theme colors and not the theme.)
7. Insert a page break at the beginning of the heading *Testing*.
8. Move the insertion point to the beginning of the document and then insert the *Austere* cover page.
9. Insert the following text in the specified fields:
   a. Insert the current year in the *[Year]* placeholder.
   b. Insert your school's name in the *[Type the company name]* placeholder. (If a company displays, select the name and then type your school's name.)
   c. If a name displays below your school's name, select the name and then type your first and last names.
   d. Insert **software life cycle** in the *[TYPE THE DOCUMENT TITLE]* placeholder (the placeholder will convert the text you type to all uppercase letters).
   e. Click the text below the document title, click the Abstract tab, and then press the Delete key.
10. Move the insertion point to any character in the title *COMMERCIAL LIFE CYCLE* and then insert the *Thin Line* page numbering at the bottom of the pages (the page numbering will not appear on the cover page).
11. Save, print, and then close **WL1-C4-A1-SoftwareCycle.docx**.

Assessment

2 FORMAT AN INTELLECTUAL PROPERTY REPORT AND INSERT HEADERS AND FOOTERS

1. Open **IntelProp.docx** and then save the document with Save As and name it **WL1-C4-A2-IntelProp**.
2. Select text from the beginning of the first paragraph of text to just above the *REFERENCES* title located toward the end of the document and then indent the first line to 0.25 inch.
3. Apply the Heading 1 style to the titles *PROPERTY PROTECTION ISSUES* and *REFERENCES* (located toward the end of the document).
4. Apply the Heading 2 style to the headings in the document.
5. Change the Quick Styles set to *Distinctive* and change the paragraph spacing to *Relaxed*. (Use the Change Styles button to make these changes.)
6. Center the *PROPERTY PROTECTION ISSUES* and *REFERENCES* titles.
7. Select and then hang indent the paragraphs below the *REFERENCES* title.
8. Insert a page break at the beginning of the *REFERENCES* title.
9. Move the insertion point to the beginning of the document and then insert the *Exposure* header. Type **Property Protection Issues** in the *[Type the document title]* placeholder and, if necessary, insert the current date in the *[Pick the date]* placeholder.
10. Insert the *Pinstripes* footer and type your first and last names in the *[Type text]* placeholder.
11. Save and then print **WL1-C4-A2-IntelProp.docx**.
12. Remove the header and footer.
13. Insert the *Austere (Odd Page)* footer and then make the following changes:
    a. Delete the *[Type the company name]* placeholder.
    b. Select the text and page number in the footer and then change the font size to 12 and turn on bold.
14. Insert the *DRAFT 1* watermark in the document.
15. Insert a page border of your choosing to the document.
16. Display the Border and Shading Options dialog box and then change the top, left, bottom, and right measurements to *31 pt*. **Hint: Display the Border and Shading Options dialog box by clicking the Options button at the Borders and Shading dialog box with the Page Border tab selected.**
17. Save, print, and then close **WL1-C4-A2-IntelProp.docx**.

Assessment

3 FORMAT A REAL ESTATE AGREEMENT

1. Open **REAgrmnt.docx** and then save the document with Save As and name it **WL1-C4-A3-REAgrmnt**.
2. Find all occurrences of *BUYER* (matching the case) and replace with *James Berman*.
3. Find all occurrences of *SELLER* (matching the case) and replace with *Mona Trammell*.
4. Find all word forms of the word *buy* and replace with *purchase*.
5. Search for 14-point Tahoma bold formatting in dark red and replace with 12-point Constantia bold formatting in black.
6. Insert page numbers at the bottom center of each page.
7. Save, print, and then close **WL1-C4-A3-REAgrmnt.docx**.

Visual Benchmark   Demonstrate Your Proficiency

FORMAT A RESUME STYLES REPORT

1. Open **ResumeStyles.docx** and then save it with Save As and name it **WL1-C4-VB-ResumeStyles**.
2. Format the document so it appears as shown in Figure 4.10 on page 143 with the following specifications:
   - Change the top margin to 1.5 inches.
   - Apply the Heading 1 style to the title and the Heading 2 style to the headings.
   - Change the Quick Styles set to *Formal*.
   - Apply the Aspect theme and then change the theme colors to *Origin*.
   - Insert the *Tiles* header and the *Tiles* footer. Insert the appropriate text in placeholders and/or delete placeholders so your headers and footers display similar to what you see in Figure 4.10 on page 143.
   - Apply other formatting so your document appears the same as the document shown in the figure.
   - Insert the *Tiles* cover page and insert the text in the placeholders and/or delete placeholders so your coverage page displays similar to what you see in Figure 4.10.
3. Save, print, and then close **WL1-C4-VB-ResumeStyles.docx**.

Case Study   Apply Your Skills

Part

1

You work for Citizens for Consumer Safety, a nonprofit organization providing information on household safety. Your supervisor, Melinda Johansson, has asked you to attractively format a document on smoke detectors. She will be using the document as an informational handout during a presentation on smoke detectors. Open the document named **SmokeDetectors.docx** and then save the document with Save As and name it **WL1-C4-CS-SmokeDetectors**. Apply a theme to the document and apply appropriate styles to the title and headings. Ms. Johansson has asked you to change the page orientation and then change the left and right margins to 1.5 inches. She wants the extra space at the left and right margins so audience members can write notes in the margins. Use the Help feature or experiment with the options in the Header & Footer Tools Design tab and figure out how to number pages on every page but the first page. Insert page numbering in the document that prints at the top right side of every page except the first page. Save, print, and then close **WL1-C4-CS-SmokeDetectors.docx**.

Figure 4.10 Visual Benchmark

After reviewing the formatted document on smoke detectors, Ms. Johansson has decided that she wants the document to print in the default orientation and she is not happy with the theme and style choices. She also noticed that the term "smoke alarm" should be replaced with "smoke detector." She has asked you to open and then format the original document. Open **SmokeDetectors.docx** and then save the document with Save As and name it **WL1-C4-CS-SmokeDetectors**. Apply a theme to the document (other than the one you chose for Part 1) and apply styles to the title and headings. Search for all occurrences of *smoke alarm* and replace with *smoke detector*. Insert a cover page of your choosing and insert the appropriate information in the page. Use the Help feature or experiment with the options in the Header & Footer Tools Design tab and figure out how to insert an odd-page and even-page footer in a document. Insert an odd-page footer that prints the page number at the right margin and insert an even-page footer that prints the page number at the left margin. You do not want the footer to print on the cover page so make sure you position the insertion point below the cover page before inserting the footers. After inserting the footers in the document, you decide that they need to be moved down the page to create more space between the last line of text on a page and the footer. Use the Help feature or experiment with the options in the Header & Footer Tools Design tab to figure out how to move the footers down and then edit each footer so they display 0.3" from the bottom of the page. Save, print, and then close **WL1-C4-CS-SmokeDetectors.docx**.

Ms. Johansson has asked you to prepare a document on infant car seats and car seat safety. She wants this informational car seat safety document available for distribution at a local community center. Use the Internet to find websites that provide information on child and infant car seats and car seat safety. Write a report on the information you find that includes at least the following information:

- Description of the types of car seats (such as rear-facing, convertible, forward-facing, built-in, and booster)
- Safety rules and guidelines
- Installation information
- Specific child and infant seat models
- Sites on the Internet that sell car seats
- Price ranges
- Internet sites providing safety information

Format the report using a theme and styles and include a cover page and headers and/or footers. Save the completed document and name it **WL1-C4-CS-CarSeats**. Print and then close the document.

Note: Before beginning unit assessments, copy to your storage medium the Word2010L1U1 subfolder from the Word2010L1 folder on the CD that accompanies this textbook and then make Word2010L1U1 the active folder.

Assessing Proficiency ■■■■■■■■■■■■

In this unit, you have learned to create, edit, save, and print Word documents. You also learned to format characters, paragraphs, and pages.

Assessment 1 Format *Designing an Effective Website* Document

1. Open **Website.docx** and then save the document with Save As and name it **WL1-U1-A1-Website**.
2. Complete a spelling and grammar check.
3. Select from the paragraph that begins *Make your home page work for you.* through the end of the document and then apply bullet formatting.
4. Select and then bold the first sentence of each bulleted paragraph.
5. Apply paragraph border and shading to the document title.
6. Save and then print **WL1-U1-A1-Website.docx**.
7. Change the top, left, and right margins to 1.5 inches.
8. Select the bulleted paragraphs, change the paragraph alignment to justified, and then insert numbering.
9. Select the entire document and then change the font to 12-point Cambria.
10. Insert the text shown in Figure U1.1 after paragraph number 2. (The number 3. should be inserted preceding the text you type.)
11. Save, print, and then close **WL1-U1-A1-Website.docx**.

Figure U1.1 Assessment 1

> **Avoid a cluttered look.** In design, less is more. Strive for a clean look to your pages, using ample margins and white space.

Assessment 2 Format *Accumulated Returns* Document

1. Open **ReturnChart.docx** and then save the document with Save As and name it **WL1-U1-A2-ReturnChart**.
2. Select the entire document and then make the following changes:
   a. Click the No Spacing style.
   b. Change the line spacing to 1.5.

c. Change the font to 12-point Cambria.

d. Apply 6 points of spacing after paragraphs.

3. Select the title *TOTAL RETURN CHARTS*, change the font to 14-point Corbel bold, change the alignment to center, and apply paragraph shading of your choosing.

4. Bold the following text that appears at the beginning of the second through the fifth paragraphs:

Average annual total return: *Annual total return:*

Accumulation units: *Accumulative rates:*

5. Select the paragraphs of text in the body of the document (all paragraphs except the title) and then change the paragraph alignment to justified.

6. Select the paragraphs that begin with the bolded words, sort the paragraphs in ascending order, and then indent the text 0.5 inch from the left margin.

7. Insert a watermark that prints *DRAFT* diagonally across the page.

8. Save, print, and then close **WL1-U1-A2-ReturnChart.docx**.

Assessment 3 Format Computer Ethics Report

1. Open **FutureEthics.docx** and then save the document with Save As and name it **WL1-U1-A3-FutureEthics.docx**.

2. Apply the Heading 1 style to the titles *FUTURE OF COMPUTER ETHICS* and *REFERENCES*.

3. Apply the Heading 2 style to the headings in the document.

4. Change the paragraph spacing to *Relaxed*. **Hint: Do this with the Change Styles button**.

5. Change the Quick Styles set to *Thatch*.

6. Apply the Hardcover theme and then change the theme colors to *Concourse*.

7. Center the two titles (*FUTURE OF COMPUTER ETHICS* and *REFERENCES*).

8. Hang indent the paragraphs of text below the *REFERENCES* title.

9. Insert page numbering that prints at the bottom center of each page.

10. Save, print, and then close **WL1-U1-A3-FutureEthics.docx**.

Assessment 4 Set Tabs and Type Division Income Text in Columns

1. At a new blank document, type the text shown in Figure U1.2 with the following specifications:

a. Bold and center the title as shown.

b. You determine the tab settings for the text in columns.

c. Select the entire document and then change the font to 12-point Arial.

2. Save the document and name it **WL1-U1-A4-Income**.

3. Print and then close **WL1-U1-A4-Income.docx**.

Figure U1.2 Assessment 4

INCOME BY DIVISION			
	2009	**2010**	**2011**
Public Relations	$14,375	$16,340	$16,200
Database Services	9,205	15,055	13,725
Graphic Design	18,400	21,790	19,600
Technical Support	5,780	7,325	9,600

Assessment 5 Set Tabs and Type Table of Contents Text

1. At a blank document, type the text shown in Figure U1.3 with the following specifications:
   a. Bold and center the title as shown.
   b. You determine the tab settings for the text in columns.
   c. Select the entire document, change the font to 12-point Bookman Old Style (or a similar serif typeface), and then change the line spacing to 1.5.
2. Save the document and name it **WL1-U1-A5-TofC**.
3. Print and then close **WL1-U1-A5-TofC.docx**.

Figure U1.3 Assessment 5

Assessment 6 Format Union Agreement Contract

1. Open **LaborContract.docx** and then save the document with Save As and name it **WL1-U1-A6-LaborContract**.
2. Find all occurrences of *REINBERG MANUFACTURING* and replace with *MILLWOOD ENTERPRISES*.
3. Find all occurrences of *RM* and replace with *ME*.
4. Find all occurrences of *LABOR WORKERS' UNION* and replace with *SERVICE EMPLOYEES' UNION*.
5. Find all occurrences of *LWU* and replace with *SEU*.
6. Select the entire document and then change the font to 12-point Cambria and the line spacing to double.
7. Select the numbered paragraphs in the *Transfers and Moving Expenses* section and change to bullets.
8. Select the numbered paragraphs in the *Sick Leave* section and change to bullets.
9. Change the page orientation to landscape and the top margin to 1.5".
10. Save and then print **WL1-U1-A6-LaborContract.docx**.
11. Change the page orientation to portrait and the left margin (previously the top margin) back to 1".
12. Insert the *Alphabet* footer and type **Union Agreement** in the *[Type text]* placeholder.
13. Insert the *Alphabet* cover page and insert *UNION AGREEMENT* as the document title and *Millwood Enterprises* as the document subtitle. Include any additional information required by the cover page.
14. Save, print, and then close **WL1-U1-A6-LaborContract.docx**.

Assessment 7 Copy and Paste Text in Health Plan Document

1. Open **KeyLifePlan.docx** and then save the document with Save As and name it **WL1-U1-A7-KeyLifePlan**.
2. Open **PlanOptions.docx** and then turn on the display of the Clipboard task pane. Make sure the Clipboard is empty.
3. Select the heading *Plan Highlights* and the six paragraphs of text below the heading and then copy the selected text to the clipboard.
4. Select the heading *Plan Options* and the two paragraphs of text below the heading and then copy the selected text to the clipboard.
5. Select the heading *Quality Assessment* and the six paragraphs of text below the heading and then copy the selected text to the clipboard.
6. Close **PlanOptions.docx**.
7. With **WL1-U1-A7-KeyLifePlan.docx** open, display the Clipboard task pane.
8. Move the insertion point to the beginning of the *Provider Network* heading, paste the *Plan Options* item from the Clipboard, and merge the formatting.
9. With the insertion point positioned at the beginning of the *Provider Network* heading, paste the *Plan Highlights* item from the Clipboard, and merge the formatting.
10. Move the insertion point to the beginning of the *Plan Options* heading, paste the *Quality Assessment* item from the Clipboard, and merge the formatting.
11. Clear the Clipboard and then close it.
12. Apply the Heading 1 style to the title, *KEY LIFE HEALTH PLAN*.
13. Apply the Heading 2 style to the headings in the document.
14. Change the top margin to 1.5 inches.
15. Change to the *Modern* Quick Styles set.
16. Apply the Grid theme.
17. Insert a double line, dark red page border.
18. Insert the *Sideline* header and type **Health Plans** in the *[Type the document title]* placeholder. Insert the *Sideline* footer.
19. Add the *Sideline* cover page. Delete the company name and document subtitle placeholders. Insert your first and last names in the Author placeholder and the current date in the Date placeholder.
20. Save, print, and then close **WL1-U1-A7-KeyLifePlan.docx**.

Writing Activities ■■■■■■■■■■■■■■■■■

The following activities give you the opportunity to practice your writing skills along with demonstrating an understanding of some of the important Word features you have mastered in this unit. Use correct grammar, appropriate word choices, and clear sentence constructions. Follow the steps explained on the next page to improve your writing skills.

The Writing Process

Plan Gather ideas, select which information to include, and choose the order in which to present the information.

Checkpoints
- What is the purpose?
- What information does the reader need in order to reach your intended conclusion?

Write Following the information plan and keeping the reader in mind, draft the document using clear, direct sentences that say what you mean.

Checkpoints
- What are the subpoints for each main thought?
- How can you connect paragraphs so the reader moves smoothly from one idea to the next?

Revise Improve what is written by changing, deleting, rearranging, or adding words, sentences, and paragraphs.

Checkpoints
- Is the meaning clear?
- Do the ideas follow a logical order?
- Have you included any unnecessary information?
- Have you built your sentences around strong nouns and verbs?

Edit Check spelling, sentence construction, word use, punctuation, and capitalization.

Checkpoints
- Can you spot any redundancies or clichés?
- Can you reduce any phrases to an effective word (for example, change *the fact that* to *because*)?
- Have you used commas only where there is a strong reason for doing so?
- Did you proofread the document for errors that your spell checker cannot identify?

Publish Prepare a final copy that could be reproduced and shared with others.

Checkpoints
- Which design elements, such as boldface or different fonts, would help highlight important ideas or sections?
- Would charts or other graphics help clarify meaning?

Activity 1 Write Hyphenation Steps and Hyphenate Text in Document

Use Word's Help feature to learn about hyphenating text in a document. Learn how to hyphenate text automatically as well as manually. Create a document following these instructions:

1. Include an appropriate title that is bolded and centered.
2. Write the steps required to automatically hyphenate text in a document.
3. Write the steps required to manually hyphenate text in a document.

Save the document and name it **WL1-U1-Act1-Hyphen**. Print and then close **WL1-U1-Act1-Hyphen.docx**. Open **WL1-U1-A3-FutureEthics.docx** and then save the document with Save As and name it **WL1-U1-Act1-FutureEthics**. Manually hyphenate text in the document. Save, print, and then close **WL1-U1-Act1-FutureEthics.docx**.

Activity 2 Write Information on Customizing Spelling and Grammar

Use Word's Help feature to learn about grammar and style options. Learn about grammar options and what they detect and style options and what they detect. Also, learn how to set rules for grammar and style. Once you have determined this information, create a document describing at least two grammar options and at least two style options. Also include in this document the steps required to change the writing style from grammar only to grammar and style. Save the completed document and name it **WL1-U1-Act2-CustomSpell**. Print and then close **WL1-U1-Act2-CustomSpell.docx**.

Internet Research ■■■■■■■■■■■■■■■■■■■■

Research Business Desktop Computer Systems

You hold a part-time job at a local newspaper, *The Daily Chronicle*, where you conduct Internet research for the staff writers. Mr. Woods, the editor, has decided to purchase new desktop computers for the staff. He has asked you to identify at least three PCs that can be purchased directly over the Internet, and he requests that you put your research and recommendations in writing. Mr. Woods is looking for solid, reliable, economical, and powerful desktop computers with good warranties and service plans. He has given you a budget of $1,300 per unit.

Search the Internet for three desktop PC computer systems from three different manufacturers. Consider price, specifications (processor speed, amount of RAM, hard drive space, and monitor type and size), performance, warranties, and service plans when making your choice of systems. Print your research findings and include them with your report. (For helpful information on shopping for a computer, read the articles "Buying and Installing a PC" and "Purchasing a Computer," posted in the Course Resources section of this book's Internet Resource Center, either at www.emcp.net/BenchmarkOffice10 or www.emcp.net/BenchmarkWord10.)

Using Word, write a brief report in which you summarize the capabilities and qualities of each of the three computer systems you recommend. Include a final paragraph detailing which system you suggest for purchase and why. If possible, incorporate user opinions and/or reviews about this system to support your decision. At the end of your report, include a table comparing the computer system. Format your report using the concepts and techniques you learned in Unit 1. Save the report and name it **WL1-U1-InternetResearch**. Print and then close the file.

Microsoft® Word

Level 1

Unit 2 ■ Enhancing and Customizing Documents

Applying Formatting and Inserting Objects

PERFORMANCE OBJECTIVES

Upon successful completion of Chapter 5, you will be able to:

- Insert section breaks
- Create and format text in columns
- Hyphenate words automatically and manually
- Create a drop cap
- Insert symbols, special characters, and the date and time
- Use the Click and Type feature
- Vertically align text
- Insert, format, and customize pictures, clip art images, text boxes, shapes, and WordArt

Tutorials

5.1	Inserting Section Breaks
5.2	Applying Columns
5.3	Hyphenating Words
5.4	Inserting Symbols and Special Characters
5.5	Creating a Drop Cap and Inserting the Date and Time
5.6	Using Click and Type
5.7	Using Vertical Alignment
5.8	Inserting, Sizing, and Moving Images
5.9	Inserting and Customizing a Pull Quote
5.10	Inserting and Formatting a Shape
5.11	Inserting and Modifying WordArt
5.12	Creating and Inserting a Screenshot

To apply page or document formatting to only a portion of the document, insert a section break. You can insert a continuous section break or a section break that begins a new page. A section break is useful when formatting text in columns. The hyphenation feature hyphenates words at the end of lines, creating a less ragged margin. Use buttons in the Text and Symbols groups in the Insert tab to insert symbols, special characters, and the date and time. With the Click and Type feature, you can position the insertion point at various locations in the document and change the paragraph alignment. Use the *Vertical alignment* option at the Page Setup dialog box with the Layout tab selected to align text vertically on the page. Along with these features, you will also learn how to increase the visual appeal of a document by inserting and customizing images such as pictures, clip art, text boxes, shapes, and WordArt. Model answers for this chapter's projects appear on the following pages.

Note: Before beginning the projects, copy to your storage medium the Word2010L1C5 subfolder from the Word2010L1 folder on the CD that accompanies this textbook and then make Word2010L1C5 the active folder.

153

COMPUTER INPUT DEVICES

Engineers have been especially creative in designing new ways to get information into computers. Some input methods are highly specialized and unusual, while common devices often undergo redesign to improve their capabilities or their ergonomics, the ways in which they affect people physically. Some common input devices include keyboards, mice, trackballs, and touchpads.

Keyboard

A keyboard can be an external device that is attached by means of a cable, or it can be attached to the CPU case itself as it is for laptop computers. Most keyboards today are QWERTY keyboards, which take their name from the first six keys at the left of the first row of letters. An alternative, the DVORAK keyboard, places the most commonly used keys close to the user's fingertips and speeds typing.

Many keyboards have a separate numeric keypad, like that of a calculator, containing numbers and mathematical operators. All keyboards have modifier keys that enable the user to change the symbol or character that is entered when a given key is pressed. The Shift key, for example, makes a letter uppercase. Keyboards also have special cursor keys that enable the user to change the position on the screen of the cursor, a symbol that appears on the monitor to show where in a document the next change will appear. Most keyboards

also have function keys, labeled F1, F2, F3, and so on. These keys allow the user to issue commands by pressing a single key.

Mouse

Graphical operating systems contain many elements that a user can choose by pointing at them. Such elements include buttons, tools, pull-down menus, and icons for file folders, programs, and document files. Often pointing to and clicking on one of these elements is more convenient than using the cursor or arrow keys on the keyboard. This pointing and clicking can be done by using a mouse. The mouse is the second most common input device, after the keyboard. A mouse operates by moving the cursor on the computer screen to correspond to movements made with the mouse.

Trackball

A trackball is like an upside-down mouse. A mouse is moved over a pad. A trackball remains stationary, and the user moves the ball with his or her fingers or palm. One or more buttons for choosing options are incorporated into the design of the trackball.

Touchpad and Touchscreen

A touchpad feels less mechanical than a mouse or trackball because the user simply moves a finger on the pad. A touchpad has two parts. One part acts as a button, while the other emulates a mouse

1

pad on which the user traces the location of the cursor with a finger. People with carpal tunnel syndrome find touchpads and trackballs easier to use than mice. Many portable computers have built-in trackballs or touchpads as input devices.

A touchscreen allows the user to choose options by pressing the appropriate part of the screen. Touchscreens are widely used in bank ATMs and in kiosks at retail outlets and in tourist areas.

Prepared by: Matthew Viña
SoftCell Technologies*
June 11, 2012
11:40 AM

2

Project 1 Format a Document on Computer Input Devices
WL1-C5-P1-InputDevices.docx

SUPERVISORY TRAINING
Maximizing Employee Potential
Wednesday, February 15, 2012
Training Center
9:00 a.m. to 3:30 p.m.

Figure 1 Uluru (Ayers Rock, Australia)

Project 2 Create an Announcement about Supervisory Training
WL1-C5-P2-Training.docx

ROBOTS AS ANDROIDS

Robotic factories are increasingly commonplace, especially in heavy manufacturing, where tolerance of repetitive movements, great strength, and untiring precision are more important than flexibility. Robots are especially useful in hazardous work, such as defusing bombs or handling radioactive materials. They also excel in constructing tiny components like those found inside notebook computers, which are often too small for humans to assemble.

Most people think of robots in science fiction terms, which generally depict them as androids, or simulated humans. Real robots today do not look human at all, and judged by human standards, they are not very intelligent. The task of creating a humanlike body has proven incredibly difficult. Many technological advances in visual perception, audio perception, touch, dexterity, locomotion, and navigation need to occur before robots that look and act like human beings will live and work among us.

VISUAL PERCEPTION

Visual perception is an area of great complexity. A large percentage of the human brain is dedicated to processing data coming from the eyes. As our most powerful sense, sight is the primary means through which we understand the world around us. A single camera is not good enough to simulate the eye. Two cameras are needed to give stereoscopic vision, which allows depth and movement perception. Even with two cameras, visual perception is incomplete because the cameras cannot understand or translate what they see. Processing the image is the difficult part. In order for

"The task of creating a humanlike body has proven incredibly difficult."

a robot to move through a room full of furniture it must build a mental map of that room, complete with obstacles. The robot must judge the distance and size of objects before it can figure out how to move around them.

AUDIO PERCEPTION

Audio perception is less complex than visual perception, but no less important. People respond to audible cues about their surroundings and the people they are with without even thinking about it. Listeners can determine someone's emotional state just by hearing the person's voice. A car starting up when someone crosses the street prompts the walker to glance in that direction to check for danger. Identifying a single voice and interpreting what is being said amid accompanying background noise is a task that is among the most important for human beings—and the most difficult.

TACTILE PERCEPTION

Tactile perception, or touch, is another critical sense. Robots can be built with any level of strength, since they are made of steel and motors. How does a robot capable of lifting a car pick up an egg in the dark without dropping or crushing it? The answer is through a sense of touch. The robot must not only be able to feel an object, but also be able to sense how much pressure it is applying to that object. With this feedback it can properly judge how hard it

Page 1

Project 3 Customize a Report on Robots
WL1-C5-P3-Robots.docx

should squeeze. This is a very difficult area, and it may prove that simulating the human hand is even more difficult than simulating the human mind.

Related to touch is the skill of dexterity, or hand-eye coordination. The challenge is to create a robot that can perform small actions, such as soldering tiny joints or placing a chip at a precise spot in a circuit board within half a millimeter.

LOCOMOTION

Locomotion includes broad movements such as walking. Getting a robot to move around is not easy. This area of robotics is challenging, as it requires balance within an endlessly changing set of variables. How does the program adjust for walking up a hill, or down a set of stairs? What if the wind is blowing hard or a foot slips? Currently most mobile robots work with wheels or treads, which limits their mobility in some circumstances but makes them much easier to control.

NAVIGATION

Related to perception, navigation deals with the science of moving a mobile robot through an environment. Navigation is not an isolated area of artificial intelligence, as it must work closely with a visual system or some other kind of perception system. Sonar, radar, mechanical "feelers," and other systems have been subjects of experimentation. A robot can plot a course to a location using an internal "map" built up by a navigational perception system. If the course is blocked or too difficult, the robot must be smart enough to backtrack so it can try another plan.

Page 2

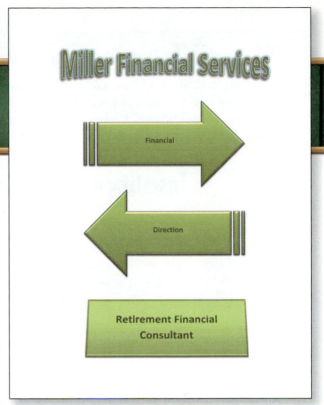

Project 4 Prepare a Company Flyer

WL1-C5-P4-FinConsult.docx

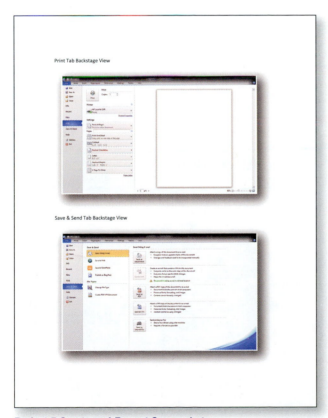

Project 5 Create and Format Screenshots

WL1-C5-P5-BackstageViews.docx

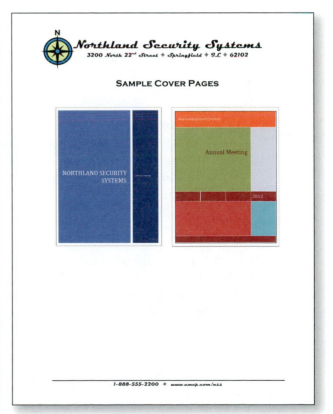

WL1-C5-P5-NSSCoverPages.docx

You will format into columns text in a document on computer input devices, improve the readability of the document by hyphenating long words, and improve the visual appeal by inserting a drop cap.

Inserting a Section Break ■■■■■■■ ■ ■■■■■■ ■■■ ■■

▼ Quick Steps

Insert a Section Break
1. Click Page Layout tab.
2. Click Breaks button.
3. Click section break type in drop-down list.

HINT

If you delete a section break, the text that follows the section break takes on the formatting of the text preceding the break.

Breaks

You can change the layout and formatting of specific portions of a document by inserting section breaks. For example, you can insert section breaks and then change margins for the text between the section breaks. If you want to format specific text in a document into columns, insert a section break.

Insert a section break in a document by clicking the Page Layout tab, clicking the Breaks button in the Page Setup group, and then clicking the desired option in the *Section Breaks* section of the drop-down list. You can insert a section break that begins a new page or a continuous section break that does not begin a new page. A continuous section break separates the document into sections but does not insert a page break. Click one of the other three options in the *Section Breaks* section of the Breaks drop-down list if you want to insert a section break that begins a new page.

A section break inserted in a document is not visible in Print Layout view. Click the Draft button and a section break displays in the document as a double row of dots with the words *Section Break* in the middle. Depending on the type of section break you insert, text follows *Section Break*. For example, if you insert a continuous section break, the words *Section Break (Continuous)* display in the middle of the row of dots. To delete a section break, change to Draft view, position the insertion point on the section break, and then press the Delete key.

Project **1a**   Inserting a Continuous Section Break   Part 1 of 8

1. Open **InputDevices.docx** and then save it with Save As and name it **WL1-C5-P1-InputDevices**.
2. Insert a continuous section break by completing the following steps:
   a. Move the insertion point to the beginning of the *Keyboard* heading.
   b. Click the Page Layout tab.
   c. Click the Breaks button in the Page Setup group and then click *Continuous* in the *Section Breaks* section of the drop-down list.
3. Click the Draft button in the view area on the Status bar and then notice the section break that displays across the screen.
4. Click the Print Layout button in the view area on the Status bar.

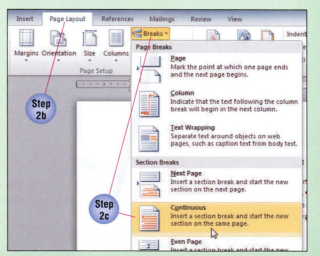

5. With the insertion point positioned at the beginning of the *Keyboard* heading, change the left and right margins to 1.5 inches. (The margin changes affect only the text after the continuous section break.)
6. Save and then print **WL1-C5-P1-InputDevices.docx**.

Creating Columns ■■■■■■■■■■■■■■■■■■■■■■■■■

When preparing a document containing text, an important point to consider is the readability of the document. Readability refers to the ease with which a person can read and understand groups of words. The line length of text in a document can enhance or detract from the readability of text. If the line length is too long, the reader may lose his or her place on the line and have a difficult time moving to the next line below. To improve the readability of some documents such as newsletters or reports, you may want to set the text in columns. One common type of column is newspaper, which is typically used for text in newspapers, newsletters, and magazines. Newspaper columns contain text that flows up and down in the document.

▼ **Quick Steps**

Create Columns
1. Click Page Layout tab.
2. Click Columns button.
3. Click on desired number of columns.

Columns

Create newspaper columns with the Columns button in the Page Setup group in the Page Layout tab or with options from the Columns dialog box. The Columns button creates columns of equal width. Use the Columns dialog box to create columns with varying widths. A document can include as many columns as room available on the page. Word determines how many columns can be included on the page based on the page width, the margin widths, and the size and spacing of the columns. Columns must be at least one-half inch in width. Changes in columns affect the entire document or the section of the document in which the insertion point is positioned.

Project 1b **Formatting Text into Columns**   **Part 2 of 8**

1. With **WL1-C5-P1-InputDevices.docx** open, make sure the insertion point is positioned below the section break and then return the left and right margins to 1 inch.
2. Delete the section break by completing the following steps:
   a. Click the Draft button in the view area on the Status bar.
   b. Position the insertion point on the section break.

   c. Press the Delete key.
   d. Click the Print Layout button in the view area on the Status bar.

3. Move the insertion point to the beginning of the first paragraph of text in the document and then insert a continuous section break.
4. Format the text into columns by completing the following steps:
   a. Make sure the insertion point is positioned below the section break.
   b. Click the Page Layout tab.
   c. Click the Columns button in the Page Setup group.
   d. Click *Two* at the drop-down list.
5. Save **WL1-C5-P1-InputDevices.docx**.

Creating Columns with the Columns Dialog Box

▼ **Quick Steps**

Create Columns with Columns Dialog Box
1. Click Page Layout tab.
2. Click Columns button.
3. Click *More Columns* at the drop-down list.
4. Specify column options.
5. Click OK.

You can use the Columns dialog box to create newspaper columns that are equal or unequal in width. To display the Columns dialog box shown in Figure 5.1, click the Columns button in the Page Setup group of the Page Layout tab and then click *More Columns* at the drop-down list.

With options at the Columns dialog box you can specify the style and number of columns, enter your own column measurements, and create unequal columns. You can also insert a line between columns. By default, column formatting is applied to the whole document. With the *Apply to* option at the bottom of the Columns dialog box, you can change this from *Whole document* to *This point forward*. At the *This point forward* option, a section break is inserted and the column formatting is applied to text from the location of the insertion point to the end of the document or until other column formatting is encountered. The *Preview* section of the dialog box displays an example of how the columns will appear in your document.

Figure 5.1 Columns Dialog Box

Choose the number of columns in this group or with this option.

Specify column width and spacing with options in this section.

Use this option to apply column formatting to the whole document, from the insertion point to the end of the document, or for a specific section.

Click this check box to insert a line between columns.

Preview column settings in this section.

Removing Column Formatting

To remove column formatting using the Columns button, position the insertion point in the section containing columns, click the Page Layout tab, click the Columns button, and then click *One* at the drop-down list. You can also remove column formatting at the Columns dialog box by selecting the *One* option in the *Presets* section.

Inserting a Column Break

When formatting text into columns, Word automatically breaks the columns to fit the page. At times, column breaks may appear in an undesirable location. You can insert a column break by positioning the insertion point where you want the column to end, clicking the Page Layout tab, clicking the Breaks button, and then clicking *Column* at the drop-down list.

You can also insert a column break with the keyboard shortcut, Ctrl + Shift + Enter.

Project 1c   **Formatting Columns at the Columns Dialog Box**   Part 3 of 8

1. With **WL1-C5-P1-InputDevices.docx** open, delete the section break by completing the following steps:
   a. Click the Draft button in the view area on the Status bar.
   b. Position the insertion point on the section break and then press the Delete key.
   c. Click the Print Layout button in the view area on the Status bar.
2. Remove column formatting by clicking the Columns button in the Page Setup group in the Page Layout tab and then clicking *One* at the drop-down list.
3. Format text in columns by completing the following steps:
   a. Position the insertion point at the beginning of the first paragraph of text in the document.
   b. Click the Columns button in the Page Setup group and then click *More Columns* at the drop-down list.
   c. At the Columns dialog box, click *Two* in the *Presets* section.
   d. Click the down-pointing arrow at the right of the *Spacing* option box until *0.3"* displays.
   e. Click the *Line between* check box to insert a check mark.
   f. Click the down-pointing arrow at the right side of the *Apply to* option box and then click *This point forward* at the drop-down list.
   g. Click OK to close the dialog box.

---

4. Insert a column break by completing the following steps:
   a. Position the insertion point at the beginning of the *Mouse* heading.
   b. Click the Breaks button in the Page Setup group and then click *Column* at the drop-down list.
5. Save and then print **WL1-C5-P1-InputDevices.docx**.

Balancing Columns on a Page

In a document containing text formatted into columns, Word automatically lines up (balances) the last line of text at the bottom of each column, except the last page. Text in the first column of the last page may flow to the end of the page, while the text in the second column may end far short of the end of the page. You can balance columns by inserting a continuous section break at the end of the text.

Project 1d   Formatting and Balancing Columns of Text   **Part 4 of 8**

1. With **WL1-C5-P1-InputDevices.docx** open, delete the column break by completing the following steps:
   a. Position the insertion point at the beginning of the *Mouse* heading.
   b. Click the Draft button in the view area on the Status bar.
   c. Position the insertion point on the column break.

   d. Press the Delete key.
   e. Click the Print Layout button in the view area on the Status bar.
2. Select the entire document and then change the font to 12-point Constantia.
3. Move the insertion point to the end of the document and then balance the columns by clicking the Page Layout tab, clicking the Breaks button, and then clicking *Continuous* at the drop-down list.
4. Apply the Aqua, Accent 5, Lighter 60% paragraph shading to the title *COMPUTER INPUT DEVICES*.
5. Apply the Aqua, Accent 5, Lighter 80% paragraph shading to each of the headings in the document.
6. Insert page numbering that prints at the bottom of each page.
7. Save **WL1-C5-P1-InputDevices.docx**.

Hyphenating Words ▪■■■■■■■■■■■■■■■■■

In some Word documents, especially documents with left and right margins wider than 1 inch, or text set in columns, the right margin may appear quite ragged. To improve the display of text lines by making line lengths more uniform, consider hyphenating long words that fall at the end of a text line. When using the hyphenation feature, you can tell Word to hyphenate words automatically in a document or you can manually insert hyphens.

Automatically Hyphenating Words

To automatically hyphenate words in a document, click the Page Layout tab, click the Hyphenation button in the Page Setup group, and then click *Automatic* at the drop-down list. Scroll through the document and check to see if hyphens display in appropriate locations within the words. If, after hyphenating words in a document, you want to remove all hyphens, immediately click the Undo button on the Quick Access toolbar. This must be done immediately after hyphenating since the Undo feature undoes only the last function.

Manually Hyphenating Words

If you want to control where a hyphen appears in a word during hyphenation, choose manual hyphenation. To do this, click the Page Layout tab, click the Hyphenation button in the Page Setup group, and then click *Manual* at the drop-down list. This displays the Manual Hyphenation dialog box as shown in Figure 5.2. (The word in the *Hyphenate at* text box will vary.) At this dialog box, click Yes to hyphenate the word as indicated in the *Hyphenate at* text box, click No if you do not want the word hyphenated, or click Cancel to cancel hyphenation. You can also reposition the hyphen in the *Hyphenate at* text box. Word displays the word with syllable breaks indicated by a hyphen. The position where the word will be hyphenated displays as a blinking black bar. If you want to hyphenate at a different location in the word, position the blinking black bar where you want the hyphen and then click Yes. Continue clicking Yes or No at the Manual Hyphenation dialog box. Be careful with words ending in *-ed*. Several two-syllable words can be divided before that final syllable, for example, *noted*. However, one-syllable words ending in *-ed* should not be divided. An example is *served*. Watch for this type of occurrence and click No to cancel the hyphenation. At the hyphenation complete message, click OK.

▼ Quick Steps

Automatic Hyphenation
1. Click Page Layout tab.
2. Click Hyphenation button.
3. Click *Automatic* at drop-down list.

Manual Hyphenation
1. Click Page Layout tab.
2. Click Hyphenation button.
3. Click *Manual* at drop-down list.
4. Click Yes or No to hyphenate indicated words.
5. When complete, click OK.

H I N T

Avoid dividing words at the ends of more than two consecutive lines.

Hyphenation

Figure 5.2 Manual Hyphenation Dialog Box

Click Yes to hyphenate the word at this location or move to a different syllable break and then click Yes.

If you want to remove all hyphens in a document, immediately click the Undo button on the Quick Access toolbar. To delete a few, but not all, of the optional hyphens inserted during hyphenation, use the Find and Replace dialog box. To do this, you would display the Find and Replace dialog box with the Replace tab selected, insert an optional hyphen symbol in the *Find what* text box (to do this, click the More button, click the Special button and then click *Optional Hyphen* at the pop-up list), and make sure the *Replace with* text box is empty. Complete the find and replace, clicking the Replace button to replace the hyphen with nothing or clicking the Find Next button to leave the hyphen in the document.

Project 1e   **Automatically and Manually Hyphenating Words**   **Part 5 of 8**

1. With **WL1-C5-P1-InputDevices.docx** open, hyphenate words automatically by completing the following steps:
   a. Press Ctrl + Home and then click the Page Layout tab.
   b. Click the Hyphenation button in the Page Setup group and then click *Automatic* at the drop-down list.

2. Scroll through the document and notice the automatic hyphenations.
3. Click the Undo button to remove the hyphens.
4. Manually hyphenate words by completing the following steps:
   a. Click the Hyphenation button in the Page Setup group and then click *Manual* at the drop-down list.
   b. At the Manual Hyphenation dialog box, make one of the following choices:
      • Click Yes to hyphenate the word as indicated in the *Hyphenate at* text box.
      • Move the hyphen in the word to a more desirable location, and then click Yes.
      • Click No if you do not want the word hyphenated.
   c. Continue clicking Yes or No at the Manual Hyphenation dialog box.
   d. At the hyphenation complete message, click OK.

5. Save **WL1-C5-P1-InputDevices.docx**.

Creating a Drop Cap ■■■■■■■ ■■■■■■■ ■■■■

Quick Steps

Create Drop Cap
1. Click Insert tab.
2. Click Drop Cap button.
3. Click desired type in drop-down list.

Drop Cap

Use a drop cap to enhance the appearance of text. A *drop cap* is the first letter of the first word of a paragraph that is set into a paragraph. Drop caps identify the beginning of major sections or parts of a document. Create a drop cap with the Drop Cap button in the Text group in the Insert tab. You can choose to set the drop cap in the paragraph or in the margin. At the Drop Cap dialog box, you can specify a font, the numbers of lines you want the letter to drop, and the distance you want the letter positioned from the text of the paragraph. You can drop cap the first word by selecting the word first and then clicking the Drop Cap button.

Step
1c

1. With **WL1-C5-P1-InputDevices.docx** open, create a drop cap by completing the following steps:
   a. Position the insertion point on the first word of the first paragraph of text (*Engineers*).
   b. Click the Insert tab.
   c. Click the Drop Cap button in the Text group.
   d. Click *In margin* at the drop-down gallery.

Step
1d

2. Looking at the drop cap, you decide that you do not like it in the margin and want it to be a little smaller. To change the drop cap, complete the following steps:
   a. With the E in the word *Engineers* selected, click the Drop Cap button in the Text group and then click *None* at the drop-down gallery.
   b. Click the Drop Cap button and then click *Drop Cap Options* at the drop-down gallery.
   c. At the Drop Cap dialog box, click *Dropped* in the *Position* section.
   d. Change the font to *Times New Roman*.
   e. Change the *Lines to drop* option to *2*.
   f. Click OK to close the dialog box.
   g. Click outside the drop cap to deselect it.
3. Save **WL1-C5-P1-InputDevices.docx**.

Step
2c

Step
2d

Step
2e

Step
2f

Inserting Symbols and Special Characters ■■■■■■■■■■

You can use the Symbol button in the Insert tab to insert special symbols in a document. Click the Symbol button in the Symbols group in the Insert tab and a drop-down list displays with the most recently inserted symbols along with a *More Symbols* option. Click one of the symbols that displays in the list to insert it in the document or click the *More Symbols* option to display the Symbol dialog box as shown in Figure 5.3. At the Symbol dialog box, double-click the desired symbol, and then click Close; or click the desired symbol, click the Insert button, and then click Close.

At the Symbol dialog box with the Symbols tab selected, you can change the font with the *Font* option. When you change the font, different symbols display in the dialog box. Click the Special Characters tab at the Symbol dialog box and a list of special characters displays along with keyboard shortcuts to create the special character.

▼ **Quick Steps**

Insert a Symbol
1. Click Insert tab.
2. Click Symbol button.
3. Click desired symbol in drop-down list.
OR
1. Click Insert tab.
2. Click Symbol button.
3. Click *More Symbols*.
4. Double-click desired symbol.
5. Click Close.

Symbol

Figure 5.3 Symbol Dialog Box with Symbols Tab Selected

Use the *Font* option to select the desired set of characters.

Project 1g Inserting Symbols and Special Characters

1. With **WL1-C5-P1-InputDevices.docx** open, press Ctrl + End to move the insertion point to the end of the document.
2. Press the Enter key once, type **Prepared by:**, and then press the spacebar once.
3. Type the first name **Matthew**.
4. Insert the last name *Viña* by completing the following steps:
   a. Type **Vi**.
   b. Click the Symbol button in the Symbols group in the Insert tab.
   c. Click *More Symbols* at the drop-down list.
   d. At the Symbol dialog box, make sure the *Font* option displays as *(normal text)* and then double-click the ñ symbol (located in approximately the twelfth row).
   e. Click the Close button.
   f. Type **a**.
5. Press Shift + Enter.
6. Insert the keyboard symbol (⌨) by completing the following steps:
   a. Click the Symbol button and then click *More Symbols*.
   b. At the Symbol dialog box, click the down-pointing arrow at the right side of the *Font* option and then click *Wingdings* at the drop-down list. (You will need to scroll down the list to display this option.)
   c. Double-click ⌨ (located approximately in the second row).
   d. Click the Close button.
7. Type **SoftCell Technologies**.

Step 4d

Step 6b   Step 6c

8. Insert the registered trademark symbol (®) by completing the following steps:
   a. Click the Symbol button and then click *More Symbols*.
   b. At the Symbol dialog box, click the Special Characters tab.
   c. Double-click the ® symbol (tenth option from the top).
   d. Click the Close button.
   e. Press Shift + Enter.
9. Select the keyboard symbol (⌨) and then change the font size to 18.
10. Save **WL1-C5-P1-InputDevices.docx**.

Step 8b

Step 8c

Inserting the Date and Time ■■■■■■■■■■■■■■■■

Use the Date & Time button in the Text group in the Insert tab to insert the current date and time in a document. Click this button and the Date and Time dialog box displays as shown in Figure 5.4. (Your date will vary from what you see in the figure.) At the Date and Time dialog box, click the desired date and/or time format in the *Available formats* list box.

If the *Update automatically* check box does not contain a check mark, the date and/or time are inserted in the document as normal text that you can edit in the normal manner. You can also insert the date and/or time as a field. The advantage to inserting the date or time as a field is that the field can be updated with the Update Field keyboard shortcut, F9. Insert a check mark in the *Update automatically* check box to insert the data and/or time as a field. You can also insert the date as a field using the keyboard shortcut Alt + Shift + D, and insert the time as a field with the keyboard shortcut Alt + Shift + T.

▼ **Quick Steps**

Insert Date and Time
1. Click Insert tab.
2. Click Date and Time button.
3. Click option in list box.
4. Click OK.

Date & Time

Figure 5.4 Date and Time Dialog Box

Click the desired option in this list box.

Insert a check mark in this option if you want the date and/or time updated each time you open the document.

1. With **WL1-C5-P1-InputDevices.docx** open, press Ctrl + End and make sure the insertion point is positioned below the company name.
2. Insert the current date by completing the following steps:
   a. Click the Date & Time button in the Text group in the Insert tab.
   b. At the Date and Time dialog box, click the third option from the top in the *Available formats* group.
   c. Click in the *Update automatically* check box to insert a check mark.
   d. Click OK to close the dialog box.
3. Press Shift + Enter.
4. Insert the current time by pressing Alt + Shift + T.
5. Save **WL1-C5-P1-InputDevices.docx**.
6. Update the time by clicking the time and then pressing F9.
7. Save, print, and then close **WL1-C5-P1-InputDevices.docx**.

Step 2b

Your dates and times may vary.

Step 2c

Step 2d

Project **2** Create an Announcement about Supervisory Training   **3 Parts**

You will create an announcement about upcoming supervisory training and use the click and type feature to center and right align text. You will vertically center the text on the page and insert and format a picture to add visual appeal to the announcement.

Using the Click and Type Feature ■■■■■■■■■■■■■■■■

Word contains a click and type feature you can use to position the insertion point at a specific location and alignment in the document. This feature allows you to position one or more lines of text as you type, rather than typing the text and then selecting and reformatting the text, which requires multiple steps.

To use click and type, make sure the document displays in Print Layout view and then hover the mouse pointer at the location where you want the insertion point positioned. As you move the mouse pointer, you will notice that the pointer displays with varying horizontal lines representing the alignment. Double-click the mouse button and the insertion point is positioned at the location of the mouse pointer.

If the horizontal lines do not display next to the mouse pointer when you double-click the mouse button, a left tab is set at the position of the insertion point. If you want to change the alignment and not set a tab, make sure the horizontal lines display near the mouse pointer before double-clicking the mouse.

▼ **Quick Steps**

Use Click and Type
1. Hover mouse at left margin, between left and right margins, or at right margin.
2. Double-click left mouse button.

1. At a blank document, create the centered text shown in Figure 5.5 by completing the following steps:
   a. Position the I-beam pointer between the left and right margins at about the 3.25-inch mark on the horizontal ruler and the top of the vertical ruler.
   b. When the center alignment lines display below the I-beam pointer, double-click the left mouse button.

Step 1b

   c. Type the centered text shown in Figure 5.5. Press Shift + Enter to end each text line.
2. Change to right alignment by completing the following steps:
   a. Position the I-beam pointer near the right margin at approximately the 1.5-inch mark on the vertical ruler until the right alignment lines display at the left side of the I-beam pointer.
   b. Double-click the left mouse button.
   c. Type the right-aligned text shown in Figure 5.5. Press Shift + Enter to end the text line.
3. Select the centered text and then change the font to 14-point Candara bold and the line spacing to double.
4. Select the right-aligned text, change the font to 10-point Candara bold, and then deselect the text.
5. Save the document and name it **WL1-C5-P2-Training**.

Figure 5.5 Project 2a

SUPERVISORY TRAINING
Maximizing Employee Potential
Wednesday, February 15, 2012
Training Center
9:00 a.m. to 3:30 p.m.

Sponsored by
Cell Systems

Vertically Aligning Text ▪■▪■▪■▪▪▪■■▪■▪■▪▪■■▪■

Text in a Word document is aligned at the top of the page by default. You can change this alignment with the *Vertical alignment* option at the Page Setup dialog box with the Layout tab selected as shown in Figure 5.6. Display this dialog box by clicking the Page Layout tab, clicking the Page Setup group dialog box launcher, and then clicking the Layout tab at the Page Setup dialog box.

Figure 5.6 Page Setup Dialog Box with Layout Tab Selected

Click this down-pointing arrow to display a list of vertical alignment options.

▼ **Quick Steps**

Vertically Align Text
1. Click Page Layout tab.
2. Click Page Setup dialog box launcher.
3. Click Layout tab.
4. Click desired alignment.
5. Click OK.

The *Vertical alignment* option from the Page Setup dialog box contains four choices — *Top, Center, Justified,* and *Bottom*. The default setting is *Top*, which aligns text at the top of the page. Choose *Center* if you want text centered vertically on the page. The *Justified* option will align text between the top and the bottom margins. The *Center* option positions text in the middle of the page vertically, while the *Justified* option adds space between paragraphs of text (not within) to fill the page from the top to bottom margins. If you center or justify text, the text does not display centered or justified on the screen in the Draft view, but it does display centered or justified in the Print Layout view. Choose the *Bottom* option to align text in the document vertically along the bottom of the page.

Project 2b | **Vertically Centering Text** | **Part 2 of 3**

1. With **WL1-C5-P2-Training.docx** open, click the Page Layout tab and then click the Page Setup group dialog box launcher.
2. At the Page Setup dialog box, click the Layout tab.
3. Click the down-pointing arrow at the right side of the *Vertical alignment* option box and then click *Center* at the drop-down list.
4. Click OK to close the dialog box.
5. Save and then print **WL1-C5-P2-Training.docx**.

Inserting an Image ■■■■■■■■■■■■■■■■■■■■■■■

You can insert an image such as a picture or clip art in a Word document with buttons in the Illustrations group in the Insert tab. Click the Picture button to display the Insert Picture dialog box where you can specify the desired picture file or click the Clip Art button and then choose from a variety of images available at the Clip Art task pane. When you insert a picture or a clip art image in a document, the Picture Tools Format tab displays. Use options on the Picture Tools Format tab to customize and format the image.

Customizing and Formatting an Image

With options in the Adjust group in the Picture Tools Format tab you can remove unwanted portions of the image, correct the brightness and contrast, change the image color, apply artistic effects, compress the size of the image file, change to a different image, and reset the image back to the original formatting. Use buttons in the Picture Styles group to apply a predesigned style to the image, change the image border, or apply other effects to the image. With options in the Arrange group, you can position the image on the page, specify how text will wrap around it, align the image with other elements in the document, and rotate the image. Use the Crop button in the Size group to remove any unnecessary parts of the image and specify the image size with the *Shape Height* and *Shape Width* measurement boxes.

Crop

In addition to the Picture Tools Format tab, you can customize and format an image with options at the shortcut menu. Display this menu by right-clicking the image. With options at the shortcut menu, you can change the picture, insert a caption, choose text wrapping, size and position the image, and display the Format Picture dialog box.

Sizing an Image

You can change the size of an image with the *Shape Height* and *Shape Width* measurement boxes in the Size group in the Picture Tools Format tab or with the sizing handles that display around the selected image. To change size with a sizing handle, position the mouse pointer on a sizing handle until the pointer turns into a double-headed arrow and then hold down the left mouse button. Drag the sizing handle in or out to decrease or increase the size of the image and then release the mouse button. Use the middle sizing handles at the left or right side of the image to make the image wider or thinner. Use the middle sizing handles at the top or bottom of the image to make the image taller or shorter. Use the sizing handles at the corners of the image to change both the width and height at the same time.

Resize a selected object horizontally, vertically, or diagonally from the center outward by holding down the Ctrl key and then dragging a sizing handle.

Moving an Image

Move an image to a specific location on the page with options from the Position button drop-down gallery. The Position button is located in the Arrange group in the Picture Tools Format tab. When you choose an option at the Position button drop-down gallery, the image is moved to the specified location on the page and square text wrapping is applied to the image.

Position

You can also move the image by dragging it to the desired location. Before dragging an image, you must first choose a text wrapping style by clicking the Wrap Text button in the Arrange group and then clicking the desired wrapping style at the drop-down list. After choosing a wrapping style, move the image by positioning the mouse pointer on the image border until the arrow pointer turns into a four-headed arrow. Hold down the left mouse button, drag the image to the desired position, and then release the mouse button. To help precisely position an image, consider turning on gridlines. Do this by clicking the Align button in the Arrange group in the Picture Tools Format tab and then clicking *View Gridlines*.

Rotate the image by positioning the mouse pointer on the green, round rotation handle until the pointer displays as a circular arrow. Hold down the left mouse button, drag in the desired direction, and then release the mouse button.

▼ **Quick Steps**

Insert Picture
1. Click Insert tab.
2. Click Picture button.
3. Double-click desired picture in Insert Picture dialog box.

Picture

Inserting a Picture

To insert a picture in a document, click the Insert tab and then click the Picture button in the Illustrations group. At the Insert Picture dialog box, navigate to the folder containing the desired picture and then double-click the picture. Use buttons in the Picture Tools Format tab to format and customize the picture. You can insert a picture from a Web page by opening the Web page, opening a Word document, and then dragging the picture from the Web page to the document. If the picture is linked, the link (rather than the image) will display in your document.

Project 2c	Inserting and Customizing a Picture	Part 3 of 3

1. With **WL1-C5-P2-Training.docx** open, return the vertical alignment back to *Top* by completing the following steps:
   a. Click the Page Layout tab.
   b. Click the Page Setup group dialog box launcher.
   c. At the Page Setup dialog box, click the Layout tab.
   d. Click the down-pointing arrow at the right side of the *Vertical alignment* option box and then click *Top* at the drop-down list.
   e. Click OK to close the dialog box.
2. Select and then delete the text *Sponsored by* and the text *Cell Systems*.
3. Select the remaining text and change the line spacing to single.
4. Move the insertion point to the beginning of the document and then press the Enter key until the first line of text displays at approximately the 3-inch mark on the vertical ruler.
5. Insert a picture by completing the following steps:
   a. Click the Insert tab.
   b. Click the Picture button in the Illustrations group.
   c. At the Insert Picture dialog box, navigate to your Word2010L1C5 folder.
   d. Double-click *Uluru.jpg* in the list box.
6. Crop the picture by completing the following steps:
   a. Click the Crop button in the Size group.
   b. Position the mouse pointer on the bottom, middle crop handle (displays as a short black line) until the pointer turns into the crop tool (displays as a small, black T).

c. Hold down the left mouse button, drag up to just below the mountain as shown at the right, and then release the mouse button.

d. Click the Crop button in the Size group to turn off the feature.

7. Change the size of the picture by clicking in the *Shape Height* measurement box in the Size group, typing 3, and then pressing Enter.

8. Move the picture behind the text by clicking the Wrap Text button in the Arrange group and then clicking *Behind Text* at the drop-down list.

9. Rotate the image by clicking the Rotate button in the Arrange group and then clicking *Flip Horizontal* at the drop-down list.

10. Change the picture color by clicking the Color button in the Adjust group and then clicking the second option from the right in the *Color Saturation* section (*Saturation: 300%*).

11. After looking at the coloring, you decide to return to the original color by clicking the Undo button on the Quick Access toolbar.

12. Sharpen the picture by clicking the Corrections button in the Adjust group and then clicking the second option from the right in the *Sharpen and Soften* section (*Sharpen: 25%*).

13. Change the contrast of the picture by clicking the Corrections button in the Adjust group and then clicking the third option from the left in the bottom row of the *Brightness and Contrast* section [*Brightness: 0% (Normal) Contrast: +40%*].

14. Apply a picture style by clicking the More button at the right side of the thumbnails in the Picture Styles section and then clicking the first option from the left in the second row (*Simple Frame, Black*).

15. Compress the picture by completing the following steps:
   a. Click the Compress Pictures button in the Adjust group.
   b. At the Compress Pictures dialog box, make sure a check mark displays in both options in the *Compression options* section and then click OK.

16. Position the mouse pointer on the border of the selected picture until the pointer displays with a four-headed arrow attached and then drag the picture so the text is positioned in the sky above Ayres Rock.

17. If the text does not fit in the sky above the rock, increase the height of the picture. To do this, position the mouse pointer on the top border middle sizing handle until the pointer displays as a two-headed arrow pointing up and down. Hold down the left mouse button, drag up until the text displays approximately one-half inch below the top border of the picture, and then release the mouse button.

18. Save and then print **WL1-C5-P2-Training.docx**.

19. With the picture selected, remove the background by completing the following steps:
   a. Click the Remove Background button in the Adjust group in the Picture Tools Format tab.
   b. Using the left middle sizing handle, drag the left border to the left side of the image.

c. Drag the right middle sizing handle to the right side of the image.

d. Drag the bottom middle sizing handle to the bottom border of the image.

e. Click the Keep Changes button in the Close group in the Background Removal tab. (The picture should now display with the sky removed.)

Step 19e

Step 20c

20. Insert a caption by completing the following steps:

a. Right-click the picture. (This displays the shortcut menu.)

b. Click the *Insert Caption* option at the shortcut menu.

c. At the Caption dialog box with the insertion point positioned in the *Caption* text box, press the spacebar and then type **Uluru (Ayers Rock, Australia)**.

d. Click OK. (The caption displays below and at the left side of the picture.)

21. Save, print, and then close **WL1-C5-P2-Training.docx**.

Step 20d

Project 3 Customize a Report on Robots   2 Parts

You will open a report on robots and then add visual appeal to the report by inserting and formatting a clip art image and a built-in text box.

Inserting a Clip Art Image

Microsoft Office includes a gallery of media images you can insert in a document such as clip art, photographs, and movie images, as well as sound clips. To insert an image in a Word document, click the Insert tab and then click the Clip Art button in the Illustrations group. This displays the Clip Art task pane at the right side of the screen as shown in Figure 5.7.

To view all picture, sound, and motion files, make sure the *Search for* text box in the Clip Art task pane does not contain any text and then click the Go button. When the desired image is visible, click the image to insert it in the document. Use buttons in the Picture Tools Format tab to format and customize the clip art image.

Unless the Clip Art task pane default settings have been customized, the task pane displays all illustrations, photographs, videos, and audio files. The *Results should be* option has a default setting of *Selected media file types*. Click the down-pointing arrow at the right side of this option to display media types. To search for a specific media type, remove the check mark before all options at the drop-down list except for the desired type. For example, if you are searching only for photograph images, remove the check mark before *Illustrations*, *Videos*, and *Audio*.

Quick Steps

Insert Clip Art Image
1. Click Insert tab.
2. Click Clip Art button.
3. Type search word or topic.
4. Press Enter.
5. Click desired image.

HINT

You can drag a clip art image from the Clip Art task pane to your document.

Clip Art

Figure 5.7 Clip Art Task Pane

Type the search word or topic in this text box.

Use this option to specify the type of files for which you are searching.

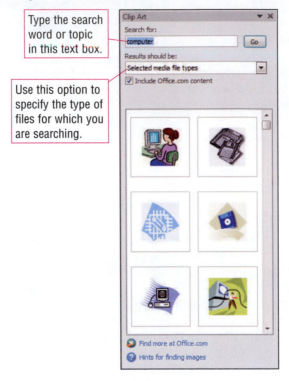

If you are searching for specific images, click in the *Search for* text box, type the desired topic, and then click the Go button. For example, if you want to find images related to business, click in the *Search for* text box, type **business**, and then click the Go button. Clip art images related to *business* display in the viewing area of the task pane. If you are connected to the Internet, Word will search for images at the Office Online website matching the topic.

Project 3a **Inserting an Image** **Part 1 of 2**

1. Open **Robots.docx** and then save the document with Save As and name it **WL1-C5-P3-Robots**.
2. Apply the Heading 1 style to the title *ROBOTS AS ANDROIDS* and apply the Heading 2 style to the headings in the document.
3. Change the Quick Styles set to *Modern*. **Hint: Do this with the Change Styles button in the Styles group in the Home tab.**
4. Insert a clip art image by completing the following steps:
   a. Move the insertion point so it is positioned at the beginning of the first paragraph of text (the sentence that begins *Robotic factories are increasingly . . .*).
   b. Click the Insert tab.
   c. Click the Clip Art button in the Illustrations group.
   d. At the Clip Art task pane, select any text that displays in the *Search for* text box, type **computer**, and then press Enter.
   e. Click the computer image in the list box as shown at the right.

Step 4d

Step 4e

f. Close the Clip Art task pane by clicking the Close button (contains an X) located in the upper right corner of the task pane.

5. Format the clip art image by completing the following steps:

a. Click the More button at the right side of the thumbnails in the Picture Styles group and then click the *Drop Shadow Rectangle* option (fourth option from the left in the top row).

Step 5a

b. Click the Color button in the Adjust group and then click the *Blue, Accent color 1 Dark* option (second option from the left in the second row).

c. Click in the *Shape Height* measurement box in the Size group, type 3, and then press Enter.

6. Reset the image and the image size by clicking the Reset Picture button arrow in the Adjust group and then clicking the *Reset Picture & Size* option at the drop-down list.

Step 6

7. Crop the clip art image by completing the following steps:

a. Click the Crop button in the Size group.

b. Position the mouse pointer on the top middle crop handle (displays as a short black line) until the pointer turns into the crop tool.

c. Hold down the left mouse button, drag down to just above the top of the computer as shown at the right, and then release the mouse button.

d. Click the Crop button in the Size group to turn off the feature.

Step 7c

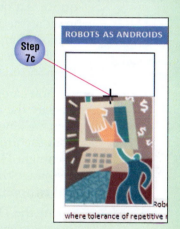

8. Decrease the size of the picture by clicking in the *Shape Height* measurement box in the Size group, typing 1.3, and then pressing Enter.

9. Change the text wrapping by clicking the Wrap Text button in the Arrange group and then clicking *Square* at the drop-down list.

10. Rotate the image by clicking the Rotate button in the Arrange group and then clicking *Flip Horizontal* at the drop-down list.

11. Click the Corrections button in the Adjust group and then click the third option from the left in the bottom row [*Brightness: 0% (Normal) Contrast: +40%*].

12. Click the Picture Effects button in the Picture Styles group, point to *Shadow*, and then click the last option in the top row of the *Outer* section (*Offset Diagonal Bottom Left*).

Step 12

13. Position the mouse pointer on the border of the selected picture until the pointer turns into a four-headed arrow and then drag the picture so it is positioned as shown at the right.
14. Click outside the clip art image to deselect it.
15. Save **WL1-C5-P3-Robots.docx**.

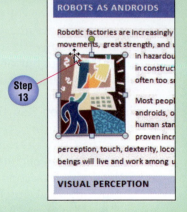

Inserting and Customizing a Pull Quote

Use a pull quote in a document such as an article to attract attention. A **pull quote** is a quote from an article that is "pulled out" and enlarged and positioned in an attractive location on the page. Some advantages of pull quotes are that they reinforce important concepts, summarize your message, and break up text blocks to make them easier to read. If you use multiple pull quotes in a document, keep them in order to ensure clear comprehension for readers.

You can insert a pull quote in a document with a predesigned built-in text box. Display the available pull quote built-in text boxes by clicking the Insert tab and then clicking the Text Box button in the Text group. Click the desired pull quote from the drop-down list that displays and the built-in text box is inserted in the document. Type the quote inside the text box and then format the text and/or customize the text box. Use buttons in the Drawing Tools Format tab to format and customize the built-in text box.

At the Drawing Tools Format tab, use options in the Insert Shapes group to insert a shape in the document. Click the Edit Shape button in the Insert Shapes group and a drop-down list displays. Click the *Change Shape* option if you want to change the shape of the selected text box. Click the *Edit Points* option and small black squares display at points around the text box. Use the mouse on these points to increase or decrease a point of the text box. Apply predesigned styles to a text box with options in the Shape Styles group. You can also change the shape fill, outline, and effects. Change the formatting of the text in the text box with options in the WordArt Styles group. Click the More button that displays at the right side of the WordArt style thumbnails and then click the desired style at the drop-down gallery. You can further customize text with the Text Fill, Text Outline, and Text Effects buttons in the Text group. Use options in the Arrange group to position the text box on the page, specify text wrapping in relation to the text box, align the text box with other objects in the document, and rotate the text box. Specify the text box size with the *Shape Height* and *Shape Width* measurement boxes in the Size group.

1. With **WL1-C5-P3-Robots.docx** open, click the Insert tab.
2. Click the Text Box button in the Text group.
3. Scroll down the drop-down list and then click the *Contrast Quote* option.
4. Type the following text in the text box: **"The task of creating a humanlike body has proven incredibly difficult."**
5. Make sure the Drawing Tools Format tab is active.
6. Click the More button at the right side of the style thumbnails in the Shape Styles group and then click the *Subtle Effect - Blue, Accent 1* option (second option from the left in the fourth row).

Step 2

Step 3

Step 6

Step 7

7. Click the Shape Effects button in the Shape Styles group, point to *Shadow*, and then click the *Offset Diagonal Bottom Right* option (first option from the left in the first row in the *Outer Section*).
8. Position the mouse pointer on the border of the selected text box until the pointer turns into a four-headed arrow and then drag the text box so it is positioned as shown above.
9. Save, print, and then close **WL1-C5-P3-Robots.docx**.

Step 8

You will prepare a company flyer by inserting and customizing shapes, text boxes, and WordArt.

Shapes

Drawing Shapes

Use the Shapes button in the Insert tab to draw shapes in a document including lines, basic shapes, block arrows, flow chart shapes, stars and banners, and callouts. Click a shape and the mouse pointer displays as crosshairs (plus sign). Position the crosshairs where you want the shape to begin, hold down the left mouse button, drag to create the shape, and then release the mouse button. This inserts the shape in the document and also displays the Drawing Tools Format tab. Use buttons in this tab to change the shape, apply a style to the shape, arrange the shape, and change the size of the shape. This tab contains many of the same options and buttons as the Picture Tools Format tab and the Text Box Tools Format tab.

If you choose a shape in the *Lines* section of the drop-down list, the shape you draw is considered a *line drawing*. If you choose an option in the other sections of the drop-down list, the shape you draw is considered an *enclosed object*. When drawing an enclosed object, you can maintain the proportions of the shape by holding down the Shift key while dragging with the mouse to create the shape.

Copying Shapes

To copy a shape, select the shape and then click the Copy button in the Clipboard group in the Home tab. Position the insertion point at the location where you want the copied image and then click the Paste button. You can also copy a selected shape by holding down the Ctrl key while dragging the shape to the desired location.

Project 4a **Drawing Arrow Shapes**

Part 1 of 3

1. At a blank document, press the Enter key twice and then draw an arrow shape by completing the following steps:
   a. Click the Insert tab.
   b. Click the Shapes button in the Illustrations group and then click the *Striped Right Arrow* shape in the *Block Arrows* section.
   c. Position the mouse pointer (displays as crosshairs) in the document at approximately the 1-inch mark on the horizontal ruler and the 0.5-inch mark on the vertical ruler.
   d. Hold down the Shift key and the left mouse button, drag to the right until the tip of the arrow is positioned at approximately the 5.5-inch mark on the horizontal ruler, and then release the mouse button and the Shift key.

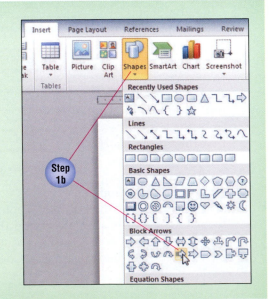

Step 1b

2. Format the arrow by completing the following steps:
   a. Click in the *Shape Height* measurement box in the Size group, type 2.4, and then press Enter.
   b. Click in the *Shape Width* measurement box in the Size group, type 4.5, and then press Enter.
   c. Click the More button at the right side of the thumbnails in the Shape Styles group and then click the *Intense Effect – Olive Green, Accent 3* option (fourth option from the left in the sixth row).

   d. Click the Shape Effects button in the Shape Styles group, point to *Bevel*, and then click the *Angle* option (first option from the left in the second row in the *Bevel* section).
   e. Click the Shape Outline button arrow in the Shape Styles group and then click the Dark Blue color (second color from the right in the *Standard Colors* section).
3. Copy the arrow by completing the following steps:
   a. With the mouse pointer positioned in the arrow (mouse pointer displays with a four-headed arrow attached), hold down the Ctrl key and the left mouse button.
   b. Drag down until the outline of the copied arrow displays just below the top arrow, release the mouse button, and then release the Ctrl key.
   c. Copy the arrow again by holding down the Ctrl key and the left mouse button and then dragging the outline of the copied arrow just below the second arrow.
4. Flip the middle arrow by completing the following steps:
   a. Click the middle arrow to select it.
   b. Click the Rotate button in the Arrange group in the Drawing Tools Format tab and then click *Flip Horizontal* at the drop-down gallery.
5. Insert the text *Financial* in the top arrow by completing the following steps:
   a. Click the top arrow to select it.
   b. Type **Financial**. (The text will appear in the middle of the arrow.)
   c. Select *Financial*.
   d. Click the Home tab.
   e. Change the font size to 16, turn on bold, and then change the font color to Olive Green, Accent 3, Darker 50%.
6. Complete steps similar to those in Step 5 to insert the word *Direction* in the middle arrow.
7. Complete steps similar to those in Step 5 to insert the word *Retirement* in the bottom arrow.
8. Save the document and name it **WL1-C5-P4-FinConsult**.
9. Print the document.

Drawing and Formatting a Text Box

▼ **Quick Steps**

Draw a Text Box
1. Click Insert tab.
2. Click Text Box button in Text group.
3. Click *Draw Text Box*.
4. Drag in document screen to create box.

You can use the built-in text boxes provided by Word or you can draw your own text box. To draw a text box, click the Insert tab, click the Text Box button in the Text group, and then click *Draw Text Box* at the drop-down list. The mouse pointer displays as crosshairs. Position the crosshairs in the document and then drag to create the text box. You can also just click in the document. When a text box is selected, the Text Box Tools Format tab displays. Use buttons in this tab to format text boxes in the same manner as formatting built-in text boxes.

Project 4b **Inserting and Formatting a Text Box** **Part 2 of 3**

1. With **WL1-C5-P4-FinConsult.docx** open, delete the bottom arrow by completing the following steps:
   a. Click the bottom arrow. (This displays a border around the arrow.)
   b. Position the mouse pointer on the border (displays with four-headed arrow attached) and then click the left mouse button. (This changes the dashed border to a solid border.)
   c. Press the Delete key.

2. Insert, size, and format a text box by completing the following steps:
   a. Click the Insert tab.
   b. Click the Text Box button in the Text group and then click *Draw Text Box* at the drop-down list.
   c. Click in the document at about the one-inch mark on the horizontal ruler and about one inch below the bottom arrow. (This inserts a text box in the document.)
   d. Click in the *Shape Height* measurement box in the Size group and then type 1.7.
   e. Click in the *Shape Width* measurement box, type 4.5, and then press Enter.
   f. Click the More button at the right side of the thumbnails in the Shape Styles group and then click the *Intense Effect – Olive Green, Accent 3* option at the drop-down gallery (fourth option from the left in the sixth row).
   g. Click the Shape Effects button in the Shape Styles group, point to *Bevel*, and then click the *Soft Round* option at the side menu (second option from the left in the second row in the *Bevel* section).

Step 2b

Step 2g

h. Click the Shape Effects button in the Shape Styles group, point to *3-D Rotation*, and then click the *Perspective Above* option (first option from the left in the second row in the *Perspective* section).

3. Insert and format text in the text box by completing the following steps:
   a. Press the Enter key twice. (The insertion point should be positioned in the text box.)
   b. Click the Home tab.
   c. Change the font size to 24 points, turn on bold, and change the font color to Olive Green, Accent 3, Darker 50%.
   d. Click the Center button in the Paragraph group.
   e. Type **Retirement Financial Consulting**. (Your text box should appear as shown below.)

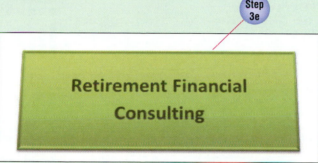

4. Save **WL1-C5-P4-FinConsult.docx**.

Creating and Modifying WordArt Text ▪▪▪▪▪▪▪▪▪▪▪▪▪

With the WordArt feature, you can distort or modify text to conform to a variety of shapes. This is useful for creating company logos, letterheads, flyer titles, or headings. To insert WordArt in a document, click the Insert tab and then click the WordArt button in the Text group. At the drop-down list that displays, click the desired option and a WordArt text box is inserted in the document containing the words *Your text here* and the Drawing Tools Format tab is active. Type the desired WordArt text and then format the WordArt with options in the Drawing Tools Format tab.

▼ **Quick Steps**
Create WordArt Text
1. Click Insert tab.
2. Click WordArt button.
3. Click desired WordArt option at drop-down list.
4. Type WordArt text.

WordArt

Project 4c **Inserting and Modifying WordArt**   **Part 3 of 3**

1. With **WL1-C5-P4-FinConsult.docx** open, press Ctrl + Home to move the insertion point to the beginning of the document.
2. Insert WordArt text by completing the following steps:
   a. Click the Insert tab.

b. Click the WordArt button in the Text group and then click the *Fill – Olive Green, Accent 3, Outline – Text 2* option.

c. Type **Miller Financial Services**.

3. Format the WordArt text by completing the following steps:

a. Click the outside border of the WordArt text so the border displays as a solid line instead of a dashed line.

b. Click the Text Fill button arrow in the WordArt Styles group in the Drawing Tools Format tab and then click the *Olive Green, Accent 3, Darker 25%* option.

c. Click the Text Effects button in the WordArt Styles group, point to *Glow*, and then click the *Aqua, 5 pt glow, Accent color 5* option in the *Glow Variations* section.

d. Click the Text Effects button in the WordArt Styles group, point to *3-D Rotation*, and then click the *Perspective Above* option in the *Perspective* section.

e. Click in the *Shape Height* measurement box in the Size group and then type **1**.

f. Click in the *Shape Width* measurement box in the Size group, type **6**, and then press Enter.

g. Click the Text Effects button in the WordArt Styles group, point to *Transform*, and then click the *Deflate* option in the *Warp* section (second option from the left in the sixth row).

h. Click the Position button in the Arrange group and then click the second option from the left in the first row in the *With Text Wrapping* section (*Position in Top Center with Square Text Wrapping*).

4. Check to make sure that the WordArt, the two arrows, and the text box all fit on one page. If they do not, consider moving and/or sizing the arrows or text box to ensure that they fit on one page.

5. Save, print, and then close **WL1-C5-P4-FinConsult.docx**.

Step 3h

$\mathcal{P}$roject **5** **Create and Format Screenshots**

2 Parts

You will create screenshots of the Print tab and Save & Send tab Backstage views and then create screen clippings of cover pages and create a sample cover pages document.

Creating and Inserting a Screenshot ■■■■■■■■■■■■■■

The Illustrations group in the Insert tab contains a Screenshot button, which you can use to capture the contents of a screen as an image or capture a portion of a screen. If you want to capture the entire screen, open a new document, click the Insert tab, click the Screenshot button in the Illustrations group, and then click the desired screen thumbnail at the drop-down list. The currently active document does not display as a thumbnail at the drop-down list, only any other documents or files that you have open. When you click the desired thumbnail, the screenshot is inserted as an image in the open document, the image is selected, and the Picture Tools Format tab is active. Use buttons in this tab to customize the screenshot image.

Screenshot

$\mathcal{P}$roject 5a   **Inserting and Formatting Screenshots**

Part 1 of 2

1. Open a blank document.
2. Open a second blank document, type **Print Tab Backstage View** at the left margin, and then press the Enter key.
3. Save the document and name it **WL1-C5-P5-BackstageViews**.
4. Click the Word button on the Taskbar, click the thumbnail representing the blank document, and then display the Print tab Backstage view by clicking the File tab and then clicking the Print tab.

Step 4

5. Click the Word button on the Taskbar and then click the thumbnail representing **WL1-C5-P5-BackstageViews.docx**.

6. Insert and format a screenshot of the Print tab Backstage view by completing the following steps:

   a. Click the Insert tab.

   b. Click the Screenshot button in the Illustrations group and then click the thumbnail that displays in the drop-down list. (This inserts a screenshot of the Print tab Backstage view in the document.)

   c. With the screenshot image selected, click the More button that displays at the right side of the thumbnails in the Picture Styles group and then click the *Drop Shadow Rectangle* option.

   d. Select the measurement in the *Shape Width* measurement box in the Size group, type 5.5, and then press Enter.

7. Press Ctrl + End and then press the Enter key twice. (This moves the insertion point below the screenshot image.)

8. Type **Save & Send Tab Backstage View** at the left margin and then press the Enter key.

9. Click the Word button on the Taskbar and then click the thumbnail representing the blank document.

10. At the Backstage view, click the Save & Send tab. (This displays the Save & Send tab Backstage view.)

11. Click the Word button on the Taskbar and then click the thumbnail representing **WL1-C5-P5-BackstageViews.docx**.

12. Insert and format a screenshot of the Save & Send tab Backstage view by completing Step 6.

13. Press Ctrl + Home to move the insertion point to the beginning of the document.

14. Save, print, and then close **WL1-C5-P5-BackstageViews.docx**.

15. At the Save & Send tab Backstage view, click the Close button to close the document without saving it.

In addition to making a screenshot of an entire screen, you can make a screenshot of a specific portion of the screen by clicking the *Screen Clipping* option at the Screenshot button drop-down list. When you click this option, the other open document, file, or Windows desktop displays in a dimmed manner and the mouse pointer displays as a crosshair. Using the mouse, draw a border around the specific area of the screen you want to capture. The specific area you identified is inserted in the other document as an image, the image is selected, and the Picture Tools Format tab is active. If you have only one document or file open when you click the Screenshot tab, clicking the *Screen Clipping* option will cause the Windows desktop to display.

1. Open **NSSLtrhd.docx** and save it with Save As and name it **WL1-C5-P5-NSSCoverPages**.
2. Type the text **Sample Cover Pages** and then press the Enter key twice.
3. Select the text you just typed, change the font to 18-point Copperplate Gothic Bold, and then center the text.
4. Press Ctrl + End to move the insertion point below the text.
5. Open the document named **NSSCoverPg01.docx**.
6. Click the Word button on the Taskbar and then click the thumbnail representing **WL1-C5-P5-NSSCoverPages.docx**.
7. Create and format a screenshot screen clipping by completing the following steps:

   a. Click the Insert tab.
   b. Click the Screenshot button in the Illustrations group and then click *Screen Clipping*.
   c. When the **NSSCoverPg01.docx** displays in a dimmed manner, position the mouse crosshairs in the upper left corner of the cover page, hold down the left mouse button, drag down to the lower right corner of the cover page, and then release the mouse button. (See image at the right.)

   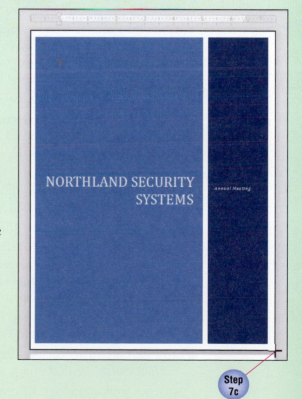

   d. With the cover page screenshot image inserted in **WL1-C5-P5-NSSCoverPages.docx**, make sure the image is selected (sizing handles display around the cover page image).
   e. Click the Wrap Text button in the Arrange group in the Picture Tools Format tab and then click *Square* at the drop-down gallery.
   f. Select the current measurement in the *Shape Width* measurement box in the Size group, type 3, and then press Enter.
8. Click the Word button on the Taskbar and then click the thumbnail representing **NSSCoverPg01.docx** and then close the document.
9. Open **NSSCoverPg02.docx**.
10. Click the Word button on the Taskbar and then click the thumbnail representing **WL1-C5-P5-NSSCoverPages.docx**.
11. Create and format a screenshot by completing steps similar to those in Step 7.
12. Position the two cover page screenshot images so they are side by side in the document.
13. Save, print, and then close **WL1-C5-P5-NSSCoverPages.docx**.
14. Close **NSSCoverPg02.docx**.

Chapter Summary

- Insert a section break in a document to apply formatting to a portion of a document. You can insert a continuous section break or a section break that begins a new page. View a section break in Draft view since section breaks are not visible in Print Layout view.

- Set text in columns to improve readability of documents such as newsletters or reports. Format text in columns using the Columns button in the Page Setup group in the Page Layout tab or with options at the Columns dialog box.

- Remove column formatting with the Columns button in the Page Layout tab or at the Columns dialog box. Balance column text on the last page of a document by inserting a continuous section break at the end of the text.

- Improve the display of text lines by hyphenating long words that fall at the end of the line. You can automatically or manually hyphenate words in a document.

- To enhance the appearance of text, use drop caps to identify the beginning of major sections or parts of a paragraph. Create drop caps with the Drop Cap button in the Text group in the Insert tab.

- Insert symbols with options at the Symbol dialog box with the Symbols tab selected and insert special characters with options at the Symbol dialog box with the Special Characters tab selected.

- Click the Date & Time button in the Text group in the Insert tab to display the Date and Time dialog box. Insert the date or time with options at this dialog box or with keyboard shortcuts. If the date or time is inserted as a field, update the field with the Update Field key, F9.

- Use the click and type feature to center, right-align, and left-align text.

- Vertically align text in a document with the *Vertical alignment* option at the Page Setup dialog box with the Layout tab selected.

- Insert an image such as a picture or clip art with buttons in the Illustrations group in the Insert tab.

- Customize and format an image with options and buttons in the Picture Tools Format tab. Size an image with the *Shape Height* and *Shape Width* measurement boxes in the Size group in the Picture Tools Format tab or with the sizing handles that display around the selected image.

- Move an image with options from the Position button drop-down gallery located in the Picture Tools Format tab or by choosing a text wrapping style and then moving the image by dragging it with the mouse.

- To insert a picture, click the Insert tab, click the Picture button, navigate to the desired folder at the Insert Picture dialog box, and then double-click the picture.

- To insert a clip art image, click the Insert tab, click the Clip Art button, and then click the desired image in the Clip Art task pane.

- Insert a pull quote in a document with a built-in text box by clicking the Insert tab, clicking the Text Box button, and then clicking the desired built-in text box at the drop-down list.

- Draw shapes in a document by clicking the Shapes button in the Illustrations group in the Insert tab, clicking the desired shape at the drop-down list, and then dragging in the document to draw the shape. Customize a shape with options at the Drawing Tools Format tab. Copy a shape by holding down the Ctrl key while dragging the selected shape.

- Draw a text box by clicking the Text Box button in the Text group in the Insert tab, clicking *Draw Text Box* at the drop-down list, and then clicking in the document or dragging in the document. Customize a text box with buttons at the Drawing Tools Format tab.

- Use WordArt to distort or modify text to conform to a variety of shapes. Customize WordArt with options at the Drawing Tools Format tab.

- Use the Screenshot button in the Illustrations group in the Home tab to capture the contents of a screen or capture a portion of a screen.

- Use buttons in the Picture Tools Format tab to customize a screenshot image.

Commands Review

FEATURE	RIBBON TAB, GROUP	BUTTON, OPTION	KEYBOARD SHORTCUT
Continuous section break	Page Layout, Page Setup	, Continuous	
Columns dialog box	Page Layout, Page Setup	, More Columns	
Columns	Page Layout, Page Setup		
Hyphenate words automatically	Page Layout, Page Setup	, Automatic	
Manual Hyphenation dialog box	Page Layout, Page Setup	, Manual	
Drop cap	Insert, Text		
Symbol dialog box	Insert, Symbols		
Date and Time dialog box	Insert, Text		
Insert date			Alt + Shift + D
Insert time			Alt + Shift + T
Update field			F9
Page Setup dialog box	Page Layout, Page Setup		
Insert Picture dialog box	Insert, Illustrations		
Clip Art task pane	Insert, Illustrations		
Pull quote (Built-in text box)	Insert, Text		

FEATURE	RIBBON TAB, GROUP	BUTTON, OPTION	KEYBOARD SHORTCUT
Shapes	Insert, Illustrations		
Text box	Insert, Text		
WordArt	Insert, Text		
Screenshot	Insert, Illustrations		

Concepts Check Test Your Knowledge

Completion: In the space provided at the right, indicate the correct term, symbol, or command.

1. View a section break in this view. _____

2. Format text into columns with the Columns button located in this group in the Page Layout tab. _____

3. Balance column text on the last page of a document by inserting this type of break at the end of the text. _____

4. The first letter of the first word of a paragraph that is set into a paragraph is called this. _____

5. The Symbol button is located in this tab. _____

6. This is the keyboard shortcut to insert the current date. _____

7. Use this feature to position the insertion point at a specific location and alignment in a document. _____

8. Vertically align text with the *Vertical alignment* option at the Page Setup dialog box with this tab selected. _____

9. Insert an image in a document with buttons in this group in the Insert tab. _____

10. Customize and format an image with options and buttons in this tab. _____

11. Size an image with the sizing handles that display around the selected image or with these measurement boxes in the Picture Tools Format tab. _____

12. Click the Picture button in the Insert tab and this dialog box displays. _____

13. Click the Clip Art button in the Insert tab and this displays at the right side of the screen. _____

14. This is the term for a quote that is enlarged and positioned in an attractive location on the page. _____

15. Apply predesigned styles to a text box with options in this group. _____

16. The Shapes button is located in this tab. _____

17. To copy a selected shape, hold down this key while dragging the shape. _____

18. Use this feature to distort or modify text to conform to a variety of shapes. _____

19. To capture a portion of a screen, click the Screenshot button in the Illustrations group in the Insert tab and then click this option at the drop-down list. _____

Skills Check Assess Your Performance

Assessment

1 ### ADD VISUAL APPEAL TO A REPORT ON THE FUTURE OF THE INTERNET

1. Open **Internet2.docx** and then save the document with Save As and name it **WL1-C5-A1-Internet2**.
2. Apply the Heading 1 style to the title of the report and apply the Heading 3 style to the headings in the report. *Hint: You may need to click the Heading 2 style to display the Heading 3 style.*
3. Change the Quick Styles set to *Thatch* and then center the title.
4. Apply the Elemental theme and then change the theme colors to *Solstice*.
5. Format the text from the first paragraph to the end of the document into two columns with 0.4 inches between columns.
6. Balance the text on the second page.
7. Insert a clip art image related to *satellite*. (Choose the clip art image that is available with Word and does not require downloading. This clip art image is blue and black and contains a satellite and a person holding a telephone and a briefcase.)
8. Make the following customizations to the clip art image:
   a. Change the height to 1.2".
   b. Apply tight text wrapping.
   c. Change the color of the clip art image to *Aqua, Accent color 1 Light*.
   d. Correct the contrast to Brightness: *0% (Normal) Contrast: –20%*.
   e. Drag the image so it is positioned at the left margin in the *Satellite Internet Connections* section.

9. Insert the *Alphabet Quote* built-in text box and then make the following customizations:
   a. Type the following text in the text box: "A remedy for the traffic clogging the information highway is Internet2."
   b. Select the text and then change the font size to 12 and change the line spacing to 1.15.
   c. Apply the Subtle Effect - Aqua, Accent 1 style to the text box (second option from the left in the fourth row).
   d. Apply the Offset Bottom shadow effect to the text box.
   e. Drag the box so it is positioned above the SATELLITE INTERNET CONNECTIONS heading in the first column, below the SECOND INTERNET heading in the second column, and centered between the left and right margins.
10. Press Ctrl + End to move the insertion point to the end of the document. (The insertion point will be positioned below the continuous section break you inserted on the second page to balance the columns of text.)
11. Change back to one column.
12. Press the Enter key twice and then draw a shape using the *Plaque* shape (located in the second row in the *Basic Shapes* section) and make the following customizations:
   a. Recolor the shape to match the color formatting in the document or the built-in text box.
   b. Position the shape centered between the left and right margins.
   c. Make any other changes to enhance the visual appeal of the shape.
   d. Type the following text inside the shape: ☙ Felicité Compagnie ❧. Insert the ☙ and ❧ symbols at the Symbol dialog box with the Wingdings font selected. Insert the é symbol at the Symbol dialog box with the *(normal text)* font selected.
   e. Insert the current date below ☙ *Felicité Compagnie* ❧ and insert the current time below the date.
13. Manually hyphenate the document (do not hyphenate headings or proper names).
14. Create a drop cap with the first letter of the word *The* that begins the first paragraph of text.
15. Save, print, and then close **WL1-C5-A1-Internet2.docx**.

Assessment

2 CREATE A SALES MEETING ANNOUNCEMENT

1. Create an announcement about an upcoming sales meeting with the following specifications:
   a. Insert the company name *Inlet Corporation* as WordArt text.
   b. Insert the following text in the document:
      National Sales Meeting
      Northwest Division
      Ocean View Resort
      August 20 through August 22, 2012
   c. Insert the picture named **Ocean.jpg** and size and position the picture behind the text.
   d. Make any formatting changes to the WordArt, text, and picture to enhance the visual appeal of the document.
2. Save the announcement document and name it **WL1-C5-A2-SalesMtg**.
3. Print and then close **WL1-C5-A2-SalesMtg.docx**.

Assessment

3 CREATE AN ANNOUNCEMENT

1. At a blank document, create the announcement shown in Figure 5.8. Insert the caduceus clip art image as shown in the figure with the following specifications:
   a. Use the word *medicine* to locate the clip art image.
   b. Change the text wrapping to *Tight*.
   c. Change the clip art image color to *Blue, Accent color 1 Dark*.
   d. Correct the brightness and contrast to *Brightness: +20% Contrast: –20%*.
   e. Size and move the clip art image as shown in the figure.
2. Apply character (set the heading in 28-point Candara and the remaining text in 14-point Candara), paragraph, and page formatting so your document appears the same as the document in Figure 5.8.
3. Save the completed announcement and name it **WL1-C5-A3-FirstAidCourse**.
4. Print and then close **WL1-C5-A3-FirstAidCourse.docx**. (If some of the page border does not print, consider increasing the measurements at the Border and Shading Options dialog box.)

Figure 5.8 Assessment 3

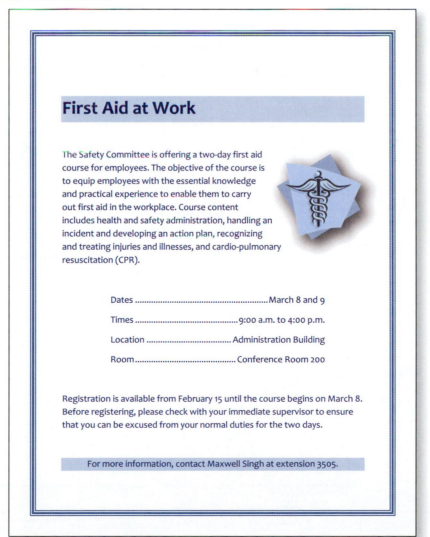

Assessment

4 INSERT SCREENSHOTS IN A MEMO

1. Open **FirstAidMemo.docx** and then save it with Save As and name it **WL1-C5-A4-FirstAidMemo**.
2. Insert screenshots so your document appears as shown in Figure 5.9. (Insert your initials in place of the XX located toward the end of the document.) Use the **FirstAidAnnounce.docx** document located in your Word2010L1C5 folder to create the first screenshot and use the document **WL1-C5-A3-FirstAidCourse.docx** you created in Assessment 3 for the second screenshot. *Hint: Decrease the size of the document so the entire document is visible on the screen*.
3. Save, print, and close **WL1-C5-A4-FirstAidMemo.docx**.

Figure 5.9 Assessment 4

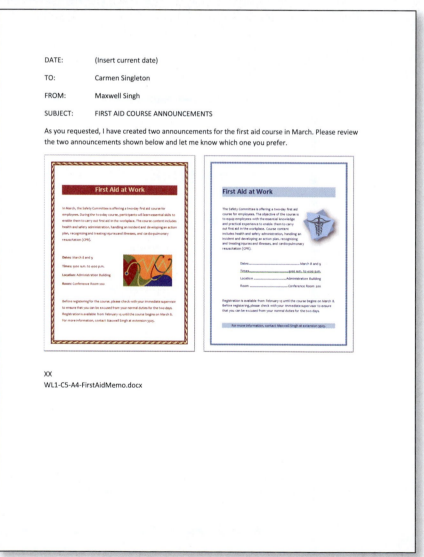

Visual Benchmark Demonstrate Your Proficiency

1 CREATE A SHAPE

1. At a blank document create the document shown in Figure 5.10 with the following specifications:
   a. Draw the shape using the *Quad Arrow Callout* located in the *Block Arrows* section.
   b. Apply the *Subtle Effect – Olive Green, Accent 3* shape style to the shape.
   c. Change the shape effect to *Soft Round* bevel.
   d. Change the height and width of the shape to 5 inches.
   e. Type the text in the shape as shown and set the text in 16-point Copperplate Gothic Bold and change the text color to dark green.
   f. Insert the truck clip art image and size and position it as shown in Figure 5.10. (If this truck clip art image is not available, choose another truck clip art image. Change the text wrap to *In Front of Text*.)
2. Center the shape on the page.
3. Save the document and name it **WL1-C5-VB1-FourCorners**.
4. Print and then close the document.

Figure 5.10 Visual Benchmark 1

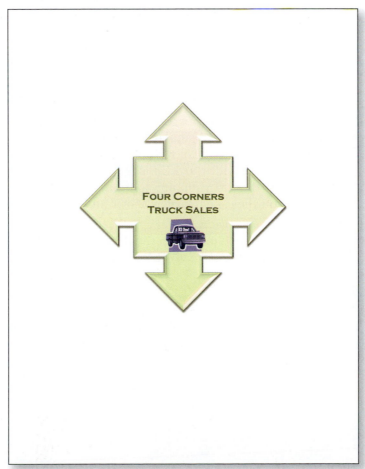

2 FORMAT A REPORT

1. Open **Resume.docx** and then save it with Save As and name it
   WL1-C5-VB2-Resume.
2. Format the report so it appears as shown in Figure 5.11 with the following
   specifications:
   a. Insert the WordArt text *Résumé Writing* with the following specifications:
      - Use the *Gradient Fill – Blue, Accent 1* option (fourth option from the left
        in the third row).
      - Type the text **Résumé Writing** and insert the é symbol using the Insert
        Symbol dialog box.
      - Change the position to *Position in Top Center with Square Text Wrapping*
        (middle option in the top row of the *With Text Wrapping* section).
      - Change the width of the WordArt to 5.5 inches and the height to 0.9 inch.
      - Apply the *Can Up* transform text effect. **Hint: Use the Transform option
        from the Text Effects button drop-down list**.
   b. Apply the Heading 3 style to the two headings in the report.
   c. Change the Quick Styles set to *Modern*.
   d. Change the theme to *Aspect* and change the theme colors to *Flow*.
   e. Format the report into two columns beginning with the first paragraph of
      text and balance the columns on the second page.
   f. Insert the pull quote with the following specifications:
      - Use the *Austere Quote*.
      - Type the text shown in the pull quote in Figure 5.11. (Use the Insert
        Symbol dialog box to insert the two é symbols in the word résumé.)
      - Change the pull quote text color to dark blue.
      - Select the text box (make sure the border displays as a solid line), make
        the Drawing Tools Format tab active, and then change the shape outline
        color to blue.
   g. Insert the cake clip art image with the following specifications:
      - Insert the clip art image shown in the figure. If this image is not
        available, choose a similar image of a cake.
      - Change the image color to *Blue, Accent color 1 Light*.
      - Change the width to 1.2 inches.
      - Change the text wrapping to *Tight*.
      - Position the cake image as shown in Figure 5.11.
   h. Insert the *Conservative* footer.
   i. Manually hyphenate text in the document.
3. Save, print, and then close **WL1-C5-VB2-Resume.docx**.

Figure 5.11 Visual Benchmark 2

winning résumé. It will be a useful list of tasks and achievements.

Writing a résumé is like baking a cake. You need all the right ingredients: flour, butter, eggs, and so on. It is what you do with the ingredients that makes the difference between a great résumé (or cake) and failure. Keeping your résumé up-to-date is like keeping a stock of ingredients in the pantry—it's potentially very useful, but do not imagine that is the end of it!

INFORMATION ABOUT THE JOB

You should tailor the information in your résumé to the main points in the job advertisement. Get as much information about the job and the company as you can. The main sources of information about a job are normally the following:

- A job advertisement
- A job description
- A friend in the company
- The media
- Gossip and rumor
- Someone already doing the job or something similar

There is no substitute for experience. Talking to someone who does a job similar to the one you wish to apply for in the same company may well provide you with a good picture of what the job is really like. Bear in mind, of course, that this source of information is not always reliable. You may react differently than the way that person does, and therefore their experience with a company may be very different from yours. However, someone with reliable information can provide a golden opportunity. Make sure you do not waste the chance to get some information.

Résumé Writing

To produce the best "fitting" résumé, you need to know about yourself and you need to know about the job you are applying for. Before you do anything else, ask yourself why you are preparing a résumé. The answer to this question is going to vary from one person to the next, and here are our top ten reasons for writing a résumé:

1. You have seen a job advertised in the paper that appeals to you.
2. You want to market yourself to win a contract or a proposal, or be elected to a committee or organization.
3. You have seen a job on an Internet job site that appeals to you.
4. Your friends or family told you of a job opening at a local company.
5. You want to work for the local company and thought that sending a résumé to them might get their attention.
6. You have seen a job advertised internally at work.
7. You are going for a promotion.
8. You are feeling fed up and writing down all your achievements will cheer you up and might motivate you to look for a better job.
9. You are thinking "Oh, so that's a résumé! I suppose I ought to try to remember what I've been doing with my life."
10. You are about to be downsized and want to update your résumé to be ready for any good opportunities.

All of these certainly are good reasons to write a résumé, but the résumé serves many different purposes. One way of seeing the differences is to ask yourself who is going to read the résumé in each case.

Résumés 1 through 5 will be read by potential employers who probably do not know you. Résumés 6 and 7 are likely to be read by your boss or other people who know you. Résumés 8 through 10 are really for your own benefit and should not be considered as suitable for sending out to employers.

> *"Updating your résumé from time to time is a good idea so you do not forget important details..."*

THE RIGHT MIX

Think about the list of reasons again. How else can you divide up these reasons? An important difference is that, in some cases, you will have a good idea of what the employer is looking for because you have a job advertisement in front of you and can tailor your résumé accordingly. For others, you have no idea what the reader might want to see. Updating your résumé from time to time is a good idea so you do not forget important details, but remember that the result of such a process will not be a

Case Study Apply Your Skills

Part 1

You work for Honoré Financial Services and have been asked by the office manager, Jason Monroe, to prepare an information newsletter. Mr. Monroe has asked you to open the document named **Budget.docx** and then format it into columns. You determine the number of columns and any additional enhancements to the columns. He also wants you to proofread the document and correct any spelling and grammatical errors. Save the completed newsletter and name it **WL1-C5-CS-Budget** and then print the newsletter. When Mr. Monroe reviews the newsletter, he decides that it needs additional visual appeal. He wants you to insert visual elements in the newsletter such as WordArt, clip art, a built-in text box, and/or a drop cap. Save **WL1-C5-CS-Budget.docx** and then print and close the document.

Part 2

Honoré Financial Services will be offering a free workshop on Planning for Financial Success. Mr. Monroe has asked you to prepare an announcement containing information on the workshop. You determine what to include in the announcement such as the date, time, location, and so forth. Enhance the announcement by inserting a picture or clip art and by applying formatting such as font, paragraph alignment, and borders. Save the completed document and name it **WL1-C5-CS-Announce**. Print and then close the document.

Part 3

Honoré Financial Services has adopted a new slogan and Mr. Monroe has asked you to create a shape with the new slogan inside. Experiment with the shadow and 3-D shape effects available at the Drawing Tools Format tab and then create a shape and enhance the shape with shadow and/or 3-D effects. Insert the new Honoré Financial Services slogan "Retirement Planning Made Easy" in the shape. Include any additional enhancements to improve the visual appeal of the shape and slogan. Save the completed document and name it **WL1-C5-CS-Slogan**. Print and then close the document.

Part 4

Mr. Monroe has asked you to prepare a document containing information on teaching children how to budget. Use the Internet to find websites and articles that provide information on how to teach children to budget their money. Write a synopsis of the information you find and include at least four suggestions on how to teach children to manage their money. Format the text in the document into newspaper columns. Add additional enhancements to improve the appearance of the document. Save the completed document and name it **WL1-C5-CS-ChildBudget**. Print and then close the document.

Word

Microsoft®

Maintaining Documents

PERFORMANCE OBJECTIVES

Upon successful completion of Chapter 6, you will be able to:

- Create and rename a folder
- Select, delete, copy, move, rename, and print documents
- Save documents in different file formats
- Open, close, arrange, split, maximize, minimize, and restore documents
- Insert a file into an open document
- Print specific pages and sections in a document
- Print multiple copies of a document
- Print envelopes and labels
- Create a document using a Word template

SNAP
Training and Assessment.
Simplified.

Tutorials

6.1 Managing Documents
6.2 Managing Folders
6.3 Saving a Document as a Web Page
6.4 Sharing Documents
6.5 Working with Windows
6.6 Creating and Printing Envelopes
6.7 Creating and Printing Labels
6.8 Creating Documents Using a Word Template

Almost every company that conducts business maintains a filing system. The system may consist of documents, folders, and cabinets; or it may be a computerized filing system where information is stored on the computer's hard drive or other storage medium. Whatever type of filing system a business uses, daily maintenance of files is important to a company's operation. In this chapter, you will learn to maintain files (documents) in Word, including such activities as creating additional folders and copying, moving, and renaming documents. You will also learn how to create and print documents, envelopes, and labels and create a document using a Word template. Model answers for this chapter's projects appear on the following pages.

Word

Word2010L1C6

Note: Before beginning the projects, copy to your storage medium the Word2010L1C6 subfolder from the Word2010L1 folder on the CD that accompanies this textbook and then make Word2010L1C6 the active folder.

Project 1 Manage Documents

COMPUTER KEYBOARDS

To give commands to a computer or to enter data into it, a user needs an input device. An input device can be built into the computer, like the keyboard in a laptop, or it can be connected to the computer by a cable. Some input devices, like remote keyboards, send directions to the computer by means of an infrared signal and use no cabling at all.

QWERTY Keyboard

Keyboards can be external devices that are attached by means of a cable, or they can be attached to the CPU case itself as they are in laptops. Most keyboards today are QWERTY keyboards, which take their name from the first six keys at the left of the first row of letters. The QWERTY design was invented in the early days of mechanical typewriters to slow down typists and thus keep keys from jamming.

DVORAK Keyboard

The DVORAK keyboard is an alternative to the QWERTY keyboard. On the DVORAK keyboard, the most commonly used keys are placed close to the user's fingertips and this increases typing speed. You can install software on a QWERTY keyboard that emulates a DVORAK keyboard. The ability to emulate other keyboards is convenient especially when working with foreign languages. Keyboards have different physical appearances. Many keyboards have a separate numeric keypad, like that of a calculator, containing numbers and mathematical operators. Some keyboards are sloped and "broken" into two pieces to reduce strain. All keyboards have modifier keys that enable the user to change the symbol or characters entered when a given key is pressed.

WL1-C6-P1-CompKeyboards.docx

APARTMENT LEASE AGREEMENT

This Apartment Lease Agreement (hereinafter referred to as the "Agreement") is made and entered into this 30th day of September, 2012, by and between Monica Spellman, Lessor, and Jack Lowell, Lessee.

Term
Lessor leases to Lessee the described premises together with any and all appurtenances thereto, for a term of 1 year, such term beginning on October 1, 2012, and ending at 12 o'clock midnight on September 30, 2013.

Rent
The total rent for the term hereof is the sum of one thousand five hundred dollars ($1,500) payable on the 5th day of each month of the term. All such payments shall be made to Lessor on or before the due date and without demand.

Damage Deposit
Upon the due execution of this Agreement, Lessee shall deposit with Lessor the sum of seven hundred dollars ($700), receipt of which is hereby acknowledged by Lessor, as security for any damage caused to the Premises during the term hereof. Such deposit shall be returned to Lessee, without interest, and less any set off for damages to the Premises upon the termination of this Agreement.

Use of Premises
The Premises shall be used and occupied by Lessee and Lessee's immediate family, exclusively, as a private single family dwelling, and no part of the Premises shall be used at any time during the term of this Agreement by Lessee for the purpose of carrying on any business, profession, or trade of any kind, or for any purpose other than as a private single family dwelling. Lessee shall not allow any other person, other than Lessee's immediate family or transient relatives and friends who are guests, to use or occupy the Premises without first obtaining written consent to such use.

WL1-C6-P1-AptLease-PlainTxt.txt

WL1-C6-P1-AptLease-RichText.rtf

Project 2 Manage Multiple Documents

SECTION 1: COMPUTERS IN ENTERTAINMENT

Possibilities in the television and film industries have soared with computer technology, especially in production. Computer games have captured the public imagination and created an enormous growth in the computer game market.

TELEVISION AND FILM

Many of the spectacular graphics and special effects on television and in movies today are created with computers. The original *Star Wars* films, for example, relied heavily on hand-constructed models and hand-drawn graphics. Twenty years after the original release of the films, they were re-released with many new special effects, including futuristic cityscape backgrounds, new alien creatures, and new sounds that were created on computers and added to the films by means of computerized video editing.

The film *Jurassic Park* brought computer simulation to a new level by combining puppetry and computer animation to simulate realistic looking dinosaurs. *Toy Story*, released in 1996, was the first wholly computer-animated commercial movie. Software products that automatically format scripts of various kinds are commercially available.

HOME ENTERTAINMENT

In the 1970s, computer games such as Pong and Pac-Man captured the public imagination. Since then, there has been enormous growth in the computer game market. Manufacturers such as Sega and Nintendo produce large, complex video arcade games as well as small computer game systems for home use. Typical arcade-style computer games include simulations of boxing, warfare, racing, skiing, and flight.

The advent of powerful desktop personal computers has led to the production of home computer games that rival those of arcade machines in complexity. Other computer games make use of televisions or of small, independent, handheld devices. Games are now able to take advantage of three-dimensional graphics that create virtual environments.

Page 1

WL1-C6-P2-CommIndustry.docx

SECTION 2: COMPUTERS IN COMMUNICATION

Computers have become central to the communications industry. They play a vital role in telecommunications, publishing, and news services.

TELECOMMUNICATIONS

The industry that provides for communication across distances is called telecommunications. The telephone industry uses computers to switch and route calls automatically over telephone lines. Today, many kinds of information move over such lines, including the spoken word, faxes, and computer data. Data can be sent over telephone lines from computer to computer using a device known as a modem. One kind of data sent by modem is electronic mail, or email, which can be sent from person to person via the Internet or an online service. A recent innovation in telecommunications is teleconferencing, which allows people in various locations to see and hear one another and thus hold virtual meetings.

PUBLISHING

Just twenty years ago, a book manuscript had to be typeset mechanically or on a typesetting machine and then reproduced on a printing press. Now anyone who has access to a computer and either a modem or a printer can undertake what has come to be known as electronic publishing. Writers and editors use word processing applications to produce text. Illustrations and photographs are digitized, or turned into computer-readable files, by means of inexpensive scanners. Artists and designers use drawing and painting applications to create original graphics. Typesetters use personal computers to combine text, illustrations, and photographs. Publishers typically send computer-generated files to printers for production of the film and plates from which books and magazines are printed.

NEWS SERVICES

News providers rely on reporters located worldwide. Reporters use email to send, or upload, their stories to wire services. Increasingly, individuals get daily news reports from online services. News can also be accessed from specific providers, such as the *New York Times* or *U.S.A. Today*, via the Internet. One of the most popular Internet sites provides continuously updated weather reports.

Page 2

SECTION 3: COMPUTERS IN EDUCATION

The widespread use of home computers has brought about an increase in the availability of educational and reference software, making the computer a popular learning and reference tool. Examples of educational and reference software include encyclopedias, dictionaries, and learning tutorials.

ENCYCLOPEDIAS AND DICTIONARIES

Almost everyone has used an encyclopedia or dictionary at one time or another. An encyclopedia is a comprehensive reference work containing detailed articles on a broad range of subjects. Before computers, encyclopedias were only available in book form. They are now available electronically and many new PCs include a CD-based encyclopedia.

A standard dictionary is a reference work containing an alphabetical listing of words, with definitions that provide the word's meaning, pronunciation, and usage. Examples include *Webster's Dictionary* and *Webster's New World Dictionary of Computer Terms*. Other specialized dictionaries, such as multi-language dictionaries, contain words along with their equivalent in another language for use in translation. Many dictionaries are available on CD.

LEARNING TUTORIALS

Many people learn skills by using CD- or Internet-based tutorials. A tutorial is a form of instruction in which students are guided step-by-step through the learning process. Tutorials are available for almost any subject, including learning how to assemble a bicycle, use a word processor, or write a letter. Once an electronic tutorial is accessed, students need only follow the instructions displayed on the screen. Many tutorials include graphics to help guide students during the learning process.

Page 3

DAVID LOWRY
12033 S 152 ST
HOUSTON TX 77340

MARCELLA SANTOS
394 APPLE BLOSSOM
FRIENDSWOOD TX 77533

KEVIN DORSEY
26302 PRAIRIE DR
HOUSTON TX 77316

AL AND DONNA SASAKI
1392 PIONEER DR
BAYTOWN TX 77903

JACKIE RHYNER
29039 107 AVE E
HOUSTON TX 77302

MARK AND TINA ELLIS
607 FORD AVE
HOUSTON TX 77307

WENDY STEINBERG
4532 S 52 ST
BOSTON MA 21002-2334

GREGORY LINCOLN
4455 SIXTH AVE
BOSTON MA 21100-4409

Project 3 Create and Print Envelopes

WL1-C6-P3-Env.docx

Project 4 Create Mailing Labels

WL1-C6-P4-Labels.docx

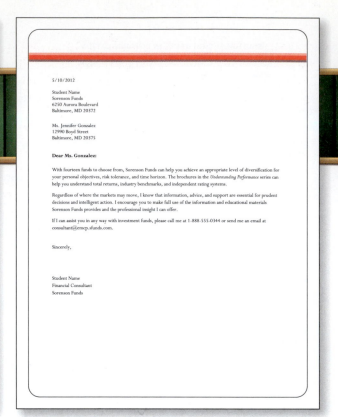

Project 5 Use a Template to Create a Business Letter

WL1-C6-P4-LAProg.docx

WL1-C6-P5-SFunds.docx

Project 1 Manage Documents   8 Parts

You will perform a variety of file management tasks including creating and renaming a folder; selecting and then deleting, copying, cutting, pasting, and renaming documents; deleting a folder; and opening, printing, and closing a document.

Maintaining Documents ▪▪▪▪▪▪▪▪▪▪▪▪▪▪▪▪▪▪▪▪

Many file (document) management tasks can be completed at the Open dialog box (and some at the Save As dialog box). These tasks can include copying, moving, printing, and renaming documents; opening multiple documents; and creating a new folder and renaming a folder.

Using Print Screen

Keyboards contain a Print Screen key that you can use to capture the contents of the screen into a file. That file can then be inserted in a Word document. The Print Screen feature is useful for file management in that you can print folder contents to help you keep track of documents and folders. To use the Print Screen key, display the desired information on the screen and then press the Print Screen key on your keyboard (generally located in the top row). When you press the Print Screen key, nothing seems to happen but, in fact, the screen image is captured in a file that is inserted in the Clipboard. To insert this file in a document, display a blank document and then click the Paste button in the Clipboard group in the Home tab. You can also paste the file by right-clicking in a blank location in a document screen and then clicking the *Paste* option at the shortcut menu.

Creating a Folder

Word documents, like paper documents, should be grouped logically and placed in *folders*. The main folder on a storage medium is called the ***root folder*** and you can create additional folders within the root folder. At the Open or Save As dialog box, documents display in the Content pane preceded by a document icon and folders are preceded by a folder icon. Create a new folder by clicking the New folder button located on the dialog box toolbar. This inserts a folder in the Content pane that contains the text *New folder*. Type a name for the folder (the name you type replaces *New folder*) and then press Enter. A folder name can contain a maximum of 255 characters. Numbers, spaces, and symbols can be used in the folder name, except those symbols explained in Chapter 1 in the "Naming a Document" section.

To make the new folder active, double-click the folder name in the Open dialog box Content pane. The current folder path displays in the Address bar in the Open dialog box. The path includes the current folder as well as any previous folders. If the folder is located in an external storage device, the drive letter and name may display in the path. For example, if you create a folder named *Correspondence* in the Word2010L1C6 folder on your storage medium, the Address bar will display *Word2010L1C6* followed by a right-pointing triangle and then *Correspondence*. Two left-pointing arrows display before *Word2010L1C6*. These arrows indicate that *Word2010L1C6* is a subfolder within a folder. Click the two left-pointing arrows and a drop-down list displays with the folder name or drive letter that is up one level from *Word2010L1C6*. The drop-down list also includes other common folders and locations.

▼ **Quick Steps**

Create a Folder
1. Display Open dialog box.
2. Click New folder button.
3. Type folder name.
4. Press Enter.

New Folder

Back

Project 1a   **Creating a Folder**   Part 1 of 8

1. Display the Open dialog box.
2. In the *Computer* list box in the Navigation pane, click the drive containing your storage medium. (You may need to scroll down the list to display the drive.)
3. Double-click the *Word2010L1C6* folder in the Content pane.
4. Click the New folder button on the dialog box toolbar.
5. Type **Correspondence** and then press Enter.
6. Print the screen contents and insert the file in a document by completing the following steps:
   a. With the Open dialog box displayed, press the Print Screen key on your keyboard (generally located in the top row of your keyboard).

b. Close the Open dialog box.
c. At the blank document, click the Paste button in the Clipboard group in the Home tab. (If a blank document does not display on your screen, press Ctrl + N to open a blank document.)
d. With the print screen file inserted in the document, print the document by clicking the File tab, clicking the Print tab, and then clicking the Print button at the Print tab Backstage view.
7. Close the document without saving it.
8. Display the Open dialog box and make Word2010L1C6 the active folder.

▼ **Quick Steps**

Rename a Folder
1. Display Open dialog box.
2. Right-click folder.
3. Click *Rename*.
4. Type new name.
5. Press Enter.

Organize

Renaming a Folder

As you organize your files and folders, you may decide to rename a folder. Rename a folder using the Organize button on the toolbar in the Open or Save As dialog box or using a shortcut menu. To rename a folder using the Organize button, display the Open or Save As dialog box, click the folder you want to rename, click the Organize button located on the toolbar in the dialog box, and then click *Rename* at the drop-down list. This selects the folder name and inserts a border around the name. Type the new name for the folder and then press Enter. To rename a folder using a shortcut menu, display the Open dialog box, right-click the folder name in the Content pane, and then click *Rename* at the shortcut menu. Type a new name for the folder and then press Enter.

Project 1b   **Renaming a Folder**   **Part 2 of 8**

1. With the Open dialog box open, right-click the *Correspondence* folder name in the Content pane.
2. Click *Rename* at the shortcut menu.
3. Type **Documents** and then press Enter.

Selecting Documents

You can complete document management tasks on one document or selected documents. To select one document, display the Open dialog box, and then click the desired document. To select several adjacent documents (documents that display next to each other), click the first document, hold down the Shift key, and then click the last document. To select documents that are not adjacent, click the first document, hold down the Ctrl key, click any other desired documents, and then release the Ctrl key.

Deleting Documents

At some point, you may want to delete certain documents from your storage medium or any other drive or folder in which you may be working. To delete a document, display the Open or Save As dialog box, select the document, click the Organize button on the toolbar, and then click *Delete* at the drop-down list. At the dialog box asking you to confirm the deletion, click Yes. To delete a document using a shortcut menu, right-click the document name in the Content pane, click *Delete* at the shortcut menu, and then click Yes at the confirmation dialog box.

Documents deleted from the hard drive are automatically sent to the Recycle Bin. If you accidentally send a document to the Recycle Bin, it can be easily restored. To free space on the drive, empty the Recycle Bin on a periodic basis. Restoring a document from or emptying the contents of the Recycle Bin is completed at the Windows desktop (not in Word). To display the Recycle Bin, minimize the Word window, and then double-click the *Recycle Bin* icon located on the Windows desktop. At the Recycle Bin, you can restore file(s) and empty the Recycle Bin.

▼ Quick Steps

Delete Folder/ Document

1. Display Open dialog box.
2. Click folder or document name.
3. Click Organize button.
4. Click *Delete* at drop-down list.
5. Click Yes.

H I N T

Remember to empty the Recycle Bin on a regular basis.

Project 1c **Selecting and Deleting Documents** **Part 3 of 8**

1. Open **FutureHardware.docx** and then save the document with Save As and name it **WL1-C6-P1-FutureHardware**.
2. Close **WL1-C6-P1-FutureHardware.docx**.
3. Delete **WL1-C6-P1-FutureHardware.docx** by completing the following steps:
   a. Display the Open dialog box.
   b. Click *WL1-C6-P1-FutureHardware.docx* to select it.
   c. Click the Organize button on the toolbar and then click *Delete* at the drop-down list.
   d. At the question asking if you want to delete **WL1-C6-P1-FutureHardware.docx**, click Yes.
4. Delete selected documents by completing the following steps:
   a. At the Open dialog box, click *CompCareers.docx*.
   b. Hold down the Shift key and then click *CompEthics.docx*.
   c. Position the mouse pointer on a selected document and then click the right mouse button.
   d. At the shortcut menu that displays, click *Delete*.
   e. At the question asking if you want to delete the items, click Yes.
5. Open **CompKeyboards.docx** and then save the document with Save As and name it **WL1-C6-P1-CompKeyboards**.
6. Save a copy of the **WL1-C6-P1-CompKeyboards.docx** document in the Documents folder by completing the following steps. (If your system does not contain this folder, check with your instructor to determine if another folder is available for you to use.)
   a. With **WL1-C6-P1-CompKeyboards.docx** open, click the File tab and then click the Save As button.

Step 3c

Step 3b

b. At the Save As dialog box, double-click the *Documents* folder located at the beginning of the Content. (Folders are listed before documents.)

c. Click the Save button located in the lower right corner of the dialog box.

7. Close **WL1-C6-P1-CompKeyboards. docx**.

8. Display the Open dialog box and then click *Word2010L1C6* in the Address bar.

Copying and Moving Documents

▼ **Quick Steps**

Copy Documents
1. Display Open dialog box.
2. Right-click document name.
3. Click *Copy*.
4. Navigate to desired folder.
5. Right-click blank area in Content pane.
6. Click *Paste*.

You can copy a document to another folder without opening the document first. To do this, use the *Copy* and *Paste* options from the Organize button drop-down list or the shortcut menu at the Open or Save As dialog box. You can copy a document or selected documents into the same folder. When you do this, Word inserts a hyphen followed by the word *Copy* to the document name. You can copy one document or selected documents into the same folder.

Remove a document from one folder and insert it in another folder using the *Cut* and *Paste* options from the Organize button drop-down list or the shortcut menu at the Open dialog box. To do this with the Organize button, display the Open dialog box, select the desired document, click the Organize button, and then click *Cut* at the drop-down list. Navigate to the desired folder, click the Organize button, and then click *Paste* at the drop-down list. To do this with the shortcut menu, display the Open dialog box, position the arrow pointer on the document to be removed (cut), click the right mouse button, and then click *Cut* at the shortcut menu. Navigate to the desired folder, position the arrow pointer in a blank area in the Content pane, click the right mouse button, and then click *Paste* at the shortcut menu.

Project 1d　**Copying Documents**　　　　　　　　　　　　　　　**Part 4 of 8**

1. At the Open dialog box with Word2010L1C6 the active folder, copy a document to another folder by completing the following steps:
   a. Click **CompTerms.docx** in the Content pane, click the Organize button, and then click *Copy* at the drop-down list.
   b. Navigate to the Documents folder by double-clicking *Documents* at the beginning of the Content pane.
   c. Click the Organize button and then click *Paste* at the drop-down list.
2. Change back to the Word2010L1C6 folder by clicking *Word2010L1C6* in the Address bar.
3. Copy several documents to the Documents folder by completing the following steps:
   a. Click once on ***IntelProp.docx***. (This selects the document.)
   b. Hold down the Ctrl key, click ***Robots.docx***, click ***TechInfo.docx***, and then release the Ctrl key. (You may need to scroll down the Content pane to display the three documents and then select the documents.)
   c. Position the arrow pointer on one of the selected documents, click the right mouse button, and then click *Copy* at the shortcut menu.
   d. Double-click the *Documents* folder.

e. Position the arrow pointer in any blank area in the Content pane, click the right mouse button, and then click *Paste* at the shortcut menu.
4. Click *Word2010L1C6* in the Address bar.
5. Move **CompIssues.docx** to the Documents folder by completing the following steps:
   a. Position the arrow pointer on **CompIssues.docx**, click the right mouse button, and then click *Cut* at the shortcut menu.
   b. Double-click *Documents* to make it the active folder.
   c. Position the arrow pointer in any blank area in the Content pane, click the right mouse button, and then click *Paste* at the shortcut menu.
6. Print the screen contents and insert the file in a document by completing the following steps:
   a. With the Open dialog box displayed, press the Print Screen key on your keyboard.
   b. Close the Open dialog box.
   c. At the blank document, click the Paste button in the Clipboard group in the Home tab. (If a blank document does not display on your screen, press Ctrl + N to open a blank document.)
   d. With the print screen file inserted in the document, print the document by clicking the File tab, clicking the Print tab, and then clicking the Print button at the Print tab Backstage view.
7. Close the document without saving it.
8. Display the Open dialog box and make Word2010L1C6 the active folder.

Renaming Documents

At the Open dialog box, use the *Rename* option from the Organize button drop-down list to give a document a different name. The *Rename* option changes the name of the document and keeps it in the same folder. To use Rename, display the Open dialog box, click once on the document to be renamed, click the Organize button, and then click *Rename* at the drop-down list. This causes a black border to surround the document name and the name to be selected. Type the desired name and then press Enter. You can also rename a document by right-clicking the document name at the Open dialog box and then clicking *Rename* at the shortcut menu. Type the desired name for the document and then press the Enter key.

▼ **Quick Steps**

Rename a Document
1. Display Open dialog box.
2. Click document name.
3. Click Organize button, *Rename*.
4. Type new name.
5. Press Enter.

Deleting a Folder

As you learned earlier in this chapter, you can delete a document or selected documents. Delete a folder and all its contents in the same manner as deleting a document.

Opening Multiple Documents

To open more than one document, select the documents in the Open dialog box, and then click the Open button. You can also open multiple documents by positioning the arrow pointer on one of the selected documents, clicking the right mouse button, and then clicking *Open* at the shortcut menu.

Open a recently opened document by clicking the File tab and then clicking the document in the *Recent Documents* list box.

1. Rename a document located in the Documents folder by completing the following steps:
   a. At the Open dialog box with the Word2010L1C6 folder open, double-click the *Documents* folder to make it active.
   b. Click once on **Robots.docx** to select it.
   c. Click the Organize button.
   d. Click *Rename* at the drop-down list.
   e. Type **Androids** and then press the Enter key.

2. Print the screen contents and insert the file in a document by completing the following steps:
   a. Press the Print Screen key on your keyboard.
   b. Close the Open dialog box.
   c. At the blank document, click the Paste button in the Clipboard group in the Home tab. (If a blank document does not display on your screen, press Ctrl + N to open a blank document.)
   d. With the print screen file inserted in the document, print the document.
3. Close the document without saving it.
4. Display the Open dialog box and make Word2010L1C6 the active folder.
5. At the Open dialog box, click the *Documents* folder to select it.
6. Click the Organize button and then click *Delete* at the drop-down list.
7. At the question asking if you want to remove the folder and its contents, click Yes.
8. Select **CompIndustry.docx**, **CompKeyboards.docx**, and **CompTerms.docx**.
9. Click the Open button located toward the lower right corner of the dialog box.
10. Close the open documents.

Sharing Documents ▪■■■▪■■■▪■■▪■■■▪■■■■▪■

Click the File tab and then click the Save & Send tab and the Save & Send tab Backstage view displays as shown in Figure 6.1. With options at this view, you can share a document by sending it as an email attachment or a fax, save your document as a different file type, and post your document to a special location such as a blog.

Figure 6.1 Save & Send Tab Backstage View

With the *Send Using E-mail* option selected, this section displays options for sending the document as an email attachment, as a PDF or XPS attachment, or as an Internet fax.

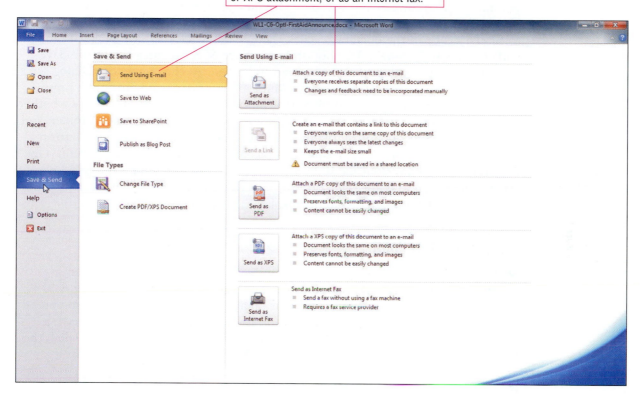

Sending a Document Using Email

When you click the *Send Using E-mail* option in the Save & Send category, options for sending a document display, such as sending a copy of the document as an attachment to an email, creating an email that contains a link to the document, attaching a PDF or XPS copy of the open document to an email, and sending an email as an Internet fax. To send the document as an attachment, you need to set up an Outlook email account. If you want to create an email that contains a link to the document, you need to save the document to a web server. Use the last button, Send as Internet Fax, to fax the current document without using a fax machine. To use this button, you must be signed up with a fax service provider. If you have not previously signed up for a service, you will be prompted to do so.

With the remaining two buttons in the Send Using E-mail category of the Save & Send tab Backstage view, you can send the document in PDF or XPS format. The letters *PDF* stand for *portable document format*, which is a document format developed by Adobe Systems® that captures all of the elements of a document as an electronic image. An XPS document is a Microsoft document format for publishing content in an easily viewable format. The letters *XPS* stand for *XML paper specification* and the letters *XML* stand for *Extensible Markup Language*, which is a set of rules for encoding documents electronically. The options below *Attach a PDF copy of this document to an e-mail* and below *Attach a XPS copy of this document to an e-mail* describe the format and the advantages of sending a document in the PDF or XPS format.

A file's format is indicated by a three- or four-letter extension after the file name.

Saving to SkyDrive

If you want to share documents with others, consider saving documents to SkyDrive, which is a file storage and sharing service that allows you to upload files that can be accessed from a web browser. To save a document to SkyDrive, you need a Windows Live ID account. If you have a Hotmail, Messenger, or Xbox LIVE account, you have a Windows Live ID account. To save a document to SkyDrive, open the document, click the File tab, click the Save & Send tab, and then click the *Save to Web* option in the Save & Send category. In the Save to Windows Live category, click the Sign In button. At the connecting dialog box, type your email address, press the Tab key, type your password, and then press Enter. Once you are connected to your Windows Live ID account, specify whether you want the file saved to your personal folder or saved to your shared folder, and then click the Save As button. At the Save As dialog box, click the Save button or type a new name in the *File name* text box and then click the Save button. One method for accessing your file from SkyDrive is to log into your Windows Live ID account and then look for the SkyDrive hyperlink. Click this hyperlink and your personal and shared folder contents display.

Saving to SharePoint

Microsoft SharePoint is a collection of products and software that includes a number of components. If your company or organization uses SharePoint, you can save a document in a library on your organization's SharePoint site so you and your colleagues have a central location for accessing documents. To save a document to a SharePoint library, open the document, click the File tab, click the Save & Send tab, and then click the *Save to SharePoint* option.

Saving a Document as a Blog Post

You can save a Word document as a blog post with the *Publish as Blog Post* option in the Save & Send tab Backstage view. To save a blog post, you must have a blog site established. Click the *Publish as Blog Post* option and information about supported blog sites displays at the right side of the Save & Send tab Backstage view. To publish a document as a blog post, open the document, click the File tab, click the Save & Send tab, click the *Publish as Blog Post* option in the Save & Send category, and then click the *Publish as Blog Post* option in the Publish as Blog Post category. If you do not have a blog site established, click the Register Now button and then complete the blog registration wizard steps. If you have a blog site established, the document will open in a new window. Type a title for the blog post and then click the Publish button that displays in the Blog group in the Blog Post tab.

Optional Project	Sending a Document as an Email Attachment, Saving to SkyDrive, and Publishing as a Blog Post

Before completing this optional exercise, check with your instructor to determine if you have Outlook set up as your email provider, if you have a Windows Live ID account, and if you have a blog site established for use in the course.

1. Open **FirstAidAnnounce.docx** and then save the document with Save As and name it **WL1-C6-Optl-FirstAidAnnounce**.
2. Send the document as an email attachment by completing the following steps:

a. Click the File tab, click the Save & Send tab, and then make sure the *Send Using E-mail* option is selected.

b. Click the Send as Attachment button in the Send Using E-mail category.

c. At the Outlook window, type your instructor's email address in the *To* text box.

d. Click the Send button.

3. With **WL1-C6-Optl-FirstAidAnnounce.docx** open, save the document to SkyDrive by completing the following steps:

a. Click the File tab, click the Save & Send tab, and then click the *Save to Web* option in the Save & Send category.

b. In the Save to Windows Live category, click the Sign In button.

c. At the connecting dialog box, type your email address, press the Tab key, type your password, and then press Enter.

d. Once you are connected to your Windows Live ID account, specify whether you want the file saved to your personal folder or saved to your shared folder, and then click the Save As button.

e. At the Save As dialog box, click the Save button.

f. Close **WL1-C6-Optl-FirstAidAnnounce.docx**.

4. If you have a blog site established, save the first aid announcement as a blog post by completing the following steps:

a. Open the **WL1-C6-Optl-FirstAidAnnounce.docx** document.

b. Click the File tab, click the Save & Send tab, and then click the *Publish as Blog Post* option in the Save & Send category.

c. Click the Publish as Blog Post button in the Publish as Blog Post category.

d. If you have a blog site established, the document will open in a new window. (If you do not have a blog site established, click the Register Now button and then complete the blog registration wizard steps.) Type a title for the blog post and then click the Publish button that displays in the Blog group in the Blog Post tab.

e. Close the blog post document.

5. Close **WL1-C6-Optl-FirstAidAnnounce.docx**.

Saving a Document in a Different Format

▼ Quick Steps

Save Document in Different Format
1. Click File tab.
2. Click Save & Send tab.
3. Click *Change File Type* option in File Types category.
4. Click desired format in Change File Type category.
5. Click Save As button.

When you save a document, the document is saved automatically as a Word document. If you need to share a document with someone who is using a different word processing program or a different version of Word, you may want to save the document in another format. At the Save & Send tab Backstage view, click the *Change File Type* option in the File Types category and the view displays as shown in Figure 6.2.

With options in the *Document File Types* section, you can choose to save a Word document with the default file format, save the document in a previous version of Word, save the document in the OpenDocument Text format, or save the document as a template. The OpenDocument Text format is an XML-based file format for displaying, storing, and editing files such as word processing, spreadsheet, or presentation files. OpenDocument Text format is free from any licensing, royalty payments, or other restrictions and, since technology changes at a rapid pace, saving a document in the OpenDocument Text format ensures that the information in the file can be accessed, retrieved, and used now and in the future.

Additional file types are available in the *Other File Types* section. If you need to send your document to another user who does not have access to Microsoft Word, consider saving the document in plain text or rich text file format. Use the *Plain Text (*.txt)* option to save the document with all formatting stripped, which is good for universal file exchange. Use the *Rich Text Format (*.rtf)* option to save the

Figure 6.2 Save & Send Tab Backstage View with *Change File Type* Option Selected

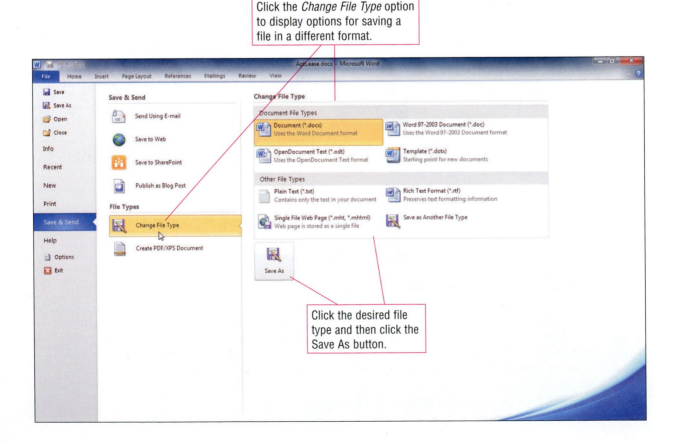

Click the *Change File Type* option to display options for saving a file in a different format.

Click the desired file type and then click the Save As button.

document with most of the character formatting applied to text in the document such as bold, italic, underline, bullets, and fonts as well as some paragraph formatting such as justification. Before the widespread use of Adobe's portable document format (PDF), rich text format was the most portable file format used to exchange files. With the *Single File Web Page (*.mht, *.mhtml)* option, you can save your document as a single page web document. Click the *Save as Another File Type* option and the Save As dialog box displays. Click the *Save as type* option box and a drop-down list displays with a variety of available file type options.

1. Open **AptLease.docx** and then save the document in Word 07-2003 format by completing the following steps:
   a. Click the File tab and then click the Save & Send tab.
   b. At the Save & Send tab Backstage view, click the *Change File Type* option in the File Types category.
   c. Click the *Word 97-2003 Document (*.doc)* option in the *Document File Types* section and then click the Save As button.

   d. At the Save As dialog box with the *Save as type* option changed to *Word 97-2003 Document (*.doc)*, type **WL1-C6-P1-AptLease-Word97-2003** and then press Enter.
2. At the document, notice the title bar displays the words *[Compatibility Mode]* after the document name.
3. Click the Page Layout tab and notice the buttons in the Themes group are dimmed. (This is because the themes features were not available in Word 97 through 2003.)
4. Close **WL1-C6-P1-AptLease-Word97-2003.doc**.
5. Open **AptLease.docx**
6. Save the document in plain text format by completing the following steps:
   a. Click the File tab and then click the Save & Send tab.
   b. At the Save & Send tab Backstage view, click the *Change File Type* option in the File Types category.

c. Click the *Plain Text (*.txt)* option in the *Other File Types* section and then click the Save As button.

d. At the Save As dialog box, type **WL1-C6-P1-AptLease-PlainTxt** and then press Enter.

e. At the File Conversion dialog box, click OK.

7. Close **WL1-C6-P1-AptLease-PlainTxt.txt**.

8. Display the Open dialog box and, if necessary, display all files. To do this, click the file type button at the right side of the *File name* text box and then click *All Files (*.*)* at the drop-down list.

9. Double-click **WL1-C6-P1-AptLease-PlainTxt.txt**. (If a File Conversion dialog box displays, click OK. Notice that the character and paragraph formatting has been removed from the document.)

10. Close **WL1-C6-P1-AptLease-PlainTxt.txt**.

▼ **Quick Steps**

Save Document in Different Format at Save As Dialog Box
1. Open document.
2. Click File tab, click Save As button.
3. Type document name.
4. Click *Save as type* option box.
5. Click desired format at drop-down list.
6. Click Save button.

In addition to options in the Save & Send tab Backstage view with the *Change File Type* option selected, you can save a document in a different format using the *Save as type* option box at the Save As dialog box. Click the *Save as type* option box and a drop-down list displays containing all available file formats for saving a document.

Project 1g **Saving a Document in a Different Format Using the**
Save as type Option Box

Part 7 of 8

1. Open **AptLease.docx**.

2. Save the document in rich text format by completing the following steps:

   a. Click the File tab and then click the Save As button.

   b. At the Save As dialog box, type **WL1-C6-P1-AptLease-RichTxt** in the *File name* text box.

   c. Click in the *Save as type* option box.

   d. Click *Rich Text Format (*.rtf)*.

   e. Click the Save button.

3. Close the document.

4. Display the Open dialog box and, if necessary, display all files.

5. Double-click **WL1-C6-P1-AptLease-RichText.rtf**. (Notice that the formatting was retained in the document.)

6. Close the document.

Saving in PDF/XPS Format

As you learned earlier, the portable document format (PDF) captures all of the elements of a document as an electronic image, and the XPS document format is a format for publishing content in an easily viewable format. To save a document in PDF or XPS format, click the File tab, click the Save & Send tab, click the *Create PDF/XPS Document* option in the File Types category, and then click the Create a PDF/XPS button in the *Create a PDF/XPS Document* section of the Backstage view. This displays the Publish as PDF or XPS dialog box with the *PDF (*.pdf)* option selected in the *Save as type* option box. If you want to save the document in XPS format, click in the *Save as type* option box and then click *XPS Document (*.xps)* at the drop-down list. At the Save As dialog box, type a name in the *File name* text box and then click the Publish button. If you save the document in PDF format, the document opens in Adobe Reader, and if you save the document in XPS format, the document opens in your browser window.

You can open a PDF file in Adobe Reader or in your web browser, and you can open an XPS file in your web browser. To open a PDF file or XPS file in your web browser, click File in the browser Menu bar and then click *Open* at the drop-down list. At the Open dialog box, click the Browse button. At the browser window Open dialog box, change the *Files of type* to *All Files (*.*)*, navigate to the desired folder, and then double-click the document.

Quick Steps

Save Document in PDF/XPS Format
1. Open document.
2. Click File tab.
3. Click Save & Send tab.
4. Click *Create PDF/XPS Document* option.
5. Click Create PDF/XPS button.
6. At Publish as PDF or XPS dialog box, specify if you want to save in PDF or XPS format.
7. Click Publish button.

Project 1h Saving a Document in PDF Format   Part 8 of 8

1. Open **NSS.docx**
2. Save the document in PDF file format by completing the following steps:
   a. Click the File tab and then click the Save & Send tab.
   b. At the Save & Send tab Backstage view, click the *Create PDF/XPS Document* option in the File Types category.
   c. Click the Create PDF/XPS button.

d. At the Publish as PDF or XPS dialog box, make sure *PDF (*.pdf)* is selected in the *Save as type* option box and then click the Publish button.

3. Scroll through the document in Adobe Reader.

4. Click the Close button located in the upper right corner of the window to close Adobe Reader.

5. Close **NSS.docx**.

6. Print the screen contents of the Word2010L1C6 folder by completing the following steps:
   a. Display the Open dialog box with the Word2010L1C6 folder active.
   b. Make sure the Files of type displays as *All Files (*.*)*. (If necessary, scroll down the content pane to display your completed project documents.)
   c. Press the Print Screen key.
   d. Close the Open dialog box.
   e. At a blank document, click the Paste button.
   f. Print the document and then close the document without saving it.

Project 2 Manage Multiple Documents — 6 Parts

You will work with windows by arranging, maximizing, restoring, and minimizing windows; move selected text between split windows; compare formatting of documents side by side; print specific text, pages, and multiple copies; and create and modify document properties.

Working with Windows ■■■■■■■■■■■■■■■■■■■■■■■■

HINT
Press Ctrl + F6 to switch between open documents.

In Word, you can open multiple documents and move the insertion point between the documents. You can also move and copy information between documents or compare the contents of documents. The maximum number of documents that you can have open at one time depends on the memory of your computer system and the amount of data in each document. When you open a new window, it displays on top of any previously opened window(s) that you have closed. Once you have multiple windows open, you can resize the windows to see all or a portion of each on the screen.

HINT
Press Ctrl + W or Ctrl + F4 to close the active document window.

When a document is open, a Word button displays on the Taskbar. Hover the mouse over this button and a thumbnail of the document displays above the button. If you have more than one document open, the Word button on the Taskbar displays another layer in a cascaded manner. The layer behind the Word button displays only a portion of the edge at the right of the button. If you have multiple documents open, hovering the mouse over the Word button on the Taskbar will cause thumbnails of all of the documents to display above the button. To change to the desired document, click the thumbnail that represents the document.

Switch Windows

Another method for determining what documents are open is to click the View tab and then click the Switch Windows button in the Window group. The document name that displays in the list with the check mark in front of it is the *active document*. The active document contains the insertion point. To make one of the other documents active, click the document name. If you are using the keyboard, type the number shown in front of the desired document.

Opening and Arranging Windows

If you open a document, click the View tab, and then click the New Window button in the Window group, Word opens a new window containing the same document. The document name in the Title bar displays followed by *:2*. Changes you make to one document are reflected in the other document.

If you have more than one document open, you can arrange them so a portion of each document displays. The portions that display are the titles (if present) and opening paragraphs of each document. To arrange a group of open documents, click the View tab and then click the Arrange All button in the Window group.

Maximizing, Restoring, and Minimizing Documents

Use the Maximize and Minimize buttons in the active document window to change the size of the window. The Maximize button is the button in the upper right corner of the active document immediately to the left of the Close button. (The Close button is the button containing the *X*.) The Minimize button is located immediately to the left of the Maximize button.

If you arrange all open documents and then click the Maximize button in the active document, the active document expands to fill the document screen. In addition, the Maximize button changes to the Restore button. To return the active document back to its size before it was maximized, click the Restore button. If you click the Minimize button in the active document, the document is reduced and a button displays on the Taskbar representing the document. To maximize a document that has been minimized, click the button on the Taskbar representing the document.

▼ Quick Steps

Open New Window
1. Open document.
2. Click View tab.
3. Click New Window button.

Arrange Windows
1. Open documents.
2. Click View tab.
3. Click Arrange All button.

Arrange All   Maximize

Minimize   Restore

Project 2a **Arranging, Maximizing, Restoring, and Minimizing Windows**   Part 1 of 6

Note: If you are using Word on a network system that contains a virus checker, you may not be able to open multiple documents at once. Continue by opening each document individually.

1. Open the following documents: **AptLease.docx**, **IntelProp.docx**, **NSS.docx**, and **CommIndustry.docx**.
2. Arrange the windows by clicking the View tab and then clicking the Arrange All button in the Window group.
3. Make **IntelProp.docx** the active document by clicking the Switch Windows button in the Window group and then clicking **IntelProp.docx** at the drop-down list.
4. Close **IntelProp.docx**.
5. Make **NSS.docx** active and then close it.
6. Make **CommIndustry.docx** active and minimize it by clicking the Minimize button in the upper right corner of the active window.
7. Maximize **AptLease.docx** by clicking the Maximize button at the right side of the Title bar. (The Maximize button is the button at the right side of the Title bar, immediately left of the Close button.)
8. Close **AptLease.docx**.
9. Restore **CommIndustry.docx** by clicking the button on the Taskbar representing the document.
10. Maximize **CommIndustry.docx**.

Step 6

Step 9

Splitting a Window

You can divide a window into two *panes*, which is helpful if you want to view different parts of the same document at one time. You may want to display an outline for a report in one pane, for example, and the portion of the report that you are editing in the other. The original window is split into two panes that extend horizontally across the screen.

▼ Quick Steps

Split Window
1. Open document.
2. Click View tab.
3. Click Split button.
4. Click in document at desired split point.
OR
Drag split bar.

Split

Split a window by clicking the View tab and then clicking the Split button in the Window group. This causes a wide gray line to display in the middle of the screen and the mouse pointer to display as a double-headed arrow pointing up and down with a small double line between. Move this double-headed arrow pointer up or down, if desired, by dragging the mouse or by pressing the up- and/or down-pointing arrow keys on the keyboard. When the double-headed arrow is positioned at the desired location in the document, click the left mouse button or press the Enter key.

You can also split the window with the split bar. The split bar is the small black horizontal bar above the View Ruler button and up scroll arrow on the vertical scroll bar. To split the window with the split bar, position the arrow pointer on the split bar until it turns into a short double line with an up- and down-pointing arrow. Hold down the left mouse button, drag the double-headed arrow into the document screen to the location where you want the window split, and then release the mouse button. With the window split, you may decide you want to move certain objects or sections of text. Do this by selecting the desired object or text and then dragging and dropping it across the split bar.

When a window is split, the insertion point is positioned in the bottom pane. To move the insertion point to the other pane with the mouse, position the I-beam pointer in the other pane, and then click the left mouse button. To remove the split line from the document, click the View tab and then click the Remove Split button in the Window group. You can also double-click the split bar or drag the split bar to the top or bottom of the screen.

Project 2b **Moving Selected Text between Split Windows** **Part 2 of 6**

1. With **CommIndustry.docx** open, save the document with Save As and name it **WL1-C6-P2-CommIndustry**.
2. Click the View tab and then click the Split button in the Window group.
3. With the split line displayed in the middle of the document screen, click the left mouse button.
4. Move the first section below the second section by completing the following steps:
   a. Click the Home tab.
   b. Select the *SECTION 1: COMPUTERS IN COMMUNICATION* section from the title to right above *SECTION 2: COMPUTERS IN ENTERTAINMENT*.
   c. Click the Cut button in the Clipboard group in the Home tab.
   d. Position the arrow pointer at the end of the document in the bottom window pane and then click the left mouse button.
   e. Click the Paste button in the Clipboard group in the Home tab.

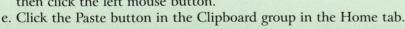

f. Change the number in the two titles to *SECTION 1: COMPUTERS IN ENTERTAINMENT* and *SECTION 2: COMPUTERS IN COMMUNICATION*.

5. Remove the split from the window by clicking the View tab and then clicking the Remove Split button in the Window group.

6. If the Section 2 title displays at the bottom of the first page, move the insertion point to the beginning of the title and then press Ctrl + Enter to insert a page break.

7. Save **WL1-C6-P2-CommIndustry.docx**.

8. Open a new window with the **WL1-C6-P2-CommIndustry.docx** document by clicking the New Window button in the Window group in the View tab. (Notice the document name in the Title bar displays followed by *:2*.)

9. Close the second version of the document by hovering the mouse pointer over the Word button on the Taskbar and then clicking the Close button in the upper right corner of the *WL1-C6-P2-CommIndustry.docx:2* thumbnail (the thumbnail that displays above the Word button on the Taskbar).

Viewing Documents Side by Side

If you want to compare the contents of two documents, open both documents, click the View tab, and then click the View Side by Side button in the Window group. Both documents are arranged in the screen side by side as shown in Figure 6.3. By default synchronous scrolling is active. With this feature active, scrolling in one document causes the same scrolling to occur in the other document. This feature is useful in situations where you want to compare text, formatting, or other features between documents. If you want to scroll in one document and not the other, click the Synchronous Scrolling button in the Window group in the View tab to turn it off.

▼ **Quick Steps**

View Side by Side
1. Open two documents.
2. Click View tab.
3. Click View Side by Side.

View Side
by Side

Figure 6.3 Viewing Documents Side by Side

Use View Side by Side to compare the formatting of two different documents.

1. With **WL1-C6-P2-CommIndustry.docx** open, open **Computers.docx**.
2. Click the View tab and then click the View Side by Side button in the Window group.
3. Scroll through both documents simultaneously. Notice the difference between the two documents. (The title and headings are set in a different font and color.) Select and then format the title and headings in **WL1-C6-P2-CommIndustry.docx** so they match the formatting in **Computers.docx**.
4. Save **WL1-C6-P2-CommIndustry.docx**.
5. Make **Computers.docx** the active document and then close it.

Insert a File
1. Click Insert tab.
2. Click Object button arrow.
3. Click *Text from File.*
4. Navigate to desired folder.
5. Double-click document.

Inserting a File ▪▪▪▪▪▪▪▪▪▪▪▪▪▪▪▪▪▪▪▪▪▪▪

If you want to insert the contents of one document into another, use the Object button in the Text group in the Insert tab. Click the Object button arrow and then click *Text from File* and the Insert File dialog box displays. This dialog box contains similar features as the Open dialog box. Navigate to the desired folder and then double-click the document you want to insert in the open document.

Object

1. With **WL1-C6-P2-CommIndustry.docx** open, move the insertion point to the end of the document.
2. Insert a file into the open document by completing the following steps:
   a. Click the Insert tab.
   b. Click the Object button arrow in the Text group.
   c. Click *Text from File* at the drop-down list.
   d. At the Insert File dialog box, navigate to the Word2010L1C6 folder and then double-click **EduComp.docx**.

3. Check the formatting of the inserted text and format it to match the formatting of the original text.
4. Save **WL1-C6-P2-CommIndustry.docx**.

Printing and Previewing a Document ■■■■■■■■■

With options at the Print tab Backstage view shown in Figure 6.4, you can specify what you want to print and also preview the pages before printing. To display the Print tab Backstage view, click the File tab and then click the Print tab.

Previewing Pages in a Document

When you display the Print tab Backstage view, a preview of the page where the insertion point is positioned displays at the right side (see Figure 6.4). Click the Next Page button (right-pointing arrow), located below and to the left of the page, to view the next page in the document and click the Previous Page button (left-pointing arrow) to display the previous page in the document. Use the Zoom slider bar to increase/decrease the size of the page, and click the Zoom to Page button to fit the page in the viewing area in the Print tab Backstage view.

Zoom to
Page

Figure 6.4 Print Tab Backstage View

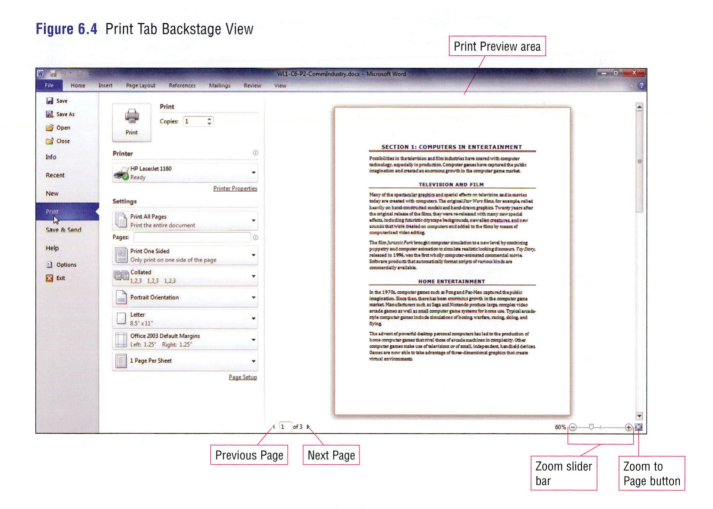

Print Preview area

Previous Page   Next Page

Zoom slider bar   Zoom to Page button

1. With **WL1-C6-P2-CommIndustry.docx** open, press Ctrl + Home to move the insertion point to the beginning of the document.
2. Preview the document by clicking the File tab and then clicking the Print tab.
3. At the Print tab Backstage view, click the Next Page button located below and to the left of the preview page. (This displays page 2 in the preview area.)
4. Click twice on the plus symbol that displays at the right side of the Zoom slider bar. (This increases the size of the preview page.)
5. Click four times on the minus symbol that displays at the left side of the Zoom slider bar. (This displays the two pages of the document in the preview area.)
6. Change the zoom at the Zoom dialog box by completing the following steps:
   a. Click the percentage number that displays at the left side of the Zoom slider bar.
   b. At the Zoom dialog box, click the *Many pages* option in the *Zoom to* section.
   c. Click OK to close the dialog box. (Notice that all pages in the document display as thumbnails in the preview area.)
7. Click the Zoom to Page button that displays at the right side of the Zoom slider bar. (This returns the page to the default size.)
8. Click the File tab to return to the document.

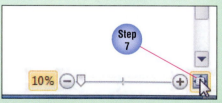

Printing Pages in a Document

Save a document before printing it.

If you want control over what prints in a document, use options at the Print tab Backstage view. Click the first gallery in the Settings category and a drop-down list displays with options for printing all pages in the document, selected text, the current page, or a custom range of pages in the document. If you want to select and then print a portion of the document, choose the *Print Selection* option.

With this option, only the text that you have selected in the current document prints. (This option is dimmed unless text is selected in the document.) Click the *Print Current Page* option to print only the page on which the insertion point is located. With the *Print Custom Range* option, you can identify a specific page, multiple pages, or a range of pages to print. If you want specific pages printed, use a comma (,) to indicate *and* and use a hyphen (-) to indicate *through*. For example, to print pages 2 and 5, you would type **2,5** in the *Pages* text box. To print pages 6 through 10, you would type **6-10**.

With the other galleries available in the Settings category of the Print tab Backstage view, you can specify on what sides of the pages you want to print, change the page orientation (portrait or landscape), specify how you want the pages collated, choose a page size, specify margins, and specify how many pages you want to print on a page.

If you want to print more than one copy of a document, use the *Copies* text box located to the right of the Print button. If you print several copies of a document that has multiple pages, Word collates the pages as they print. For example, if you print two copies of a three-page document, pages 1, 2, and 3 print, and then the pages print a second time. Printing collated pages is helpful for assembly but takes more printing time. To reduce printing time, you can tell Word *not* to print collated pages. To do this, click the Collated gallery in the Settings category and then click *Uncollated*.

If you want to send a document directly to the printer without displaying the Print tab Backstage view, consider adding the Quick Print button to the Quick Access toolbar. To do this click the Customize Quick Access Toolbar button located at the right side of the toolbar and then click *Quick Print* at the drop-down gallery. Click the Quick Print button and all pages of the active document print.

Project 2f   Printing Specific Text and Pages   Part 6 of 6

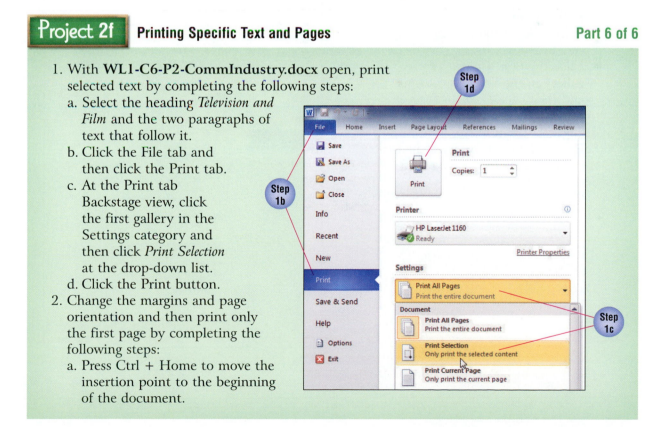

1. With **WL1-C6-P2-CommIndustry.docx** open, print selected text by completing the following steps:
   a. Select the heading *Television and Film* and the two paragraphs of text that follow it.
   b. Click the File tab and then click the Print tab.
   c. At the Print tab Backstage view, click the first gallery in the Settings category and then click *Print Selection* at the drop-down list.
   d. Click the Print button.
2. Change the margins and page orientation and then print only the first page by completing the following steps:
   a. Press Ctrl + Home to move the insertion point to the beginning of the document.

b. Click the File tab and then click the Print tab.

c. At the Print tab Backstage view, click the *Portrait Orientation* gallery in the Settings category and then click *Landscape Orientation* at the drop-down list.

d. Click the *Custom Margins* gallery in the Settings category and then click *Narrow* at the drop-down list.

e. Click the *Print All Pages* gallery in the Settings category and then click *Print Current Page* at the drop-down list.

f. Click the Print button. (The first page of the document prints in landscape orientation with 0.5-inch margins.)

3. Print all of the pages as thumbnails on one page by completing the following steps:

a. Click the File tab and then click the Print tab.

b. At the Print tab Backstage view, click the *1 Page Per Sheet* gallery in the Settings category and then click *4 Pages Per Sheet* at the drop-down list.

c. Click the *Print Current Page* gallery in the Settings category and then click *Print All Pages* at the drop-down list.

d. Click the Print button.

4. Select the entire document, change the line spacing to *1.5*, and then deselect the text.

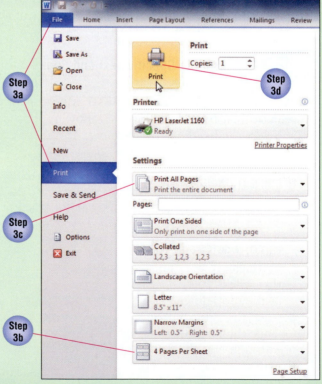

5. Print two copies of specific pages by completing the following steps:
   a. Click the File tab and then click the Print tab.
   b. Click the *Landscape Orientation* gallery in the Settings category and then click *Portrait Orientation* in the drop-down list.
   c. Click in the *Pages* text box located below the *Print Custom Range* gallery in the Settings category and then type 1,3.
   d. Click the up-pointing arrow at the right side of the *Copies* text box (located to the right of the Print button) to display *2*.
   e. Click the *Collated* gallery in the Settings category and then click *Uncollated* at the drop-down list.
   f. Click the *4 Pages Per Sheet* gallery in the Settings category and then click *1 Page Per Sheet* at the drop-down list.
   g. Click the Print button. (The first page of the document will print twice and then the third page will print twice.)
6. Save and then close **WL1-C6-P2-CommIndustry.docx**.

Project 3 — Create and Print Envelopes   2 Parts

You will create an envelope document and type the return address and delivery address using envelope addressing guidelines issued by the United States Postal Service. You will also open a letter document and then create an envelope using the inside address.

Creating and Printing Envelopes ■■■■■■■■■■■■■■■

Word automates the creation of envelopes with options at the Envelopes and Labels dialog box with the Envelopes tab selected as shown in Figure 6.5. Display this dialog box by clicking the Mailings tab and then clicking the Envelopes button in the Create group. At the dialog box, type the delivery address in the *Delivery address* text box and the return address in the *Return address* text box. You can send the envelope directly to the printer by clicking the Print button or insert the envelope in the current document by clicking the Add to Document button.

Envelopes

Figure 6.5 Envelopes and Labels Dialog Box with Envelopes Tab Selected

Type the delivery name and address in this text box.

Type the return name and address in this text box.

▼ **Quick Steps**

Create Envelope
1. Click Mailings tab.
2. Click Envelopes button.
3. Type delivery address.
4. Click in *Return address* text box.
5. Type return address.
6. Click Add to Document button or Print button.

If you enter a return address before printing the envelope, Word will display the question *Do you want to save the new return address as the default return address?* At this question, click Yes if you want the current return address available for future envelopes. Click No if you do not want the current return address used as the default. If a default return address displays in the *Return address* section of the dialog box, you can tell Word to omit the return address when printing the envelope. To do this, click the *Omit* check box to insert a check mark.

The Envelopes and Labels dialog box contains a *Preview* sample box and a *Feed* sample box. The *Preview* sample box shows how the envelope will appear when printed and the *Feed* sample box shows how the envelope should be inserted into the printer.

When addressing envelopes, consider following general guidelines issued by the United States Postal Service (USPS). The USPS guidelines suggest using all capital letters with no commas or periods for return and delivery addresses. Figure 6.6 shows envelope addresses following the USPS guidelines. Use abbreviations for street suffixes (such as *ST* for *Street* and *AVE* for *Avenue*). For a complete list of address abbreviations, visit the www.emcp.net/usps site and then search for *Official USPS Abbreviations*.

Project 3a   **Printing an Envelope**   **Part 1 of 2**

1. At a blank document, create an envelope that prints the delivery address and return address shown in Figure 6.6. Begin by clicking the Mailings tab.
2. Click the Envelopes button in the Create group.
3. At the Envelopes and Labels dialog box with the Envelopes tab selected, type the delivery address shown in Figure 6.6 (the one containing the name *GREGORY LINCOLN*). (Press the Enter key to end each line in the name and address.)
4. Click in the *Return address* text box. (If any text displays in the *Return address* text box, select and then delete it.)

5. Type the return address shown in Figure 6.6 (the one containing the name *WENDY STEINBERG*). (Press the Enter key to end each line in the name and address.)
6. Click the Add to Document button.
7. At the message *Do you want to save the new return address as the default return address?*, click No.
8. Save the document and name it **WL1-C6-P3-Env**.
9. Print and then close **WL1-C6-P3-Env.docx**. *Note: Manual feed of the envelope may be required. Please check with your instructor.*

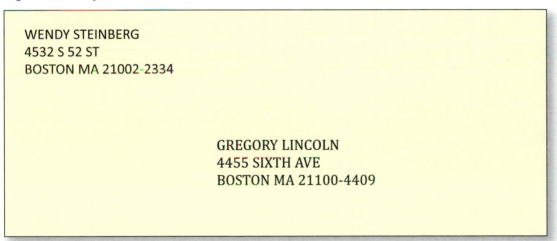

Figure 6.6 Project 3a

WENDY STEINBERG
4532 S 52 ST
BOSTON MA 21002-2334

GREGORY LINCOLN
4455 SIXTH AVE
BOSTON MA 21100-4409

If you open the Envelopes and Labels dialog box in a document containing a name and address (the name and address lines must end with a press of the Enter key and not Shift + Enter), the name and address are automatically inserted in the *Delivery address* section of the dialog box. To do this, open a document containing a name and address and then display the Envelopes and Labels dialog box. The name and address are inserted in the *Delivery address* section as they appear in the letter and may not conform to the USPS guidelines. The USPS guidelines for addressing envelopes are only suggestions, not requirements.

1. Open **LAProg.docx**.
2. Click the Mailings tab.
3. Click the Envelopes button in the Create group.
4. At the Envelopes and Labels dialog box (with the Envelopes tab selected), make sure the delivery address displays properly in the *Delivery address* section.
5. If any text displays in the *Return address* section, insert a check mark in the *Omit* check box (located to the right of the *Return address* option). (This tells Word not to print the return address on the envelope.)
6. Click the Print button.
7. Close **LAProg.docx** without saving changes.

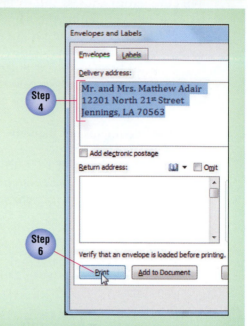

Step 4

Step 6

Project 4 **Create Mailing Labels** **2 Parts**

You will create mailing labels containing names and addresses and then create mailing labels containing the inside address of a letter.

Creating and Printing Labels ■■■■■■■■■■■■■■■■■■■■

▼ Quick Steps

Create Labels
1. Click Mailings tab.
2. Click Labels button.
3. Type desired address(es).
4. Click New Document button or Print button.

Use Word's labels feature to print text on mailing labels, file labels, disc labels, or other types of labels. Word includes a variety of predefined formats for labels that can be purchased at an office supply store. To create a sheet of mailing labels with the same name and address using the default options, click the Labels button in the Create group in the Mailings tab. At the Envelopes and Labels dialog box with the Labels tab selected as shown in Figure 6.7, type the desired address in the *Address* text box. Click the New Document button to insert the mailing label in a new document or click the Print button to send the mailing label directly to the printer.

Labels

Changing Label Options

Click the Options button at the Envelopes and Labels dialog box with the Labels tab selected and the Label Options dialog box displays as shown in Figure 6.8. At the Label Options dialog box, choose the type of printer, the desired label product, and the product number. This dialog box also displays information about the selected label such as type, height, width, and paper size. When you select a label, Word automatically determines label margins. If, however, you want to customize these default settings, click the Details button at the Label Options dialog box.

Figure 6.7 Envelopes and Labels Dialog Box with Labels Tab Selected

Type the label address in this text box.

Click the New Document button to insert the mailing label in a new document.

Click the Print button to send the label directly to the printer.

Figure 6.8 Label Options Dialog Box

Click this down-pointing arrow to display a list of available label products.

Choose the desired label product number from this list box.

Project 4a Creating Customized Mailing Labels

Part 1 of 2

1. At a blank document, click the Mailings tab.
2. Click the Labels button in the Create group.
3. At the Envelopes and Labels dialog box with the Labels tab selected, click the Options button.
4. At the Label Options dialog box, click the down-pointing arrow at the right side of the *Label vendors* option and then click *Avery US Letter* at the drop-down list.
5. Scroll down the *Product number* list box and then click *5160 Easy Peel Address Labels*.
6. Click OK or press Enter.

Step 4

Step 5

7. At the Envelopes and Labels dialog box, click the New Document button.
8. At the document screen, type the first name and address shown in Figure 6.9 in the first label.
9. Press the Tab key twice to move the insertion point to the next label and then type the second name and address shown in Figure 6.9.
10. Continue in this manner until all names and addresses in Figure 6.9 have been typed.
11. Save the document and name it **WL1-C6-P4-Labels**.
12. Print and then close **WL1-C6-P4-Labels.docx**.
13. At the blank document, close the document without saving changes.

Figure 6.9 Project 4a

DAVID LOWRY
12033 S 152 ST
HOUSTON TX 77340

MARCELLA SANTOS
394 APPLE BLOSSOM
FRIENDSWOOD TX 77533

KEVIN DORSEY
26302 PRAIRIE DR
HOUSTON TX 77316

AL AND DONNA SASAKI
1392 PIONEER DR
BAYTOWN TX 77903

JACKIE RHYNER
29039 107 AVE E
HOUSTON TX 77302

MARK AND TINA ELLIS
607 FORD AVE
HOUSTON TX 77307

If you open the Envelopes and Labels dialog box with the Labels tab selected in a document containing a name and address, the name and address are automatically inserted in the *Address* section of the dialog box. To enter different names in each of the mailing labels, start at a clear document screen, display the Envelopes and Labels dialog box with the Labels tab selected, and then click the New Document button. The Envelopes and Labels dialog box is removed from the screen and the document displays with label forms. The insertion point is positioned in the first label form. Type the name and address in this label and then press the Tab key once or twice (depending on the label) to move the insertion point to the next label. Pressing Shift + Tab will move the insertion point to the preceding label.

Project 4b **Creating Mailing Labels**   **Part 2 of 2**

1. Open **LAProg.docx** and create mailing labels with the delivery address. Begin by clicking the Mailings tab.
2. Click the Labels button in the Create group.

3. At the Envelopes and Labels dialog box with the Labels tab selected, make sure the delivery address displays properly in the *Address* section.
4. Click the New Document button.
5. Save the mailing label document and name it **WL1-C6-P4-LAProg.docx**.
6. Print and then close **WL1-C6-P4-LAProg.docx**.
7. Close **LAProg.docx**.

Step 3

Step 4

Project **5** **Use a Template to Create a Business Letter**   **1 Part**

You will use a letter template provided by Word to create a business letter.

Creating a Document Using a Template ■■■■■■■■■■■■

Word includes a number of template documents formatted for specific uses. Each Word document is based on a template document with the *Normal* template the default. With Word templates, you can easily create a variety of documents, such as letters, faxes, and awards, with specialized formatting. Display templates by clicking the File tab and then clicking the New tab. This displays the New tab Backstage view as shown in Figure 6.10.

Click the Sample templates button in the Available Templates category and installed templates display. Click the desired template in the *Sample templates* list box and a preview of the template displays at the right side of the screen. With options below the template preview, you can choose to open the template as a document or as a template. Click the Create button and the template opens and displays on the screen. Locations for personalized text display in placeholders in the template document. Select the placeholder text and then type the personalized text.

If you are connected to the Internet, you can download a number of predesigned templates that Microsoft offers. Templates are grouped into categories and the category names display in the *Office.com Templates* section of the New tab Backstage view. Click the desired template category and available templates display. Click the desired template and then click the Download button.

▼ **Quick Steps**

Create Document Using a Template
1. Click File tab.
2. Click New tab.
3. Click Sample templates button.
4. Double-click desired template.

Figure 6.10 New Tab Backstage View

Click this button to display installed templates.

Use this option to search for templates at the Office.com site.

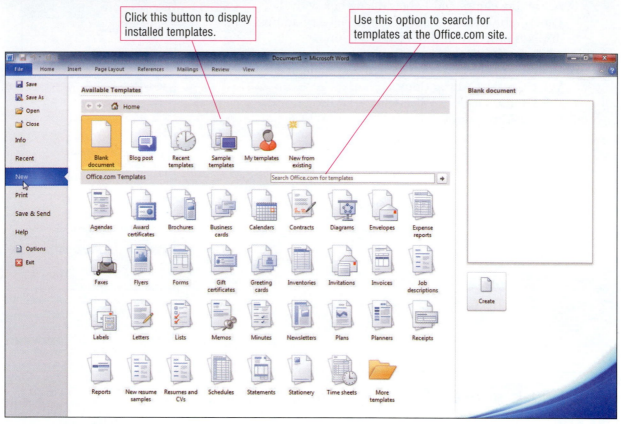

Project 5   **Creating a Letter Using a Template**   **Part 1 of 1**

1. Click the File tab and then click the New tab.
2. At the New tab Backstage view, click the Sample templates button in the Available Templates category.

Step 1

Step 2

3. Double-click the *Equity Letter* template.

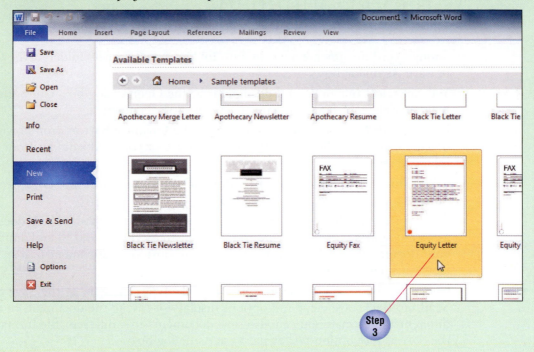

Step 3

4. At the letter document, click the placeholder text *[Pick the date]*, click the down-pointing arrow at the right side of the placeholder, and then click the Today button located at the bottom of the calendar.
5. Click in the name that displays below the date, select the name, and then type your first and last names.
6. Click the placeholder text *[Type the sender company name]* and then type **Sorenson Funds**.
7. Click the placeholder text *[Type the sender company address]*, type **6250 Aurora Boulevard**, press the Enter key, and then type **Baltimore, MD 20372**.
8. Click the placeholder text *[Type the recipient name]* and then type **Ms. Jennifer Gonzalez**.
9. Click the placeholder text *[Type the recipient address]*, type **12990 Boyd Street**, press the Enter key, and then type **Baltimore, MD 20375**.
10. Click the placeholder text *[Type the salutation]* and then type **Dear Ms. Gonzalez:**.
11. Insert a file in the document by completing the following steps:
    a. Click anywhere in the three paragraphs of text in the body of the letter and then click the Delete key.
    b. Click the Insert tab.
    c. Click the Object button arrow in the Text group and then click *Text from File* at the drop-down list.
    d. At the Insert File dialog box, navigate to the Word2010L1C6 folder on your storage medium and then double-click **SFunds.docx**.
12. Click the placeholder text *[Type the closing]* and then type **Sincerely,**.
13. Delete one blank line above Sincerely.
14. Click the placeholder text *[Type the sender title]* and then type **Financial Consultant**.
15. Save the document and name it **WL1-C6-P5-SFunds**.
16. Print and then close **WL1-C6-P5-SFunds.docx**.

Chapter Summary

- Group Word documents logically into folders. Create a new folder at the Open or Save As dialog box.

- You can select one or several documents at the Open dialog box. Copy, move, rename, delete, or open a document or selected documents.

- Use the *Cut*, *Copy*, and *Paste* options from the Organize button drop-down list or the Open dialog box shortcut menu to move or copy a document from one folder to another.

- Delete documents and/or folders with the *Delete* option from the Organize button drop-down list or shortcut menu.

- With options at the Save & Send tab Backstage view, you can send a document as an email attachment, save your document to SkyDrive and SharePoint, save your document in a different file format, and post your document to a special location such as a blog.

- Click the Change File Type button in the File Types category at the Save & Send tab Backstage view, and options display for saving the document in a different file format. You can also save documents in a different file format with the *Save as type* option box at the Save As dialog box.

- Move among the open documents by clicking the button on the Taskbar representing the desired document, or by clicking the View tab, clicking the Switch Windows button in the Window group, and then clicking the desired document name.

- View a portion of all open documents by clicking the View tab and then clicking the Arrange All button in the Window group.

- Use the Minimize, Restore, and Maximize buttons located in the upper right corner of the window to reduce or increase the size of the active window.

- Divide a window into two panes by clicking the View tab and then clicking the Split button in the Window group. This enables you to view different parts of the same document at one time.

- View the contents of two open documents side by side by clicking the View tab, and then clicking the View Side by Side button in the Window group.

- Insert a document into the open document by clicking the Insert tab, clicking the Object button arrow, and then clicking *Text from File* at the drop-down list. At the Insert File dialog box, double-click the desired document.

- Preview a document at the Print tab Backstage view. Scroll through the pages in the document with the Next Page and the Previous Page buttons that display below the preview page. Use the Zoom slider bar to increase/decrease the display size of the preview page.

- At the Print tab Backstage view you can customize the print job by changing the page orientation, size, and margins; specify how many pages you want to print on one page; the number of copies and whether or not to collate the pages; and specify the printer.

- With Word's envelope feature you can create and print an envelope at the Envelopes and Labels dialog box with the Envelopes tab selected.

- If you open the Envelopes and Labels dialog box in a document containing a name and address (with each line ending with a press of the Enter key), that information is automatically inserted in the *Delivery address* text box in the dialog box.

- Use Word's labels feature to print text on mailing labels, file labels, disc labels, or other types of labels.

- Word includes a number of template documents you can use to create a variety of documents. Display the list of template documents by clicking the File tab, clicking the New tab, and then clicking the Sample templates button.

Commands Review

FEATURE	RIBBON TAB, GROUP	BUTTON, OPTION	KEYBOARD SHORTCUT
Open dialog box	File	Open	Ctrl + O
Save As dialog box	File	Save As	
Print tab Backstage view	File	Print	Ctrl + P
Arrange all documents	View, Window		
Minimize document			
Maximize document			Ctrl + F10
Restore			
Split window	View, Window		Alt + Ctrl + S
View documents side by side	View, Window		
Insert file	Insert, Text	, Text from File	
Envelopes and Labels dialog box with Envelopes tab selected	Mailings, Create		
Envelopes and Labels dialog box with Labels tab selected	Maililngs, Create		
New tab Backstage view	File	New	

Concepts Check Test Your Knowledge

Completion: In the space provided at the right, indicate the correct term, command, or number.

1. Create a new folder with this button at the Open or Save As dialog box.

2. At the Open dialog box, the current folder path displays in this.

3. Using the mouse, select nonadjacent documents at the Open dialog box by holding down this key while clicking the desired documents.

4. Documents deleted from the hard drive are automatically sent here.

5. Copy a document to another folder without opening the document at the Open or Save As dialog box with the Organize button drop-down list or this menu

6. The letters PDF stand for this.

7. Saving a document in this format strips out all formatting.

8. Click this button in the Window group in the View tab to arrange all open documents so a portion of each document displays.

9. Click this button and the active document fills the editing window.

10. Click this button to reduce the active document to a button on the Taskbar.

11. To display documents side by side, click this button in the Window group in the View tab.

12. Display the Insert File dialog box by clicking the Object button arrow in the Insert tab and then clicking this option.

13. Type this in the *Pages* text box at the Print tab Backstage view to print pages 3 through 6 of the open document.

14. Type this in the *Pages* text box at the Print tab Backstage view to print pages 4 and 9 of the open document.

15. The Envelopes button is located in the Create group in this tab.

16. Click the Sample templates button at this Backstage view to display a list of templates.

Skills Check Assess Your Performance

Assessment

1 MANAGE DOCUMENTS

1. Display the Open dialog box with Word2010L1C6 the active folder and then create a new folder named *CheckingTools*.
2. Copy (be sure to copy and not cut) all documents that begin with *SpellGrammar* into the CheckingTools folder.
3. With the CheckingTools folder as the active folder, rename **SpellGrammar01.docx** to **Technology.docx**.
4. Rename **SpellGrammar02.docx** to **Software.docx**.
5. Print the screen contents by completing the following steps:
   a. With the Open dialog box displayed, press the Print Screen key on your keyboard.
   b. Close the Open dialog box.
   c. At a blank document, click the Paste button.
   d. Print the document.
   e. Close the document without saving it.
6. Display the Open dialog box and make Word2010L1C6 the active folder.
7. Delete the CheckingTools folder and all documents contained within it.
8. Open **StaffMtg.docx**, **Agreement.docx**, and **Robots.docx**.
9. Make **Agreement.docx** the active document.
10. Make **StaffMtg.docx** the active document.
11. Arrange all of the windows.
12. Make **Robots.docx** the active document and then minimize it.
13. Minimize the remaining documents.
14. Restore **StaffMtg.docx**.
15. Restore **Agreement.docx**.
16. Restore **Robots.docx**.
17. Maximize and then close **StaffMtg.docx** and then maximize and close **Robots.docx**.
18. Maximize **Agreement.docx** and then save the document and name it **WL1-C6-A1-Agreement**.
19. Open **AptLease.docx**.
20. View the **WL1-C6-A1-Agreement.docx** document and **AptLease.docx** document side by side.
21. Scroll through both documents simultaneously and notice the formatting differences between the title and headings in the two documents. Change the font and apply shading to the title and headings in **WL1-C6-A1-Agreement.docx** to match the font and shading of the title and headings in **AptLease.docx**.
22. Make **AptLease.docx** active and then close it.
23. Save **WL1-C6-A1-Agreement.docx**.
24. Move the insertion point to the end of the document and then insert the document named **Terms.docx**.
25. Apply formatting to the inserted text so it matches the formatting of the original text.

26. If the heading, *Damage to Premises*, displays at the bottom of page 1, insert a page break at the beginning of the heading.
27. Move the insertion point to the end of the document and then insert the document named **Signature.docx**.
28. Save, print, and then close **WL1-C6-A1-Agreement.docx**.

Assessment

2 CREATE AN ENVELOPE

1. At a blank document, create an envelope with the text shown in Figure 6.11.
2. Save the envelope document and name it **WL1-C6-A2-Env**.
3. Print and then close **WL1-C6-A2-Env.docx**.

Figure 6.11 Assessment 2

```
DR ROSEANNE HOLT
21330 CEDAR DR
LOGAN UT 84598




                    GENE MIETZNER
                    4559 CORRIN AVE
                    SMITHFIELD UT 84521
```

Assessment

3 CREATE MAILING LABELS

1. Create mailing labels with the names and addresses shown in Figure 6.12. Use a label option of your choosing. (You may need to check with your instructor before choosing an option.)
2. Save the document and name it **WL1-C6-A3-Labels**.
3. Print and then close **WL1-C6-A3-Labels.docx**.
4. At the clear document screen, close the document screen without saving changes.

Figure 6.12 Assessment 3

SUSAN LUTOVSKY	JIM AND PAT KEIL	IRENE HAGEN
1402 MELLINGER DR	413 JACKSON ST	12930 147TH AVE E
FAIRHOPE OH 43209	AVONDALE OH 43887	CANTON OH 43296
VINCE KILEY	LEONARD KRUEGER	HELGA GUNDSTROM
14005 288TH S	13290 N 120TH	PO BOX 3112
CANTON OH 43287	CANTON OH 43291	AVONDALE OH 43887

Assessment

4 PREPARE A FAX

1. Open the Equity fax template at the New tab Backstage view with sample templates selected and then insert the following information in the specified fields.

    To: Frank Gallagher
    From: (your first and last names)
    Fax: (206) 555-9010
    Pages: 3
    Phone: (206) 555-9005
    Date: (insert current date)
    Re: Consultation Agreement
    CC: Jolene Yin
    Insert an X in the *For Review* check box.
    Comments: Please review the Consultation Agreement and advise me of any legal issues.

2. Save the fax document and name it **WL1-C6-A4-Fax**.
3. Print and then close the document.

Assessment

5 SAVE A DOCUMENT AS A WEB PAGE

1. Experiment with the Save as type button at the Save As dialog box and figure out how to save a document as a single file web page.
2. Open **NSS.docx**, display the Save As dialog box, and then change Save as Type to a single file web page. Click the Change Title button that displays in the Save As dialog box. At the Enter Text dialog box, type **Northland Security Systems** in the *Page title* text box and then close the dialog box by clicking the OK button. Click the Save button in the Save As dialog box.
3. Close the **NSS.mht** file.
4. Open your web browser and then open the **NSS.mht** file.
5. Close your web browser.

Assessment

6 CREATE PERSONAL MAILING LABELS

1. At a blank document, type your name and address and then apply formatting to enhance the appeal of the text (you determine the font, font size, and font color).
2. Create labels with your name and address (you determine the label vendor and product number).
3. Save the label document and name it **WL1-C6-A6-PersonalLabels**.
4. Print and then close the document.

Assessment

7 DOWNLOAD AND COMPLETE A STUDENT AWARD CERTIFICATE

1. Display the New tab Backstage view and then search for and download a student of the month award certificate template in the *Office.com Templates* section of the Available Templates category. (To find a student of the month award, click the *Award certificates* option in the *Office.com Templates* section, click the *Academic* folder, and then look for the *Basic certificate for student of the month* template.)
2. Insert the appropriate information in the award template placeholder identifying yourself as the recipient of the student of the month award.
3. Save the completed award and name the document **WL1-C6-A7-Award**.
4. Print and then close the document.

Visual Benchmark Demonstrate Your Proficiency

CREATE CUSTOM LABELS

1. You can create a sheet of labels with the same information in each label by typing the information in the Address text box at the Envelopes and Labels dialog box or you can type the desired information, select it, and then create the label. Using this technique, create the sheet of labels shown in Figure 6.13 with the following specifications:

   - Open **NSSLabels.docx**.
   - Set the text in 12-point Magneto.
   - Select the entire document and then create the labels by displaying the Envelopes and Labels dialog box with the Labels tab selected. Change to the Avery US Letter label, product number 5161, and then click the New Document button.

2. Save the label document and name it **WL1-C6-VB-NSSLabels**.
3. Print and then close the document.
4. Close **NSSLabels.docx** without saving it.

Figure 6.13 Visual Benchmark

 Northland Security Systems
3200 *North 22ⁿᵈ Street*
Springfield, IL 62102

 Northland Security Systems
3200 *North 22ⁿᵈ Street*
Springfield, IL 62102

 Northland Security Systems
3200 *North 22ⁿᵈ Street*
Springfield, IL 62102

 Northland Security Systems
3200 *North 22ⁿᵈ Street*
Springfield, IL 62102

 Northland Security Systems
3200 *North 22ⁿᵈ Street*
Springfield, IL 62102

 Northland Security Systems
3200 *North 22ⁿᵈ Street*
Springfield, IL 62102

 Northland Security Systems
3200 *North 22ⁿᵈ Street*
Springfield, IL 62102

 Northland Security Systems
3200 *North 22ⁿᵈ Street*
Springfield, IL 62102

 Northland Security Systems
3200 *North 22ⁿᵈ Street*
Springfield, IL 62102

 Northland Security Systems
3200 *North 22ⁿᵈ Street*
Springfield, IL 62102

 Northland Security Systems
3200 *North 22ⁿᵈ Street*
Springfield, IL 62102

 Northland Security Systems
3200 *North 22ⁿᵈ Street*
Springfield, IL 62102

 Northland Security Systems
3200 *North 22ⁿᵈ Street*
Springfield, IL 62102

 Northland Security Systems
3200 *North 22ⁿᵈ Street*
Springfield, IL 62102

 Northland Security Systems
3200 *North 22ⁿᵈ Street*
Springfield, IL 62102

 Northland Security Systems
3200 *North 22ⁿᵈ Street*
Springfield, IL 62102

 Northland Security Systems
3200 *North 22ⁿᵈ Street*
Springfield, IL 62102

 Northland Security Systems
3200 *North 22ⁿᵈ Street*
Springfield, IL 62102

 Northland Security Systems
3200 *North 22ⁿᵈ Street*
Springfield, IL 62102

 Northland Security Systems
3200 *North 22ⁿᵈ Street*
Springfield, IL 62102

Case Study Apply Your Skills

Part 1

You are the office manager for the real estate company, Macadam Realty, and have been asked by the senior sales associate, Lucy Hendricks, to organize contract forms into a specific folder. Create a new folder named *RealEstate* and then copy into the folder documents that begin with the letters "RE." Ms. Hendricks has also asked you to prepare mailing labels for Macadam Realty. Include the name, Macadam Realty, and the address 100 Third Street, Suite 210, Denver, CO 80803, on the labels. Use a decorative font for the label and make the *M* in *Macadam* and the *R* in *Realty* larger and more pronounced than surrounding text. ***Hint: Format text in the label by selecting text, right-clicking in the selected text, and then choosing the desired option at the shortcut menu.*** Save the completed document and name it **WL1-C6-CS-RELabels**. Print and then close the document.

Part 2

One of your responsibilities is to format contract forms. Open the document named **REConAgrmnt.docx** and then save it and name it **WL1-C6-CS-REConAgrmnt**. The sales associate has asked you to insert signature information at the end of the document and so you decide to insert at the end of the document the file named **RESig.docx**. With **WL1-C6-CS-REConAgrmnt.docx** still open, open **REBuildAgrmnt.docx**. Format the **WL1-C6-CS-REConAgrmnt.docx** document so it is formatted in a manner similar to the **REBuildAgrmnt.docx** document. Consider the following when specifying formatting: margins, fonts, and paragraph shading. Save, print, and then close **WL1-C6-CS-REConAgrmnt.docx**. Close **REBuildAgrmnt.docx**.

Part 3

As part of the organization of contracts, Ms. Hendricks has asked you to insert document properties for the **REBuildAgrmnt.docx** and **WL1-C6-CS-REConAgrmnt.docx** documents. Use the Help feature to learn how to insert document properties. With the information you learn from the Help feature, open each of the two documents separately, display the Info tab Backstage view, click the Show All Properties hyperlink, and then insert document properties in the following fields (you determine the information to type): *Title, Subject, Categories,* and *Company*. Print the document properties for each document (change the first gallery in the Settings category in the Print tab Backstage view to *Document Properties*). Save each document with the original name and close the documents.

Part 4

A client of the real estate company, Anna Hurley, is considering purchasing several rental properties and has asked for information on how to locate real estate rental forms. Using the Internet, locate at least three websites that offer real estate rental forms. Write a letter to Anna Hurley at 2300 South 22nd Street, Denver, CO 80205. In the letter, list the websites you found and include information on which site you thought offered the most resources. Also include in the letter that Macadam Realty is very interested in helping her locate and purchase rental properties. Save the document and name it **WL1-C6-CS-RELtr**. Create an envelope for the letter and add it to the letter document. Save, print, and then close **WL1-C6-CS-RELtr.docx**. (You may need to manually feed the envelope in the printer.)

Creating Tables and SmartArt

PERFORMANCE OBJECTIVES

Upon successful completion of Chapter 7, you will be able to:
- Create, edit, and format a table
- Change the table design and layout
- Sort text in a table
- Perform calculations on data in a table
- Create and format a SmartArt diagram
- Create and format a SmartArt organizational chart

Tutorials

Some Word data can be organized in a table, which is a combination of columns and rows. With the Tables feature, you can insert data in columns and rows. This data can consist of text, values, and formulas. In this chapter you will learn how to create and format a table and insert and format data in the table. Word includes a SmartArt feature that provides a number of predesigned diagrams and organizational charts. Use this feature to create and then customize a diagram or organizational chart. Model answers for this chapter's projects appear on the following pages.

Word2010L1C7

Note: Before beginning the projects, copy to your storage medium the Word2010L1C7 subfolder from the Word2010L1 folder on the CD that accompanies this textbook and then make Word2010L1C7 the active folder.

Page 1

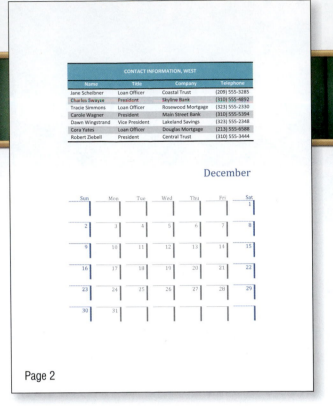

Page 2

Project 1 Create and Format Tables with Company Information

WL1-C7-P1-Tables.docx

Project 2 Create and Format Tables with Employee Information

WL1-C7-P2-TSPTables.docx

Project 3 Sort and Calculate Sales Data

WL1-C7-P3-TSPSalesTables.docx

Page 1

CONTACT INFORMATION, NORTH			
Name	**Title**	**Company**	**Telephone**
Maggie Rivera	Vice President	First Trust Bank	(203) 555-3440
Cecilia Nordyke	Loan Officer	American Financial	(509) 555-3995
Regina Stahl	Account Manager	United Fidelity	(301) 555-1221 x453

OPTIONAL PLAN PREMIUM RATES		
Waiting Period	*Plan 2012 Employees*	*Basic Plan Employees*
30 days	0.85%	0.81%
60 days	0.79%	0.67%
90 days	0.59%	0.49%
120 days	0.35%	0.30%
180 days	0.26%	0.23%

CONTACT INFORMATION, WEST			
Name	**Title**	**Company**	**Telephone**
Steven Adams	Vice President	Valley Bank	(213) 555-9002
Denise Bridgman	President	Freestone Mortgage	(323) 555-5300
Laura Coulter	Loan Officer	Pacific Savings	(310) 555-1048
Jack Gillespie	Vice President	Evergreen Trust	(323) 555-2102
Jessica Higgins	President	First Mortgage	(213) 555-4215
Eric Marquez	Vice President	Cascade Savings	(213) 555-0033
Cheryl Parente	President	Hillside Mortgage	(310) 555-1050

Page 2

CONTACT INFORMATION, WEST			
Name	**Title**	**Company**	**Telephone**
Jane Scheibner	Loan Officer	Coastal Trust	(209) 555-3285
Charles Swayze	President	Skyline Bank	(310) 555-4892
Tracie Simmons	Loan Officer	Rosewood Mortgage	(323) 555-2330
Carole Wagner	President	Main Street Bank	(310) 555-5394
Dawn Wingstrand	Vice President	Lakeland Savings	(323) 555-2348
Cora Yates	Loan Officer	Douglas Mortgage	(213) 555-6588
Robert Ziebell	President	Central Trust	(310) 555-3444

December

Sun	Mon	Tue	Wed	Thu	Fri	Sat
						1
2	3	4	5	6	7	8
9	10	11	12	13	14	15
16	17	18	19	20	21	22
23	24	25	26	27	28	29
30	31					

Project 2

Tri-State Products

Name	Department
Charles Hartman	Technical Support
Erin Dodd-Trent	Public Relations
Grace Murakami	Research and Development
Elizabeth Gentry	Technical Support
William Thatcher	Technical Support
Stewart Zimmerman	Research and Development

TRI-STATE PRODUCTS		
Name	**Employee #**	**Department**
Whitaker, Christine	1432-323-09	Financial Services
Higgins, Dennis	1230-933-21	Public Relations
Coffey, Richard	1321-843-22	Research and Development
Porter, Robbie	1122-361-38	Public Relations
Buchanan, Lillian	1432-857-87	Research and Development
Kensington, Jacob	1112-473-31	Human Resources

TRI-STATE PRODUCTS	
Title	**Name**
President	Martin Sherwood
Vice President	Gina Lopez
Vice President	Sydney Fox
Manager	Stephen Powell
Manager	Linda Wu

Tri-State Products		
Washington Division	Oregon Division	California Division

Project 3

TRI-STATE PRODUCTS Sales Division		
Salesperson	**Sales, 2010**	**Sales, 2011**
Lagasa, Brianna	$294,653	$300,211
Sogura, Jeffrey	$375,630	$399,120
Whittier, Michelle	$395,630	$376,522
Kurkova, Martina	$490,310	$476,005
Byers, Darren	$490,655	$500,210
Novak, Diana	$543,241	$651,438
Guthrie, Jonathon	$623,214	$635,099
Total	$3,213,333	$3,338,605
Average	$459,048	$476,944
Top Sales	$623,214	$651,438

Region	First Qtr.	Second Qtr.	Third Qtr.	Fourth Qtr.	Total
Northwest	$125,430	$157,090	$139,239	$120,340	$542,099
Southwest	$133,450	$143,103	$153,780	$142,498	$572,831
Northeast	$275,340	$299,342	$278,098	$266,593	$1,119,373
Southeast	$211,349	$222,330	$201,849	$239,432	$874,960
Total	$745,569	$821,865	$772,966	$768,863	$3,109,263
Average	$186,392	$205,466	$193,242	$192,216	$777,316

Page 1

Page 2

Project 4 Prepare and Format a Diagram
WL1-C7-P4-Diagrams.docx

Project 5 Prepare and Format a Company Organizational Chart
WL1-C7-P5-OrgChart.docx

Project 1 Create and Format Tables with Company Information

9 Parts

You will create a table containing contact information and another containing information on plans offered by the company. You will then change the design and layout of both tables.

Creating a Table

Use the Tables feature to create boxes of information called *cells*. A cell is the intersection between a row and a column. A cell can contain text, characters, numbers, data, graphics, or formulas. Create a table by clicking the Insert tab, clicking the Table button, dragging down and to the right until the correct number of rows and columns displays, and then clicking the mouse button. You can also create a table with options at the Insert Table dialog box. Display this dialog box by clicking the Table button in the Tables group in the Insert tab and then clicking *Insert Table* at the drop-down list.

Figure 7.1 shows an example of a table with three columns and four rows. Various parts of the table are identified in Figure 7.1 such as the gridlines, move table column marker, end-of-cell marker, end-of-row marker, and the resize handle. In a table, nonprinting characters identify the end of a cell and the end of a row. To view these characters, click the Show/Hide ¶ button in the Paragraph group in the Home

Quick Steps

Create a Table
1. Click Insert tab.
2. Click Table button.
3. Drag to create desired number of columns and rows.
4. Click mouse button.
OR
1. Click Insert tab.
2. Click Table button.
3. Click *Insert Table*.
4. Specify number of columns and rows.
5. Click OK.

Figure 7.1 Table

table move handle   move table column marker   end-of-row marker

gridline   end-of-cell marker   resize handle

Table

You can create a table within a table, creating a *nested* table.

Pressing the Tab key in a table moves the insertion point to the next cell. Pressing Ctrl + Tab moves the insertion point to the next tab within a cell.

tab. The end-of-cell marker displays inside each cell and the end-of-row marker displays at the end of a row of cells. These markers are identified in Figure 7.1.

When you create a table, the insertion point is located in the cell in the upper left corner of the table. Cells in a table contain a cell designation. Columns in a table are lettered from left to right, beginning with *A*. Rows in a table are numbered from top to bottom beginning with *1*. The cell in the upper left corner of the table is cell A1. The cell to the right of A1 is B1, the cell to the right of B1 is C1, and so on.

When the insertion point is positioned in a cell in the table, move table column markers display on the horizontal ruler. These markers represent the end of a column and are useful in changing the width of columns. Figure 7.1 identifies a move table column marker.

Entering Text in Cells

With the insertion point positioned in a cell, type or edit text. Move the insertion point to other cells with the mouse by clicking in the desired cell. If you are using the keyboard, press the Tab key to move the insertion point to the next cell or press Shift + Tab to move the insertion point to the previous cell.

If the text you type does not fit on one line, it wraps to the next line within the same cell. Or, if you press Enter within a cell, the insertion point is moved to the next line within the same cell. The cell vertically lengthens to accommodate the text, and all cells in that row also lengthen. Pressing the Tab key in a table causes the insertion point to move to the next cell in the table. If you want to move the insertion point to a tab stop within a cell, press Ctrl + Tab. If the insertion point is located in the last cell of the table and you press the Tab key, Word adds another row to the table. Insert a page break within a table by pressing Ctrl + Enter. The page break is inserted between rows, not within.

Moving the Insertion Point within a Table

To move the insertion point to a different cell within the table using the mouse, click in the desired cell. To move the insertion point to different cells within the table using the keyboard, refer to the information shown in Table 7.1.

Table 7.1 Insertion Point Movement within a Table Using the Keyboard

To move the insertion point	Press these keys
To next cell	Tab
To preceding cell	Shift + Tab
Forward one character	Right Arrow key
Backward one character	Left Arrow key
To previous row	Up Arrow key
To next row	Down Arrow key
To first cell in the row	Alt + Home
To last cell in the row	Alt + End
To top cell in the column	Alt + Page Up
To bottom cell in the column	Alt + Page Down

Project 1a   Creating a Table   Part 1 of 9

1. At a blank document, turn on bold, and then type the title **CONTACT INFORMATION** shown in Figure 7.2.
2. Turn off bold and then press the Enter key.
3. Create the table shown in Figure 7.2. To do this, click the Insert tab, click the Table button in the Tables group, drag down and to the right until the number above the grid displays as *3x5*, and then click the mouse button.
4. Type the text in the cells as indicated in Figure 7.2. Press the Tab key to move to the next cell or press Shift + Tab to move to the preceding cell. (If you accidentally press the Enter key within a cell, immediately press the Backspace key. Do not press Tab after typing the text in the last cell. If you do, another row is inserted in the table. If this happens, immediately click the Undo button on the Quick Access toolbar.)
5. Save the table and name it **WL1-C7-P1-Tables**.

Figure 7.2 Project 1a

CONTACT INFORMATION

Maggie Rivera	First Trust Bank	(203) 555-3440
Les Cromwell	Madison Trust	(602) 555-4900
Cecilia Nordyke	American Financial	(509) 555-3995
Regina Stahl	United Fidelity	(301) 555-1221
Justin White	Key One Savings	(360) 555-8966

Using the Insert Table Dialog Box

You can also create a table with options at the Insert Table dialog box shown in Figure 7.3. To display this dialog box, click the Insert tab, click the Table button in the Tables group, and then click *Insert Table.* At the Insert Table dialog box, enter the desired number of columns and rows and then click OK.

Figure 7.3 Insert Table Dialog Box

Use these options to specify the numbers of columns and rows.

Project 1b **Creating a Table with the Insert Table Dialog Box** **Part 2 of 9**

1. With **WL1-C7-P1-Tables.docx** open, press Ctrl + End to move the insertion point below the table.
2. Press the Enter key twice.
3. Turn on bold and then type the title **OPTIONAL PLAN PREMIUM RATES** shown in Figure 7.4.
4. Turn off bold and then press the Enter key.
5. Click the Insert tab, click the Table button in the Tables group, and then click *Insert Table* at the drop-down list.
6. At the Insert Table dialog box, type **3** in the *Number of columns* text box. (The insertion point is automatically positioned in this text box.)
7. Press the Tab key (this moves the insertion point to the *Number of rows* text box) and then type **5**.
8. Click OK.
9. Type the text in the cells as indicated in Figure 7.4. Press the Tab key to move to the next cell or press Shift + Tab to move to the preceding cell. To indent the text in cells B2 through B5 and cells C2 through C5, press Ctrl + Tab to move the insertion to a tab within cells and then type the text.
10. Save **WL1-C7-P1-Tables.docx**.

Step 6

Step 7

Step 8

Figure 7.4 Project 1b

OPTIONAL PLAN PREMIUM RATES

Waiting Period	Basic Plan Employees	Plan 2012 Employees
60 days	0.67%	0.79%
90 days	0.49%	0.59%
120 days	0.30%	0.35%
180 days	0.23%	0.26%

Changing the Table Design ■■■■■■■■■■■■■■■■■■■■

When you create a table, the Table Tools Design tab is selected and the tab contains a number of options for enhancing the appearance of the table as shown in Figure 7.5. With options in the Table Styles group, apply a predesigned style that applies color and border lines to a table. Maintain further control over the predesigned style formatting applied to columns and rows with options in the Table Style Options group. For example, if your table contains a total column, you would insert a check mark in the *Total Row* option. Apply additional design formatting to cells in a table with the Shading and Borders buttons in the Table Styles group. Draw a table or draw additional rows and/or columns in a table by clicking the Draw Table button in the Draw Borders group. Click this button and the mouse pointer turns into a pencil. Drag in the table to create the desired columns and rows. Click the Eraser button and the mouse pointer turns into an eraser. Drag through the column and/or row lines you want to erase in the table.

HINT

Draw a freeform table by clicking the Insert tab, clicking the Table button, and then clicking the *Draw Table* option. Drag in the document to create the table.

Shading

Draw Table

Figure 7.5 Table Tools Design Tab

1. With **WL1-C7-P1-Tables.docx** open, click in any cell in the top table.
2. Apply a table style by completing the following steps:

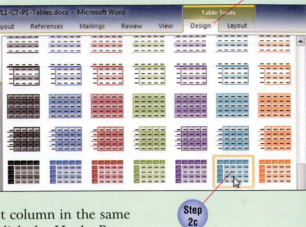

Step 2a

   a. Make sure the Table Tools Design tab is active.
   b. Click the More button at the right side of the table style thumbnails in the Table Styles group.
   c. Click the *Medium Grid 3 - Accent 5* style (second table style from the right in the tenth row in the *Built-in* section).

Step 2c

3. After looking at the table, you realize that the first row is not a header row and the first column should not be formatted differently than the other columns. To format the first row and first column in the same manner as the other rows and columns, click the *Header Row* check box and the *First Column* check box in the Table Style Options group to remove the check marks.

Step 3

4. Click in any cell in the bottom table, apply the Dark List - Accent 5 table style (second option from the right in the eleventh row in the Built-in section), and then remove the check mark from the *First Column* check box.
5. Add color borders to the top table by completing the following steps:
   a. Click in any cell in the top table.
   b. Click the Pen Color button arrow in the Draw Borders group and then click the *Orange, Accent 6, Darker 50%* color.

Step 5b

   c. Click the Line Weight button arrow in the Draw Borders group and then click *1 ½ pt* at the drop-down list. (When you choose a line weight, the Draw Table button is automatically activated.)

Step 5c

   d. Using the mouse (mouse pointer displays as a pen), drag along each side of the table. (As you drag with the mouse, a thick, brown border line is inserted. If you make a mistake or the line does not display as you intended, click the Undo button and then continue drawing along each side of the table.)
6. Drag along each side of the bottom table.
7. Click the Line Weight button in the Draw Borders group and then click *1 pt* at the drop-down list.
8. Drag along the row boundary separating the first row from the second row in the bottom table.
9. Click the Draw Table button to turn off the feature.
10. Save **WL1-C7-P1-Tables.docx**.

Selecting Cells ■■■■■■■■■■■■■■■■■■■■■■■■

You can format data within a table in several ways. For example, you can change the alignment of text within cells or rows, select and then move or copy rows or columns, or you can add character formatting such as bold, italic, or underlining. To format specific cells, rows, or columns, you must first select them.

Selecting in a Table with the Mouse

Use the mouse pointer to select a cell, row, column, or an entire table. Table 7.2 describes methods for selecting a table with the mouse. The left edge of each cell, between the left column border and the end-of-cell marker or first character in the cell, is called the *cell selection bar*. When you position the mouse pointer in the cell selection bar, it turns into a small, black arrow pointing up and to the right. Each row in a table contains a *row selection bar*, which is the space just to the left of the left edge of the table. When you position the mouse pointer in the row selection bar, the mouse pointer turns into a white arrow pointing up and to the right.

Table 7.2 Selecting in a Table with the Mouse

To select this	Do this
A cell	Position the mouse pointer in the cell selection bar at the left edge of the cell until it turns into a small, black arrow pointing up and to the right and then click the left mouse button.
A row	Position the mouse pointer in the row selection bar at the left edge of the table until it turns into an arrow pointing up and to the right and then click the left mouse button.
A column	Position the mouse pointer on the uppermost horizontal gridline of the table in the appropriate column until it turns into a short, black down-pointing arrow and then click the left mouse button.
Adjacent cells	Position the mouse pointer in the first cell to be selected, hold down the left mouse button, drag the mouse pointer to the last cell to be selected, and then release the mouse button.
All cells in a table	Click the table move handle or position the mouse pointer in the row selection bar for the first row at the left edge of the table until it turns into an arrow pointing up and to the right, hold down the left mouse button, drag down to select all rows in the table, and then release the left mouse button.
Text within a cell	Position the mouse pointer at the beginning of the text and then hold down the left mouse button as you drag the mouse across the text. (When a cell is selected, the cell background color changes to blue. When text within cells is selected, only those lines containing text are selected.)

Selecting in a Table with the Keyboard

In addition to the mouse, you can also use the keyboard to select specific cells within a table. Table 7.3 displays the commands for selecting specific amounts of a table.

If you want to select only text within cells, rather than the entire cell, press F8 to turn on the Extend mode and then move the insertion point with an arrow key. When a cell is selected, the cell background color changes to blue. When text within a cell is selected, only those lines containing text are selected.

Table 7.3 Selecting in a Table with the Keyboard

To select	Press
The next cell's contents	Tab
The preceding cell's contents	Shift + Tab
The entire table	Alt + 5 (on numeric keypad with Num Lock off)
Adjacent cells	Hold down Shift key and then press an arrow key repeatedly.
A column	Position insertion point in top cell of column, hold down Shift key, and then press down-pointing arrow key until column is selected.

Project 1d   Selecting, Moving and Formatting Cells in a Table   Part 4 of 9

1. With **WL1-C7-P1-Tables.docx** open, move two rows in the top table by completing the following steps:
   a. Position the mouse pointer in the row selection bar at the left side of the row containing the name *Cecilia Nordyke*, hold down the left mouse button, drag down to select two rows (the *Cecilia Nordyke* row and the *Regina Stahl* row).
   b. Click the Home tab and then click the Cut button in the Clipboard group.
   c. Move the insertion point so it is positioned at the beginning of the name *Les Cromwell* and then click the Paste button in the Clipboard group.
2. Move the third column in the bottom table by completing the following steps:
   a. Position the mouse pointer on the top border of the third column in the bottom table until the pointer turns into a short, black, down-pointing arrow and then click the left mouse button. (This selects the entire column.)
   b. Click the Cut button in the Clipboard group in the Home tab.
   c. With the insertion point positioned at the beginning of the text *Basic Plan Employees*, click the Paste button in the Clipboard group in the Home tab. (Moving the column removed the right border.)
   d. Insert the right border by clicking the Table Tools Design tab, clicking the Line Weight button arrow, and then clicking *1 ½ pt* at the drop-down list.

e. Hold down the left mouse button and then drag along the right border of the bottom table.

f. Click the Line Weight button arrow and then click *1 pt* at the drop-down list.

g. Click the Draw Table button to turn off the feature.

3. Apply shading to a row by completing the following steps:

Step 3b

a. Position the mouse pointer in the row selection bar at the left edge of the first row in the bottom table until the pointer turns into an arrow pointing up and to the right and then click the left mouse button. (This selects the entire first row of the bottom table.)

b. Click the Shading button arrow in the Table Styles group and then click the *Red, Accent 2, Darker 50%* color.

4. Apply a border line to a column by completing the following steps:

a. Position the mouse pointer on the top border of the first column in the bottom table until the pointer turns into a short, black, down-pointing arrow and then click the left mouse button.

Step 4b

b. Click the Borders button arrow in the Table Styles group and then click *Right Border* at the drop-down list. (This inserts a 1 point dark orange border line at the right side of the column.)

5. Complete steps similar to those in Step 2 to insert a border line at the right side of the second column.

6. Apply italic formatting to a column by completing the following steps:

a. Position the insertion point in the first cell of the first row in the top table.

b. Hold down the Shift key and then press the Down Arrow key four times. (This should select all cells in the first column.)

c. Press Ctrl + I.

7. Save **WL1-C7-P1-Tables.docx**.

Changing Table Layout

To further customize a table, consider changing the table layout by inserting or deleting columns and rows and specifying cell alignments. Change table layout with options at the Table Tools Layout tab shown in Figure 7.6. Use options and buttons in the tab to select specific cells, delete and insert rows and columns, merge and split cells, specify cell height and width, sort data in cells, and insert a formula.

HINT

Some table layout options are available at a shortcut menu that can be viewed by right-clicking a table.

Figure 7.6 Table Tools Layout Tab

Selecting with the Select Button

Select

Along with selecting cells with the keyboard and mouse, you can also select specific cells with the Select button in the Table group in the Table Tools Layout tab. To select with this button, position the insertion point in the desired cell, column, or row and then click the Select button. At the drop-down list that displays, specify what you want to select — the entire table or a column, row, or cell.

View Gridlines

Viewing Gridlines

Insert Above

When you create a table, cell borders are identified by horizontal and vertical thin, black gridlines. You can remove a cell border gridline but maintain the cell border. If you remove cell border gridlines or apply a table style that removes gridlines, nonprinting gridlines display as dashed lines. This helps you visually determine cell borders. You can turn on or off the display of these nonprinting, dashed gridlines with the View Gridlines button in the Table group in the Table Tools Layout tab.

Insert Below

Inserting and Deleting Rows and Columns

Insert Left

Insert Right

Delete

With buttons in the Rows & Columns group in the Table Tools Layout tab, you can insert a row or column and delete a row or column. Click the button in the group that inserts the row or column in the desired location such as above, below, to the left, or to the right. Add a row to the bottom of a table by positioning the insertion point in the last cell and then pressing the Tab key. To delete a table, row, or column, click the Delete button and then click the option identifying what you want to delete. If you make a mistake while formatting a table, immediately click the Undo button on the Quick Access toolbar.

Project 1e   Selecting, Inserting, and Deleting Columns and Rows   Part 5 of 9

1. Make sure **WL1-C7-P1-Tables.docx** is open.
2. The table style applied to the bottom table removed row border gridlines. If you do not see dashed gridlines in the bottom table, turn on the display of these nonprinting gridlines by positioning your insertion point in the table, clicking the Table Tools Layout tab, and then clicking the View Gridlines button in the Table group. (The button should display with an orange background indicating it is active.)
3. Select a column and apply formatting by completing the following steps:
   a. Click in any cell in the first column in the top table.
   b. Click the Select button in the Table group and then click *Select Column* at the drop-down list.
   c. With the first column selected, press Ctrl + I to remove italics and then press Ctrl + B to apply bold formatting.
4. Select a row and apply formatting by completing the following steps:
   a. Click in any cell in the first row in the bottom table.
   b. Click the Select button in the Table group and then click *Select Row* at the drop-down list.
   c. With the first row selected in the bottom table, press Ctrl + I to apply italic formatting.

---

5. Insert a new row in the bottom table and type text in the new cells by completing the following steps:

   a. Click in the cell containing the text *60 days*.

   b. Click the Insert Above button in the Rows & Columns group.

   c. Type **30 days** in the first cell of the new row, type **0.85%** in the middle cell of the new row (make sure you press Ctrl + Tab before typing the text), and type **0.81%** in the third cell of the new row. (Make sure you press Ctrl + Tab before typing the text.)

6. Insert three new rows in the top table and type text in the new cells by completing the following steps:

   a. Select the three rows of cells that begin with the names *Cecilia Nordyke*, *Regina Stahl*, and *Les Cromwell*.

   b. Click the Insert Below button in the Rows & Columns group.

   c. Type the following text in the new cells:

Teresa Getty	**Meridian Bank**	**(503) 555-9800**
Michael Vazquez	**New Horizon Bank**	**(702) 555-2435**
Samantha Roth	**Cascade Mutual**	**(206) 555-6788**

7. Delete a row by completing the following steps:
   a. Click in the cell containing the name *Les Cromwell*.
   b. Click the Delete button in the Rows & Columns group and then click *Delete Rows* at the drop-down list.
8. Insert a new column and type text in the new cells by completing the following steps:
   a. Click in the cell containing the text *First Trust Bank*.
   b. Click the Insert Left button in the Rows & Columns group.
   c. Type the following text in the new cells:
      B1 = Vice President
      B2 = Loan Officer
      B3 = Account Manager
      B4 = Branch Manager
      B5 = President
      B6 = Vice President
      B7 = Regional Manager
9. Save **WL1-C7-P1-Tables.docx**.

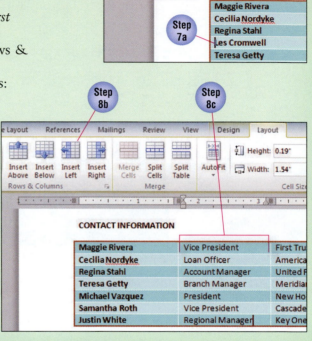

Merging and Splitting Cells and Tables

Merge Cells

Split Cells

Split Table

Click the Merge Cells button in the Merge group in the Table Tools Layout tab to merge selected cells and click the Split Cells button to split the currently active cell. When you click the Split Cells button, the Split Cells dialog box displays where you specify the number of columns or rows into which you want to split the active cell. If you want to split one table into two tables, position the insertion point in a cell in the row that you want to be the first row in the new table and then click the Split Table button.

Project 1f **Merging and Splitting Cells and Splitting a Table** Part 6 of 9

1. With **WL1-C7-P1-Tables.docx** open, insert a new row and merge cells in the row by completing the following steps:
   a. Click in the cell containing the text *Waiting Period* (located in the bottom table).
   b. Click the Insert Above button in the Rows & Columns group in the Table Tools Layout tab.

c. With all of the cells in the new row selected, click the Merge Cells button in the Merge group.

d. Type **OPTIONAL PLAN PREMIUM RATES** and then press Ctrl + E to center-align the text in the cell. (The text you type will be italicized.)

2. Select and then delete the text *OPTIONAL PLAN PREMIUM RATES* that displays above the bottom table.

3. Insert rows and text in the top table and merge cells by completing the following steps:
   a. Click in the cell containing the text *Maggie Rivera*.
   b. Click the Table Tools Layout tab.
   c. Click the Insert Above button twice. (This inserts two rows at the top of the table.)
   d. With the cells in the top row selected, click the Merge Cells button in the Merge group.
   e. Type **CONTACT INFORMATION, NORTH** and then press Ctrl + E to change the paragraph alignment to center.
   f. Type the following text in the four cells in the new second row.

   Name   **Title**   **Company**   **Telephone**

4. Apply heading formatting to the new top row by completing the following steps:
   a. Click the Table Tools Design tab.
   b. Click the *Header Row* check box in the Table Style Options dialog box.
5. Select and then delete the text *CONTACT INFORMATION* that displays above the top table.
6. Split a cell by completing the following steps:
   a. Click in the cell containing the telephone number *(301) 555-1221*.
   b. Click the Table Tools Layout tab.
   c. Click the Split Cells button in the Merge group.
   d. At the Split Cells dialog box, click OK. (The telephone number will wrap to a new line. You will change this in the next project.)

e. Click in the new cell.

f. Type x453 in the new cell. If AutoCorrect automatically capitalizes the *x*, hover the mouse pointer over the *X* until the AutoCorrect Options button displays. Click the AutoCorrect Options button and then click *Undo Automatic Capitalization* or click *Stop Auto-capitalizing First Letter of Table Cells*.

7. Split the cell containing the telephone number *(206) 555-6788* and then type x2310 in the new cell. (If necessary, make the *x* lowercase.)

8. Split the top table into two tables by completing the following steps:
   a. Click in the cell containing the name *Teresa Getty*.
   b. Click the Split Table button in the Merge group.
   c. Click in the cell containing the name *Teresa Getty* (in the first row of the new table).
   d. Click the Insert Above button in the Rows and Columns group in the Table Tools Layout tab.
   e. With the new row selected, click the Merge Cells button.
   f. Type CONTACT INFORMATION, SOUTH in the new row and then press Ctrl + E to center-align the text.

9. Draw a dark orange border at the bottom of the top table and the top of the middle table by completing the following steps:
   a. Click the Table Tools Design tab.
   b. Click the Line Weight button arrow in the Draw Borders group and then click *1 ½ pt* at the drop-down list. (This activates the Draw Table button.)
   c. Using the mouse (mouse pointer displays as a pen), drag along the bottom border of the top table.
   d. Click the top border of the middle table.
   e. Click the Draw Table button to turn it off.

10. Save and then print **WL1-C7-P1-Tables.docx**.

11. Delete the middle table by completing the following steps:
    a. Click in any cell in the middle table.
    b. Click the Table Tools Layout tab.
    c. Click the Delete button in the Rows & Columns group and then click *Delete Table* at the drop-down list.

12. Save **WL1-C7-P1-Tables.docx**.

Customizing Cell Size

When you create a table, column width and row height are equal. You can customize the width of columns or height of rows with buttons in the Cell Size group in the Table Tools Layout tab. Use the *Table Row Height* measurement box to increase or decrease the height of rows and use the *Table Column Width* measurement box to increase or decrease the width of columns. The Distribute Rows button will distribute equally the height of selected rows and the Distribute Columns button will distribute equally the width of selected columns.

Distribute Rows

Distribute Columns

You can also change column width using the move table column markers on the horizontal ruler or by using the table gridlines. To change column width using the horizontal ruler, position the mouse pointer on a move table column marker until it turns into a left and right arrow, and then drag the marker to the desired position. Hold down the Shift key while dragging a table column marker and the horizontal ruler remains stationary while the table column marker moves. Hold down the Alt key while dragging a table column marker and measurements display on the horizontal ruler. To change column width using gridlines, position the arrow pointer on the gridline separating columns until the insertion point turns into a left and right arrow with a vertical line between and then drag the gridline to the desired position. If you want to see the column measurements on the horizontal ruler as you drag a gridline, hold down the Alt key.

Adjust row height in a manner similar to adjusting column width. You can drag the adjust table row marker on the vertical ruler or drag the gridline separating rows. Hold down the Alt key while dragging the adjust table row marker or the row gridline and measurements display on the vertical ruler.

Use the AutoFit button in the Cell Size group to make the column widths in a table automatically fit the contents. To do this, position the insertion point in any cell in the table, click the AutoFit button in the Cell Size group, and then click *AutoFit Contents* at the drop-down list.

AutoFit

Project 1g   **Changing Column Width and Row Height**

1. With **WL1-C7-P1-Tables.docx** open, change the width of the first column in the top table by completing the following steps:
   a. Click in the cell containing the name *Maggie Rivera*.
   b. Position the mouse pointer on the move table column marker that displays just right of the 1.5-inch marker on the horizontal ruler until the pointer turns into an arrow pointing left and right.
   c. Hold down the Shift key and then the left mouse button.
   d. Drag the marker to the 1.25-inch mark, release the mouse button, and then release the Shift key.

Step 1d

2. Complete steps similar to those in Step 1 to drag the move table column marker that displays just right of the 3-inch mark on the horizontal ruler to the 2.75-inch mark. (Make sure the text *Account Manager* in the second column does not wrap to the next line. If it does, slightly increase the width of the button.)

3. Change the width of the third column in the top table by completing the following steps:
   a. Position the mouse pointer on the gridline separating the third and fourth columns until the pointer turns into a left- and right-pointing arrow with a vertical double line between.
   b. Hold down the Alt key and then the left mouse button, drag the gridline to the left until the measurement for the third column on the horizontal ruler displays as *1.3"*, and then release the Alt key and then the mouse button.

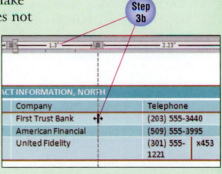

Step 3b

4. Position the mouse pointer on the gridline that separates the telephone number *(301) 555-1221* from the extension *x453* and then drag the gridline to the 5.25-inch mark on the horizontal ruler.

Step 4

5. Drag the right border of the top table to the 5.75-inch marker on the horizontal ruler.

6. Automatically fit the columns in the bottom table by completing the following steps:
   a. Click in any cell in the bottom table.
   b. Click the AutoFit button in the Cell Size group in the Table Tools Layout tab and then click *AutoFit Contents* at the drop-down list.

7. Increase the height of the first row in the bottom table by completing the following steps:
   a. Make sure the insertion point is located in one of the cells in the bottom table.
   b. Position the mouse pointer on the top adjust table row marker on the vertical ruler.
   c. Hold down the left mouse button and hold down the Alt key.
   d. Drag the adjust table row marker down until the first row measurement on the vertical ruler displays as *0.36"*, release the mouse button and then the Alt key.
8. Increase the height of the first row in the top table by completing the following steps:
   a. Click in any cell in the top table.
   b. Position the arrow pointer on the gridline that displays at the bottom of the top row until the arrow pointer turns into an up- and down-pointing arrow with a vertical double line between.
   c. Hold down the left mouse button and then hold down the Alt key.
   d. Drag the gridline down until the first row measurement on the vertical ruler displays as *0.36"* and release the mouse button and then the Alt key.
9. Save **WL1-C7-P1-Tables.docx**.

Changing Cell Alignment

The Alignment group in the Table Tools Layout tab contains a number of buttons for specifying the horizontal and vertical alignment of text in cells. The buttons contain a visual representation of the alignment and you can also hover the mouse pointer over a button to determine the alignment.

Repeating a Header Row

If a table is divided between pages, consider adding the header row at the beginning of the table that extends to the next page. This helps the reader understand the data that displays in each column. To repeat a header row, click in the header row, and then click the Repeat Header Rows button in the Data group in the Table Tools Layout tab. If you want to repeat more than one header row, select the rows and then click the Repeat Header Rows button.

1. With **WL1-C7-P1-Tables.docx** open, click in the top cell in the top table (the cell containing the title *CONTACT INFORMATION, NORTH*).

Step 2

2. Click the Align Center button in the Alignment group in the Table Tools Layout tab.

3. Format and align text in the second row in the top table by completing the following steps:
   a. Select the second row.
   b. Press Ctrl + B (this turns off bold for the entry in the first cell) and then press Ctrl + B again (this turns on bold for all entries in the second row).
   c. Click the Align Top Center button in the Alignment group.

4. Click in the top cell in the bottom table and then click the Align Center button in the Alignment group.

5. Press Ctrl + End to move the insertion point to the end of the document, press the Enter key six times, and then insert a table into the current document by completing the following steps:
   a. Click the Insert tab.
   b. Click the Object button arrow in the Text group and then click *Text from File* at the drop-down list.
   c. At the Insert File dialog box, navigate to the Word2010L1C7 folder on your storage medium and then double-click **ContactsWest.docx**.

Step 6c

6. Repeat the header row by completing the following steps:
   a. Select the first two rows in the table you just inserted.
   b. Click the Table Tools Layout tab.
   c. Click the Repeat Header Rows button in the Data group.

7. Save **WL1-C7-P1-Tables.docx**.

Inserting a Quick Table

Word includes a Quick Tables feature you can use to insert predesigned tables in a document. To insert a quick table, click the Insert tab, click the Table button, point to *Quick Tables*, and then click the desired table at the side menu. A quick table has formatting applied but you can further format the table with options at the Table Tools Design tab and the Table Tools Layout tab.

▼ **Quick Steps**

Insert Quick Table
1. Click Insert tab.
2. Click Table button.
3. Point to *Quick Tables*.
4. Click desired table.

1. With **WL1-C7-P1-Tables.docx** open, press Ctrl + End to move the insertion point to the end of the document and then press the Enter key.
2. Insert a quick table by clicking the Insert tab, clicking the Table button, pointing to *Quick Tables*, and then clicking the *Calendar 3* option at the side menu.

3. Edit text in each of the cells so the calendar reflects the current month.
4. Save, print, and then close **WL1-C7-P1-Tables.docx**.

Project 2 Create and Format Tables with Employee Information

5 Parts

You will create and format a table containing information on the names and departments of employees of Tri-State Products and also insert a table containing additional information on employees and then format the table.

Changing Cell Margin Measurements

Cell Margins

By default, cells in a table contain specific margin settings. Top and bottom margins in a cell have a default measurement of *0"* and left and right margins have a default setting of *0.08"*. Change these default settings with options at the Table Options dialog box shown in Figure 7.7. Display this dialog box by clicking the Cell Margins button in the Alignment group in the Table Tools Layout tab. Use the options in the *Default cell margins* section to change the top, bottom, left, and/ or right cell margin measurements.

Figure 7.7 Table Options Dialog Box

Use options in this section to increase and/or decrease margin measurements in cells.

Changes to cell margins will affect all cells in a table. If you want to change the cell margin measurements for one cell or for selected cells, position the insertion point in the cell or select the desired cells and then click the Properties button in the Table group in the Table Tools Layout tab. (You can also click the Cell Size group dialog box launcher.) At the Table Properties dialog box that displays, click the Cell tab and then the Options button that displays in the lower right corner of the dialog box. This displays the Cell Options dialog box shown in Figure 7.8.

Properties

Before setting the new cell margin measurements, remove the check mark from the *Same as the whole table* option. With the check mark removed from this option, the cell margin options become available. Specify the new cell margin measurements and then click OK to close the dialog box.

Figure 7.8 Cell Options Dialog Box

Remove the check mark from this option and the cell margin options become available.

Project 2a   **Changing Cell Margin Measurements**   **Part 1 of 5**

1. Open **TSPTables.docx** and then save the document with Save As and name it **WL1-C7-P2-TSPTables**.
2. Change the top and bottom margins for all cells in the table by completing the following steps:
   a. Position the insertion point in any cell in the table and then click the Table Tools Layout tab.

b. Click the Cell Margins button in the Alignment group.

c. At the Table Options dialog box, change the *Top* and *Bottom* measurements to *0.05"*.

d. Click OK to close the Table Options dialog box.

3. Change the top and bottom cell margin measurements for the first row of cells by completing the following steps:

a. Select the first row of cells (the cells containing *Name* and *Department*).

b. Click the Properties button in the Table group.

c. At the Table Properties dialog box, click the Cell tab.

d. Click the Options button.

e. At the Cell Options dialog box, remove the check mark from the *Same as the whole table* option.

f. Change the *Top* and *Bottom* measurements to *0.1"*.

g. Click OK to close the Cell Options dialog box.

h. Click OK to close the Table Properties dialog box.

4. Change the left cell margin measurement for specific cells by completing the following steps:

a. Select all rows in the table *except* the top row.

b. Click the Cell Size group dialog box launcher.

c. At the Table Properties dialog box, make sure the Cell tab is active.

d. Click the Options button.

e. At the Cell Options dialog box, remove the check mark from the *Same as the whole table* option.

f. Change the *Left* measurement to *0.3"*.

g. Click OK to close the Cell Options dialog box.

h. Click OK to close the Table Properties dialog box.

5. Save **WL1-C7-P2-TSPTables.docx**.

Changing Cell Direction

Text
Direction

Change the direction of text in a cell using the Text Direction button in the Alignment group in the Table Tools Layout tab. Each time you click the Text Direction button, the text rotates in the cell 90 degrees.

Changing Table Alignment

By default, a table aligns at the left margin. Change this alignment with options at the Table Properties dialog box with the Table tab selected as shown in Figure 7.9. To change the alignment, click the desired alignment option in the *Alignment* section of the dialog box.

Figure 7.9 Table Properties Dialog Box with Table Tab Selected

Specify the horizontal alignment of the table with options in this section.

Project 2b **Changing Table Alignment** **Part 2 of 5**

1. With **WL1-C7-P2-TSPTables.docx** open, insert a new column and change text direction by completing the following steps:
   a. Click in any cell in the first column.
   b. Click the Insert Left button in the Rows & Columns group.
   c. With the cells in the new column selected, click the Merge Cells button in the Merge group.
   d. Type **Tri-State Products**.
   e. Click the Align Center button in the Alignment group.
   f. Click twice on the Text Direction button in the Alignment group.
   g. With *Tri-State Products* selected, click the Home tab, and then increase the font size to *16*.

Step 1f

Step 1e

2. Automatically fit the contents by completing the following steps:
   a. Click in any cell in the table.
   b. Click the Table Tools Layout tab.
   c. Click the AutoFit button in the Cell Size group and then click the *AutoFit Contents* at the drop-down list.
3. Change the table alignment by completing the following steps:
   a. Click the Properties button in the Table group in the Table Tools Layout tab.

b. At the Table Properties dialog box, click the Table tab.
c. Click the *Center* option in the *Alignment* section.
d. Click OK.
4. Select the two cells containing the text *Name* and *Department* and then click the Align Center button in the Alignment group.
5. Save **WL1-C7-P2-TSPTables.docx**.

Step 3b

Step 3c

Changing Table Size with the Resize Handle

▼ **Quick Steps**

Move a Table
1. Position mouse pointer on table move handle until pointer displays as a four-headed arrow.
2. Hold down left mouse button.
3. Drag table to desired position.
4. Release mouse button.

When you hover the mouse pointer over a table, a resize handle displays in the lower right corner of the table. The resize handle displays as a small, white square. Drag this resize handle to increase and/or decrease the size and proportion of the table.

Moving a Table

Position the mouse pointer in a table and a table move handle displays in the upper left corner. Use this handle to move the table in the document. To move a table, position the mouse pointer on the table move handle until the pointer turns into a four-headed arrow, hold down the left mouse button, drag the table to the desired position, and then release the mouse button.

Project 2c | **Resizing and Moving Tables** | **Part 3 of 5**

1. With **WL1-C7-P2-TSPTables.docx** open, insert a table into the current document by completing the following steps:
   a. Press Ctrl + End to move the insertion point to the end of the document and then press the Enter key.
   b. Click the Insert tab.
   c. Click the Object button arrow in the Text group and then click *Text from File* at the drop-down list.
   d. At the Insert File dialog box, navigate to the Word2010L1C7 folder and then double-click ***TSPEmps.docx***.
2. Automatically fit the bottom table by completing the following steps:
   a. Click in any cell in the bottom table.
   b. Click the Table Tools Layout tab.
   c. Click the AutoFit button in the Cell Size group and then click *AutoFit Contents* at the drop-down list.
3. Format the bottom table by completing the following steps:
   a. Click the Table Tools Design tab.

b. Click the More button that displays at the right side of the styles thumbnails in the Table Styles group and then click the *Medium Shading 1 - Accent 2* style (third style from the left in the fourth row of the *Built-In* section).

c. Click the *First Column* check box in the Table Style Options group to remove the check mark.

d. Select the first and second rows, click the Table Tools Layout tab, and then click the Align Center button in the Alignment group.

e. Select the second row and then press Ctrl + B to turn on bold.

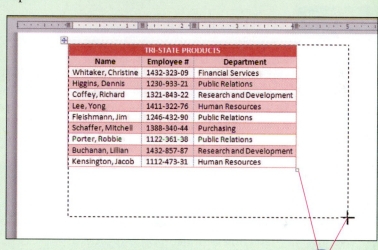

Step
3b

4. Resize the bottom table by completing the following steps:

a. Position the mouse pointer on the resize handle located in the lower right corner of the bottom table.

b. Hold down the left mouse button, drag down and to the right until the width and height of the table increases approximately one inch, and then release the mouse button.

Steps
4a-4b

5. Move the bottom table by completing the following steps:

a. Hover the mouse pointer over the bottom table.

b. Position the mouse pointer on the table move handle until the pointer displays with a four-headed arrow attached.

c. Hold down the left mouse button, drag the table so it is positioned equally between the left and right margins, and then release the mouse button.

Step
5c

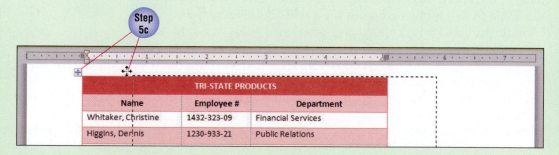

6. Select the cells in the column below the heading *Employee #* and then click the Align Top Center button in the Alignment group.

7. Save **WL1-C7-P2-TSPTables.docx**.

▼ Quick Steps

Convert Text to Table
1. Select text.
2. Click Insert tab.
3. Click Table button.
4. Click *Convert Text to Table*.

Convert Table to Text
1. Click Table Tools Layout tab.
2. Click *Convert to Text*.
3. Specify desired separator.
4. Click OK.

Converting Text to a Table and a Table to Text

You can create a table and then enter data in the cells or you can create the data and then convert it to a table. To convert text to a table, type the text and separate it with a separator character such as a comma or tab. The separator character identifies where you want text divided into columns. To convert text, select the text, click the Insert tab, click the Table button in the Tables group, and then click *Convert Text to Table* at the drop-down list.

You can convert a table to text by positioning the insertion point in any cell of the table, clicking the Table Tools Layout tab, and then clicking the Convert to Text button in the Data group. At the Convert Table to Text dialog box, specify the desired separator and then click OK.

Project 2d   **Converting Text to a Table**   **Part 4 of 5**

1. With **WL1-C7-P2-TSPTables.docx** open, press Ctrl + End to move the insertion point to the end of the document and then press the Enter key until the insertion point is positioned approximately a double space below the bottom table.
2. Insert the document named **TSPExecs.docx** into the current document.
3. Convert the text to a table by completing the following steps:
   a. Select the text you just inserted.
   b. Make sure the Insert tab is active.
   c. Click the Table button in the Tables group and then click *Convert Text to Table* at the drop-down list.
   d. At the Convert Text to Table dialog box, type **2** in the *Number of columns* text box.
   e. Click the *AutoFit to contents* option in the *AutoFit behavior* section.
   f. Click the *Commas* option in the *Separate text at* section.
   g. Click OK.

4. Select and merge the cells in the top row (the row containing the title *TRI-STATE PRODUCTS*) and then change the alignment to Align Center.
5. Apply the Medium Shading 1 - Accent 2 style (third style from the left in the fourth row of the *Built-In* section) and remove the check mark from the *First Column* check box in the Table Style Options group in the Table Tools Design tab.
6. Drag the table so it is centered and positioned below the table above.
7. Apply the Medium Shading 1 - Accent 2 style to the top table. Increase the width of the columns so the text *TRI-STATE PRODUCTS* is visible and the text in the second and third columns displays on one line.
8. Drag the table so it is centered and positioned above the middle table. Make sure the three tables fit on one page.
9. Click in the middle table and then convert the table to text by completing the following steps:
   a. Click the Table Tools Layout tab and then click the Convert to Text button in the Data group.
   b. At the Convert Table to Text dialog box, click *Tabs* and then click OK.
10. Click the Undo button to return the text to a table.
11. Save **WL1-C7-P2-TSPTables.docx**.

Drawing a Table ■■■■■■■■■■■■■■■■■■■■■■■■■■

In Project 1 you used options in the Draw Borders group in the Table Tools Design tab to draw borders around an existing table. You can also use these options to draw an entire table. To draw a table, click the Insert tab, click the Table button in the Tables group, and then click *Draw Table* at the drop-down list. This turns the mouse pointer into a pen. Drag the pen pointer in the document to create the table. The first time you release the mouse button when drawing a table, the Table Tools Design tab becomes active. Use buttons in this table to customize the table. If you make a mistake while drawing a table, click the Eraser button in the Draw Borders group (this changes the mouse pointer to an eraser) and then drag over any border lines you want to erase. You can also click the Undo button to undo your most recent action.

Eraser

Project 2e **Drawing and Formatting a Table** Part 5 of 5

1. With **WL1-C7-P2-TSPTables.docx** open, select and then delete three rows in the middle table from the row that begins with the name *Lee, Yong* through the row that begins with the name *Schaffer, Mitchell*.
2. Move the insertion point to the end of the document (outside of any table) and then press the Enter key.
3. Click the Insert tab, click the Table button, and then click the *Draw Table* option at the drop-down list. (This turns the insertion point into a pen.)
4. Using the mouse, drag in the document (below the bottom table) to create the table shown at the right. If you make a mistake, click the Undo button. You can also click the Erase button and drag over a border line to erase it. Click the Draw Table button to turn it off.

Step 4

5. After drawing the table, type **Tri-State Products** in the top cell, **Washington Division** in the cell at the left, **Oregon Division** in the middle bottom cell, and **California Division** in the cell at the right.
6. Apply the Light Grid - Accent 2 style to the table.
7. Select the table, change the font size to 12, turn on bold, and then center-align the text in the cells.
8. Make any adjustments needed to border lines so text displays on one line in each cell.
9. Drag the table so it is centered and positioned below the bottom table.
10. Save, print, and then close **WL1-C7-P2-TSPTables.docx**.

---

roject **3** **Sort and Calculate Sales Data** **2 Parts**

You will sort data in tables on Tri-State Products sales and then insert formulas to calculate total sales, average sales, and top sales.

Quick Steps

Sort Text in Tables
1. Select desired rows in table.
2. Click Sort button in Table Tools Layout tab.
3. Specify the column containing text to sort.
4. Click OK.

Sorting Text in a Table ■■■■■■■■■■■■■■■■■■■■■

With the Sort button in the Data group in the Table Tools Layout tab, you can sort text in selected cells in a table in ascending alphabetic or numeric order. To sort text, select the desired rows in the table and then click the Sort button in the Data group. At the Sort dialog box, specify the column containing the text on which you want to sort, and then click OK.

Sort

Project 3a   **Sorting Text in a Table**   **Part 1 of 2**

1. Open **TSPSalesTables.docx** and then save the document with Save As and name it **WL1-C7-P3-TSPSalesTables**.
2. Sort text in the top table by completing the following steps:
   a. Select all of the rows containing names (from *Novak, Diana* through *Sogura, Jeffrey*).
   b. Click Table Tools Layout tab.
   c. Click the Sort button in the Data group.
   d. At the Sort dialog box, click OK. (This sorts the last names in the first column in alphabetical order.)
3. After looking at the table, you decide to sort by 2010 Sales. To do this, complete the following steps:
   a. With the rows still selected, click the Sort button in the Data group.
   b. At the Sort dialog box, click the down-pointing arrow at the right side of the *Sort by* option box and then click *Column 2* at the drop-down list.
   c. Click OK.
   d. Deselect the rows.
4. Save **WL1-C7-P3-TSPSalesTables.docx**.

Step 2d

Performing Calculations in a Table ■■■■■■■■■■■■■■

fx

Formula

You can use the Formula button in the Data group in the Table Tools Layout tab to insert formulas that calculate data in a table. Numbers in cells in a table can be added, subtracted, multiplied, and divided. In addition, you can calculate averages, percentages, and minimum and maximum values. You can calculate data in a Word table, but for complex calculations use an Excel worksheet.

To perform a calculation on data in a table, position the insertion point in the cell where you want the result of the calculation inserted and then click the Formula button in the Data group in the Table Tools Layout tab. This displays the Formula dialog box shown in Figure 7.10. At this dialog box, accept the default formula that displays in the *Formula* text box or type the desired calculation, and then click OK.

Figure 7.10 Formula Dialog Box

Type the desired formula in this text box.

Click this down-pointing arrow to display a list of number formatting choices.

Click this down-pointing arrow to display a list of functions.

You can use four basic operators when writing a formula including the plus sign (+) for addition, the minus sign (hyphen) for subtraction, the asterisk (*) for multiplication, and the forward slash (/) for division. If a calculation contains two or more operators, Word calculates from left to right. If you want to change the order of calculation, use parentheses around the part of the calculation to be performed first.

In the default formula, the **SUM** part of the formula is called a *function*. Word provides other functions you can use to write a formula. These functions are available with the *Paste function* option in the Formula dialog box. For example, you can use the AVERAGE function to average numbers in cells.

Specify the numbering format with the *Number format* option at the Formula dialog box. For example, if you are calculating money amounts, you can specify that the calculated numbers display with no numbers or two numbers following the decimal point.

Project 3b **Inserting Formulas** **Part 2 of 2**

1. With **WL1-C7-P3-TSPSalesTables.docx** open, insert a formula by completing the following steps:
   a. Click in cell B9 (the empty cell located immediately below the cell containing the amount *$623,214*).
   b. Click the Table Tools Layout tab.
   c. Click the Formula button in the Data group.
   d. At the Formula dialog box, make sure *=SUM(ABOVE)* displays in the *Formula* option box.
   e. Click the down-pointing arrow at the right side of the *Number format* option box and then click *#,##0* at the drop-down list (top option in the list).
   f. Click OK to close the Formula dialog box.
   g. At the table, type a dollar sign ($) before the number just inserted in cell B9.
2. Complete steps similar to those in Steps 1c through 1g to insert a formula in cell C9 (the empty cell located immediately below the cell containing the amount *$635,099*).

Step 1d

Step 1e

Step 1f

3. Complete steps similar to those in Steps 1c through 1g to insert in the bottom table formulas that calculate totals. Insert formulas in the cells in the *Total* row and *Total* column. When inserting formulas in cells F3 through F6, you will need to change the formula to =*SUM(LEFT)*.

4. Insert a formula that calculates the average of amounts by completing the following steps:
   a. Click in cell B10 in the top table. (Cell B10 is the empty cell immediately right of the cell containing the word *Average*.)
   b. Click the Formula button in the Data group.
   c. At the Formula dialog box, delete the formula in the *Formula* text box *except* the equals sign.
   d. With the insertion point positioned immediately right of the equals sign, click the down-pointing arrow at the right side of the *Paste function* option box and then click *AVERAGE* at the drop-down list.
   e. With the insertion point positioned between the left and right parentheses, type **B2:B8**. (When typing cell designations in a formula, you can type either uppercase or lowercase letters.)
   f. Click the down-pointing arrow at the right side of the *Number format* option box and then click *#,##0* at the drop-down list (top option in the list).
   g. Click OK to close the Formula dialog box.
   h. Type a dollar sign (**$**) before the number just inserted in cell B10.

5. Complete steps similar to those in Steps 4b through 4h to insert a formula in cell C10 in the top table that calculates the average of cells C2 through C8.

6. Complete steps similar to those in Steps 4b through 4h to insert a formula in cell B7 in the bottom table that calculates the average of cells B2 through B5. Complete similar steps to insert in cell C7 the average of cells C2 through C5; insert in cell D7 the average of cells D2 through D5; insert in cell E7 the average of cells E2 through E5; and insert in cell F7 the average of cells F2 through F5.

7. Insert a formula that calculates the maximum number by completing the following steps:
   a. Click in cell B11 in the top table. (Cell B11 is the empty cell immediately right of the cell containing the words *Top Sales*.)
   b. Click the Formula button in the Data group.
   c. At the Formula dialog box, delete the formula in the *Formula* text box *except* the equals sign.
   d. With the insertion point positioned immediately right of the equals sign, click the down-pointing arrow at the right side of the *Paste function* option box and then click *MAX* at the drop-down list. (You will need to scroll down the list to display the *MAX* option.)
   e. With the insertion point positioned between the left and right parentheses, type **B2:B8**.
   f. Click the down-pointing arrow at the right side of the *Number format* option box and then click *#,##0* at the drop-down list (top option in the list).
   g. Click OK to close the Formula dialog box.
   h. Type a dollar sign (**$**) before the number just inserted in cell B11.

Step 4e

Steps 7d-7e

Step 7f

Step 7g

8. Complete steps similar to those in Steps 7b through 7h to insert the maximum number in cell C11.

9. Apply formatting to each table to enhance the visual appeal of the tables.

10. Save, print, and then close **WL1-C7-P3-TSPSalesTables.docx**.

<table>
<tr><td>**P**roject **4** **Prepare and Format a Diagram**</td><td>**2 Parts**</td></tr>
</table>

You will prepare a process diagram identifying steps in the production process and then apply formatting to enhance the diagram.

Creating SmartArt ■■■■■■■■■■■■■■■■■■■■■

With Word's SmartArt feature you can insert diagrams and organizational charts in a document. SmartArt offers a variety of predesigned diagrams and organizational charts that are available at the Choose a SmartArt Graphic dialog box shown in Figure 7.11. At this dialog box, *All* is selected in the left panel and all available predesigned diagrams display in the middle panel.

HINT

Use SmartArt to communicate your message and ideas in a visual manner.

SmartArt

Figure 7.11 Choose a SmartArt Graphic Dialog Box

Double-click the desired SmartArt graphic in this panel.

Choose the SmartArt graphic category from options in this panel.

Click a SmartArt graphic in the middle panel and then read a description of the graphic here.

Inserting and Formatting a SmartArt Diagram

Predesigned diagrams display in the middle panel of the Choose a SmartArt Graphic dialog box. Use the scroll bar at the right side of the middle panel to scroll down the list of diagram choices. Click a diagram in the middle panel and the name of the diagram displays in the right panel along with a description of the diagram type. SmartArt includes diagrams for presenting a list of data; showing data processes, cycles, and relationships; and presenting data in a matrix or pyramid. Double-click a diagram in the middle panel of the dialog box and the diagram is inserted in the document.

When you double-click a diagram at the dialog box, the diagram is inserted in the document and a text pane displays at the left side of the diagram. You can type text in the diagram in the text pane or directly in the diagram. Apply design formatting to a diagram with options at the SmartArt Tools Design tab. This tab

▼ **Quick Steps**

Insert a SmartArt Diagram
1. Click Insert tab.
2. Click SmartArt button.
3. Double-click desired diagram.

HINT

Limit the number of shapes and the amount of text to key points.

is active when the diagram is inserted in the document. With options and buttons in this tab you add objects, change the diagram layout, apply a style to the diagram, and reset the diagram back to the original formatting.

Apply formatting to a diagram with options at the SmartArt Tools Format tab. With options and buttons in this tab you can change the size and shape of objects in the diagram; apply shape styles and WordArt styles; change the shape fill, outline, and effects; and arrange and size the diagram.

Project 4a   **Inserting and Formatting a Diagram**   **Part 1 of 2**

1. At a blank document, insert the diagram shown in Figure 7.12 by completing the following steps:
   a. Click the Insert tab.
   b. Click the SmartArt button in the Illustrations group.
   c. At the Choose a SmartArt Graphic dialog box, click *Process* in the left panel and then double-click the *Alternating Flow* diagram (see image at the right).
   d. If a *Type your text here* text pane does not display at the left side of the diagram, click the Text Pane button in the Create Graphic group to display the pane.
   e. With the insertion point positioned after the top bullet in the *Type your text here* text pane, type **Design**.
   f. Click *[Text]* that displays below *Design* and then type **Mock-up**.
   g. Continue clicking occurrences of *[Text]* and typing text so the text pane displays as shown at the right.
   h. Close the text pane by clicking the Close button (contains an X) that displays in the upper right corner of the pane. (You can also click the Text Pane button in the Create Graphic group.)
2. Change the diagram colors by clicking the Change Colors button in the SmartArt Styles group and then clicking the first option in the *Colorful* section (*Colorful - Accent Colors*).

3. Apply a style by clicking the More button that displays at the right side of the thumbnails in the SmartArt Styles group and then clicking the second option from the left in the top row of the *3-D* section (*Inset*).

4. Copy the diagram and then change the layout by completing the following steps:

   a. Click inside the diagram border but outside of any shapes.

   b. Click the Home tab and then click the Copy button in the Clipboard group.

   c. Press Ctrl + End, press the Enter key once, and then press Ctrl + Enter to insert a page break.

   d. Click the Paste button in the Clipboard group.

   e. Click the bottom diagram in the document.

   f. Click the SmartArt Tools Design tab.

   g. Click the More button that displays at the right side of the thumbnails in the Layouts group and then click the Continuous Block Process layout (see image at the right).

   h. Click outside the diagram to deselect it.

5. Save the document and name it **WL1-C7-P4-Diagrams**.

Figure 7.12 Project 4a

Arranging and Moving a SmartArt Diagram

Before moving a SmartArt diagram, you must select a text wrapping style. Select a text wrapping style with the Arrange button in the SmartArt Tools Format tab. Click the Position button, and then click the desired position at the drop-down gallery. You can also choose a text wrapping style by clicking the Wrap Text button

Position

Text Wrap

and then clicking the desired wrapping style at the drop-down list. Move the diagram by positioning the arrow pointer on the diagram border until the pointer turns into a four-headed arrow, holding down the left mouse button, and then dragging the diagram to the desired location. Nudge selected shape(s) with the up, down, left, or right arrow keys on the keyboard.

Project 4b **Formatting Diagrams**   **Part 2 of 2**

1. With **WL1-C7-P4-Diagrams.docx** open, format shapes by completing the following steps:
   a. Click the diagram on the first page to select it (light gray border surrounds the diagram).
   b. Click the SmartArt Tools Format tab.
   c. In the diagram, click the rectangle shape containing the word *Design*.
   d. Hold down the Shift key and then click the shape containing the word *Development*.
   e. With the Shift key still down, click the shape containing the word *Implementation*. (All three shapes should now be selected.)
   f. Click the Change Shape button in the Shapes group.
   g. Click the seventh shape from the left in the second row of the *Block Arrows* section (the Pentagon shape).
   h. With the shapes still selected, click the Larger button in the Shapes group.
   i. With the shapes still selected, click the Shape Outline button arrow in the Shape Styles group and then click the red color *Red, Accent 2*.
   j. Click inside the diagram border but outside any shape. (This deselects the shapes but keeps the diagram selected.)

2. Change the size of the diagram by completing the following steps:
   a. Click the Size button located at the right side of the SmartArt Tools Format tab.
   b. Click in the *Height* measurement box, type 4, and then press Enter.
3. Position the diagram by completing the following steps:
   a. Click the Position button in the Arrange group in the SmartArt Tools Format tab.
   b. Click the middle option in the second row of the *With Text Wrapping* section (the *Position in Middle Center with Square Text Wrapping* option).

4. Format the bottom diagram by completing the following steps:

a. Press Ctrl + End to move to the end of the document and then click in the bottom diagram to select it.

b. Hold down the Shift key and then click each of the three shapes.

c. Click the More button at the right side of the style thumbnail in the WordArt Styles group in the SmartArt Tools Format tab.

d. Click the last WordArt style in the lower right corner of the drop-down gallery (*Fill - Blue, Accent 1, Metal Bevel, Reflection*).

e. Click the Text Outline button arrow in the WordArt Styles group and then click the light blue color in the *Standard Colors* section (the seventh color from the left).

f. Click the Text Effects button in the WordArt Styles group, point to *Glow* at the drop-down list, and then click the last option in the top row (*Orange, 5 pt glow, Accent color 6*).

g. Click inside the diagram border but outside any shape.

5. Arrange the diagram by clicking the Position button in the Arrange group and then clicking the middle option in the second row of the *With Text Wrapping* section (the *Position in Middle Center with Square Text Wrapping* option).

6. Save, print, and then close **WL1-C7-P4-Diagrams.docx**.

Step 4d

Step 4f

 roject **5** **Prepare and Format a Company Organizational Chart** **1 Part**

You will prepare an organizational chart for a company and then apply formatting to enhance the visual appeal of the organizational chart.

Creating an Organizational Chart with SmartArt

If you need to visually illustrate hierarchical data, consider creating an organizational chart with a SmartArt option. To display organizational chart SmartArt options, click the Insert tab and then click the SmartArt button in the Illustrations group. At the Choose a SmartArt Graphic dialog box, click *Hierarchy* in the left panel. Organizational chart options display in the middle panel of the dialog box. Double-click the desired organizational chart and the chart is inserted

▼ **Quick Steps**

Insert an Organizational Chart
1. Click Insert tab.
2. Click SmartArt button.
3. Click *Hierarchy*.
4. Double-click desired organizational chart.

in the document. Type text in a diagram by selecting the shape and then typing text in the shape or you can type text in the *Type your text here* window that displays at the left side of the diagram. Format a SmartArt organizational chart with options and buttons in the SmartArt Tools Design tab and the SmartArt Tools Format tab.

Project 5   Creating and Formatting an Organizational Chart   Part 1 of 1

1. At a blank document, create the organizational chart shown in Figure 7.13. To begin, click the Insert tab.
2. Click the SmartArt button in the Illustrations group.
3. At the Choose a SmartArt Graphic dialog box, click *Hierarchy* in the left panel of the dialog box and then double-click the first option in the middle panel, *Organization Chart*.
4. If a *Type your text here* window displays at the left side of the organizational chart, close the pane by clicking the Text Pane button in the Create Graphic group.
5. Delete one of the boxes in the organizational chart by clicking the border of the box in the lower right corner to select it and then pressing the Delete key. (Make sure that the selection border that surrounds the box is a solid line and not a dashed line. If a dashed line displays, click the box border again. This should change it to a solid line.)
6. With the bottom right box selected, click the Add Shape button arrow in the Create Graphic group and then click the *Add Shape Below* option.
7. Click *[Text]* in the top box, type **Blaine Willis**, press Shift + Enter, and then type **President**. Click in each of the remaining boxes and type the text as shown in Figure 7.13. (Press Shift + Enter after typing the name.)
8. Click the More button located at the right side of the style thumbnails in the SmartArt Styles group and then click the *Inset* style in the *3-D* section (second option from the left in the top row of the *3-D* section).
9. Click the Change Colors button in the SmartArt Styles group and then click the *Colorful Range - Accent Colors 4 to 5* in the *Colorful* section (fourth option from the left in the *Colorful* row).
10. Click the SmartArt Tools Format tab.
11. Click the tab (displays with a right-pointing and a left-pointing triangle) that displays at the left side of the diagram border. (This displays the *Type your text here* window.)
12. Using the mouse, select the text that displays in the *Type your text here* window.

13. Click the Change Shape button in the Shapes group and then click the *Round Same Side Corner Rectangle* option (second option from the *right* in the top row).

14. Click the Shape Outline button arrow in the Shape Styles group and then click the dark blue color (second color from the *right* in the *Standard Colors* section).

15. Close the *Type your text here* window by clicking the Close button (marked with an X) located in the upper right corner of the window.

16. Click inside the organizational chart border but outside any shape.

17. Click the Size button located at the right side of the ribbon in the SmartArt Tools Format tab, click in the *Height* measurement box, and type **4**. Click in the *Width* measurement box, type **6.5**, and then press Enter.

18. Click outside the chart to deselect it.

19. Save the document and name it **WL1-C7-P5-OrgChart**.

20. Print and then close the document.

Figure 7.13 Project 5

Chapter Summary

- Use the Tables feature to create columns and rows of information. Create a table with the Table button in the Tables group in the Insert tab or with options at the Insert Table dialog box.

- A cell is the intersection between a row and a column. The lines that form the cells of the table are called gridlines.

- Move the insertion point to cells in a document using the mouse by clicking in the desired cell or use the keyboard commands shown in Table 7.1.

- Change the table design with options and buttons in the Table Tools Design tab.

- Refer to Table 7.2 for a list of mouse commands for selecting specific cells in a table and Table 7.3 for a list of keyboard commands for selecting specific cells in a table.

- Change the layout of a table with options and buttons in the Table Tools Layout tab.

- You can select a table, column, row, or cell using the Select button in the Table group in the Table Tools Layout tab.

- Turn on and off the display of gridlines by clicking the Table Tools Layout tab and then clicking the View Gridlines button in the Table group.

- Insert and delete columns and rows with buttons in the Rows & Columns group in the Table Tools Layout tab.

- Merge selected cells with the Merge Cells button and split cells with the Split Cells button, both located in the Merge group in the Table Tools Layout tab.

- Change column width and row height using the height and width measurement boxes in the Cell Size group in the Table Tools Layout tab; by dragging move table column markers on the horizontal ruler, adjust table row markers on the vertical ruler, or gridlines in the table; or with the AutoFit button in the Cell Size group.

- Change alignment of text in cells with buttons in the Alignment group in the Table Tools Layout tab.

- If a table spans two pages, you can insert a header row at the beginning of the rows that extend to the next page. To do this, click in the header row, or select the desired header rows, and then click the Repeat Header Rows button in the Data group in the Table Tools Layout tab.

- Quick Tables are predesigned tables you can insert in a document by clicking the Insert tab, clicking the Table button, pointing to *Quick Tables*, and then clicking the desired table at the side menu.

- Change cell margins with options in the Table Options dialog box.

- Change text direction in a cell with the Text Direction button in the Alignment group.

- Change the table alignment at the Table Properties dialog box with the Table tab selected.

- You can use the resize handle to change the size of the table and the table move handle to move the table.

- Convert text to a table with the *Convert Text to Table* option at the Table button drop-down list. Convert a table to text with the Convert to Text button in the Data group in the Table Tools Layout tab.

- Draw a table in a document by clicking the Insert tab, clicking the Table button, and then clicking *Draw Table*. Using the mouse, drag in the document to create the table.

- Sort selected rows in a table with the Sort button in the Data group.

- Perform calculations on data in a table by clicking the Formula button in the Data group in the Table Tools Layout tab and then specifying the formula and number format at the Formula dialog box.

- Use the SmartArt feature to insert predesigned diagrams and organizational charts in a document. Click the SmartArt button in the Insert tab to display the Choose a SmartArt Graphic dialog box.

- Format a SmartArt diagram or organizational chart with options and buttons in the SmartArt Tools Design tab and the SmartArt Tools Format tab.

- To move a SmartArt diagram, first choose a position or a text wrapping style with the Arrange button in the SmartArt Tools Format tab.

Commands Review

FEATURE	RIBBON TAB, GROUP	BUTTON	OPTION
Table	Insert, Tables		
Insert Table dialog box	Insert, Tables		Insert Table
Draw table	Insert, Tables		Draw Table
View gridlines	Table Tools Layout, Table		
Insert column left	Table Tools Layout, Rows & Columns		
Insert column right	Table Tools Layout, Rows & Columns		
Insert row above	Table Tools Layout, Rows & Columns		
Insert row below	Table Tools Layout, Rows & Columns		
Delete table	Table Tools Layout, Rows & Columns		Delete Table
Delete row	Table Tools Layout, Rows & Columns		Delete Rows
Delete column	Table Tools Layout, Rows & Columns		Delete Columns
Merge cells	Table Tools Layout, Merge		
Split cells dialog box	Table Tools Layout, Merge		
AutoFit table contents	Table Tools Layout, Cell Size		
Cell alignment	Table Tools Layout, Alignment		
Repeat header row	Table Tools Layout, Data		
Insert Quick Table	Insert, Tables		Quick Tables
Table Options dialog box	Table Tools Layout, Alignment		
Text direction	Table Tools Layout, Alignment		
Convert text to table	Insert, Tables		Convert Text to Table
Convert table to text	Table Tools Layout, Data		
Sort text in table	Table Tools Layout, Data		
Formula dialog box	Table Tools Layout, Data		
Choose a SmartArt Graphic dialog box	Insert, Illustrations		

Concepts Check Test Your Knowledge

Completion: In the space provided at the right, indicate the correct term, command, or number.

1. The Table button is located in this tab. _____

2. This is another name for the lines that form the cells of the table. _____

3. Use this keyboard shortcut to move the insertion point to the previous cell. _____

4. Use this keyboard shortcut to move the insertion point to a tab within a cell. _____

5. This tab contains table styles you can apply to a table. _____

6. Click this button in the Table Tools Layout tab to insert a column at the left side of the column containing the insertion point. _____

7. Insert and delete columns and rows with buttons in this group in the Table Tools Layout tab. _____

8. One method for changing column width is dragging this on the horizontal ruler. _____

9. Use this button in the Cell Size group to make the column widths in a table automatically fit the contents. _____

10. Change the table alignment at this dialog box with the Table tab selected. _____

11. Hover the mouse pointer over a table and this displays in the lower right corner of the table. _____

12. Position the mouse pointer in a table and this displays in the upper left corner. _____

13. Display the Formula dialog box by clicking the Formula button in this group in the Table Tools Layout tab. _____

14. A variety of predesigned diagrams and organizational charts are available at this dialog box. _____

15. The SmartArt button is located in this tab. _____

16. If you need to visually illustrate hierarchical data, consider creating this with the SmartArt feature. _____

Skills Check Assess Your Performance

Assessment

1 CREATE AND FORMAT A PROPERTY REPLACEMENT COSTS TABLE

1. At a blank document, create the table shown in Figure 7.14 with the following specifications:
   a. Create a table with two columns and eight rows.
   b. Merge the cells in the top row.
   c. Type the text in the cells as shown in Figure 7.14.
   d. Right-align the cells containing the money amounts as well as the blank line below the last amount (cells B2 through B8).
   e. Automatically fit the contents of the cells.
   f. Apply the *Light List - Accent 4* table style.
   g. Remove the check mark from the *First Column* check box.
   h. Draw a green (*Olive Green, Accent 3, Darker 25%*) 1½ pt border around the table.
   i. Change the font size to 14 for the text in cell A1 and change the alignment to Align Center.
   j. Use the resize handle located in the lower right corner of the table and increase the width and height of the table by approximately one inch.
2. Click in the *Accounts receivable* cell and insert a row below. Type **Equipment** in the new cell at the left and type **$83,560** in the new cell at the right.
3. Insert a formula in cell B9 that sums the amounts in cell B2 through B8. (Insert a dollar sign before the amount in cell B9.)
4. Save the document and name it **WL1-C7-A1-CostsTable**.
5. Print and then close **WL1-C7-A1-CostsTable.docx**.

Figure 7.14 Assessment 1

PROPERTY Replacement Costs	
Business personal property	$1,367,340
Earnings and expenses	$945,235
Domestic and foreign transit	$123,400
Accounts receivable	$95,460
Legal liability	$75,415
Computer coverage	$53,098
Total	

Assessment

2 ### FORMAT A TABLE CONTAINING TRANSPORTATION SERVICE INFORMATION

1. Open **ServicesTable.docx** and then save the document with Save As and name it **WL1-C7-A2-ServicesTable**.
2. Format the table so it appears as shown in Figure 7.15.
3. Position the table in the middle of the page.
4. Save, print, and then close **WL1-C7-A2-ServicesTable.docx**.

Figure 7.15 Assessment 2

Metro Area Transportation Services	Service	Telephone
	Langley City Transit	
	Subway and bus information	(507) 555-3049
	Service status hotline	(507) 555-4123
	Travel information	(507) 555-4993
	Valley Rail Road	
	Railway information	(202) 555-2300
	Status hotline	(202) 555-2343
	Travel information	(202) 555-2132
	Mainline Bus	
	Bus routes	(507) 555-6530
	Emergency hotline	(507) 555-6798
	Travel information	(507) 555-7542
	Village Travel Card	
	Village office	(507) 555-1232
	Card inquiries	(507) 555-1930

Assessment

3 ### CREATE AND FORMAT A COMPANY DIAGRAM

1. At a blank document, create the SmartArt diagram shown in Figure 7.16 with the following specifications:
   a. Use the Titled Matrix diagram.
   b. Apply the *Colorful - Accent Colors SmartArt* style.
   c. Type all of the text shown in Figure 7.16.
   d. Select all of the text and then apply the *Fill - Red, Accent 2, Matte Bevel WordArt* style.
2. Save the document and name it **WL1-C7-A3-SDCDiagram**.
3. Print and then close **WL1-C7-A3-SDCDiagram.docx**.

Figure 7.16 Assessment 3

Assessment

4 CREATE AND FORMAT A COMPANY ORGANIZATIONAL CHART

1. At a blank document, create the organizational chart shown in Figure 7.17 with the following specifications:
   a. Use the Hierarchy chart.
   b. Select the top text box and insert a shape above.
   c. Select the top right text box and then add a shape below.
   d. Type the text shown in the organizational chart in Figure 7.17.
   e. Apply the *Colorful Range - Accent Colors 2 to 3* option.
   f. Increase the height to 4.5" and the width to 6.5".
   g. Position the organizational chart in the middle of the page.
2. Save the document and name it **WL1-C7-A4-OrgChart**.
3. Print and then close **WL1-C7-A4-OrgChart.docx**.

Figure 7.17 Assessment 4

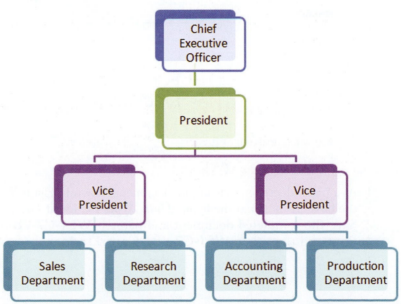

Assessment

5 INSERT FORMULAS IN A TABLE

1. In this chapter, you learned how to insert formulas in a table. Experiment with writing formulas (consider using the Help feature or other reference) and then open **FinAnalysis.docx**. Save the document with Save As and name it **WL1-C7-A5-FinAnalysis**.
2. Format the table so it appears as shown in Figure 7.18.
3. Insert a formula in cell B13 that sums the amounts in cells B6 through B12. Complete similar steps to insert a formula in cell C13, D13, and E13.
4. Insert a formula in cell B14 that subtracts the amount in B13 from the amount in B4. *Hint: The formula should look like this:* **=(B4-B13)**. Complete similar steps to insert a formula in cells C14, D14, and E14.
5. Save, print, and then close **WL1-C7-A5-FinAnalysis.docx**.

Figure 7.18 Assessment 5

TRI-STATE PRODUCTS

Financial Analysis

	2009	2010	2011	2012
Revenue	$1,450,348	$1,538,239	$1,634,235	$1,523,455
Expenses				
Facilities	$250,220	$323,780	$312,485	$322,655
Materials	$93,235	$102,390	$87,340	$115,320
Payroll	$354,390	$374,280	$380,120	$365,120
Benefits	$32,340	$35,039	$37,345	$36,545
Marketing	$29,575	$28,350	$30,310	$31,800
Transportation	$4,492	$5,489	$5,129	$6,349
Miscellaneous	$4,075	$3,976	$4,788	$5,120
Total				
Net Revenue				

Visual Benchmark Demonstrate Your Proficiency

1 CREATE A COVER LETTER CONTAINING A TABLE

1. At a blank document, create the document shown in Figure 7.19. Create and format the table as shown in the figure. *Hint: Apply the* **Light Grid - Accent 5** *table style*.
2. Save the completed document and name it **WL1-C7-VB1-CoverLtr**.
3. Print and then close **WL1-C7-VB1-CoverLtr.docx**.

Figure 7.19 Visual Benchmark 1

10234 Larkspur Drive
Cheyenne, WY 82002
July 15, 2012

Dr. Theresa Solberg
Rocky Mountain News
100 Second Avenue
Cheyenne, WY 82001

Dear Dr. Solberg:

Your advertised opening for a corporate communications staff writer describes interesting challenges. As you can see from the table below, my skills and experience are excellent matches for the position.

QUALIFICATIONS AND SKILLS	
Your Requirements	**My Experience, Skills, and Value Offered**
Two years of business writing experience	Four years of experience creating diverse business messages, from corporate communications to feature articles and radio broadcast material.
Ability to complete projects on deadline	Proven project coordination skills and tight deadline focus. My current role as producer of a daily three-hour talk-radio program requires planning, coordination, and execution of many detailed tasks, always in the face of inflexible deadlines.
Oral presentation skills	Unusually broad experience, including high-profile roles as an on-air radio presence and "the voice" for an on-hold telephone message company.
Relevant education (BA or BS)	BA in Mass Communications; one year post-graduate study in Multimedia Communications.

As you will note from the enclosed résumé, my experience encompasses corporate, print media, and multimedia environments. I offer a diverse and proven skill set that can help your company create and deliver its message to various audiences to build image, market presence, and revenue. I look forward to meeting with you to discuss the value I can offer your company.

Sincerely,

Marcus Tolliver

Enclosure: Résumé

2 CREATE AND FORMAT A SMARTART DIAGRAM

1. At a blank document, create the document shown in Figure 7.20. Create and format the SmartArt diagram as shown in the figure. *Hint: Use the* **Step Up Process** *diagram*.
2. Save the completed document and name it **WL1-C7-VB2-SalesDiagram**.
3. Print and then close **WL1-C7-VB2-SalesDiagram.docx**.

Figure 7.20 Visual Benchmark 2

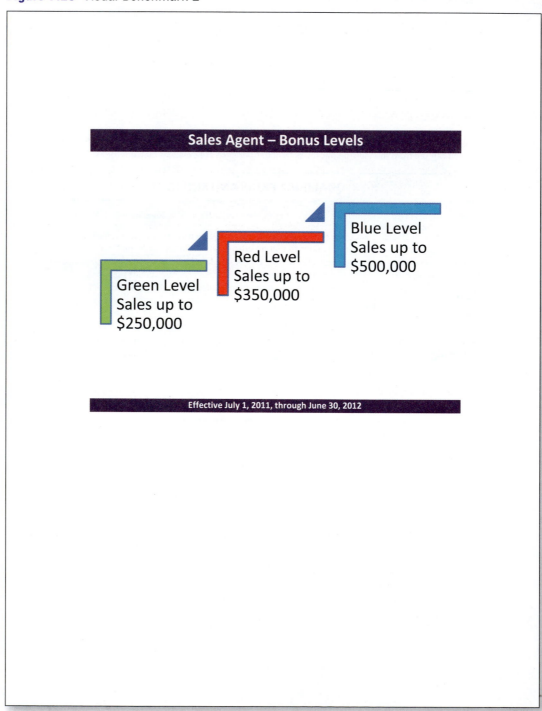

Case Study Apply Your Skills

Part 1

You have recently been hired as an accounting clerk for a landscaping business, Landmark Landscaping, which has two small offices in your city. The accounting clerk prior to you kept track of monthly sales using Word, and the manager would prefer that you continue using that application. Open the file named **LLMoSales.docx** and then save the document with Save As and name it **WL1-C7-CS-LLMoSales**. After reviewing the information, you decide that a table would be a better way of maintaining and displaying the data. Convert the data to a table and modify its appearance so that it is easy to read and understand. Insert a total row at the bottom of the table and then insert formulas to sum the totals in the columns containing amounts. Apply formatting to the table to enhance the visual appeal. Determine a color theme for the table and then continue that same color theme when preparing other documents for Landmark Landscaping. Save, print, and then close the document.

Part 2

The president of Landmark Landscaping has asked you to prepare an organizational chart for the company that will become part of the company profile. Use a SmartArt organizational chart and create a chart with the following company titles (in the order shown below):

Format the organizational chart to enhance the visual appeal and apply colors that match the color scheme you chose for the company in Part 1. Save the document and name it **WL1-C7-CS-LLOrgChart**. Print and then close the document.

Part 3

As part of the company profile, the president of the company would like to include a diagram that represents the services offered by the company and use the diagram as a company marketing tool. Use SmartArt to create a diagram that contains the following services: Maintenance Contracts, Planting Services, Landscape Design, and Landscape Consultation. Format the diagram to enhance the visual appeal and apply colors that match the color scheme you chose for the company in Part 1. Save the document and name it **WL1-C7-CS-LLServices**. Print and then close the document.

Part 4

The office manager has started a training document with information on using SmartArt. He has asked you to add information on keyboard shortcuts for working with shapes in a SmartArt graphic. Use the Help feature to learn about the keyboard shortcuts available for working with shapes and then create a table and insert the information in the table. Format the table to enhance the visual appeal and apply colors that match the color scheme you chose for the company in Part 1. Save the document and name it **WL1-C7-CS-SAShortcuts**. Print and then close the document.

Part 5

One of the landscape architects has asked you to prepare a table containing information on trees that need to be ordered next month. She would also like to have you include the Latin name for the trees since this is important when ordering. Create a table that contains the common name of the tree, the Latin name, the number required, and the price per tree as shown in Figure 7.21. Use the Internet (or any other resource available to you) to find the Latin name of each tree listed in Figure 7.21. Create a column in the table that multiplies the number of trees required by the price and include this formula for each tree. Format and enhance the table so it is attractive and easy to read. Save the document and name it **WL1-C7-CS-LLTrees**. Print and then close the document.

Figure 7.21 Case Study, Part 5

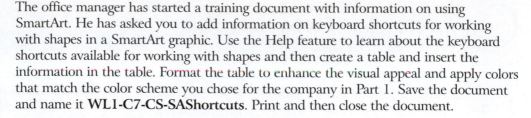

Douglas Fir, 15 required, $1.99 per tree
White Elm, 10 required, $2.49 per tree
Western Hemlock, 10 required, $1.89 per tree
Red Maple, 8 required, $6.99 per tree
Ponderosa Pine, 5 required, $2.69 per tree

Word Microsoft

Merging Documents

PERFORMANCE OBJECTIVES

Upon successful completion of Chapter 8, you will be able to:

- **Create and merge letters, envelopes, labels, and a directory**
- **Create custom fields for a merge**
- **Edit main documents and data source files**
- **Input text during a merge**

Tutorials

8.1 Creating a Data Source File

8.2 Creating a Main Document

8.3 Creating Form Letters Using Mail Merge

8.4 Merging Envelopes

8.5 Editing a Data Source File

Word includes a Mail Merge feature you can use to create customized letters, envelopes, labels, directories, e-mail messages, and faxes. The Mail Merge feature is useful for situations where you need to send the same letter to a number of people and create an envelope for each letter. Use Mail Merge to create a main document that contains a letter, envelope, or other data and then merge the main document with a data source. In this chapter, you will use Mail Merge to create letters, envelopes, labels, and directories. Model answers for this chapter's projects appear on the following pages.

Word2010L1C8

Note: Before beginning the projects, copy to your storage medium the Word2010L1C8 subfolder from the Word2010L1 folder in the CD that accompanies this textbook and then make Word2010L1C8 the active folder.

February 23, 2012

«AddressBlock»

«GreetingLine»

McCormack Funds is lowering its expense charges beginning May 1, 2012. The reductions in expense charges mean that more of your account investment performance in the «Fund» is returned to you, «Title» «Last_Name». The reductions are worth your attention because most of our competitors' fees have gone up.

Lowering expense charges is noteworthy because before the reduction, McCormack expense deductions were already among the lowest, far below most mutual funds and variable annuity accounts with similar objectives. At the same time, services for you, our client, will continue to expand. If you would like to discuss this change, please call us at (212) 555-2277. Your financial future is our main concern at McCormack.

Sincerely,

Jodie Langstrom
Director, Financial Services

XX
WL1-C8-P1-MFMD.docx

February 23, 2012

Mr. Kenneth Porter
7645 Tenth Street
Apt. 314
New York, NY 10192

Dear Mr. Porter:

McCormack Funds is lowering its expense charges beginning May 1, 2012. The reductions in expense charges mean that more of your account investment performance in the Mutual Investment Fund is returned to you, Mr. Porter. The reductions are worth your attention because most of our competitors' fees have gone up.

Lowering expense charges is noteworthy because before the reduction, McCormack expense deductions were already among the lowest, far below most mutual funds and variable annuity accounts with similar objectives. At the same time, services for you, our client, will continue to expand. If you would like to discuss this change, please call us at (212) 555-2277. Your financial future is our main concern at McCormack.

Sincerely,

Jodie Langstrom
Director, Financial Services

XX
WL1-C8-P1-MFMD.docx

Page 1

Project 1 Merge Letters to Customers

WL1-C8-P1-MFMD.docx

February 23, 2012

Ms. Carolyn Renquist
13255 Meridian Street
New York, NY 10435

Dear Ms. Renquist:

McCormack Funds is lowering its expense charges beginning charges mean that more of your account investment perfo to you, Ms. Renquist. The reductions are worth your atten have gone up.

Lowering expense charges is noteworthy because before were already among the lowest, far below most mutual fu objectives. At the same time, services for you, our client, discuss this change, please call us at (212) 555-2277. Your McCormack.

Sincerely,

Jodie Langstrom
Director, Financial Services

XX
WL1-C8-P1-MFMD.docx

Page 2

February 23, 2012

Dr. Amil Ranna
433 South 17th
Apt. 17-D
New York, NY 10322

Dear Dr. Ranna:

McCormack Funds is lowering its expense charges beginni charges mean that more of your account investment perfe to you, Dr. Ranna. The reductions are worth your attentio gone up.

Lowering expense charges is noteworthy because before were already among the lowest, far below most mutual fu objectives. At the same time, services for you, our client, discuss this change, please call us at (212) 555-2277. Your McCormack.

Sincerely,

Jodie Langstrom
Director, Financial Services

XX
WL1-C8-P1-MFMD.docx

Page 3

February 23, 2012

Mrs. Wanda Houston
566 North 22nd Avenue
New York, NY 10634

Dear Mrs. Houston:

McCormack Funds is lowering its expense charges beginning May 1, 2012. The reductions in expense charges mean that more of your account investment performance in the Quality Care Fund is returned to you, Mrs. Houston. The reductions are worth your attention because most of our competitors' fees have gone up.

Lowering expense charges is noteworthy because before the reduction, McCormack expense deductions were already among the lowest, far below most mutual funds and variable annuity accounts with similar objectives. At the same time, services for you, our client, will continue to expand. If you would like to discuss this change, please call us at (212) 555-2277. Your financial future is our main concern at McCormack.

Sincerely,

Jodie Langstrom
Director, Financial Services

XX
WL1-C8-P1-MFMD.docx

Page 4

Mr. Kenneth Porter
7645 Tenth Street
Apt. 314
New York, NY 10192

Ms. Carolyn Renquist
13255 Meridian Street
New York, NY 10435

Project 2 Merge Envelopes

WL1-C8-P2-MFEnvs.docx

Project 3 Merge Mailing Labels

WL-C8-P3-LabelsMD.docx

Last Name	First Name	Fund
Porter	Kenneth	Mutual Investment Fund
Renquist	Carolyn	Quality Care Fund
Ranna	Amil	Priority One Fund
Houston	Wanda	Quality Care Fund

Project 4 Merge a Directory

WL1-C8-P4-Directory.docx

Name	Home Phone	Cell Phone
Saunders, Martin	413-555-3492	410-555-1249
Delaney, Antonia	410-555-2009	413-555-3492
Perkins, Amanda	410-555-5743	410-555-0695
Hogan, Gregory	410-555-3448	410-555-9488
Grenwald, Anita	410-555-6784	413-555-1200
Childers, Jillian	410-555-3833	410-555-7522
Bellamy, Rebecca	410-555-4755	410-555-8833
Benoit, Victoria	410-555-3482	413-555-9378
Fernandez, Darlene	410-555-7833	410-555-4261
Kaszycki, Brian	410-555-3842	410-555-9944
Stahl, Kaycee	410-555-2331	413-555-2321
Davis, Jennae	410-555-5774	410-555-9435

Mr. Martin Saunders
231 South 41st Street
P.O. Box 3321
Baltimore, MD 20156

Ms. Amanda Perkins
9033 North Ridge Drive
Apt. #401
Baltimore, MD 20487

Ms. Anita Grenwald
580 Capital Lane
#1002-B
Baltimore, MD 20384

Mr. Steve Dutton
3490 East 145th
Apt. B
Baltimore, MD 20468

Mrs. Darlene Fernandez
12115 South 42nd
#20-G
Baltimore, MD 20376

Mrs. Kaycee Stahl
450 Washington Ave.
Baltimore, MD 20376

Project 5 Select Records and Merge Mailing Labels

WL1-C8-P5-SFLabels.docx

Project 6 Edit Records in a Data Source File

WL1-C8-P6-Directory.docx

Page 1

February 23, 2012

Mr. Kenneth Porter
7645 Tenth Street
Apt. 314
New York, NY 10192

Dear Mr. Porter:

McCormack Funds is lowering its expense charges beginning May 1, 2012. The reductions in expense charges mean that more of your account investment performance in the Mutual Investment Fund is returned to you, Mr. Porter. The reductions are worth your attention because most of our competitors' fees have gone up.

Lowering expense charges is noteworthy because before the reduction, McCormack expense deductions were already among the lowest, far below most mutual funds and variable annuity accounts with similar objectives. At the same time, services for you, our client, will continue to expand. If you would like to discuss this change, please call our service representative, Marilyn Smythe, at (646) 555-8944.

Sincerely,

Jodie Langstrom
Director, Financial Services

XX
WL1-C8-P1-MFMD.docx

Page 2

February 23, 2012

Ms. Carolyn Renquist
13255 Meridian Street
New York, NY 10435

Dear Ms. Renquist:

McCormack Funds is lowering its exp
charges mean that more of your acco
to you, Ms. Renquist. The reductions
have gone up.

Lowering expense charges is notewo
were already among the lowest, far b
objectives. At the same time, service
discuss this change, please call our se

Sincerely,

Jodie Langstrom
Director, Financial Services

XX
WL1-C8-P1-MFMD.docx

Page 3

February 23, 2012

Dr. Amil Ranna
433 South 17th
Apt. 17-D
New York, NY 10322

Dear Dr. Ranna:

McCormack Funds is lowering its exp
charges mean that more of your acco
to you, Dr. Ranna. The reductions are
gone up.

Lowering expense charges is notewo
were already among the lowest, far b
objectives. At the same time, service
discuss this change, please call our se

Sincerely,

Jodie Langstrom
Director, Financial Services

XX
WL1-C8-P1-MFMD.docx

Page 4

February 23, 2012

Mrs. Wanda Houston
566 North 22nd Avenue
New York, NY 10634

Dear Mrs. Houston:

McCormack Funds is lowering its expense charges beginning May 1, 2012. The reductions in expense charges mean that more of your account investment performance in the Quality Care Fund is returned to you, Mrs. Houston. The reductions are worth your attention because most of our competitors' fees have gone up.

Lowering expense charges is noteworthy because before the reduction, McCormack expense deductions were already among the lowest, far below most mutual funds and variable annuity accounts with similar objectives. At the same time, services for you, our client, will continue to expand. If you would like to discuss this change, please call our service representative, Thomas Rivers, at (646) 555-0793.

Sincerely,

Jodie Langstrom
Director, Financial Services

XX
WL1-C8-P1-MFMD.docx

Project 7 Add Fill-in Fields to a Main Document

WL1-C8-P7-MFMD.docx

Page 1

Sorenson Funds

January 22, 2013

Mr. Martin Saunders
231 South 41st Street
P.O. Box 3321
Baltimore, MD 20156

Dear Mr. Saunders:

Last year, a law went into effect that changes the maximum amounts that may be contributed to defined contribution pension and tax-deferred annuity plans, such as those using Sorenson Funds annuities. Generally, the changes slow down the rate at which the maximums will increase in the future. A likely result is that more people will reach the maximum and, if they wish to save more for their retirement, they will have to use after-tax savings instruments.

The amount of money you can voluntarily contribute to your fund was expected to rise above the current maximum. The amendments will delay any cost-of-living adjustments, and the limit will probably not go up for several years. The changes in the law will have an effect on your next annuity statement. If you want to increase or decrease the amount you contribute to your fund, please let us know.

Sincerely,

Jennifer Tann
Director of Financial Services

XX
SFLtrMD.docx

6250 Aurora Boulevard ✦ Baltimore, MD 20372 ✦ 1-888-555-0344

Page 2

Sorenson Funds

January 22, 2013

Mrs. Antonia Delaney
11220 East Madison
Rosedale, MD 21237

Dear Mrs. Delaney:

Last year, a law went into effect that changes the maximum amounts that may be contributed to defined contribution pension and tax-deferred annuity plans, such as those using Sorenson Funds annuities. Generally, the changes slow down the rate at which the maximums will increase in the future. A likely result is that more people will reach the maximum and, if they wish to save more for their retirement, they will have to use after-tax savings instruments.

The amount of money you can voluntarily contribute to your fund was expected to rise above the current maximum. The amendments will delay any cost-of-living adjustments, and the limit will probably not go up for several years. The changes in the law will have an effect on your next annuity statement. If you want to increase or decrease the amount you contribute to your fund, please let us know.

Sincerely,

Jennifer Tann
Director of Financial Services

XX
SFLtrMD.docx

6250 Aurora Boulevard ✦ Baltimore, MD 20372 ✦ 1-888-555-0344

Project 8 Use Mail Merge Wizard

WL1-C8-P8-SFLtrs.docx

<table>
<tr><td>**P**roject **1**</td><td>**Merge Letters to Customers**</td><td>**3 Parts**</td></tr>
</table>

You will create a data source file and a letter main document, and then merge the main document with the records in the data source file.

Completing a Merge ■■■■■■■■■■■■■■■■■■■■■■■■■■■

Use buttons and options in the Mailings tab to complete a merge. A merge generally takes two files — the ***data source*** file and the ***main document***. The main document contains the standard text along with fields identifying where variable information is inserted during the merge. The data source file contains the variable information that will be inserted in the main document.

Start Mail Merge

Use the Start Mail Merge button in the Mailings tab to identify the type of main document you want to create and use the Select Recipients button to create a data source file or to specify an existing data source file. You can also use the Mail Merge Wizard to guide you through the merge process. Start the wizard by clicking the Mailings tab, clicking the Start Mail Merge button, and then clicking *Step by Step Mail Merge Wizard*.

Select Recipients

Creating a Data Source File

Before creating a data source file, determine what type of correspondence you will be creating and the type of information you will need to insert in the correspondence. Word provides predetermined field names you can use when creating the data source file. Use these field names if they represent the data you are creating. Variable information in a data source file is saved as a ***record***. A record contains all of the information for one unit (for example, a person, family, customer, client, or business). A series of fields makes one record, and a series of records makes a data source file.

Create a data source file by clicking the Select Recipients button in the Start Mail Merge group in the Mailings tab and then clicking *Type New List* at the drop-down list. At the New Address List dialog box shown in Figure 8.1, use the predesigned fields offered by Word or edit the fields by clicking the Customize

▼ **Quick Steps**

Create Data Source File
1. Click Mailings tab.
2. Click Select Recipients button.
3. Click *Type New List* at drop-down list.
4. Type data in predesigned or custom fields.
5. Click OK.

Figure 8.1 New Address List Dialog Box

The fields in one row make a record.

Type text in a field in this dialog box and then press Tab to move to the next field.

Columns button. At the Customize Address List dialog box that displays, insert new fields or delete existing fields and then click OK. With the desired fields established, type the required data. Note that fields in the main document correspond to the column headings in the data source file. When all records have been entered, click OK. At the Save Address List dialog box, navigate to the desired folder, type a name for the data source file, and then click OK. Word saves a data source file as an Access database. You do not need Access on your computer to complete a merge with a data source file.

Project 1a Creating a Data Source File

Part 1 of 3

1. At a blank document, click the Mailings tab.
2. Click the Start Mail Merge button in the Start Mail Merge group and then click *Letters* at the drop-down list.
3. Click the Select Recipients button in the Start Mail Merge group and then click *Type New List* at the drop-down list.

4. At the New Address List dialog box, Word provides a number of predesigned fields. Delete the fields you do not need by completing the following steps:
   a. Click the Customize Columns button.
   b. At the Customize Address List dialog box, click *Company Name* to select it and then click the Delete button.
   c. At the message asking if you are sure you want to delete the field, click the Yes button.
   d. Complete steps similar to those in 4b and 4c to delete the following fields:
      Country or Region
      Home Phone
      Work Phone
      E-mail Address

5. Insert a custom field by completing the following steps:
   a. At the Customize Address List dialog box, click the Add button.
   b. At the Add Field dialog box, type **Fund** and then click OK.
   c. Click the OK button to close the Customize Address List dialog box.

6. At the New Address List dialog box, enter the information for the first client shown in Figure 8.2 by completing the following steps:
   a. Type **Mr.** in the Title field and then press the Tab key. (This moves the insertion point to the *First Name* field. You can also press Shift + Tab to move to the previous field.)
   b. Type **Kenneth** and then press the Tab key.
   c. Type **Porter** and then press the Tab key.
   d. Type **7645 Tenth Street** and then press the Tab key.

e. Type **Apt. 314** and then press the Tab key.
f. Type **New York** and then press the Tab key.
g. Type **NY** and then press the Tab key.
h. Type **10192** and then press the Tab key.
i. Type **Mutual Investment Fund** and then press the Tab key. (This makes the Title field active in the next row.)
j. With the insertion point positioned in the *Title* field, complete steps similar to those in 6a through 6i to enter the information for the three other clients shown in Figure 8.2.

7. After entering all of the information for the last client in Figure 8.2 (Mrs. Wanda Houston), click the OK button located in the bottom right corner of the New Address List dialog box.

8. At the Save Address List dialog box, navigate to the Word2010L1C8 folder on your storage medium, type **WL1-C8-P1-MFDS** in the *File name* text box, and then click the Save button.

Steps 6a–6i

Figure 8.2 Project 1a

Title	= Mr.		Title	= Ms.
First Name	= Kenneth		First Name	= Carolyn
Last Name	= Porter		Last Name	= Renquist
Address Line 1	= 7645 Tenth Street		Address Line 1	= 13255 Meridian Street
Address Line 2	= Apt. 314		Address Line 2	= (leave this blank)
City	= New York		City	= New York
State	= NY		State	= NY
Zip Code	= 10192		Zip Code	= 10435
Fund	= Mutual Investment Fund		Fund	= Quality Care Fund
Title	= Dr.		Title	= Mrs.
First Name	= Amil		First Name	= Wanda
Last Name	= Ranna		Last Name	= Houston
Address Line 1	= 433 South 17th		Address Line 1	= 566 North 22nd Avenue
Address Line 2	= Apt. 17-D		Address Line 2	= (leave this blank)
City	= New York		City	= New York
State	= NY		State	= NY
Zip Code	= 10322		Zip Code	= 10634
Fund	= Priority One Fund		Fund	= Quality Care Fund

Creating a Main Document

When you begin a mail merge, you specify the type of main document you are creating. After creating and typing the records in the data source file, type the main document. Insert in the main document fields identifying where you want the variable information inserted when the document is merged with the data source file. Use buttons in the Write & Insert Fields group to insert fields and field blocks in the main document.

▼ Quick Steps

Create Main Document
1. Click Mailings tab.
2. Click Start Mail Merge button.
3. Click desired document type at drop-down list.
4. Type main document text and insert fields as needed.

HINT

A field name is inserted in the main document surrounded by chevrons (« and »), which distinguish fields in the main document and do not display in the merged document.

Insert all of the fields required for the inside address of a letter with the Address Block button in the Write & Insert Fields group. Click this button and the Insert Address Block dialog box displays with a preview of how the fields will be inserted in the document to create the inside address; the dialog box also contains buttons and options for customizing the fields. Click OK and the «AddressBlock» field is inserted in the document. The «AddressBlock» field is an example of a composite field that groups a number of fields together.

Click the Greeting Line button and the Insert Greeting Line dialog box displays with options for customizing how the fields are inserted in the document to create the greeting line. When you click OK at the dialog box, the «GreetingLine» composite field is inserted in the document.

If you want to insert an individual field from the data source file, click the Insert Merge Field button. This displays the Insert Merge Field dialog box with a list of fields from the data source file. Click the Insert Merge Field button arrow and a drop-down list displays containing the fields in the data source file. If you want merged data formatted, you can format the merge fields at the main document.

Address Block

Greeting Line

Insert Merge Field

Project 1b Creating a Main Document
Part 2 of 3

1. At the blank document, create the letter shown in Figure 8.3. Begin by clicking the No Spacing style in the Styles group in the Home tab.
2. Press the Enter key six times and then type **February 23, 2012**.
3. Press the Enter key four times and then insert the address fields by completing the following steps:
   a. Click the Mailings tab and then click the Address Block button in the Write & Insert Fields group.
   b. At the Insert Address Block dialog box, click the OK button.
   c. Press the Enter key twice.
4. Insert the greeting line fields by completing the following steps:
   a. Click the Greeting Line button in the Write & Insert Fields group.
   b. At the Insert Greeting Line dialog box, click the down-pointing arrow at the right of the option box containing the comma (the box to the right of the box containing *Mr. Randall*).
   c. At the drop-down list that displays, click the colon.
   d. Click OK to close the Insert Greeting Line dialog box.
   e. Press the Enter key twice.

5. Type the letter to the point where «Fund» displays and then insert the «Fund» field by clicking the Insert Merge Field button arrow and then clicking *Fund* at the drop-down list.

6. Type the letter to the point where the «Title» field displays and then insert the «Title» field by clicking the Insert Merge Field button arrow and then clicking *Title* at the drop-down list.

7. Press the spacebar and then insert the «Last_Name» field by clicking the Insert Merge Field button arrow and then clicking *Last_Name* at the drop-down list.

8. Type the remainder of the letter shown in Figure 8.3. (Insert your initials instead of the *XX* at the end of the letter.)

9. Save the document and name it **WL1-C8-P1-MFMD**.

Figure 8.3 Project 1b

February 23, 2012

«AddressBlock»

«GreetingLine»

McCormack Funds is lowering its expense charges beginning May 1, 2012. The reductions in expense charges mean that more of your account investment performance in the «Fund» is returned to you, «Title» «Last_Name». The reductions are worth your attention because most of our competitors' fees have gone up.

Lowering expense charges is noteworthy because before the reduction, McCormack expense deductions were already among the lowest, far below most mutual funds and variable annuity accounts with similar objectives. At the same time, services for you, our client, will continue to expand. If you would like to discuss this change, please call us at (212) 555-2277. Your financial future is our main concern at McCormack.

Sincerely,

Jodie Langstrom
Director, Financial Services

XX
WL1-C8-P1-MFMD.docx

Previewing a Merge

Preview Results

First Record   Last Record

Previous Record   Next Record

To view how the main document will appear when merged with the first record in the data source file, click the Preview Results button in the Mailings tab. You can view the main document merged with other records by using the navigation buttons in the Preview Results group. This group contains the First Record buttons, Previous Record, Go to Record, Next Record, and Last Record buttons. Click the button that will display the main document merged with the desired record. Viewing the merged document before printing is helpful to ensure that the merged data is correct. To use the Go to Record button, click the button, type the number of the desired record, and then press Enter. Turn off the preview feature by clicking the Preview Results button.

The Preview Results group in the Mailings tab also includes a Find Recipient button. If you want to search for and preview merged documents with specific entries, click the Preview Results button and then click the Find Recipient button. At the Find Entry dialog box that displays, type the specific field entry for which you are searching in the *Find* text box and then click the Find Next button. Continue clicking the Find Next button until Word displays a message telling you that there are no more entries that contain the text you typed.

Checking for Errors

Auto Check for Errors

Before merging documents, you can check for errors using the Auto Check for Errors button in the Preview Results group in the Mailings tab. Click this button and the Checking and Reporting Errors dialog box shown in Figure 8.4 displays containing three options. Click the first option, *Simulate the merge and report errors in a new document,* to tell Word to test the merge, not make any changes, and report errors in a new document. Choose the second option, *Complete the merge, pausing to report each error as it occurs,* and Word will merge the documents and display errors as they occur during the merge. Choose the third option, *Complete the merge without pausing. Report errors in a document,* and Word will complete the merge without pausing and insert any errors in a new document.

Merging Documents

Finish & Merge

To complete the merge, click the Finish & Merge button in the Finish group in the Mailings tab. At the drop-down list that displays, you can choose to merge the records and create a new document, send the merged documents directly to the printer, or send the merged documents by email.

Figure 8.4 Checking and Reporting Errors Dialog Box

Choose an option at this dialog box to tell Word to simulate the merge and then check for errors; or complete the merge and then pause to report errors; or report errors without pausing.

To merge the documents and create a new document with the merged records, click the Finish & Merge button and then click *Edit Individual Documents* at the drop-down list. At the Merge to New Document dialog box, make sure *All* is selected in the *Merge records* section and then click OK. This merges the records in the data source file with the main document and inserts the merged documents in a new document. You can also display the Merge to New Document dialog box by pressing Alt + Shift + N. Press Alt + Shift + M to display the Merge to Printer dialog box.

You can identify specific records you want merged with options at the Merge to New Document dialog box. Display this dialog box by clicking the Finish & Merge button in the Mailings tab and then clicking the *Edit Individual Documents* option at the drop-down list. Click the *All* option in the Merge to New Document dialog box to merge all records in the data source and click the *Current record* option if you want to merge only the current record. If you want to merge specific adjacent records, click in the *From* text box, type the beginning record number, press the Tab key, and then type the ending record number in the *To* text box.

Project 1c   Merging the Main Document with the Data Source File   **Part 3 of 3**

1. With **WL1-C8-P1-MFMD.docx** open, preview the main document merged with the first record in the data source file by clicking the Preview Results button in the Mailings tab.
2. Click the Next Record button to view the main document merged with the second record in the data source file.
3. Click the Preview Results button to turn it off.
4. Automatically check for errors by completing the following steps:
   a. Click the Auto Check for Errors button in the Preview Results group in the Mailings tab.
   b. At the Checking and Reporting Errors dialog box, click the first option, *Simulate the merge and report errors in a new document*.
   c. Click OK.
   d. If a new document displays with any errors, print the document and then close it without saving it. If a message displays telling you that no errors were found, click OK.
5. Click the Finish & Merge button in the Finish group and then click *Edit Individual Documents* at the drop-down list.
6. At the Merge to New Document dialog box, make sure *All* is selected and then click OK.
7. Save the merged letters and name the document **WL1-C8-P1-MFLtrs**.
8. Print **WL1-C8-P1-MFLtrs.docx**. (This document will print four letters.)
9. Close **WL1-C8-P1-MFLtrs.docx**.
10. Save and then close **WL1-C8-P1-MFMD.docx**.

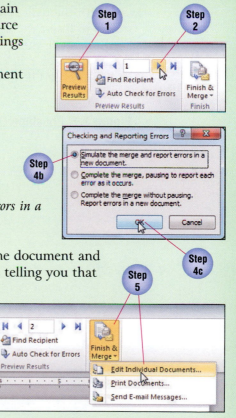

Project **2** **Merge Envelopes** 1 Part

You will use Mail Merge to prepare envelopes with customer names and addresses.

Merging Envelopes ■■■■■■■■■■■■■■■■■■■■■■■■

If you create a letter as a main document and then merge it with a data source file, more than likely you will need properly addressed envelopes in which to send the letters. To prepare an envelope main document that is merged with a data source file, click the Mailings tab, click the Start Mail Merge button, and then click *Envelopes* at the drop-down list. This displays the Envelope Options dialog box as shown in Figure 8.5. At this dialog box, specify the desired envelope size, make any other changes, and then click OK.

The next step in the envelope merge process is to create the data source file or identify an existing data source file. To identify an existing data source file, click the Select Recipients button in the Start Mail Merge group and then click *Use Existing List* at the drop-down list. At the Select Data Source dialog box, navigate to the folder containing the desired data source file and then double-click the file.

With the data source file attached to the envelope main document, the next step is to insert the appropriate fields. Click in the envelope in the approximate location where the recipient's address will appear and a box with a dashed blue border displays. Click the Address Block button in the Write & Insert Fields group and then click OK at the Insert Address Block dialog box.

Figure 8.5 Envelope Options Dialog Box

Click this down-pointing arrow to display a list of available envelope options.

1. At a blank document, click the Mailings tab.
2. Click the Start Mail Merge button in the Start Mail Merge group and then click *Envelopes* at the drop-down list.
3. At the Envelope Options dialog box, make sure the envelope size is 10 and then click OK.
4. Click the Select Recipients button in the Start Mail Merge group and then click *Use Existing List* at the drop-down list.
5. At the Select Data Source dialog box, navigate to the Word2010L1C8 folder on your storage medium and then double-click the data source file named *WL1-C8-P1-MFDS.mdb*.
6. Click in the approximate location in the envelope document where the recipient's address will appear. (This causes a box with a dashed blue border to display. If you do not see this box, try clicking in a different location on the envelope.)

7. Click the Address Block button in the Write & Insert Fields group.
8. At the Insert Address Block dialog box, click the OK button.
9. Click the Preview Results button to see how the envelope appears merged with the first record in the data source file.
10. Click the Preview Results button to turn it off.
11. Click the Finish & Merge button in the Finish group and then click *Edit Individual Documents* at the drop-down list.

12. At the Merge to New Document dialog box, specify that you want only the first two records to merge by completing the following steps:
   a. Click in the *From* text box and then type **1**.
   b. Click in the *To* text box and then type **2**.
   c. Click OK. (This merges only the first two records and opens a document with two merged envelopes.)
13. Save the merged envelopes and name the document **WL1-C8-P2-MFEnvs**.
14. Print **WL1-C8-P2-MFEnvs.docx**. (This document will print two envelopes. Manual feed of the envelopes may be required. Please check with your instructor.)
15. Close **WL1-C8-P2-MFEnvs.docx**.
16. Save the envelope main document and name it **WL1-C8-P2-EnvMD**.
17. Close **WL1-C8-P2-EnvMD.docx**.

P**roject** **3** **Merge Mailing Labels**   1 Part

You will use Mail Merge to prepare mailing labels with customer names and addresses.

Merging Labels

Create mailing labels for records in a data source file in much the same way that you create envelopes. Click the Start Mail Merge button and then click *Labels* at the drop-down list. This displays the Label Options dialog box as shown in Figure 8.6. Make sure the desired label is selected and then click OK to close the dialog box. The next step is to create the data source file or identify an existing data source file. With the data source file attached to the label main document, insert the appropriate fields and then complete the merge.

Figure 8.6 Label Options Dialog Box

1. At a blank document, click the Mailings tab.
2. Click the Start Mail Merge button in the Start Mail Merge group and then click *Labels* at the drop-down list.
3. At the Label Options dialog box, complete the following steps:
   a. If necessary, click the down-pointing arrow at the right side of the *Label vendors* option and then click *Avery US Letter* at the drop-down list. (If this product vendor is not available, choose a vendor name that offers labels that print on a full page.)
   b. Scroll in the *Product number* list box and then click *5160 Easy Peel Address Labels*. (If this option is not available, choose a label number that prints labels in two or three columns down a full page.)
   c. Click OK to close the dialog box.

4. Click the Select Recipients button in the Start Mail Merge group and then click *Use Existing List* at the drop-down list.
5. At the Select Data Source dialog box, navigate to the Word2010L1C8 folder on your storage medium and then double-click the data source file named *WL1-C8-P1-MFDS.mdb*.
6. At the labels document, click the Address Block button in the Write & Insert Fields group.
7. At the Insert Address Block dialog box, click the OK button. (This inserts «AddressBlock» in the first label. The other labels contain the «Next Record» field.)
8. Click the Update Labels button in the Write & Insert Fields group. (This adds the «AddressBlock» field after each «Next Record» field in the second and subsequent labels.)
9. Click the Preview Results button to see how the labels appear merged with the records in the data source file.
10. Click the Preview Results button to turn it off.

11. Click the Finish & Merge button in the Finish group and then click *Edit Individual Documents* at the drop-down list.
12. At the Merge to New Document dialog box, make sure *All* is selected, and then click OK.
13. Format the labels by completing the following steps:
    a. Click the Table Tools Layout tab.
    b. Click the Select button in the Table group and then click *Select Table*.
    c. Click the Align Center Left button in the Alignment group.
    d. Click the Home tab and then click the Paragraph group dialog box launcher.
    e. At the Paragraph dialog box, click the up-pointing arrow at the right of *Before* and also at the right of *After* to change the measurement to 0 pt. Click the up-pointing arrow at the right of the *Inside* option to change the measurement to 0.3" and then click OK.
14. Save the merged labels and name the document **WL1-C8-P3-MFLabels**.
15. Print and then close **WL1-C8-P3-MFLabels.docx**.
16. Save the label main document and name it **WL1-C8-P3-LabelsMD**.
17. Close **WL1-C8-P3-LabelsMD.docx**.

Step 13e

Paragraph

Indents and Spacing   Line and Page

General

Alignment:

Outline level:

Indentation

Inside: 0.3"

Outside:

☐ Mirror indents

Spacing

Before: 0 pt

After: 0 pt

☐ Don't add space between paragr

Project **4** **Merge a Directory**   1 Part

You will use Mail Merge to prepare a directory list containing customer names and type of financial investment funds.

Merging a Directory

When merging letters, envelopes, or mailing labels, a new form is created for each record. For example, if the data source file merged with the letter contains eight records, eight letters are created. If the data source file merged with a mailing label contains twenty records, twenty labels are created. In some situations, you may want merged information to remain on the same page. This is useful, for example, when creating a list such as a directory or address list.

Begin creating a merged directory by clicking the Start Mail Merge button and then clicking *Directory* at the drop-down list. Create or identify an existing data source file and then insert the desired fields in the directory document. You may want to set tabs to insert text in columns.

1. At a blank document, click the Mailings tab.
2. Click the Start Mail Merge button in the Start Mail Merge group and then click *Directory* at the drop-down list.
3. Click the Select Recipients button in the Start Mail Merge group and then click *Use Existing List* at the drop-down list.

4. At the Select Data Source dialog box, navigate to the Word2010L1C8 folder on your storage medium and then double-click the data source file named **WL1-C8-P1-MFDS.mdb**.
5. At the document screen, set left tabs at the 1-inch mark, the 2.5-inch mark, and the 4-inch mark on the Ruler and then press the Tab key. (This moves the insertion point to the tab set at the 1-inch mark.)
6. Click the Insert Merge Field button arrow and then click *Last_Name* at the drop-down list.
7. Press the Tab key to move the insertion point to the 2.5-inch mark.
8. Click the Insert Merge Field button arrow and then click *First_Name* at the drop-down list.
9. Press the Tab key to move the insertion point to the 4-inch mark.
10. Click the Insert Merge Field button arrow and then click *Fund* at the drop-down list.
11. Press the Enter key once.
12. Click the Finish & Merge button in the Finish group and then click *Edit Individual Documents* at the drop-down list.
13. At the Merge to New Document dialog box, make sure *All* is selected and then click OK. (This merges the fields in the document.)
14. Press Ctrl + Home, press the Enter key once, and then press the Up Arrow key once.
15. Press the Tab key, turn on bold, and then type **Last Name**.
16. Press the Tab key and then type **First Name**.
17. Press the Tab key and then type **Fund**.

18. Save the directory document and name it **WL1-C8-P4-Directory**.
19. Print and then close the document.
20. Close the directory main document without saving it.

You will use Mail Merge to prepare mailing labels with names and addresses of customers living in Baltimore.

Editing a Data Source File ■■■■■■■■■■■■■■■■■■■■

Edit a main document in the normal manner. Open the document, make the required changes, and then save the document. Since a data source is actually an Access database file, you cannot open it in the normal manner. Open a data source file for editing using the Edit Recipient List button in the Start Mail Merge group in the Mailings tab. When you click the Edit Recipient List button, the Mail Merge Recipients dialog box displays as shown in Figure 8.7. Select or edit records at this dialog box.

Selecting Specific Records

All of the records in the Mail Merge Recipients dialog box contain a check mark before the first field. If you want to select specific records, remove the check mark from those records you do not want included in a merge. In this way you can select and then merge specific records in the data source file with the main document.

Figure 8.7 Mail Merge Recipients Dialog Box

Select specific records by removing the check marks from those records you do not want included in the merge.

1. At a blank document, create mailing labels for customers living in Baltimore. Begin by clicking the Mailings tab.
2. Click the Start Mail Merge button in the Start Mail Merge group and then click *Labels* at the drop-down list.
3. At the Label Options dialog box, make sure *Avery US Letter* displays in the *Label products* option box, and *5160 Easy Peel Address Labels* displays in the *Product number* list box, and then click OK.
4. Click the Select Recipients button in the Start Mail Merge group and then click *Use Existing List* at the drop-down list.
5. At the Select Data Source dialog box, navigate to the Word2010L1C8 folder on your storage medium and then double-click the data source file named ***SFClients.mdb***.
6. Click the Edit Recipient List button in the Start Mail Merge group.
7. At the Mail Merge Recipients dialog box, complete the following steps:
   a. Click the check box located immediately left of the *Last Name* field column heading to remove the check mark. (This removes all of the check marks from the check boxes.)

      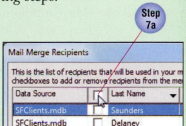

   b. Click the check box immediately left of each of the following last names: *Saunders, Perkins, Grenwald, Dutton, Fernandez,* and *Stahl.* (These are the customers who live in Baltimore.)
   c. Click OK to close the dialog box.
8. At the labels document, click the Address Block button in the Write & Insert Fields group.
9. At the Insert Address Block dialog box, click the OK button.
10. Click the Update Labels button in Write & Insert Fields group.
11. Click the Preview Results button and then click the Previous Record button to display each of the labels and make sure only those customers living in Baltimore display.
12. Click the Preview Results button to turn it off.
13. Click the Finish & Merge button in the Finish group and then click *Edit Individual Documents* at the drop-down list.
14. At the Merge to New Document dialog box, make sure *All* is selected, and then click OK.
15. Format the labels by completing the following steps:
   a. Click the Table Tools Layout tab.
   b. Click the Select button in the Table group and then click *Select Table.*
   c. Click the Align Center Left button in the Alignment group.
   d. Click the Home tab and then click the Paragraph group dialog box launcher.
   e. At the Paragraph dialog box, click the up-pointing arrow at the right of *Before* and also at the right of *After* to change the measurement to 0 pt. Click the up-pointing arrow at the right of the *Inside* option to change the measurement to 0.3" and then click OK.
16. Save the merged labels and name the document **WL1-C8-P5-SFLabels**.
17. Print and then close **WL1-C8-P5-SFLabels.docx**.
18. Close the main labels document without saving it.

Project 6 Edit Records in a Data Source File

1 Part

You will edit records in a data source file and then use Mail Merge to prepare a directory with the edited records that contains customer names, telephone numbers, and cell phone numbers.

Editing Records

A data source file may need editing on a periodic basis to add or delete customer names, update fields, insert new fields, or delete existing fields. To edit a data source file, click the Edit Recipient List button in the Start Mail Merge group. At the Mail Merge Recipients dialog box, click the data source file name in the *Data Source* list box and then click the Edit button that displays below the list box. This displays the Edit Data Source dialog box shown in Figure 8.8. At this dialog box you can add a new entry, delete an entry, find a particular entry, and customize columns.

Figure 8.8 Edit Data Source Dialog Box

Edit the fields in the records in the data source file at this dialog box.

Project 6 Editing Records in a Data Source File

Part 1 of 1

1. Make a copy of the **SFClients.mdb** file by completing the following steps:
   a. Display the Open dialog box and make Word2010L1C8 the active folder.
   b. If necessary, change the file type button to *All Files (*.*)*.
   c. Right-click on the **SFClients.mdb** file and then click *Copy* at the shortcut menu.
   d. Position the mouse pointer in a white portion of the Open dialog box Content pane (outside of any file name), click the right mouse button, and then click *Paste* at the shortcut menu. (This inserts a copy of the file in the dialog box Content pane and names the file **SFClients-Copy.mdb**.)
   e. Right-click on the file name *SFClients-Copy.mdb* and then click *Rename* at the shortcut menu.

f. Type **WL1-C8-P6-DS** and then press Enter.

g. Close the Open dialog box.

2. At a blank document, click the Mailings tab.

3. Click the Select Recipients button and then click *Use Existing List* from the drop-down list.

4. At the Select Data Source dialog box, navigate to the Word2010L1C8 folder on your storage medium and then double-click the data source file named ***WL1-C8-P6-DS.mdb***.

5. Click the Edit Recipient List button in the Start Mail Merge group.

6. At the Mail Merge Recipients dialog box, click ***WL1-C8-P6-DS.mdb*** that displays in the *Data Source* list box and then click the Edit button.

7. Delete the record for Steve Dutton by completing the following steps:

a. Click the square that displays at the beginning of the row for *Mr. Steve Dutton*.

b. Click the Delete Entry button.

c. At the message asking if you want to delete the entry, click the Yes button.

8. Insert a new record by completing the following steps:

a. Click the New Entry button in the dialog box.

b. Type the following text in the new record in the specified fields:

> Title = **Ms.**
> First Name = **Jennae**
> Last Name = **Davis**
> Address Line 1 = **3120 South 21st**
> Address Line 2 = (none)
> City = **Rosedale**
> State = **MD**
> ZIP Code = **20389**

9. Insert a new field and type text in the field by completing the following steps:

a. At the Edit Data Source dialog box, click the Customize Columns button.

b. At the message asking if you want to save the changes made to the data source file, click Yes.

c. At the Customize Address List dialog box, click *ZIP Code* in the *Field Names* list box. (A new field is inserted below the selected field.)

d. Click the Add button.

e. At the Add Field dialog box, type **Cell Phone** and then click OK.

f. You decide that you want the *Cell Phone* field to display after the *Home Phone* field. To move the *Cell Phone* field, make sure it is selected and then click the Move Down button.

g. Click OK to close the Customize Address List dialog box.

h. At the Edit Data Source dialog box, scroll to the right to display the *Cell Phone* field (last field in the file) and then type the following cell phone numbers (after typing each cell phone number, except the last number, press the Down Arrow key to make the next cell below active):

Record 1 = 410-555-1249
Record 2 = 413-555-3492
Record 3 = 410-555-0695
Record 4 = 410-555-9488
Record 5 = 413-555-1200
Record 6 = 410-555-7522
Record 7 = 410-555-8833
Record 8 = 413-555-9378
Record 9 = 410-555-4261
Record 10 = 410-555-9944
Record 11 = 413-555-2321
Record 12 = 410-555-9435

i. Click OK to close the Edit Data Source dialog box.
j. At the message asking if you want to update the recipient list and save changes, click Yes.
k. At the Mail Merge Recipients dialog box, click OK.

10. Create a directory by completing the following steps:
a. Click the Start Mail Merge button and then click *Directory* at the drop-down list.
b. At the blank document, set left tabs on the horizontal ruler at the 1-inch mark, the 3-inch mark, and the 4.5-inch mark.
c. Press the Tab key. (This moves the insertion point to the first tab set at the 1-inch mark.)
d. Click the Insert Merge Field button arrow and then click *Last_Name* at the drop-down list.
e. Type a comma and then press the spacebar.
f. Click the Insert Merge Field button arrow and then click *First_Name* at the drop-down list.
g. Press the Tab key, click the Insert Merge Field button arrow, and then click *Home_Phone* at the drop-down list.
h. Press the Tab key, click the Insert Merge Field button arrow, and then click *Cell_Phone* at the drop-down list.
i. Press the Enter key once.
j. Click the Finish & Merge button in the Finish group and then click *Edit Individual Documents* at the drop-down list.
k. At the Merge to New Document dialog box, make sure *All* is selected and then click OK. (This merges the fields in the document.)

11. Press Ctrl + Home, press the Enter key once, and then press the Up Arrow key once.
12. Press the Tab key, turn on bold, and then type **Name**.
13. Press the Tab key and then type **Home Phone**.
14. Press the Tab key and then type **Cell Phone**.

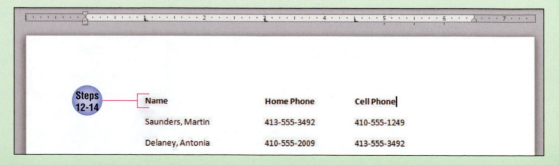

15. Save the directory document and name it **WL1-C8-P6-Directory**.
16. Print and then close the document.
17. Close the directory main document without saving it.

Project **7** **Add Fill-in Fields to a Main Document** **1 Part**

You will edit a form letter and insert sales representative contact information during a merge.

Inputting Text during a Merge ■■■■■■■■■ ■ ■■■ ■■

Word's Merge feature contains a large number of Word fields you can insert in a main document. In this chapter, you will learn about the *Fill-in* field that is used for information input at the keyboard during a merge. For more information on the other Word fields, please refer to the on-screen help.

Situations may arise in which you do not need to keep all variable information in a data source file. For example, variable information that changes on a regular basis might include a customer's monthly balance, a product price, and so on. Word lets you input variable information into a document during the merge using the keyboard. A Fill-in field is inserted in a main document by clicking the Rules button in the Write & Insert Fields group in the Mailings tab and then clicking *Fill-in* at the drop-down list. This displays the Insert Word Field: Fill-in dialog box shown in Figure 8.9. At this dialog box, type a short message indicating what should be entered at the keyboard and then click OK. At the Microsoft Word dialog box with the message you entered displayed in the upper left corner, type text you want to display in the document and then click OK. When the Fill-in field or fields are added, save the main document in the normal manner. A document can contain any number of Fill-in fields.

When you merge the main document with the data source file, the first record is merged with the main document and the Microsoft Word dialog box displays with the message you entered displayed in the upper left corner. Type the required information for the first record in the data source file and then click the OK

▼ **Quick Steps**

Insert *Fill-in* Field in Main Document
1. Click Mailings tab.
2. Click Rules button.
3. Click *Fill-in* at drop-down list.
4. Type prompt text.
5. Click OK.
6. Type text to be inserted in document.
7. Click OK.

Rules

Figure 8.9 Insert Word Field: Fill-in Dialog Box

In this text box, type a short message indicating what should be entered at the keyboard.

button. Word displays the dialog box again. Type the required information for the second record in the data source file and then click OK. Continue in this manner until the required information has been entered for each record in the data source file. Word then completes the merge.

1. Open the document named **WL1-C8-P1-MFMD.docx** (at the message asking if you want to continue, click Yes) and then save the document with Save As and name it **WL1-C8-P7-MFMD**.

2. Change the second paragraph in the body of the letter to the paragraph shown in Figure 8.10. Insert the first Fill-in field (representative's name) by completing the following steps:
   a. Click the Mailings tab.
   b. Click the Rules button in the Write & Insert Fields group and then click *Fill-in* at the drop-down list.
   c. At the Insert Word Field: Fill-in dialog box, type **Insert rep name** in the *Prompt* text box and then click OK.
   d. At the Microsoft Word dialog box with *Insert rep name* displayed in the upper left corner, type **(representative's name)** and then click OK.

3. Complete steps similar to those in Step 2 to insert the second Fill-in field (phone number), except type **Insert phone number** in the *Prompt* text box at the Insert Word Field: Fill-in dialog box and type **(phone number)** at the Microsoft Word dialog box.

4. Save **WL1-C8-P7-MFMD.docx**.

5. Merge the main document with the data source file by completing the following steps:
   a. Click the Finish & Merge button and then click *Edit Individual Documents* at the drop-down list.
   b. At the Merge to New Document dialog box, make sure *All* is selected, and then click OK.
   c. When Word merges the main document with the first record, a dialog box displays with the message *Insert rep name* and the text *(representative's name)* selected. At this dialog box, type **Marilyn Smythe** and then click OK.
   d. At the dialog box with the message *Insert phone number* and *(phone number)* selected, type **(646) 555-8944** and then click OK.

e. At the dialog box with the message *Insert rep name*, type **Anthony Mason** (over *Marilyn Smythe*) and then click OK.

f. At the dialog box with the message *Insert phone number*, type **(646) 555-8901** (over the previous number) and then click OK.

g. At the dialog box with the message *Insert rep name*, type **Faith Ostrom** (over *Anthony Mason*) and then click OK.

h. At the dialog box with the message *Insert phone number*, type **(646) 555-8967** (over the previous number) and then click OK.

i. At the dialog box with the message *Insert rep name*, type **Thomas Rivers** (over *Faith Ostrom*) and then click OK.

j. At the dialog box with the message *Insert phone number*, type **(646) 555-0793** (over the previous number) and then click OK.

6. Save the merged document and name it **WL1-C8-P7-MFLtrs**.

7. Print and then close **WL1-C8-P7-MFLtrs.docx**.

8. Save and then close **WL1-C8-P7-MFMD.docx**.

Figure 8.10 Project 7

Lowering expense charges is noteworthy because before the reduction, McCormack expense deductions were already among the lowest, far below most mutual funds and variable annuity accounts with similar objectives. At the same time, services for you, our client, will continue to expand. If you would like to discuss this change, please call our service representative, **(representative's name)**, at **(phone number)**.

roject **8** **Use Mail Merge Wizard**   **1 Part**

You will use the Mail Merge wizard to merge a main document with a data source file and create letters to clients of Sorenson Funds.

Merging Using the Mail Merge Wizard ■■■■■■■■■■■■■■

The Mail Merge feature includes a Mail Merge wizard that guides you through the merge process. To access the Wizard, click the Mailings tab, click the Start Mail Merge button, and then click the *Step By Step Mail Merge Wizard* option at the drop-down list. The first of six Mail Merge task panes displays at the right side of the screen. Completing the tasks at one task pane displays the next task pane. The options in each task pane may vary depending on the type of merge you are performing. Generally, you complete one of the following steps at each task pane:

- Step 1: Select the type of document you want to create such as a letter, email message, envelope, label, or directory.

- Step 2: Specify whether you want to use the current document to create the main document, start from a template, or start from an existing document.

- Step 3: Specify whether you are typing a new list, using an existing list, or selecting from an Outlook contacts list.

- Step 4: Use the items in this task pane to help you prepare the main document such as inserting fields in the main document.
- Step 5: Preview the merged documents.
- Step 6: Complete the merge.

Project 8 — Preparing Form Letters Using the Mail Merge Wizard — Part 1 of 1

1. At a blank document, click the Mailings tab, click the Start Mail Merge button in the Start Mail Merge group, and then click *Step by Step Mail Merge Wizard* at the drop-down list.
2. At the first Mail Merge task pane, make sure *Letters* is selected in the *Select document type* section and then click the <u>Next: Starting document</u> hyperlink located toward the bottom of the task pane.
3. At the second Mail Merge task pane, click the *Start from existing document* option in the *Select starting document* section.
4. Click the Open button in the *Start from existing* section of the task pane.
5. At the Open dialog box, navigate to the Word2010L1C8 folder on your storage medium and then double-click **SFLtrMD.docx**.
6. Click the <u>Next: Select recipients</u> hyperlink located toward the bottom of the task pane.
7. At the third Mail Merge task pane, click the <u>Browse</u> hyperlink that displays in the *Use an existing list* section of the task pane.
8. At the Select Data Source dialog box, navigate to the Word2010L1C8 folder on your storage medium and then double-click **SFClients.mdb**.
9. At the Mail Merge Recipients dialog box, click OK.
10. Click the <u>Next: Write your letter</u> hyperlink that displays toward the bottom of the task pane.
11. At the fourth Mail Merge task pane, enter fields in the form letter by completing the following steps:
    a. Position the insertion point a double space above the first paragraph of text in the letter.
    b. Click the <u>Address block</u> hyperlink located in the *Write your letter* section of the task pane.
    c. At the Insert Address Block dialog box, click the OK button.
    d. Press the Enter key twice and then click the <u>Greeting line</u> hyperlink located in the *Write your letter* section of the task pane.
    e. At the Insert Greeting Line dialog box, click the down-pointing arrow at the right of the option box containing the comma (the box to the right of the box containing *Mr. Randall*).
    f. At the drop-down list that displays, click the colon.
    g. Click OK to close the Insert Greeting Line dialog box.

Step 3

Step 4

Step 7

Step 11b

Step 11d

12. Click the <u>Next: Preview your letters</u> hyperlink located toward the bottom of the task pane.
13. At the fifth Mail Merge task pane, look over the letter that displays in the document window and make sure the information merged properly. If you want to see the letters for the other recipients, click the button in the Mail Merge task pane containing the right-pointing arrow.
14. Click the Preview Results button in the Preview Results group to turn off the preview feature.
15. Click the <u>Next: Complete the merge</u> hyperlink that displays toward the bottom of the task pane.
16. At the sixth Mail Merge task pane, click the <u>Edit individual letters</u> hyperlink that displays in the *Merge* section of the task pane.
17. At the Merge to New Document dialog box, make sure *All* is selected and then click the OK button.
18. Save the merged letters documents with the name **WL1-C8-P8-SFLtrs**.
19. Print only the first two pages of **WL1-C8-P8-SFLtrs.docx**.
20. Close the document.
21. At the sixth Mail Merge task pane, close the letter main document without saving it.

Chapter Summary

- Use the Mail Merge feature to create letters, envelopes, labels, directories, email messages, and faxes, all with personalized information.

- Generally, a merge takes two documents — the data source file containing the variable information and the main document containing standard text along with fields identifying where variable information is inserted during the merge process.

- Variable information in a data source file is saved as a record. A record contains all of the information for one unit. A series of fields makes one record, and a series of records makes a data source file.

- A data source file is saved as an Access database but you do not need Access on your computer to complete a merge with a data source.

- You can use predesigned fields when creating a data source file or you can create your own custom field at the Customize Address List dialog box.

- Use the Address Block button in the Write & Insert Fields group in the Mailings tab to insert all of the fields required for the inside address of a letter. This inserts the «AddressBlock» field, which is considered a composite field because it groups a number of fields together.

- Click the Greeting Line button in the Write & Insert Fields group in the Mailings tab to insert the «GreetingLine» composite field in the document.

- Click the Insert Merge Field button arrow in the Write & Insert Fields group in the Mailings tab to display a drop-down list of fields contained in the data source file.

- Click the Preview Results button in the Mailings tab to view the main document merged with the first record in the data source. Use the navigation buttons in the Preview Results group in the Mailings tab to display the main document merged with the desired record.
- Before merging documents, check for errors by clicking the Auto Check for Errors button in the Preview Results group in the Mailings tab. This displays the Checking and Reporting Errors dialog box with three options for checking errors.
- Click the Finish & Merge button in the Mailings tab to complete the merge.
- Select specific records for merging by inserting or removing check marks from the desired records in the Mail Merge Recipients dialog box. Display this dialog box by clicking the Edit Recipient List button in the Mailings tab.
- Edit specific records in a data source file at the Edit Data Source dialog box. Display this dialog box by clicking the Edit Recipient List button in the Mailings tab, clicking the desired data source file name in the *Data Source* list box, and then clicking the Edit button.
- Use the Fill-in field in a main document to insert variable information at the keyboard during a merge.
- Word includes a Mail Merge wizard you can use to guide you through the process of creating letters, envelopes, labels, directories, and email messages with personalized information.

Commands Review

FEATURE	RIBBON TAB, GROUP	BUTTON	OPTION
New Address List dialog box	Mailings, Start Mail Merge		Type New List
Letter main document	Mailings, Start Mail Merge		Letters
Checking and Reporting Errors dialog box	Mailings, Preview Results		
Envelopes main document	Mailings, Start Mail Merge		Envelopes
Labels main document	Mailings, Start Mail Merge		Labels
Directory main document	Mailings, Start Mail Merge		Directory
Preview merge results	Mailings, Preview Results		
Mail Merge Recipients dialog box	Mailings, Start Mail Merge		
Address Block field	Mailings, Write & Insert Fields		
Greeting Line field	Mailings, Write & Insert Fields		
Insert merge fields	Mailings, Write & Insert Fields		

FEATURE	RIBBON TAB, GROUP	BUTTON	OPTION
Fill-in merge field	Mailings, Write & Insert Fields		Fill-in
Mail Merge wizard	Mailings, Start Mail Merge		Step by Step Mail Merge Wizard

Concepts Check Test Your Knowledge

Completion: In the space provided at the right, indicate the correct term, command, or number.

1. A merge generally takes two files — a data source file and this. _____

2. This term refers to all of the information for one unit in a data source file. _____

3. Create a data source file by clicking this button in the Mailings tab and then clicking *Type New List* at the drop-down list. _____

4. A data source file is saved as this type of file. _____

5. Create your own custom fields in a data source file with options at this dialog box. _____

6. Use this button in the Mailings tab to insert all of the required fields for the inside address in a letter. _____

7. The «GreetingLine» field is considered this type of field because it includes all of the fields required for the greeting line. _____

8. Click this button in the Mailings tab to display the first record merged with the main document. _____

9. Before merging a document, check for errors using this button in the Preview Results group in the Mailings tab. _____

10. To complete a merge, click this button in the Finish group in the Mailings tab. _____

11. When creating the envelope main document, click in the approximate location where the recipient's address will appear and then click this button in the Write & Insert Fields group. _____

12. Select specific records in a data source file by inserting or removing check marks from the records in this dialog box. _____

13. Use this field to insert variable information at the keyboard during a merge. _____

14. Click this option at the Start Mail Merge button drop-down list to begin the Mail Merge wizard. _____

Skills Check Assess Your Performance

Assessment

1 PREPARE AND MERGE LETTERS, ENVELOPES, AND LABELS

1. Open **CCLtrhd.docx** and then save the document with Save As and name it **WL1-C8-A1-CCMD**.
2. Look at the information in Figure 8.11 and Figure 8.12 and then use the Mail Merge feature to prepare four letters. Create the data source file with the information in Figure 8.11 and then save the file and name it **WL1-C8-A1-CCDS**.
3. Merge the **WL1-C8-A1-CCMD** main document with the **WL1-C8-A1-CCDS.mdb** data source file and then save the merged letters document and name it **WL1-C8-A1-CCLtrs**.
4. Print and then close **WL1-C8-A1-CCLtrs.docx** and then save and close **WL1-C8-A1-CCMD.docx**.
5. Create an envelope main document and then merge it with the **WL1-C8-A1-CCDS.mdb** data source file.
6. Save the merged envelopes document and name it **WL1-C8-A1-CCEnvs**. Print and then close the envelopes document. (Check with your instructor before printing the envelopes.) Close the envelope main document without saving it.
7. Create a labels main document (use the Avery US Letter product number 5160 label) and then merge it with the **WL1-C8-A1-CCDS.mdb** data source file. When the labels are merged, press Ctrl + A to select the entire document, click the Home tab, and then click the No Spacing style in the Styles group.
8. Save the merged labels document and name it **WL1-C8-A1-CCLabels**. Print and then close the labels document and then close the labels main document without saving it.

Figure 8.11 Assessment 1

Mr. Tony Benedetti	Ms. Theresa Dusek
1315 Cordova Road	12044 Ridgway Drive
Apt. 402	(leave this blank)
Santa Fe, NM 87505	Santa Fe, NM 87505
Home Phone: 505-555-0489	Home Phone: 505-555-1120
Mrs. Mary Arguello	Mr. Preston Miller
2554 Country Drive	120 Second Street
#105	(leave this blank)
Santa Fe, NM 87504	Santa Fe, NM 87505
Home Phone: 505-555-7663	Home Phone: 505-555-3551

Figure 8.12 Assessment 1

May 8, 2012

«AddressBlock»

«GreetingLine»

The Cordova Children's Community Center is a nonprofit agency providing educational and recreational activities to children in the Cordova community. We are funded by donations from the community and rely on you and all of our volunteers to provide quality care and services to our children. As a member of our outstanding volunteer team, we are inviting you to attend our summer volunteer open house on Saturday, May 26, at the community center from 1:00 to 4:30 p.m. We want to honor you and our other volunteers for your commitment to children so please plan to attend so we can thank you in person.

The Center's summer volunteer session begins Friday, June 1, and continues through August 31. According to our volunteer roster, you have signed up to volunteer during the summer session. Throughout the summer we will be offering a variety of services to our children including tutoring, creative art classes, recreational activities, and a science camp. At the open house, you can sign up for the specific area or areas in which you want to volunteer. We look forward to seeing you at the open house and during the upcoming summer session.

Sincerely,

Andy Amura
Volunteer Coordinator

XX
WL1-C8-A1-CCMD.docx

Assessment

2 EDIT AND MERGE LETTERS

1. Open **WL1-C8-A1-CCMD.docx** (at the message asking if you want to continue, click Yes) and then save the main document with Save As and name it **WL1-C8-A2-CCMD**.
2. Edit the **WL1-C8-A1-CCDS.mdb** data source file by making the following changes:
   a. Display the record for Ms. Theresa Dusek and then change the address from *12044 Ridgway Drive* to *1390 Fourth Avenue*.
   b. Display the record for Mr. Preston Miller and change the home phone number from *505-555-3551* to *505-555-1289*.
   c. Delete the record for Mrs. Mary Arguello.
   d. Insert a new record with the following information:
      > Mr. Cesar Rivera
      > 3201 East Third Street
      > Santa Fe, NM 87505
      > 505-555-6675
3. At the main document, edit the second sentence of the second paragraph so it reads as follows (insert a *Fill-in* field for the *(number of hours)* shown in the sentence below):
   > According to our volunteer roster, you have signed up to volunteer for *(number of hours)* during the summer session.
4. Merge the main document with the data source file and type the following text for each of the records:
   > Record 1 = four hours a week
   > Record 2 = six hours a week
   > Record 3 = twelve hours a week
   > Record 4 = four hours a week
5. Save the merged document and name it **WL1-C8-A2-CCLtrs**.
6. Print and then close **WL1-C8-A2-CCLtrs.docx**.
7. Save and then close **WL1-C8-A2-CCMD.docx**.

Assessment

3 CREATE A DIRECTORY

1. At a blank document, create a directory main document and specify **WL1-C8-A1-CCDS.mdb** as the data source file. Insert a left tab at the 1.5-inch mark and the 4-inch mark on the Ruler. Press the Tab key and then insert the «First_Name» field at the 1.5-inch tab. Press the spacebar and then insert the «Last_Name» field. Press the Tab key, insert the «Home_Phone» field at the second tab, and then press the Enter key.
2. Merge the directory main document with the data source.
3. Insert the heading *Volunteer* in bold above the first column and insert the heading *Telephone* in bold above the second column.
4. Save the directory document and name it **WL1-C8-A3-CCDir**.
5. Print and then close the document.
6. Close the directory main document without saving it.

Assessment

4 MERGE LETTERS AND ENVELOPES USING THE MAIL MERGE WIZARD

1. Open **TTSLtrMD.docx** from the Word2010L1C8 folder on your storage medium. Insert your initials in place of the *XX* that display toward the bottom of the letter.
2. Use the Mail Merge wizard to prepare letters using the **TTSLtrMD.docx** document as the main document and specify **TTSClients.mdb** as the data source file.
3. When the merge is complete save the merged letters document and name it **WL1-C8-A4-TTSLtrs**.
4. Print only the first two pages (letters) in the document.
5. Close **WL1-C8-A4-TTSLtrs.docx**.
6. Close **TTSLtrMD.docx** without saving the changes.

Visual Benchmark Demonstrate Your Proficiency

PREPARE AND MERGE LETTERS

1. Open **FPLtrhd.docx** and then save the document with Save As and name it **WL1-C8-VB-FPMD**.
2. Look at the information in Figure 8.13 and Figure 8.14 and then use Mail Merge to prepare four letters. (When creating the main document as shown in Figure 8.14, insert the appropriate fields where you see the text Title; First Name; Last Name; Street Address; and City, State ZIP. Insert the appropriate field where you see the text Title and Last Name in the first paragraph of text.) Create the data source file with the information in Figure 8.13 and then save the file and name it **WL1-C8-VB-FPDS**.
3. Merge the **WL1-C8-VB-FPMD.docx** main document with the **WL1-C8-VB-FPDS.mdb** data source file and then save the merged letters document and name it **WL1-C8-VB-FPLtrs**.
4. Print and then close **WL1-C8-VB-FPLtrs.docx**.
5. Save and then close **WL1-C8-VB-FPMD.docx**.

Figure 8.13 Visual Benchmark Data Source Records

Mr. and Mrs. Chris Gallagher
17034 234th Avenue
Newport, VT 05855

Ms. Heather Segarra
4103 Thompson Drive
Newport, VT 05855

Mr. Gene Goodrich
831 Cromwell Lane
Newport, VT 05855

Mrs. Sonya Kraus
15933 Ninth Street
Newport, VT 05855

Figure 8.14 Visual Benchmark Main Document

Frontline Photography Equipment and Supplies

(Current Date)

Title First Name Last Name
Street Address
City, State ZIP

Dear Title Last Name:

We have enjoyed being a part of the Newport community for the past two years. Our success in the community is directly related to you, Title Last Name, and all of our other loyal customers. Thank you for shopping at our store for all of your photography equipment and supply needs.

To show our appreciation for your loyalty and your business, we are enclosing a coupon for 20 percent off any item in our store, even our incredibly low-priced clearance items. Through the end of the month, all of our camera accessories are on sale. So, use your coupon and take advantage of additional savings on items such as camera lenses, tripods, cleaning supplies, and camera bags.

To accommodate our customers' schedules, we have increased our weekend hours. Our store will be open Saturdays until 7:00 p.m. and Sundays until 5:00 p.m. Come by and let our sales associates find just the right camera and camera accessories for you.

Sincerely,

(Student Name)

XX
WL1-C8-VB-FPMD.docx
Enclosure

559 Tenth Street, Suite A ◈ Newport, VT 05855 ◈ (802) 555-4411

Case Study   Apply Your Skills

Part 1

You are the office manager for Freestyle Extreme, a sporting goods store that specializes in snowboarding and snow skiing equipment and supplies. The store has two branches, one on the east side of town and the other on the west side. One of your job responsibilities is to send letters to customers letting them know about sales, new equipment, and upcoming events. Next month, both stores are having a sale and all snowboard and snow skiing supplies will be 15% off the regular price. Create a data source file that contains the following customer information: first name, last name, address, city, state, ZIP code, and branch. Add six customers to the data source file and indicate that three usually shop at the East branch and the other three usually shop at the West branch. Create a letter as a main document that includes information about the upcoming sale. The letter should contain at least two paragraphs and, in addition to the information on the sale, might include information about the store, snowboarding, and/or snow skiing. Save the data source file with the name **WL1-C8-CS-FEDS**, save the main document with the name **WL1-C8-CS-FEMD**, and save the merged document with the name **WL1-C8-CS-FELtrs**. Create envelopes for the six merged letters and name the merged envelope document **WL1-C8-CS-FEEnvs**. Do not save the envelope main document. Print the merged letters document and the merged envelopes document.

Part 2

A well-known extreme snowboarder will be visiting both branches of the store to meet with customers and sign autographs. Use the Help feature to learn how to insert an If . . . Then . . . Else merge field in a document and then create a letter that includes the name of the extreme snowboarder (you determine the name), the time, which is 1:00 p.m. to 4:30 p.m., and any additional information that might interest the customer. Also include in the letter an If . . . Then . . . Else merge field that will insert *Wednesday, September 26* if the customer's Branch is *East* and will insert *Thursday, September 27* if the Branch is *West*. Add visual appeal to the letter by inserting a picture, clip art image, WordArt, or any other feature that will attract the reader's attention. Save the letter main document and name it **WL1-C8-CS-MD**. Merge the letter main document with the **WL1-C8-CS-FEDS.mdb** data source. Save the merged letters document and name it **WL1-C8-CS-AnnLtrs**. Print the merged letters document.

Part 3

The store owner wants to try selling shorter skis known as "snow blades" or "skiboards." He has asked you to research the shorter skis and identify one type and model to sell only at the West branch of the store. If the model sells well, he will consider selling it at the East branch at a future time. Prepare a main document letter that describes the new snow blade or skiboard that the West branch is selling. Include information about pricing and tell customers that the new item is being offered at a 40% discount if purchased within the next week. Merge the letter main document with the **WL1-C8-CS-FEDS.mdb** data source file and include only those customers that shop at the West branch. Save the merged letters document and name it **WL1-C8-CS-SBLtrs**. Print the merged letters document. Save the letter main document and name it **WL1-C8-CS-SBMD**. Print and then close the main document.

Performance Assessment

Note: Before beginning unit assessments, copy to your storage medium the Word2010L1U2 subfolder from the Word2010L1 folder on the CD that accompanies this textbook and then make Word2010L1U2 the active folder.

Word2010L1U2

Assessing Proficiency

In this unit, you have learned to format text into columns; insert, format, and customize objects to enhance the visual appeal of a document; manage files, print envelopes and labels, and create documents using templates; create and edit tables; visually represent data in SmartArt diagrams and organizational charts; and use Mail Merge to create letters, envelopes, labels, and directions.

Assessment 1 Format a Technology Occupations Document

1. Open **TechOccs.docx** and then save the document with Save As and name it **WL1-U2-A01-TechOccs**.
2. Move the insertion point to the beginning of the heading *Telecommuting* and then insert the file named **CommMedia.docx**.
3. Apply the Heading 1 style to the title and the Heading 2 style to the headings in the document.
4. Change the Quick Styles set to *Formal* and change the paragraph spacing to *Open*.
5. Insert a continuous section break at the beginning of the first paragraph of text (the paragraph that begins *The march of computer technology . . .*).
6. Format the text below the section break into two columns.
7. Balance the columns on the second page.
8. Insert a pull quote of your choosing on the first page of the document that includes the text *"As the future of wireless unfolds, many new jobs will emerge as well."*
9. Create a drop cap with the first letter of the first word *The* that begins the first paragraph of text and make the drop cap two lines in height.
10. Manually hyphenate words in the document.
11. Insert page numbering that prints at the bottom of each page (you determine the page number formatting).
12. Save, print, and then close **WL1-U2-A01-TechOccs.docx**.

Assessment 2 Create a Workshop Flyer

1. Create the flyer shown in Figure U2.1 with the following specifications:
   a. Create the WordArt with the following specifications:
      - Use the *Fill - Tan, Text 2, Outline - Background 2* option (first option from the left in the top row) at the WordArt button drop-down gallery.
      - Increase the width to 6.5 inches and the height to 1 inch.
      - Apply the *Deflate* text effect transform shape.
      - Change the text fill color to *Olive Green, Accent 3, Lighter 40%*.
   b. Type the text shown in the figure set in 22-point Calibri bold and center the text.
   c. Insert the clip art image shown in the figure (use the keyword *buildings* to find the clip art) and then change the wrapping style to *Square*. Position and size the image as shown in the figure.
2. Save the document and name it **WL1-U2-A02-TravelFlyer**.
3. Print and then close **WL1-U2-A02-TravelFlyer.docx**.

Figure U2.1 Assessment 2

Assessment 3 Create a Staff Meeting Announcement

1. Create the announcement shown in Figure U2.2 with the following specifications:
   a. Use the *Hexagon* shape in the *Basic Shapes* section of the Shapes drop-down list to create the shape.
   b. Apply the *Subtle Effect - Aqua, Accent 5* shape style.
   c. Apply the *Art Deco* bevel shape effect.
   d. Type the letter **A** (this makes active many of the tab options), click the Home tab, and then click the No Spacing style in the Styles group.
   e. Type the remaining text in the shape as shown in the figure. Insert the ñ as a symbol (in the *(normal text)* font and insert the clock as a symbol (in the *Wingdings* font). Set the text and clock symbol in larger font sizes.
2. Save the completed document and name it **WL1-U2-A03-MeetNotice**.
3. Print and then close **WL1-U2-A03-MeetNotice.docx**.

Figure U2.2 Assessment 3

Assessment 4 Create a River Rafting Flyer

1. At a blank document, insert the picture named **River.jpg**. (Insert the picture using the Picture button.)
2. Crop out a portion of the trees at the left and right and a portion of the hill at the top.
3. Correct the brightness and contrast to *Brightness: +20% Contrast: +40%*.
4. Specify that the picture should wrap behind text.
5. Insert the text *River Rafting Adventures* on one line, *Salmon River, Idaho* on the next line, and *1-888-555-3322* on the third line.
6. Increase the size of the picture so it is easier to see and the size of the text so it is easier to read. Center the text and position it on the picture on top of the river so the text is readable.
7. Save the document and name it **WL1-U2-A04-RaftingFlyer**.
8. Print and then close **WL1-U2-A04-RaftingFlyer.docx**.

Assessment 5 Create an Envelope

1. At a blank document, create an envelope with the text shown in Figure U2.3.
2. Save the envelope document and name it **WL1-U2-A05-Env**.
3. Print and then close **WL1-U2-A05-Env.docx**.

Figure U2.3 Assessment 5

Mrs. Eileen Hebert
15205 East 42nd Street
Lake Charles, LA 71098

Mr. Earl Robicheaux
1436 North Sheldon Street
Jennings, LA 70542

Assessment 6 Create Mailing Labels

1. Create mailing labels with the name and address for Mrs. Eileen Hebert shown in Figure U2.3 using a label vendor and product of your choosing.
2. Save the document and name it **WL1-U2-A06-Labels**.
3. Print and then close **WL1-U2-A06-Labels.docx**.

Assessment 7 Create and Format a Table with Software Training Information

1. At a blank document, create the table shown in Figure U2.4. Format the table and the text in a manner similar to what is shown in Figure U2.4.
2. Insert a formula in B8 that totals the numbers in cells B4 through B7.
3. Insert a formula in C8 that totals the numbers in cells C4 through C7.
4. Save the document and name it **WL1-U2-A07-TechTraining**.
5. Print and then close **WL1-U2-A07-TechTraining.docx**.

TRI-STATE PRODUCTS		
Computer Technology Department Microsoft® Office 2010 Training		
Application	**# Enrolled**	**# Completed**
Access 2010	20	15
Excel 2010	62	56
PowerPoint 2010	40	33
Word 2010	80	72
Total		

Assessment 8 Create and Format a Table Containing Training Scores

1. Open **TrainingScores.docx** and then save the document with Save As and name it **WL1-U2-A08-TrainingScores**.
2. Insert formulas that calculate the averages in the appropriate row and column. (When writing the formulas, change the *Number format* option to *0*.)
3. Autofit the contents of the table.
4. Apply a table style of your choosing to the table.
5. Appy any other formatting to improve the visual appeal of the table.
6. Save, print, and then close **WL1-U2-A08-TrainingScores.docx**.

Assessment 9 Create an Organizational Chart

1. Use SmartArt to create an organizational chart for the following text (in the order displayed). Change the colors to *Colorfuttl Range - Accent Colors 2 to 3* and apply the *Metallic Scene* SmartArt style.
2. Save the completed document and name it **WL1-U2-A09-OrgChart**.
3. Print and then close **WL1-U2-A09-OrgChart.docx**.

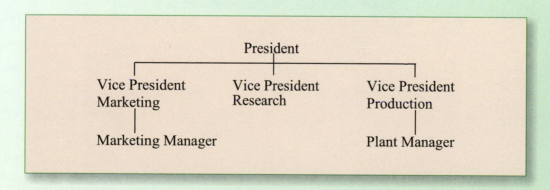

Assessment 10 Create a SmartArt Diagram

1. At a blank document, create the WordArt and diagram shown in Figure U2.5 with the following specifications:
   a. Insert the WordArt text with the *Gradient Fill - Blue, Accent 1, Outline - White* option. Change the shape height to 1 inch and the shape width to 6 inches and then apply the *Square* transform text effect.
   b. Create the diagram using the Vertical Picture Accent List diagram. Click the picture icon that displays in the top circle and then insert the picture named **Seagull.jpg** located in the Word2010L1U2 folder. Insert the same picture in the other two circles. Type the text in each rectangle shape as shown in Figure U2.5. Change the colors to *Colorful Range - Accent Colors 4 to 5* and apply the *Cartoon* SmartArt style.
2. Save the document and name it **WL1-U2-A10-SPDiagram**.
3. Print and then close **WL1-U2-A10-SPDiagram.docx**.

Figure U2.5 Assessment 10

Assessment 11 Merge and Print Letters

1. Look at the information shown in Figure U2.6 and Figure U2.7. Use the Mail Merge feature to prepare six letters using the information shown in the figures. When creating the letter main document, open **SMLtrhd.docx** and then save the document with Save As and name it **WL1-U2-A11-MD**. Insert Fill-in fields in the main document in place of the *(coordinator name)* and *(telephone number)* text. Create the data source file with the text shown in Figure U2.6 and name the file **WL1-U2-A11-DS**.

2. Type the text in the main document as shown in Figure U2.7 and then merge the document with the **WL1-U2-A11-DS.mdb** data source file. When merging, enter the first name and telephone number shown below for the first three records and enter the second name and telephone number shown below for the last three records.

   Jeff Greenswald   (813) 555-9886
   Grace Ramirez   (813) 555-9807

3. Save the merged letters document and name it **WL1-U2-A11-Ltrs**. Print and then close the document.

4. Save and then close the main document.

Figure U2.6 Assessment 11

Mrs. Antonio Mercado
3241 Court G
Tampa, FL 33623

Ms. Kristina Vukovich
1120 South Monroe
Tampa, FL 33655

Ms. Alexandria Remick
909 Wheeler South
Tampa, FL 33620

Mr. Minh Vu
9302 Lawndale Southwest
Tampa, FL 33623

Mr. Curtis Iverson
10139 93rd Court South
Tampa, FL 33654

Mrs. Holly Bernard
8904 Emerson Road
Tampa, FL 33620

December 12, 2012

«AddressBlock»

«GreetingLine»

Sound Medical is switching hospital care in Tampa to St. Jude's Hospital beginning January 1, 2013. As mentioned in last month's letter, St. Jude's Hospital was selected because it meets our requirements for high-quality, customer-pleasing care that is also affordable and accessible. Our physicians look forward to caring for you in this new environment.

Over the past month, staff members at Sound Medical have been working to make this transition as smooth as possible. Surgeries planned after January 1 are being scheduled at St. Jude's Hospital. Mothers delivering babies any time after January 1 are receiving information about delivery room tours and prenatal classes available at St. Jude's. Your Sound Medical doctor will have privileges at St. Jude's and will continue to care for you if you need to be hospitalized.

You are a very important part of our patient family, «Title» «Last_Name», and we hope this information is helpful. If you have any additional questions or concerns, please call your Sound Medical health coordinator, (coordinator name), at (telephone number), between 8:00 a.m. and 4:30 p.m.

Sincerely,

Jody Tiemann
District Administrator

XX
WL1-U2-A11-MD.docx

Assessment 12 Merge and Print Envelopes

1. Use the Mail Merge feature to prepare envelopes for the letters created in Assessment 11.
2. Specify **WL1-U2-A11-DS.mdb** as the data source document.
3. Save the merged envelopes document and name the document **WL1-U2-A12-Envs**.
4. Print and then close **WL1-U2-A12-Envs.docx**.
5. Do not save the envelope main document.

Writing Activities ■■■■■■■■■■■■■■■■■■

The following activities give you the opportunity to practice your writing skills along with demonstrating an understanding of some of the important Word features you have mastered in this unit. Use correct grammar, appropriate word choices, and clear sentence constructions.

Activity 1 Compose a Letter to Volunteers

You are an employee for the City of Greenwater and are responsible for coordinating volunteers for the city's Safe Night program. Compose a letter to the volunteers listed below and include the following information in the letter:

- Safe Night event scheduled for Saturday, June 16, 2012.

- Volunteer orientation scheduled for Thursday, May 17, 2012, at 7:30 p.m. At the orientation, participants will learn about the types of volunteer positions available and the work schedule.

Include any additional information in the letter, including a thank you to the volunteers. Use the Mail Merge feature to create a data source with the names and addresses shown below that is attached to the main document, which is the letter to the volunteers. Save the merged letters as **WL1-U2-Act01-Ltrs** and then print the letters.

Mrs. Laura Reston 376 Thompson Avenue Greenwater, OR 99034	Mr. Matthew Klein 7408 Ryan Road Greenwater, OR 99034
Ms. Cecilia Sykes 1430 Canyon Road Greenwater, OR 99034	Mr. Brian McDonald 8980 Union Street Greenwater, OR 99034
Mr. Ralph Emerson 1103 Highlands Avenue Greenwater, OR 99034	Mrs. Nola Alverez 598 McBride Street Greenwater, OR 99034

Activity 2 Create a Business Letterhead

You have just opened a new mailing and shipping business and need letterhead stationery. Create a letterhead for your company in a header and/or footer. Use Word's Help feature to learn about creating a header that only displays and prints on the first page. Create the letterhead in a header that displays and prints only on the first page and include *at least* one of the following: a clip art image, a picture, a shape, a text box, and/or WordArt. Include the following information in the header:

Global Mailing
4300 Jackson Avenue
Toronto, ON M4C 3X4
(416) 555-0095
www.emcp.net/globalmailing

Save the completed letterhead and name it **WL1-U2-Act02-Ltrhd**. Print and then close the document.

Internet Research ■■■■■■■■■■ ■■■■■■■

Create a Flyer on an Incentive Program

The owner of Terra Travel Services is offering an incentive to motivate travel consultants to increase travel bookings. The incentive is a sales contest with a grand prize of a one-week paid vacation to Cancun, Mexico. The owner has asked you to create a flyer that will be posted on the office bulletin board that includes information about the incentive program and some information about Cancun. Create this flyer using information about Cancun that you find on the Internet. Include a photo you find on a website (make sure it is not copyrighted) or include a clip art image representing travel. Include any other information or object to add visual appeal to the flyer. Save the completed flyer and name it **WL1-U2-InternetResearch**. Print and then close the document.

Job Study ■■■■■■■■■■ ■■■■■■■■■■ ■■■

Develop Recycling Program Communications

The Chief Operating Officer of Harrington Engineering has just approved your draft of the company's new recycling policy (see the file named **RecyclingPolicy.docx** located in the Word2010L1U2 folder). Edit the draft and prepare a final copy of the policy along with a memo to all employees describing the new guidelines. To support the company's energy resources conservation effort, you will send hard copies of the new policy to the Somerset Recycling Program president and to directors of Somerset Chamber of Commerce.

Using the concepts and techniques you learned in this unit, prepare the following documents:

- Format the recycling policy manual, including a cover page, appropriate headers and footers, and page numbers. Add at least one graphic and one diagram where appropriate. Format the document using a Quick Styles set and styles. Save the manual and name it **WL1-U2-JobStudyManual**. Print the manual.

- Download a memo template from Office.com Templates (at the New tab Backstage view) and then create a memo from Susan Gerhardt, Chief Operating Officer of Harrington Engineering to all employees introducing the new recycling program. Copy the *Procedure* section of the recycling policy manual into the memo where appropriate. Include a table listing five employees who will act as Recycling Coordinators at Harrington Engineering (make up the names). Add columns for the employees' department names and their telephone extensions. Save the memo and name it **WL1-U2-JobStudyMemo**. Print the memo.
- Write a letter to the President of the Somerset Recycling Program, William Elizondo, enclosing a copy of the recycling policy manual. Add a notation indicating copies with enclosures were sent to all members of the Somerset Chamber of Commerce. Save the letter and name it **WL1-U2-JobStudyLetter**. Print the letter.
- Create mailing labels (see Figure U2.8). Save the labels and name the file **WL1-U2-JobStudyLabels**. Print the file.

Figure U2.8 Mailing Labels

William Elizondo, President Somerset Recycling Program 700 West Brighton Road Somerset, NJ 55123	Paul Schwartz Somerset Chamber of Commerce 45 Wallace Road Somerset, NJ 55123
Ashley Crighton Somerset Chamber of Commerce 45 Wallace Road Somerset, NJ 55123	Carol Davis Somerset Chamber of Commerce 45 Wallace Road Somerset, NJ 55123
Robert Knight Somerset Chamber of Commerce 45 Wallace Road Somerset, NJ 55123	

Index

Text Box Tools Format tab,
178, 179
Text Effects button, 42
Text Highlight Color button, 42
Theme Colors button, 49, 50
Theme Effects button, 49, 50
Theme Fonts button, 49, 50
themes
    applying, 49–50
    changing, 49–50
    defined, 49
this point forward option, 158
time, inserting, 165–166
Title bar, 6
typeface
    defined, 37
    monospaced, 37–38
    proportional, 5, 7, 38
    sans serif, 38
    serif, 38
type size, 38
type styles, 38
    choosing, 40–41

U

Undo button, 21–22, 92
United States Postal Service
    (USPS) guidelines for
    addresses, 224, 225
unpinning of document, 13

V

vertical alignment option, 153
vertically aligning text, 167–168
vertically centering text, 168
vertical ruler, 6
vertical scroll bar, 6, 15
view, changing, 109–110
View buttons, 109
viewing, documents side by side,
    217–218
View Options button, 109
View Ruler button, 85
View Side by Side button, 217

W

watermark, 125
    inserting, 125
web browser, opening XPS files
    in, 213
white space
    at end of sentence, 7
    hiding/showing in Print
    Layout view, 112–113
windows
    arranging, 215
    opening, 215
    splitting, 216–218
    working with, 214–217
Windows Live ID account, 208

Word, exiting, 14
WordArt, creating and
    modifying, 181–183
word forms, finding and
    replacing, 134–135
Word Options dialog box, 76
words
    automatically hyphenating,
    161
    manually hyphenating,
    161–162
word wrap, 5
Write & Insert Fields group,
    295–296

X

XML (Extensible Markup
    Language), 207
XPS (XML paper specification)
    format, 207
    saving document as,
    213–214

Z

Zoom In button, 109
Zoom Out button, 109
Zoom slider bar, 109, 219
Zoom to Page button, 219